Made in France

Made in France: Studies in Popular Music serves as a comprehensive introduction to the history, sociology, and musicology of contemporary French popular music. The volume consists of essays by scholars of French popular music, and covers the major figures, styles, and social contexts of pop music in France. The book first presents a general description of the history and background of popular music in France, followed by essays that are organized into thematic sections: The Mutations of French Popular Music During the *"Trente Glorieuses"*; Politicising Popular Music; Assimilation, Appropriation, French Specificity; and From Digital Stakes to Cultural Heritage: French Contemporary Topics.

Gérôme Guibert is a doctor in sociology and associate professor at the Paris III Sorbonne Nouvelle University. He has published many books, including *La Production de la culture: Le cas des musiques amplifiées en France* (2006). He is also editor-in-chief of *Volume!*, the French journal of popular music studies. His research is in the fields of economic sociology, solidarity economy and local music scenes, with interests in the cultural development of music genres in France (including metal).

Catherine Rudent is a doctor and an associate professor in musicology at Paris-Sorbonne University (Paris IV). Interested in style and social determination within the area of (mainly French) popular music, she has published *L'Album de chansons: Entre processus social et œuvre musicale* (2011). A founding member of the European francophone branch of the International Association for the Study of Popular Music (IASPM), in 2011 she created a book series about popular music, *Musiques Populaires Actuelles/Amplifiées*.

Routledge Global Popular Music Series

Series Editors: Franco Fabbri, Conservatorio di Musica Arrigo Boito di Parma, Italy, and Goffredo Plastino, Newcastle University, UK

The *Routledge Global Popular Music Series* provides popular music scholars, teachers, students and musicologists with a well-informed and up-to-date introduction to different world popular music scenes. The series of volumes can be used for academic teaching in popular music studies, or as a collection of reference works. Written by those living and working in the countries about which they write, this series is devoted to popular music largely unknown to Anglo-American readers.

Made in Italy: Studies in Popular Music
Edited by Franco Fabbri and Goffredo Plastino

Made in Japan: Studies in Popular Music
Edited by Tōru Mitsui

Made in Brazil: Studies in Popular Music
Edited by Martha Tupinambá de Ulhôa, Cláudia Azevedo and Felipe Trotta

Made in Latin America: Studies in Popular Music
Edited by Julio Mendívil and Christian Spencer Espinosa

Made in Korea: Studies in Popular Music
Edited by Hyunjoon Shin and Seung-Ah Lee

Made in Sweden: Studies in Popular Music
Edited by Alf Björnberg and Thomas Bossius

Made in Hungary: Studies in Popular Music
Edited by Emília Barna and Tamás Tófalvy

Made in France: Studies in Popular Music
Edited by Gérôme Guibert and Catherine Rudent

Made in the Low Countries: Studies in Popular Music
Edited by Lutgard Mutsaers and Gert Keunen

Made in France

Studies in Popular Music

Edited by

**Gérôme Guibert and
Catherine Rudent**

LONDON AND NEW YORK

First published 2018 by Routledge

2 Park Square, Milton Park, Abingdon, Oxfordshire OX14 4RN
52 Vanderbilt Avenue, New York, NY 10017

Routledge is an imprint of the Taylor & Francis Group, an informa business

First issued in paperback 2019

Library of Congress Cataloging-in-Publication Data
Names: Guibert, Gérôme. | Rudent, Catherine.
Title: Made in France : studies in popular music / edited by Gérôme
    Guibert and Catherine Rudent.
Description: New York, NY : Routledge, 2018. | Series: Routledge global
popular music series | Includes bibliographical references and index.
Identifiers: LCCN 2017016064 (print) | LCCN 2017016697 (ebook) |
    ISBN 9781315761619 (E-book) | ISBN 9781138793040 (hardback : alk.
    paper)
Subjects: LCSH: Popular music—France—History and criticism. | Popular
music—Social aspects—France—History.
Classification: LCC ML3489 (ebook) | LCC ML3489 .M33 2018 (print) |
    DDC 781.640944—dc23
LC record available at https://lccn.loc.gov/2017016064

ISBN: 978-1-138-79304-0 (hbk)
ISBN: 978-0-367-86977-9 (pbk)

Typeset in Minion Pro
by Apex CoVantage, LLC

Support for this project provided by IReMus

IReMUS
institut de recherche
en musicologie

Contents

Figures

Tables

Contributors

Christian Béthune completed his doctorate, titled *Jazz as a Critic of Aesthetic Categories*, in 1991. Between 1979 and 2001, he was a regular contributor to France's *Jazz Magazine*. His books on rap and jazz, all published by Klincksieck, include *Le Rap: une esthétique hors-la-loi*, *Pour une esthétique du rap* and *Le Jazz et l'Occident*. He is currently a research associate at the Centre Interdisciplinaire d'Etudes et de Recherches sur les Expressions Contemporaines (CIEREC), based in Jean Monnet University at Saint-Etienne.

Juliette Dalbavie holds a PhD in information science and communication, and is a lecturer at the University of Lille III and a member of the Geriico research laboratory. Her research interests relate to the constitution, circulation and transmission of popular music culture. She is specifically interested in exhibitions devoted to singers and their repertoires, and in the processes of emotional attachment and memorialisation.

Sylvain Dejean is an associate professor in economics at the University of La Rochelle. His research interest is focused in digital economics at the Centre for Research in Management (CEREGE). He has conducted studies about the impact of online digital piracy on the cultural industry and has also studied the determinants of voluntary contributions in open online communities. He has more recently been interested in the economics issues raised by the development of the so called "sharing" economy.

Gérôme Guibert is a doctor in sociology and associate professor at the Paris III Sorbonne Nouvelle University. He has published many books, including *La Production de la culture: Le cas des musiques amplifiées en France* (2006). He is also editor-in-chief of *Volume!*, the French journal of popular music studies. His research is in the fields of economic sociology, solidarity economy and local music scenes, with interests in the cultural development of music genres in France (including metal).

Fabien Hein is a senior lecturer in sociology at the University of Lorraine (Metz) and a researcher at the Lorraine Lab of Social Sciences (2L2S). His research mainly focuses on cultural entrepreneurship.

Olivier Julien is a lecturer in popular music at Paris-Sorbonne University (Paris IV). A referee for the French Centre National du Livre, the Belgian Fonds national de la Recherche

Scientifique, the Canadian Fonds Québécois de Recherche sur la Société et la Culture and the journals *Popular Music, Musurgia* and *Volume!*, he is the editor of *Sgt. Pepper and the Beatles: It Was Forty Years Ago Today* (Ashgate 2009, ARSC Award for Best Research in Recorded Rock and Popular Music).

Marc Kaiser recently completed his PhD at Sorbonne Nouvelle University, with a historical and comparative study of French popular music policies. He has given lectures and presented seminars on communication and cultural studies and has worked as a research engineer on the economy of live popular music in France, and as a research scholar at the French National Library. He is currently a teaching assistant (Attaché Temporaire d'Enseignement et de Recherche) at Charles de Gaulle University in Lille.

Barbara Lebrun is a lecturer in contemporary French Culture at the University of Manchester, and a French popular music specialist. She is the author of *Protest Music in France* (Ashgate 2009, winner of the 2011 IASPM Best Monograph prize), and editor of *Chanson et Performance* (L'Harmattan, 2012). She has published articles in France, the United Kingdom and the United States, and is currently working on a monograph contextualising the career of female singer Dalida.

David Looseley is an emeritus professor at the University of Leeds. His research deals with French contemporary culture, the subject of many of his publications. His latest book, *Édith Piaf: A Cultural History*, was published in 2015. He also published *Popular Music in Contemporary France: Authenticity, Politics, Debate* (2003) and *The Politics of Fun: Cultural Policy and Debate in Contemporary France* (1997). In 2010, he was nominated Chevalier de L'Ordre des Palmes Académiques.

Stéphanie Molinero holds a PhD in sociology. After several years as an assistant professor, she now works for the cultural agency of the region Île-de-France (Paris). In 2009, she published her first monograph *Les Publics du rap: Enquête sociologique*, based on her doctoral research into rap audiences in France.

Anne Petiau is a sociologist. Since completing her PhD on electronic music, she has been working in the fields of youth, popular culture and deviance. She is currently a researcher and a teacher at the Institut de Travail Social et de Recherche Sociale Île-de-France (ITSRS).

Cécile Prévost-Thomas is a lecturer in the sociology of music and musicology at Sorbonne Nouvelle University (Paris III). A member of the Centre de Recherche sur les Liens Sociaux (CERLIS), she is the co-editor of *La Chanson francophone engagée* (2008) and of *25 ans de sociologie de la musique en France* (2012). Her research focuses on francophone *chanson*, its genres and symbolic functions.

Vincent Rouzé is a lecturer in culture and communication at Paris VIII University. His research focuses on digitalization and globalization processes, and their impact on the production and valorisation of music and the arts. His PhD examined the role of music broadcasting in public spaces in France, and he is the author of *Mythologie de l'iPod: À l'écoute du temps présent* (2010). His current research deals with the uses and functions of crowdfunding and crowdsourcing in the creative industries, and the role of music as a strategic tool in communication businesses.

Catherine Rudent is a doctor and an associate professor in musicology at Paris-Sorbonne University (Paris IV). Interested in style and social determination within the area of (mainly French) popular music, she has published *L'Album de chansons: Entre processus social et œuvre musicale* (2011). A founding member of the European francophone branch of the International Association for the Study of Popular Music (IASPM), in 2011 she created a book series about popular music, *Musiques Populaires Actuelles/Amplifiées*.

Matthieu Saladin holds a PhD in aesthetics and is a professor of philosophy of the arts at the Graduate School of Art in Mulhouse. He is editor-in-chief of *Tacet* (*Experimental Music Review*). In 2010, he directed a two-volume special issue of *Volume!* about covers in popular music.

Jedediah Sklower is a PhD student in communication sciences and cultural history. His research deals with French popular music history in the 1960s. He is a member of the editorial team of *Volume!*. He published *Free Jazz, la catastrophe féconde* (L'Harmattan, 2006), and co-edited *Countercultures and Popular Music* with Sheila Whiteley (Ashgate, 2014), as well as *Politiques des musiques populaires au XXIe siècle* with Elsa Grassy (Mélanie Seteun, 2016).

Raphaël Suire is an associate professor in economics at the University of Rennes I. His research interests are in Internet usage and digital economics at the Centre for Research in Economics and Management (CREM-CNRS). He has conducted many studies about digital usage, the cultural sector and market dynamics. His most recent work examines the place of illegal download and digital file sharing in the context of France's HADOPI law.

Florence Tamagne is an associate professor in contemporary history at the University of Lille III. She has published *A History of Homosexuality in Europe: Berlin, London, Paris, 1919–1939* (Algora Pub., 2004) and contributed to R. Aldrich (ed.), *Gay Life and Culture* (Universe, 2006) and G. Hekma (ed.), *A Cultural History of Sexuality in the Modern Age* (Berg, 2011). She is currently working on rock music, youth cultures and politics in France, Britain and Germany (1950s–1980s).

Translators

Preface: Jack Sims
Introduction: Jack Sims

Preamble to Part I: Henry Jones
  1 Saladin: Jack Sims
  2 Tamagne (written in English)
  3 Julien (originally in English, checked by Orlene McMahon and Jerrold Levinson)
  4 Kaiser: Orlene McMahon

Preamble to Part II: Jack Sims
  5 Sklower (written in English)
  6 Guibert: Marc Naimark
  7 Lebrun (written in English)

Preamble to Part III: Raphaël Costambeys-Kempczynski
  8 Prévost-Thomas: Marc Naimark
  9 Rudent: Marc Naimark
10 Molinero: Henry Jones
11 Béthune: Henry Jones
12 Hein: Jedediah Sklower

Preamble to Part IV: Jack Sims
13 Dalbavie: Delia Morris
14 Petiau: Rónán MacDubhghaill, Angela Davis and Jack Sims
15 Dejean and Suire (written in English)
16 Rouzé: Marc Naimark

Coda Looseley (written in English)
Afterword Godin and Guibert: Jack Sims

Series Foreword

Popular music studies have progressed from the initial focus on methodologies to exploring a variety of genres, scenes, works, and performers. British and North-American music have been privileged and studied first, not only for their geographic and generational proximity to scholars, but also for their tremendous impact. Everything else has been often relegated to the dubious "world music" category, with a "folk" (or "roots," or "authentic") label attached.

However, world popular music is no less popular than rock 'n' roll, R&B, disco, rap, singer-songwriters, punk, grunge, Brit-pop, or nu-gaze. It is no less full of history and passion, no less danceable, socially relevant, and commercialized. Argentinian tango, Brazilian bossa nova, Mexican reggaeton, Cuban *son* and *timba*, Spanish and Latin American *cantautores*, French *auteurs-compositeurs-interprètes*, Italian *cantautori* and electronic dance music, J-pop, German cosmic music and *Schlager*, Neapolitan Song, Greek *entechno*, Algerian *raï*, Ghanaian highlife, Portuguese fado, Nigerian *jùjú*, Egyptian and Lebanese Arabic pop, Israeli *mizrahit*, and Indian *filmi* are just a few examples of locally and transnationally successful genres that, with millions of records sold, are an immensely precious key to understand different cultures, societies, and economies.

More than in the past, there is now a widespread awareness of the "Other" popular music: however, we still lack access to the original sources, or to texts to rely on. The *Routledge Global Popular Music Series* has been devised to offer to scholars, teachers, students, and general readers worldwide direct access to scenes, works, and performers that have been mostly not much or at all considered in the current literature, and at the same time to provide a better understanding of the different approaches in the field of non-Anglophone scholarship. Uncovering the wealth of studies flourishing in so many countries, inaccessible to those who do not speak the local language, is by now no less urgent than considering the music itself.

The series website (www.globalpopularmusic.net) includes hundreds of audiovisual examples that complement the volumes. The interaction with the website is intended to give a well-informed introduction to the world's popular music from entirely new perspectives, and at the same time to provide updated resources for academic teaching.

The Routledge Global Popular Music Series ultimately aims at establishing a truly international arena for a democratic musicology, through authoritative and accessible books. We hope that our work will help the creation of a different polyphony of critical approaches, and that you will enjoy listening to and being part of it.

Franco Fabbri
University of Turin, Italy

Goffredo Plastino
Newcastle University, UK

Series Editors

Preface

Catherine Rudent

Is there anything specifically French in French music, and if so, what? Can a French identity be made out across the whole of French national music production? Is there something that lends its stamp to the nation's works, innovations, musical practices and the processes that structure them? Do we see this stamp at work in the field of popular music, even when we're "only" talking about entertainment, even when it's "popular"? Is it present even outside of the field of art music, even where the music is culturally less elaborate, less controlled, less subject to cultural, educational and social filters?

Historians specialising in French culture and the French identity sometimes mention characteristic French tendencies. In *Le temps des masses*, Jean-François Sirinelli and Jean-Pierre Rioux look at twentieth-century French culture. They talk, for example, about various political, intellectual and cultural turning points that marked French history in the twentieth century and evoke a specifically French, particularly individualistic way of breaking with the past:

> When it comes to unprecedented creativity and new thinking, we need to analyse the particularly French propensity to cast any break in individual terms and to individualise more markedly than elsewhere, more than in Germany, Austria-Hungary, Russia or Italy, the very approach that has led to this break.
>
> (Sirinelli and Rioux 2005, 135)

This statement applies rather well in the context of French popular music, especially in the second half of the twentieth century, with its social, cultural and economic revolutions, the major innovations in sound techniques and the many popular music artists who upset conventions. Take, for example, the *chanson* artists who developed out of post-war Parisian cabaret (Brassens, Ferré, Gainsbourg, Nougaro, etc.); rock artists (Manset, Thiéfaine, Bashung, Les Rita Mitsouko, etc.); and punk, rap or French Touch artists (Daft Punk, Air, Dimitri from Paris, Justice, David Guetta, etc.). In this context, like the broader historical and political one, new departures tend to be associated with outstanding individuals who generally succeed as an exception, following on from previous outstanding individuals and not being easily identified as part of a general and collective trend.

Celebrated historian Fernand Braudel links this quest for the new to the characteristic diversity of France. According to him, the "plural" is a fundamental principle of the French nation—an omnipresent geographical, cultural and linguistic diversity. For him, "the identity of France," is based on

> the dazzling triumph of the plural, of the heterogeneous, of the never-quite-the-same, of the never-quite-what-you-find-elsewhere. No doubt England, Germany, Italy or Spain, examined in detail have a perfect claim to be named diversity too, but not perhaps with quite the same exuberance or obstinacy. [. . .] [In France] the plural submerges and swallows up the singular. [. . .] It is at any rate impossible, in this dialogue between plural and singular, to brush aside the first term. Unless it is restored to pride of place, we shall never grasp the problem of problems in our national past, the fragmentation underlying it, the contrasts, tensions, misunderstandings or complementary compromises—they do exist—but also the quarrels, bitter antagonisms and mutual taunts.
>
> (Braudel 1986, 29–31)

France is seen as being marked by a resistance to embracing a collective identity and a constant and productive tendency to self-reinvention.

This book provides an in-depth examination of the various trends in French popular music and thus offers some answers to the aforementioned questions. Indeed, it starts with an examination of two innovative figures, with Gérôme Guibert's general introduction beginning by drawing a parallel between the two inventors of phonographic recording: one in the United States, Edison, who combined his role as an inventor and his technical knowledge with an entrepreneurial nature; the other in France, Charles Cros, an engineer and poet, less pragmatic, and more interested in both the abstract dimension of technical invention and the aesthetic aspects of creativity.

However, this book focuses on the second half of the twentieth century and the start of the twenty-first. It deals with French popular music from after the Second World War up to the present.

First of all, the 1960s take quite some comprehending, there being a lot to take in. The 1960s was a turbulent decade in Western history from a social and political point of view, and this also goes for musical forms and technological and media developments. Nationally speaking, two major phenomena that have structured the entire history of French popular music originate in this decade: the first was *yéyé*, the expression of the shock wave of rock on the French popular musical landscape, achieving an almost adolescent, intensive and relatively superficial synthesis of rock and *chanson*. What was established through *yéyé*, therefore, in the field of the music and entertainment industry, was a relationship between national specificities and globalised perspectives. It was the major turning point of that moment of the twentieth century—in France as elsewhere in Europe, but with national characteristics that are described in detail throughout the book.

Over the same period, the second crucial component was the culmination of the production of text-based *chanson* with artists like Barbara, Anne Sylvestre, Léo Ferré, Jacques Brel, Georges Brassens, Claude Nougaro, early Gainsbourg and so on. These artists are considered to have been at the top of their game in this decade, which was also a high point for arrangers and orchestrators (who were also sometimes composers) such as François Rauber, André

Popp, Jean-Michel Defaye, Alain Goraguer and Michel Legrand. Also to be noted, and still during this same decade, is the triumph, in terms of popularity and commercial success, of certain stars of a more consensual and more widely publicised *chanson* style, such as Charles Aznavour and Gilbert Bécaud.

The 1960s are, here, the focus of the first part and resound across many subsequent chapters. One of the aims of the book is to detail and expound on the landscape of this dense coexistence of trends in France. What aesthetic, cultural, ideological and economic issues result from this and what are the consequences of these issues? The reader will, for example, find a section on the *yéyé* aesthetic, another on the cultural history of the first festivals, a reflection on the poetic ambiguities of Gainsbourg's writing (which came to the fore in the 1960s), and yet another on aspects of the music industry at the same time. This important decade is approached from numerous angles right from the start of the book.

From the 1960s onwards, the question of political developments in general and cultural policy in France in particular also plays out. The place of popular music (but also one of its most aesthetically legitimate branches, jazz) within the French political landscape from the left to the right, from the 1960s to the 1990s, are the focus of the second part. We are reminded that the cultural policy of the second half of the twentieth century at first chose to ignore entertainment, placing "art music" above it. Political considerations in French popular music came to the fore in the 1970s (with a specific positioning of punk and heavy metal in France, addressed by G. Guibert) and evolved in the 1980s and 1990s around issues of integration—musical, as well as general—of people from immigrant backgrounds and the post-colonial context (B. Lebrun).

Another great unifying theme of the book is the deconstruction of the confusion between French popular music and French *chanson*. They are all too often conflated, particularly outside France. However, although the authenticity of singer-songwriters features in this book (Prévost-Thomas), the richness and breadth of musical production that bears little relation to *chanson* is also emphasised. But what do we mean by saying that this production "bears little relation to *chanson*"? Does a specific form of musical production called "*chanson française*" exist (Rudent)? Several chapters of the book, especially in the third part, invite us to question this rather approximate and rigid designation and instead take measure of the changing and diverse reality of French popular music, from *chanson* to rock (Lebrun, Guibert), punk (Hein) and rap (Molinero, Béthune). The third part of the book thus takes a closer look at French *chanson* and its related issues of identity (two chapters) and then at the poetic aspects of French rap. Artistic singularity *à la française* would seem to be very characteristic throughout French popular music.

There is therefore a duality in France's positioning vis-à-vis its popular music. As "*musiques actuelles*" ("current music")—the ministerial name for popular music since the 1990s—popular music is in the now, with all the peculiarities, constant adjustments and future prospects this entails. At the same time, it is a heritage from the past, making it subject to memorial and conservation strategies. The fourth part of the book goes into some of the issues of contemporary French popular music studies. It deals with both a past that is subject to contemporary heritage making (Dalbavie), legal issues related to the digitisation of music and musical uses on the Web (Suire) and considerations related to aesthetics and current musical practices (Petiau, Rouzé). It thus shows how French popular music is part of a global music industry, both integrating itself within it and marking out its peculiarities.

Bibliography

Braudel, Fernand. 1986. *L'identité de la France. Espace et histoire*. Paris: Les éditions Arthaud.
Sirinelli, Jean-François, and Jean-Pierre Rioux. 2005 [1998]. *Le temps des masses: Histoire culturelle de la France*, vol. 4. Paris: Editions du Seuil.

Introduction
What's the French Touch in French Popular Music? A Sociohistorical Introduction to *Chanson* and Other French Repertoires

Gérôme Guibert

An attempt to denote what characterises France in terms of popular music can be made by setting its economic processes and cultural foundations against the Weberian model of *The Protestant Ethic and the Spirit of Capitalism* (Weber 1967 [1905]), using the question of sound recording[1] as an example. Thus, historically, the first two patents related to "talking machines," those of Edison in the United States and Charles Cros in France, are contemporary to each other, both dating back to the year 1877, yet an examination of the cultural contexts of the filings in the two countries shows the extent to which they were divergent. In the United States, Thomas Edison was as much entrepreneur as inventor. He had a research laboratory, worked with fifteen employees and sought to commercialise the phonograph soon after developing it (Tournès 1999). Its technical implementation was, here, just one step along the way, so much so that Edison's development process has been studied by Mark Granovetter (2008, 217–220) from the point of view of economic sociology (2008, 217–220), underlining the importance of social relations from a strategic perspective. More broadly speaking, the pragmatic approach, the importance of doing (Lallement 2015), was emphasised over ideological aspects or any symbolic battle of wills in the domain. The French context would appear to have been markedly different. Cros is described as a lone inventor, "a bit of a dreamer" (Flichy 1991, 193–196), who, due to a lack of finances and the desire to pursue technical achievement, never build a prototype. An inventor dabbling in many fields, Cros was also a poet, who even described the processes behind his palaeograph in verse (Ibid.). His approach, it could be said, cannot have encouraged investors to support him. Furthermore, on neither side of the Atlantic did our inventors themselves see music as a possible application of sound recording. Cros conceived of it primarily as a method to preserve memory, and even Edison saw it as being used as an answering machine or Dictaphone in a professional setting. It would nevertheless be Edison, rather than his French counterpart, who eventually adapted to demand and the uses to which the invention was put, even though he had not foreseen them (Maisonneuve 2006). Of course, he went on to affect the rest of the world through the Edison Phonograph Company.

Without wishing to construct a comparative history based on stereotypes, it seems important to note, and the areas of musical production and reception prove no exception, that France has, first and foremost, long since been characterised by a deliberate separation between the domains of economics and art (Poirrier 2000), a phenomenon particularly characteristic of the Romantic period (Heinich 1996). The artistic quality of music is moreover, or at least it was from the 1930s to the 1970s, associated with independence and disinterestedness, as we can see from the critical writings of Adorno and the Frankfurt School. The same position would be adopted in public policies that sought, as of the establishment of a Ministry for Culture in 1959, to protect authorship, including that in popular cultures, via state (national) and local (regional and municipal) authorities. Nevertheless, since even the time of the Third Republic (1870), public action should be understood from an often-hierarchical perspective by no means exempt from elitism and distrust of the people and democratic processes (Maigret 2003). Thus, popular music was often suspected of artificiality or inauthenticity (Grignon and Passeron 1989), at least before Bourdieu highlighted the structural homology between social class and musical genres. His perspective did not, however, credit popular culture with an emancipatory dimension, but rather stigmatised the processes of social domination associated with popular music. In fact, for more than thirty years, from the 1970s until at least the beginning of this new century, academic research in France focused on the reproductive mechanisms at work in historical or contemporary popular music. It thus largely neglected discussions and contributions originating in cultural studies, particularly issues of resistance, agency and empowerment (Fabiani 2015) or those of interdisciplinary debates developed in many arenas, including those of popular music studies.

Republicanism

Why does French *chanson* hold such an important place in the national narrative (Naudin 1968)? Indeed, its importance is such that the notion of French popular music has often been understood as a synonym of the expression *chanson française* (Guibert 2005). Understanding the peculiarities of French popular music therefore also necessitates an examination of civilizational cultural attributes. One of them is extremely deep-rooted: the role of the French language. French was imposed universally across France during the Third Republic (1870–1940), in line with a political will to unite the French regions. The spread of French was centrally organised and propagated from the top down through the republic's school system (Ozouf 1989). School education became successively compulsory, free and, as of 1905, secular. The imposition of French in the provinces was contemporaneous with two other movements. The first was the development of cultural industries, starting with books and the daily press (Kalifa 2001) and the second was a rural exodus to the cities (and specifically to Paris) caused by the industrial revolution. While the desire to extend the influence of French as the national language was motivated by a republican, egalitarian ideal, it had a decisive impact on French popular musical heritage (folk music). Indeed, this heritage was transformed by the rapid depletion of languages and dialects spoken throughout France. This occurred in the context of a country that took little (and belated) interest in transcribing oral memory (Goffre 1984), partly because traces of singularity were seen as countering the construction of a collective national consciousness.

Town and Country

Without going into the details of a history that is described elsewhere (Duneton 1998), the genesis of "popular music" as a product of the dialectical opposition between folk music and *art music*[2] in mid- and late-nineteenth-century France, can only be understood, both for *chanson* and folk music in general (Guibert 2006), through a simultaneous examination of rural and urban contexts. It took on heterogeneous forms at least until the advent of broadcast media (radio, cinema) in the early 1930s. In the first case, that of the countryside and small towns, the development of French in school was, in the second half of the nineteenth century, accompanied by a growth in the number of instrumental bands (*harmonies*, wind bands; *cliques*, bugles and drums; and *fanfares*, brass) and vocal societies (choirs), whether through the Church, secular political organisations or factories (employing a large workforce). These bands and choral societies, which reached an apogee in the first quarter of the twentieth century, were organised both with a view to popular education and control of the masses.[3] Their rise was contemporaneous with new manufactured instruments like the saxophone and, more generally, brass made from scrap from the army, as well as with new infrastructure such as bandstands, patronage halls, municipal theatres and, later, music schools (Mussat 1992).

In urban areas, in prominent places in towns, the street singer was an important figure (sometimes accompanied by a barrel organ or other mechanical device in vogue since the July Monarchy [1830–1848]) (Gétreau 1997). In the second half of the century, singers also performed in *café-concerts*. Between 1850 and 1914, these were major venues for popular entertainment and *chanson* performance. Located in Paris and the largest French towns, there were enormous numbers of them, from the most luxurious and famous (in Paris, Les Ambassadeurs, L'Alcazar d'Eté, L'Eldorado, Les Folies Bergères, Ba-Ta-Clan, Le Moulin Rouge, etc.) to the more modest (De Langle 1990). They could house an average of 400–500 people, but the largest had a capacity of 1,500 spectators. They combined the consumption of drinks, live musical entertainment and "the staging of the female body" (Condemi 1992) with the practice of *la corbeille*, for example, whereby attractive singers were spread across the stage during part of the program (Condemi 1992, 85). The rest of the time, they brightened up the room and were described by female singer Polaire as "half artists, half *demi-mondaines*" (Ibid., 91). For over fifty years, from the Second Empire to the First World War, the success and reputation of *cafés-concerts* were very much part of what gave Paris its image as world capital of pleasure. Male and female singers of national or international renown made their careers there (Thérésa, Mayol, Dranem, Paulus, Yvette Guilbert, Polaire, etc.). Even Aristide Bruant, a major figure in the cabarets of Montmartre in the late nineteenth century (Le Chat Noir, Le Mirliton)[4] and who played a vital role in the history of French *chanson*, was also a star of the *cafés-concerts* where he triumphed as a singer (e.g., at Les Ambassadeurs) and also as a director.

Furthermore, in contrast to practices in the provinces, by the early twentieth century, dances were no longer organised around collective celebrations but to a certain extent responded to the rules of supply and demand. If you paid, you could dance midweek at *bal musettes* (street dances) to accordion music brought to Paris by Italian immigrants in the late nineteenth century (Defrance 1984).

The early twentieth century saw the emergence of theatres dedicated to popular music that went beyond operetta, with the beginnings of Parisian and French music hall venues. The genre of "realist" *chanson*, first heard at the turn of the twentieth century in cabarets and *café-concerts*, reached its apogee in *music-hall* in the twenties. Realist *chanson* was based on urban, mostly Parisian themes: the *faubourgs*, buildings and streets in working-class neigh-bourhoods, criminals, prostitutes and pimps, the urban poverty of children, simple and car-nal, often ephemeral sexual relationships; *javas* danced to the sound of the accordion in taverns on the banks of the Marne and so on. These songs were sung by singers like Damia, Fréhel, Lys Gauty, Yvonne George, Marie Dubas and, a little later, Piaf. Realist *chanson* was rooted in earlier sung genres: the lament (*complainte*), the romance, the vaudeville and their successor, the *goualante* (Charpentier-Leroy 2014; Dutheil-Pessin 2004).

With *music-hall*, the audience no longer paid primarily to drink or eat but rather to see a show. Through "the mechanics of emotion" (Kalifa 2001, 43), a rationalisation of the business of shows was sought through the pursuit of "American methods." The term *variété*, which would be used in France to designate popular music production, originated in this context in the succession of scenes in *music-hall* shows (Klein 1988). With the costumes, sets, dancers and, from the 1920s, *la meneuse de revue* or lead dancer, show producers sought to provide a total spectacle based on visual impact and the volume of sound. This was made possible through two elements: firstly, the accentuation of rhythm and secondly, an increase in num-bers in the orchestra. The expansion of the orchestra in terms of size was accompanied by the appropriation of jazz drums from US military troops at the end of the First World War. Elec-tric amplification of the voice, and then instruments, arose from the development of talkies and therefore the concomitant equipment of theatres. Indeed, with the end of the musical as a popular genre in the early 1930s, performance venues with a room equipped with amplifi-cation equipment would alternate between film projection and singing tours (*tours de chant*) (Basile and Gavouyère 1996).

The Establishment of a Professional Sector

In addition to these facilities, the construction of a music industry in France was made possible by the gradual professionalization of several functions. From the early years of the twentieth century (Lesueur 1999), publishers began selling *petits formats*, small-format sheet music transcribing the lyrics and melodies of popular songs. They were sold by street singers and then at *café-concerts*, as well as musical instrument stores that also sold sheet music. During the 1930s, the talkies, which capitalised on the image of the star, enabled the trade in small-format sheet music to continue because songs from hit movies were sung by singers in markets or public squares (Basile 1999, 14). At the same time, the Société des Auteurs, Compositeurs et Éditeurs de Musique (SACEM), a copyright society set up in 1858, gradu-ally increased its membership (Duneton 1998, 926). Even though public performance rights were negligible due to a lack of control and collection of copyright fees for the use of reper-toires, authors and composers gradually negotiated a share of revenue with publishers from sales of small-format sheet music and then from recordings (Szendy 2001). Indeed, with the rapid development of radio and cinema during the 1930s, it became possible to collect broadcasting rights. Reproduction rights from the sale of phonographs were also gradually acknowledged. It should be noted that, unlike in the United States and most English-speaking countries, the company which managed authors' rights was rooted in popular music, since it came from an initiative by song composers and lyricists who thought it unfair that street singers should perform works that these composers and lyricists had written and sold to

Figure 0.1 Académie du disque Français (ADF), *Almanach du disque*, 1958, Paris, Editions Pierre Horay, 1959, back cover advertising.

publishers for a fixed fee (Duneton 1998). What further characterised the situation in France, however, in terms of the dissemination of popular music, was that records did not become a mass consumer product before the 1950s and the appearance of vinyl. Records—like the piano for private use—were primarily something bought by the upper classes, with the historic firm Pathé (acquired by British company EMI in the mid-1930s) dominating phonographic production in France until this period (Tournès 2002). Besides film and radio, and photographs in magazines or on small-format sheet music, the "media" image of singers on whom attention was focused was strengthened with singing tours in private venues in towns and cities (Olympia, Alhambra, Florida, Katorza, etc.) and summer tours in the casinos of seaside towns (on the Atlantic coast and the Riviera) (Guibert 2006). These specific elements had an impact on the development of popular music in France after the Second World War and up to the contemporary period, the period focused on in this book.

The Sustainable Establishment of Popular Music

In terms of musical offering, the economic and media system functioning in the late 1940s persisted until at least the early 1980s. This period was characterised in particular by a public broadcasting system, with the notorious Office de Radiodiffusion-Télévision Française (ORTF), which had a monopoly on radio and television. The only exceptions were what were known as the *radios périphériques*, of which there were three and which broadcast from countries bordering France (Europe n° 1, Radio Luxembourg and Radio Monte-Carlo). Faced with a state system that favoured establishment culture alongside an ambition to take it to the people, these radios differentiated themselves by broadcasting a lot of popular music, especially new artists from Great Britain and the United States, as well as French popular music production recorded by major labels.

Recorded Music as a Badge of Youth

While French *chanson* was not specifically linked to younger audiences, or rather teenagers (Galland 1985), things took a new direction in the 1960s. Baby boomers, born after 1945, were particularly influenced by the show *Salut les Copains* (which was broadcast on Europe n° 1) and other programs following the same model that broadcast "French 'music-hall'[5] for young people" (Sohn 2001). Specialised generational magazines, which developed in the early 1960s, were added to this, following on from the magazines that appeared in the 1930s dedicated to certain currents of popular music (primarily jazz and *chanson*). Two chapters are dedicated to this period in this book, one on repertoires (Saladin), the other on this generation and perceptions of it (Tamagne), a time when what are commonly known as *les Trente Glorieuses*, the post-war boom years, were beginning in France. In a context in which listening media was changing, in particular with the popularisation of vinyl in the mid- to late 1950s,[6] record production exploded and the musical offering took on the form we are familiar with today in most cultural industries, that of an oligopoly with a competitive fringe with a few companies dominating production. Some were majors, like Pathé Marconi EMI (the historic French company after its takeover by British company EMI), the German Philips, and the American RCA (CBS that established itself in France in the second half of the 1960s) and Warner (in the early 1970s after linking up with Filipacchi). M. Kaiser's chapter covers these developments. The industry gradually became globalised through successive sales, mergers and acquisitions, before developing into the sector we know today. Nevertheless in the French context, two large national record companies were established, sharing over 10% of the market until the end of the 1970s (Huet et al. 1978, 88) and playing an important role in signing and supporting artists, before being bought by majors in the 1990s. Several of the contributors to this book include mention of them (Kaiser, Julien and Béthune). They were headed up by two figures who began their pre-war careers in jazz. One, Eddie Barclay, a musician, set up the Barclay label (including artists like Dalida, Aznavour, Brel, Ferré, Ferrat, Mitchell and Polnareff), which dominated French *chanson* and *variété* (French pop) after jazz. The other, journalist (*Jazz Hot*) and producer (Grappelli and Reinhardt's group, the Quintette du Hot Club de France) Charles Delaunay, set up the Vogue label (starting the careers of Johnny Hallyday, Françoise Hardy, Jacques Dutronc, Antoine and even Colette Renard and Martin Circus) after helping build a community of jazz listeners in the 1930s through the Hot Club de France jazz association and *Jazz Hot* magazine.

What characterised French repertoires from the 1960s to the 1980s was a kind of "great divide" between French *variété* and Anglo-American rock (produced abroad and distributed in France).[7] The media (magazines, television and radio) and recorded music were split in two opposing directions and were aimed at two types of audiences. The youngest, especially those at middle school (*collégiens*) and from working-class backgrounds, were targeted by new French *variété* that would become known under the name *yéyé*, after the rapid disappearance of the first wave of French rock 'n' roll (1961 to 1963) (Guibert 2006). While rock 'n' roll was played in groups, *yéyé* adopted the classical model of individual singer performers. Meanwhile, more and more *lycéens* (senior high school students) and university students, particularly those from the middle classes, were taking an interest in Anglo-American popular music, with star turns from groups such as the Beatles (from 1963) and then Pink Floyd (from the turn of the 1970s) or the Clash in the late 1970s, the Cure, U2 in the second half of the 1980s and, later, Nirvana or Radiohead, each of which were to play a generational role and spark off vocations in terms of amateur performance. Therefore, from the mid-1960s until at least the late 1980s, no media space was given to French rock bands, even though subculture movements were in evidence here and there (Tamagne).

Artists who managed to bring audiences together and overcome the divide between French *variété* and English or American rock were very rare. Mention can be made of Serge Gainsbourg (see the chapter by Olivier Julien in this book), whose career began in small cabaret *chanson* venues in the late 1950s, but who found *variété* success from 1965 until the late 1980s. From the 1980s, some artists belonged to both worlds: groups like Téléphone, Trust, Indochine and Les Rita Mitsouko, and musicians like Bashung or Manu Chao and a few singers who were seen as having a rock background, like Etienne Daho. This situation naturally leads today to a re-examination of many forgotten singers from what is sometimes a nostalgic perspective (see the chapters by Dalbavie or Rouzé in this book). In any case, this period of the rise of the economic and social importance of popular music led to youth asserting itself as an age group, partly in opposition to the previous generation. If the 1960s witnessed a new consumer desire within a context of growth, the 1970s saw increased criticism of the political and social models established therein. This took place before the arrival of the more superficial 1980s (Neyrand and Guilot 1983), which were nevertheless marked by issues of identity differentiation, with the emergence of post-colonial questions (Lebrun in this book).

The Dynamics of Independent and Community-Based Development

The massive introduction of recorded music had an impact in the field of live music. Concerts became, from the 1980s onwards, pretexts to promote new records, at the same time that the business of live concerts was being optimised through the activities of private promoters (Guibert and Sagot-Duvauroux 2013). However, recorded music also led to a transformation of contexts in which dance music was presented—in France and elsewhere—with the growth of nightclubs where musicians gave way to recorded music. Nightclubs took hold as of the mid- to late 1960s. At the request of DJs, a musical offering was developed that was designed with dance in mind, such as disco music in the 1970s.

In economic terms, what characterised disco, like many specialised music markets (whether jazz related, or music that came out of the resurgence of the regional folk movement or even protest song), was the assertion of the role of independent producers, who, working closely with artists, worked under contract for large record producers to ensure the visibility and distribution of their artists. From an organisational perspective, this represented the gradual transition from the "craftsman/bureaucrat" pairing to that of the "entrepreneur/showman" as theorised by Richard Peterson and translated into French by A. Hennion (Peterson 1991).

Yet the notion of subcontracting innovation in the field of "hit-parades" and niche repertoires did not call into question the oligopolistic dominance of big labels in respect of mainstream artists signed to the majors (whether French *variété* or Anglo-American rock).

In respect of the music, three simultaneous developments—which could be qualified as organisational, aesthetic and political—were characteristic of the last two decades of the twentieth century in France. The first concerned the economic structure of an alternative channel of recorded music (from recording to the distribution of records to retailers—independent record stores). This took place following the re-appropriation of the punk and DIY ethic in France in the late 1970s. Indeed, above and beyond the countercultural ideology, a pro-active philosophy developed, stimulated by small music production organisations. There was also a favourable context in terms of technological innovations (in particular, multi-track cassette recorders, cassette decks, photocopiers and the FM radio network). This dynamic, which soon affected all DIY post-punk currents (including subcultures such as psychobilly, garage, ska, hardcore, alternative rock, new wave, indie pop, neo-realist *chanson*, thrash metal and then death metal and black metal), can also be explained through the spread of individual and collective musical practice among young people (notably through collective rehearsal; Touché 1994). The collective sharing of music through popular education leisure facilities seems to have been freer from this time (Belleville 1985).

New independent initiatives in local music scenes around the country (as opposed to the Paris-centric industry) had an impact on the economics of music in France. This extended to the community-based organisation of music rehearsal and distribution activities, whether amateur or in support of professionalization (Hein, in this book; Hein 2006; Guibert 2006).

Figure 0.2 Mustang, "Anne-Sophie," A Rag/Sony, 2009, single front cover.

The second movement was connected to the increased internationalisation of local musical propositions and the link-up between global and local musical trends. At a time when, from the 1980s onwards, *chanson* and rock were criticised for their sometimes Western-centric performances and focus on limited or traditional instruments, other movements asserted themselves in France.

This was the case of rap and more broadly speaking hip hop (Molinero and Béthune in this book), reflecting perspectives related to issues surrounding immigration. The arrival of electronic music can also be mentioned here (Petiau in this book), questioning ways of doing and responding to popular music, but also establishing a dialogue with conceptual art (Jouannais and Kihm 1998).

Figure 0.3 Justice, *D.A.N.C.E Remixes*, Ed Banger Records, 2007, single front cover.

We must also mention world music as a commercial category, giving access both to a discography of the musical heritage of French regions (folk) and that of foreign countries, primarily countries in the south (Olivier 2012). In the early 1990s, moreover, artists (Les Négresses Vertes and Mano Negra, whose lead singer Manu Chao went on to pursue a solo career) mixed post-colonial influences, alternative rock and realist *chanson* to achieve a significant international impact.

Finally, what was particularly characteristic of France, compared to many countries, was national and also local-level public cultural policy (Poirrier 2000; Dubois 1999). From the beginning of the Third Republic (1870) until the end of the 1950s, the entertainment sector—like the cultural industries sector—was developed through private initiatives. In 1959, the creation of a Ministry of Culture, headed by André Malraux, constituted the initial change.

Public policy at that time aimed to support autonomous art and protect it from the market, particularly through the creation of *Maisons de la Culture* (arts centres). In wanting to celebrate the works of humanity from a perspective that could be described as Kantian, the Ministry of Culture well and truly separated them from commercial leisure practices (the entertainment and cultural industries) that were not included in its scope. Nor were amateur community-based practices considered to be artistic. Nevertheless, the Ministry of Culture did have a remit to broaden artistic appeal (democratisation) and works had to be brought closer to the people. With the election of François Mitterrand to the presidency in 1981, cultural policy under the leadership of J. Lang was partly modified. In particular, rock and *chanson* were supported from the mid-1990s under the remit known as "*musiques actuelles*"[8] (Teillet 2002). These elements resulted in numerous French specificities, particularly in terms of remuneration for artists (Menger 2005), the construction of a network of venues with public financial support and support for festivals (Guibert and Sagot-Duvauroux 2013). Facing increasing globalised communication in a sector where the attraction of "foreign" English-language productions was significant, another Ministry of Culture action was to put into place a quota for the broadcast of French-language songs (1994),[9] which in particular promoted the development of the local rap scene (Molinero 2009), as well as discussion on the place of rap over *chanson* (Pecqueux 2007).[10]

Consolidation of Digital Technology, Reaffirmation of Local Musical Activity and Reshuffling the Deck

In addition to financial support for music, public policy from the 1980s onwards acted to limit noise levels of concerts, conditions for reception of audiences, copyright compliance in the field of performing arts and the creation of a support fund for the sector. Coulangeon (1999) speaks of a "cleansing" of the professional music sector, with a disappearance of the "*noir de chauffe*."[11]

From the late twentieth century, with the steady decline in turnover for recording production and the corollary of the rise of digital applications (Hesmondhalgh 2008), the state legislated to restrict peer-to-peer and illegal downloading (Dadvsi law 2006, transposing European Directive 29 from 2001 and the HADOPI law, 2009), provoking much discussion (see the chapter by Suire in this book).

We then saw a transformation of the economic model of production and distribution of recorded music (Beuscart 2007). Although an oligopolistic pattern continued, it was no longer simply based on companies in the music sector, but more broadly on those at work in the media and digital technology industries (Bouquillion and Matthews 2010). Television, like traditional media, ensured the promotion of established Francophone artists, but also acted as promoter of young talent through reality shows (*Star Academy* and *Popstars* from 2001, *Nouvelle Star* in 2003 and then *The Voice* in 2012). After more than a decade of such TV talent shows, it is notable that several contestants have become permanent fixtures on the media landscape (Jenifer, Nolwenn Leroy, Christophe Willem, Julien Doré, Olivia Ruiz, Amel Bent and so on).

Meanwhile, in France, popular music has taken on great prominence in the leisure time of the French (Donnat 2008), as well as increasing amounts of public space (Rouzé, this book). Interest in the study of listeners and fans shows the extent to which meaning given to how music is received has gained in complexity in line with the complexity of processes and behaviours (Glevarec and Pinet 2009). A specific example is given in this book with *tectonik*, a current in electronic music which combines independent artistic performance, large distribution companies and the use of social networks (Petiau).

The turn of the century also saw the development of popular music heritage actions, through dedicated museums or exhibitions (see the Dalbavie chapter in this book). At the municipal level in towns and cities throughout France, local music histories have been written by enthusiasts (Guibert and Le Guern 2010). Yet internationally, music has also come to be considered as a "creative industry" that can generate revenue and become a factor in promoting a region, particularly from the point of view of tourism (Bennett and Peterson 2004). While some cities have used this to transform the image of their city, others have focused communication on authenticity linked to the region and its traditions (Martin 2006).

A Summary of Research Activities

In France, the historical weight of cultural legitimacy and the role of historical materialism remained decisive until the 1980s. Thus, research on music was almost exclusively approached from the perspective of the dual opposition between "independent art" and "functional music" or, in other words, between "serious music" and "light music," or between "music in the written tradition" and "music in the oral tradition." There was no place for other modes of analysis or dialectics, such as those evoked by Tagg (1982) and Cutler (1985). Encyclopaedias and histories of music therefore often devoted no more than a small space to "non-art" music, dealing briefly with jazz, traditional music and *chanson* and forgetting "other popular music" altogether (Roland 1963; Souriau 1999). Work on French *chanson* and *"music-hall"* was the first to be developed, in the form of literature and linguistics research (Calvet 1981). But, to use Michel De Certeau's analogy on "the beauty of death" (1974), works on *chanson*, like those on rural popular music, has often focused on endangered repertoires and taken little interest in music as experienced, or its creative dimension (Olivier 2012).

International research activity under the guidance of the International Association for the Study of Popular Music (IASPM) and the theorisation of the concept of "popular music" helped to structure French research from the mid- to late 1980s. From this perspective, mention must be made of the role of the journal *Vibrations* under the supervision of Antoine Hennion and other young researchers of the time (Louis-Jean Calvet, Philippe Gumplowicz, Jean-Claude Klein, etc.) who published six issues with Éditions Privat (Grenier 1991) and hosted the International IASPM Biennial in Paris in 1989 (200 years after the French Revolution). Sociological research then began to develop. Besides Hennion's work on *variété* producers (Hennion 1981), this included the coordination of a seminal work with Patrick Mignon (1991): *Rock, de l'histoire au mythe*. As well as bringing together researchers working on rock music from the perspective of various social science disciplines at the time (C. Dutheil, sociology; J.M. Lucas, economics; P. Teillet, political science, etc.), this work offered translated contributions from two sociologists who were precursors in the field of popular music research internationally: Simon Frith and Richard Peterson offered analysis on rock music production. Popular music was then gradually addressed in France from the point of view of the sociology of work, art and culture, youth and deviance.

Meanwhile, the creation of the French Musical Observatory (OMF) at Paris 4 University (Paris-Sorbonne) in 1989 gave rise to several musicological and sociological publications on popular music (following research by Anne-Marie Green and then Catherine Rudent, Laurent Cugny and Olivier Julien) after teaching in this musicology department began to cover *chanson* (Chantal Brunschwig) and rock (Patrick Mignon) in the mid-1980s. To this can be added the pioneering work of several other researchers, such as Denis-Constant Martin on reggae (1982), which hinged on sociology and semiotics, Jean-Marie Seca's social psychology doctoral thesis on rock (1988) and sociological and anthropological research on *chanson* carried out by Joëlle Deniot and Catherine Dutheil at the University of Nantes, particularly the 1997 conference on realist *chanson* (Deniot and Dutheil 1997).

Faced with academic institutions influenced by critical theories that, beyond a few minor initiatives, proved reticent to studying popular cultures, many trainee researchers conducted research drawing on the growth of amateur activities in the sector and studying a popular music sector under construction. These included, during the 1990s, among others, Marc Touché and H. Bazin, the work of E. Brandl, G. Guibert, F. Ribac, A. Petiau, D. Tassin, C. Prevost-Thomas and O. Roueff.

Building on this foundation, as of the late 1990s, a multidisciplinary group of doctoral students (S. Etienne, G. Guibert, M.P. Bonniol and then E. Parent and M. Saladin) established the "music and society" collection of works and the multidisciplinary academic journal *Volume!*, which instituted a new generation of researchers (at the same time as publishing research from the first generation). An inventory of social science research on music can be found in Prevost-Thomas (2010). Several special issues of human and social sciences journals were also dedicated to popular music during the first decade of the twenty-first century (*Musurgia, Terrain, Réseaux*).

Therefore, by the early 2000s, the general context of the perception of popular music can be said to have begun to change in academic circles, in parallel with the translation of English and American journalistic literature (S. Reynolds, D. Toop, G. Marcus) related to the world of research and, in particular, cultural studies (Éditions Allia, Kargo, Tristan). After reports on the International IASPM Biennials from several French researchers who had attended, a new "European Francophone branch" was set up again by Christophe Pirenne, Catherine Rudent and François Ribac in 2005. It organised a symposium in francophone Belgium—the first president of the association, Christophe Pirenne, was a professor at Louvain-la-Neuve. In France, these initiatives have allowed an interdisciplinary dynamic on an international scale to be combined with the emergence of disciplinary initiatives above and beyond a purely musicological or sociological approach. These have thus included research in the fields of geography (Guiu 2006), the political economics of communication (Matthews and Perticoz 2012), history (Baubérot and Tamagne 2016), law (Mastor et al. 2010), management sciences (Sohier 2010; Le Rendu-Lizée 2014) and research emanating from language departments.

In each chapter of this book, we will return in detail to the issues touched on previously. It is hoped that the reader will be able to gain an accurate picture, in context, of how popular music is experienced in France today, as well as the various traditions of French research into popular music. Indeed, this work brings together researchers from very diverse backgrounds and disciplines, with very different objectives, but who, collectively, would seem to be representative of the dynamics of French and Francophone research, nationally and internationally.

Notes

1 French specificities in other technological innovations, such as the cinema and the beginnings of communication through digital networks (which took the form of the Minitel in France in the 1980s), might also be mentioned here.
2 According to the definition given in multidisciplinary research in the 1980s and the birth of the IASPM and the journal *Popular Music*. See, in particular, Cutler (1984) on this dialectical mechanism.
3 The growth of instrumental and vocal societies was not without resistance or opposition however (Amaouche-Antoine Cordonnier 1984), and the musical knowledge acquired was sometimes appropriated for dances and other popular secular festivals.
4 Smaller places are very different in spirit, both in terms of their audience (made up mostly of artists or students) and their entertainment (where *chanson* blended with poetry and readings, Penet 1999).
5 Translator's note: In France, the term "*music-hall*" was also used to refer to the music industry.
6 As well as the electric guitar or the Teppaz portable record player—which can be seen as symbols of industrial modernity, but also of youth (Morin 1963)
7 This is of course an oversimplification. At the least, a third force was French *chanson* in its more poetic or political forms.
8 Translator's note: Literally meaning "current music," the term *musiques actuelles* was the official term chosen in the framework of public policies in France.
9 Between 1992 and 1998, the weighting for local repertoires in France increased from 39.9% to 49.8%, making it one of the highest, ahead of Great Britain (48.3%) and Germany (43.5%), Syndicat National des Producteurs de Phonographes (SNEP), *L'économie du disque 1999*, p. 45.
10 As well as the ongoing debate on this issue between C. Rubin (2004) and A. Pecqueux (2005).
11 Which is to say, whereby, previously, initiation to the profession took place outside legal or official frameworks. See Marc Perrenoud's work on musicians ("*musicos*") (2007) and Fabien Hein's chapter in this book for more information on the practical conditions of exercising in the music profession in this context.

Bibliography

Amaouche-Antoine, Marie-Dominique. 1984. "Espéraza 1870–1940: Une ville ouvrière qui chante." *Ethnologie Française* 14(3):237–250.
Basile, Giusy, and Chantal Gavouyère. 1996. *La chanson française dans le cinéma des années 30*. Paris: Bibliothèque Nationale de France.
———. 1999. "La chanson et la musique des rues à travers la production phonographique et cinématographique." *Ethnologie Française* 29(1):11–21.
Baubérot, Arnaud, and Florence Tamagne. 2016. *This is a Modern World: Histoire sociale du rock*. Lille: Presses du Septentrion.
Belleville, Pierre. 1985. "Demain L'Education populaire." In *Guide de L'éducation populaire*, edited by Benigno Caseres, 220–225. Paris: La Découverte.
Bennett, Andy, and Richard A. Peterson. 2004. *Music Scenes, Local, Translocal and Virtual*. Nashville: Vanderbilt University Press.
Beuscart, Jean-Samuel. 2007. "Les transformations de L'intermédiation musicale La construction de L'offre commerciale de musique en ligne en france." *Réseaux* 25(141–142): 143–176.
———. 2008. "Sociabilité en ligne, notoriété virtuelle et carrière artistique: Les usages de MySpace par les musiciens autoproduits." *Réseaux* 152:139–168.
Bouquillion, Philippe, and Jacob T. Matthews. 2010. *Le Web collaboratif: Mutations des industries de la culture et de la communication*. Grenoble: Presses universitaires de Grenoble.
Calvet, Louis-Jean. 1981. *Chanson et société*. Paris: Payot.
Charpentier-Leroy, Marie. 2014. "La chanson réaliste : histoire d'un genre." Master thesis diss., Paris-Sorbonne University.
Condemi, Concetta. 1992. *Les Cafés-concerts: Histoire d'un divertissement*. Paris: Quai Voltaire.
Constant, Denis. 1982. *Aux Sources du Reggae: Musique, société et politique en Jamaïque*. Roquevaire: Parenthèses.
Cordonnier, Pierrick. 1994. "Harmonies fanfares et danses populaires." *Marsyas* 29:7–9.

Coulangeon, Philippe. 1999. "Les musiciens de jazz: les chemins de la professionnalisation." *Genèses* 36:54–68.

Cutler, Chris. 1984. *File Under Popular: Theoretical and Critical Writings on Music*. London: November Books.

De Certeau, Michel. 1974. *La Culture au pluriel*. Paris: UGE.

Defrance, Yves. 1984. "Traditions populaires et industrialisation: Le cas de L'accordéon." *Ethnologie Française* 14(3):223–236.

De Langle, Henry-Melchior. 1990. *Le petit monde des cafés et débits parisiens au xixᵉ siècle*. Paris: PUF.

Deniot, Joëlle, and Catherine Dutheil. 1997. "La voix et son document." *Sociologie de L'Art* 10:53–70.

Donnat, Olivier. 1997. *Les Pratiques Culturelles des Français: Enquête 1997*. Paris: La Documentation Française.

———. 2008. *Les pratiques culturelles des Français à L'ère numérique: Enquête 2008*. Paris: La Documentation Française.

Dubois, Vincent. 1999. *La Politique culturelle: Genèse d'une catégorie d'intervention publique*. Paris: Belin.

Duneton, Claude. 1998. *Histoire de la chanson française, 1780–1860, tome 2*. Paris: Éditions du Seuil.

Dutheil-Pessin, Catherine. 2004. *La Chanson réaliste: Sociologie d'un genre: le visage et la voix*. Paris: L'Harmattan.

Fabiani, Jean-Louis. 2015. *La sociologie comme elle s'écrit: De Bourdieu à Latour*. Paris: Éditions de L'EHESS.

Flichy, Patrice. 1991. *Une Histoire de la communication moderne: Espace public et vie privée*. Paris: La Découverte.

Frith, Simon. 1989. "Why Do Songs Have Words?" *Contemporary Music Review* 5(1):77–96.

Galland, Olivier. 1985. *Les Jeunes*. Paris: La Découverte.

Gétreau, Florence, ed. 1997. *Musiciens des rues de Paris*. Paris: RMN.

Girard Augustin. 1978. "Industries culturelles." *Futuribles: Analyse—prévision—prospectives* 17:597–605.

Glevarec, Hervé, and Michel Pinet. 2009. *La radio et ses publics: Sociologie d'une fragmentation*. Paris: Seteun/Irma.

Goffre, Annie. 1984. "Exploitation raisonnée de la musique folklorique en France et ses artisans depuis la fin du xixᵉ siècle." *Ethnologie Française* 14(3):295–318.

Granovetter, Mark. 2008. *Sociologie Économique*. Paris: Seuil.

Grenier, Line. 1991. "*Vibrations*: musiques, médias, sociétés. Nos. 1–6. Paris: Privat, 1985–1988." *Popular Music* 10(1):93–97.

Grignon, Claude, and Jean-Claude Passeron. 1989. *Le savant et le populaire. Misérabilisme et populisme en sociologie et en littérature*. Paris: Seuil.

Guibert, Gérôme. 2005. "Is the French Word 'chanson' Equivalent to the English Term 'popular music'?" In *Making Music, Making Meaning, IASPM International Conference Proceedings*, edited by Geoff Stahl, 275–282. Rome: IASPM. www.iaspm.net/archive/IASPM05LIGHT.pdf.

———. 2006. *La production de la culture: Le cas des musiques amplifiées en France: Genèse, structuration, industries, alternatives*. Paris and St Amant Tallende: Irma/editions Seteun.

Guibert, Gérôme, and Philippe Le Guern. 2007. "Faire L'histoire des musiques amplifies en France." In *Stereo: Sociologie compare des musiques populaires France-G.B*, edited by Hugh Dauncey and Philippe Le Guern, 27–44. Paris: Seteun/Irma.

———. 2010. "Charting the History of Amplified Musics in France." In *Stereo: Comparative Perspectives on the Sociological Study of Popular Music in France and Britain*, edited by Hugh Dauncey and Philippe Le Guern, 23–42. London: Ashgate.

Guibert, Gérôme, and Dominique Sagot-Duvauroux. 2013. *Musiques actuelles, ça part en live: Analyse économique d'une filière culture*. Paris: Irma/DEPS.

Guiu, Claire, ed. 2006. "Géographies et musiques: quelles perspectives?" *Géographie et cultures* 59.

Hein, Fabien. 2006. *Le monde du rock: Ethnographie du réel*. Clermont-Ferrand and Paris: Mélanie Seteun/IRMA.

Heinich, Nathalie. 1996. *Être artiste*. Paris: Klincksiek.

Hennion, Antoine. 1981. *Les professionnels du disque: Une sociologie des variétés*. Paris: Métailié.

Hennion, Antoine, Émilie Gomart, and Sophie Maisonneuve. 2000. *Figures de L'amateur: Formes, objets et pratiques de L'amour de la musique aujourd'hui*. Paris: La Documentation Française.

Hesmondhalgh, David. 2008 "La musique et le numérique: au-delà du battage." In *Sound Factory: Musique et logiques de L'industrialisation*, edited by Stéphane Dorin, 141–151. Paris: Seteun.

Huet, Armel, Jacques Ion, Alain Lefebvre, Bernard Miège, and René Peron. 1978. *Capitalisme et industries culturelles*. Grenoble: PUG.

Jouannais, Jean-Yves, and Christophe Kihm, eds. 1998. "Techno. Anatomie des cultures électroniques." Special issue, *Art Press hors-série 9*.

Kalifa, Dominique. 2001. *La culture de masse en France. 1: 1860–1930*. Paris: La Découverte.

Klein, Jean-Claude. 1985. "Emprunt, synchrétisme, métissage: la revue à grand spectacle des années folles." *Vibrations* 1:39–53.

———. 1988. "Chanson et music-hall des années 20." In *La chanson française et son histoire*, edited by Rieger Dietmar, 299–305. Tübingen: Gunter Narr Verlag.

Lallement, Michel. 2015. *L'âge du faire: Hacking, travail, anarchie*. Paris: Le Seuil.

Le Rendu-Lizée, Carole. 2014. "Enjeux et conditions de la mise en oeuvre d'un groupement d'employeur dans le secteur culturel: une application aux musiques actuelles." PhD diss., Angers University.

Lesueur, Daniel. 1999. *Hit-parades: 1950–1998*. Paris: Alternatives et Parallèles.

Maigret, Eric. 2003. *Sociologie de la communication et des médias*. Paris: Armand Colin.

Maisonneuve, Sophie. 2006. "De la machine parlante au disque: une innovation technique, commerciale et culturelle." *XXe siècle* 92:17–32.

Martin, Denis-Constant. 2006. "*Le myosotis, et puis la rose . . . Pour une sociologie des 'musiques de masse.'*" L'Homme 177–178:131–154.

Mastor, Wanda, Jean-Pierre Marguénaud, and Fabien Marchadier, eds. 2010. *Droit et Rock*. Paris: Dalloz.

Matthews, Jacob, and Lucien Perticoz, eds. 2012. *L'industrie musicale à L'aube du XXIe siècle*. Paris: L'Harmattan.

Menger, Pierre Michel. 2005. *Profession artiste: Extension du domaine de la création*. Paris: Textuel.

Mignon, Patrick, and Hennion Antoine, eds. 1991. *Rock, de L'histoire au mythe*. Paris: Anthropos.

Molinero, Stéphanie. 2009. *Les Publics du rap: Enquête sociologique*. Paris: L'Harmattan.

Morin, Edgar. 1963. "Salut les copains I: Une nouvelle classe d'âge." *Le Monde* 6 juillet:1.

Mussat, Marie-Claire. 1992. *La belle époque des kiosques à musique*. Paris: Éditions du May.

Naudin, Marie. 1968. *Évolution parallèle de la poésie et de la musique en France: Rôle unificateur de la chanson*. Paris: Nizet.

Neyrand, Gérard, and Caroline Guillot. 1983. *Entre clips et looks: Les pratiques de consommation des adolescents*. Paris: L'Harmattan.

Olivier, Emmanuelle. 2012. *Musiques au monde: La tradition au prisme de la creation*. Sampzac: Éditions Delatour.

Ozouf, Jacques, and Mona Ozouf. 1989. *La république des instituteurs*. Paris: Gallimard.

Pecqueux, Anthony. 2007. *Voix du rap: Essai de sociologie de L'action musicale*. Paris. L'Harmattan.

———. 2005. "Le rap français comme pratique chansonnière: Réponse à Christophe Rubin." *Volume! La revue des musiques populaires* 4(1):151–154.

Penet, Martin. 1999. "L'âge d'or de la chanson littéraire." *Revue de la Bibliothèque Nationale de France* 3:61–67.

Perrenoud, Marc. 2007. *Les Musicos: Enquête sur des musiciens ordinaires*. Paris: La Découverte.

Peterson, Richard. 1991. "Mais pourquoi en 1955? Comment expliquer la naissance du rock." In *Rock, de L'histoire au mythe*, edited by Antoine Hennion and Patrick Mignon, 9–40. Paris: Anthropos, coll. "Vibrations."

Poirrier, Philippe. 2000. *L'État et la culture en France au XXe siècle*. Paris: Le Livre de Poche.

Prévost-Thomas, Cécile. 2010. "Les nouvelles perspectives en sociologie de la musique." *L'Année sociologique* 60(2): 403–417.

Roland, Manuel. 1963. *Histoire de la musique, tome 2, du XVIIIe siècle à nos jours*. Paris: Galimmard, La Pléiade.

Rubin, Christophe. 2004. "Le rap est-il soluble dans la chanson française?" *Volume! La revue des musiques populaires* 3(2): 29–42.

Rypko Schub, Louise. 1976. "La chanson naturaliste: Aristide Bruant, ou le revers de la Belle Époque." *Cahiers de L'Association internationale des études françaises* 28:195–212.

Schaeffner, André. 1997 [1926]. *Le jazz*. Paris: Jean Michel Place.

Schlesser, Gilles. 2006. *Le Cabaret "rive gauche": De la Rose rouge au Bateau ivre (1946–1974)*. Paris: L'Archipel.

Seca, Jean-Marie. 1988. *Vocations Rock*. Paris: Klincksiek.

Sohier, Alice. 2010. "Le rôle de L'expérience vécue et de ses antécédents sur la satisfaction envers un spectacle vivant. Le cas des festivals de rock." Phd. diss., Caen University.

Sohn, Anne-Marie. 2001. *Âge tendre et tête de bois: Histoire des jeunes des années 60*. Paris: Hachette.

Souriau, Etienne, ed. 1999. *Vocabulaire d'esthétique*. Paris: PUF.

Szendy, Peter. 2001. *Écoute: Une histoire de nos oreilles*. Paris: Minuit.

Tagg, Philip. 1982. "Analysing Popular Music: Theory, Method and Practice." *Popular Music* 2:37–67.

Teillet, Philippe. 2002. "Éléments pour une histoire des politiques publiques en faveur des 'musiques amplifies.'" In *Les Collectivités locales et la culture: Les formes de L'institutionnalisation, XIXe–XXe siècles*, edited by Poirrier Philippe, 361–393. Paris: La Documentation Française/Comité d'Histoire du Ministère de la Culture— Fondation Maison des Sciences de L'Homme.

Touché, Marc. 1994. *Connaissance de L'environnement sonore urbain: L'exemple des lieux de répétitions*. Vaucresson: Rapport de recherche CRIV-CNRS.

Tournès, Ludovic. 1999. *New Orleans sur Seine, Histoire du jazz en France*. Paris: Fayard.

———. 2002. "Jalons pour une histoire internationale de L'industrie du disque; expansion, déclin et absorption de la branche phonographique de Pathé (1894–1936)." In *Histoire des industries culturelles en France, XIXe–XXe siècles*, edited by Jacques Marseille and Patrick Eveno, 465–477. Paris: ADHE.

Weber, Max. 1967 [1905]. *L'éthique protestante et L'esprit du capitalisme*. Paris: Plon.

PART I

Zeitgeist

The Mutations of French Popular Music
During the "*Trente Glorieuses*"

Gérôme Guibert and Catherine Rudent

From the end of the Second World War through to the beginning of the 1970s, French pop-ular music underwent a period of renewal.

The war and its fallout transformed the global balance of power, with the influence of the United States becoming increasingly prominent in the economy, politics and culture of the Western world. International politics revolved around issues linked to the Cold War, as well as the violent upheavals of decolonisation. In France, the 1960s and 1970s formed a period that Henri Mendras (1994) has described as the "Second French Revolution," affecting every aspect of society. As Mendras has shown, it was between 1965 and 1984 that

> four large and antagonistic classes [the farmers, the labourers, the bourgeoisie and the middle classes] crumbled [. . .]. The dominant institutions—the Church, the military, the Republic, education, the Communist Party and the unions—lost their symbolic aura and their authority [. . .].

Amongst other factors, this multi-faceted and radical transformation of French society was brought about by the so-called baby boom—that is, the exceptional number of births occur-ring after the end of the war. In France, this occurred particularly between 1946 and 1951 (Bernstein & Milza 2, 367). At the beginning of the 1960s, these individuals were becoming teenagers, and the demographic composition of the French state was thus profoundly altered and renewed, with a lower average age and a significant proportion of the population aged under twenty. This facilitated the arrival of new cultural practices, themselves reinforced by the economic prosperity of the nation between 1945 and 1975. This was a time commonly known in France as the "*Trente Glorieuses*," a "period of significant and steady growth, ben-efitting from a favourable international trade environment, an opening-up of foreign mar-kets, a strong increase in population, and state intervention" (Berstein & Milza 2, 365). This period of growth would only be cut short by the global financial crises of 1973–1974, when "a succession of disturbances [. . .] rocked the international monetary system created by the Bretton-Woods agreements, upset global oil prices, and affected a wide range of older or maturing industries" (Berstein & Milza 3, 7).

As for the world of music, the baby boomers of the 1960s showed tremendous enthusi-asm in adopting new popular music styles (that of the so-called *yéyés* in particular), and in embracing the new, light, practical and cheap recording formats and broadcasting equipment (transistor radios, 45 rpm vinyl "singles," portable "turntables"). Indeed, it was this young generation that made the radio show *Salut les Copains* (lit. *Hi There, Buddies*) so successful. This show was created in 1959 by Daniel Filipacchi and Frank Ténot for the Europe n° 1 station (which was also young itself, having been started in 1955). Aimed at school-age teen-agers, it was broadcast daily at the end of the school day and featured the "smash hits" of artists who themselves were only just entering adulthood: Johnny Hallyday, Sylvie Vartan, France Gall, Sheila, Françoise Hardy, Eddy Mitchell, Claude François. This was a group of perhaps a dozen or so artists in all, according to Jean-Marie Périer, the photographer who found himself at the heart of this musical phenomenon. The music of the *yéyés* represented a significant stage in the history of French popular music in the second half of the twentieth century: it is analysed here from both a cultural and aesthetic perspective in the chapters by Florence Tamagne and Matthieu Saladin.

French music, like French society in general, has undergone some major transformations, and yet, it is important to situate these in an extremely divided national and cultural context. During this period, the hierarchies between "high" culture and "pop" culture remained strong. Excellent and complex analyses of this divide can be found in the work of Bourdieu, and particularly in his book *La Distinction*, published in 1979, for which sociological surveys were conducted in 1963 and in 1967–1968. This work proposes sociological explanations for the structuration of tastes, crystallised around the notions of "legitimate" taste, "middle-brow" taste and "popular" taste.

And yet, from a historical perspective, it seems that all musical fields, both "legitimate" and "popular," underwent major changes in the post-war period through to the 1960s. Indeed, in the world of "legitimate" music, Boulez revived the principles of serialism, seeking to make a break with the recent French past. The studios of the Radiodiffusion-Télévision Française (RTF) also broadcast the musical experiments of Pierre Schaeffer and Pierre Henry—experiments that parallel those of Stockhausen in Cologne and Berio in Milan. At the same time, musical revolutions were occurring in *chanson*—that is, on the other side of the art music / popular music divide.

In Paris, an extraordinary renaissance occurred in cabaret music in the 1950s and 1960s: from the end of the 1940s onwards, the "*cabarets d'esprit rive gauche*" (Schlesser 2006, 87–111) saw the arrival of a great number of talents. These venues were the first springboards for the careers of Gréco, Brassens, Brel, Ferré, Barbara, Anne Sylvestre, Nougaro, Gainsbourg and others. At the end of the 1950s, a series of further shake-ups occurred, starting with the arrival of rock music in France from 1956 onwards. Initially, this came via the humorous par-odies performed by Henri Salvador who, whilst maintaining a certain critical distance, fitted pun-filled lyrics by Boris Vian to music by Michel Legrand ("Rock and roll-mops") or Henri Salvador himself ("Rock hoquet"). At the same time, American 45 rpm vinyl "singles" began to arrive in France, where they provoked quite a different, and indeed enthusiastic, response from the youngest generation of musicians who subsequently became the first French "rock-ers."[1] Next, France saw the rise of the *yéyé* phenomenon, which had its roots firmly in this first wave of rock music, but which was nevertheless distinct from it, occurring a few years later from 1960 onwards. Issuing directly out of the *Salut les Copains* programme, the *yéyé* movement was borne along by a handful of artists aired on this show, whose singles fre-quently sold more than a million copies. In their music, they reworked the styles that were proving particularly commercially successful in the United States for a French audience—of which the twist is a notable example. Most of the time, the *yéyé* groups simply adapted French lyrics to pre-existing music—an analysis of these adaptations is provided here in the chapter by Matthieu Saladin. It was only in 1963 that this musical style was baptised "*yéyé*" by Edgar Morin: in two articles published by the newspaper *Le Monde*, the sociologist analysed this musical phenomenon as the expression of a new way of growing into adulthood, one in which one's "friends" ("*copains*") played an essential role.

The first section of *Made in France* traces the history of these profound transformations: Florence Tamagne thus highlights the difference between the societal anxieties raised by the violence of the so-called *blousons noirs* and by the first year of the *yéyé* movement, on the one hand, and the conservative values associated with the *yéyé* groups during their heyday in the years after 1963, on the other. The fear of rock music, she shows, continued through into the 1970s with the rise of rock festivals.

Julien's chapter calls attention to the extent to which Gainsbourg—whose production precisely is at its best between 1958 ("Le poinçonneur des Lilas") and 1979 (*Aux armes et caetera*)—borrowed from the many contradictory trends present in France during this turbulent time. In a blend which is his own, Gainsbourg not only assumed the high poetic ambitions of cabaret music but also managed to incorporate new styles imported from the English-speaking world.

Kaiser, on the other hand, focuses on the French vinyl industry. In this domain also, the changes of the era did not occur all at once: as he shows with examples drawn from archive research, this industry regularly underwent cycles of obsolescence and of regrowth. As for the post-war revival, Kaiser demonstrates that it was already well underway in the form of the variety shows of the 1950s, many years before *yéyé* music exploded onto the scene.

It is therefore necessary to put the *yéyé* revolution (1960–1965) into perspective, position it within its wider chronological context and consider it as the result of a series of broader and more complex changes in terms of the economics, technology, demography, society and culture of the time. It is also important to realise that this musical movement—which seemed so short, so boisterous and so instantly recognisable—did not break out from a tradition of French *chanson* that was sedate, poetic, homogenous and refined, whose progression had until then been seamless and uniform. This simplistic narrative of a stimulating, and without exception authentic, French *chanson* movement—running from Bruant (at the end of the nineteenth century) through to Brel, Ferré and Brassens—is questioned by a number of researchers. In *En avant la zizique*, Boris Vian (1959, 114–117), himself a prominent actor in the history of French *chanson*, calls attention to the tasteless records that occasionally characterised *chanson* during France's Belle Epoque; Jean-Claude Klein (1988) shows the aesthetic divides at play in *music-hall chanson* during the 1920s; Gérôme Guibert (2006) traces the constitutive tensions in the field, which go back to well before the twentieth century. French *chanson* before 1960 is not a uniform and calm landscape, living out a golden age which would be destroyed by the *yéyé* cataclysm.

The *yéyé* revolution must also be reinterpreted in terms of what is happening today: the older members of the baby-boom generation are now in their seventies. As a result, there has been what commentators have called a "*papyboom*." For these individuals, who represent a considerable proportion of French society, the years of the 1960s and the music of the *yéyés* are those of their youth and their teenage obsessions. They are invested therefore with an aura of nostalgia, an important sentiment in cultural and musical practice. As a sign of this renewed interest in the *yéyé* phenomenon, we might cite the recent "*Vieilles Canailles*" (lit. the "old rabble") concerts: Johnny Hallyday, Eddy Mitchell and Jacques Dutronc, all over the age of seventy, performed in six concerts at the Palais Omnisport Paris-Bercy arena in November 2014. The hall was filled to capacity (17,000 seats), and the performance was screened in cinemas a few days later, and then again on 15 January 2015, because of the popularity of the show. It was undoubtedly hugely well received amongst a very broad audience and its success has been prolonged further still by the recent release of a DVD version. Vast swathes of the French public have turned out to listen to these three artists who, it must be said, have not always been to everybody's liking; and this audience is, in all probability, more homogenous in terms of age than social or cultural standing.

The history of French popular music and the upheavals it underwent during the thirty years following 1945 is thus a complex one which demands nuanced analysis. But those actors who were implicated at the time in supporting (or resisting) the rise of the *yéyé* did not always recognise these subtleties. On the whole, the *yéyés* shared with their teenage audience an unbridled fascination with the musical hits imported from the United States and used this to fashion a new local generational identity based around these new musical styles and new ways of thinking about teenage culture. It is on the subject of this founding period, filled with a certain violence inherent in the speed and extent of the transformations taking place, that this first section of the book begins with the chapter by Matthieu Saladin. The adaptations made by the *yéyés* on which his analysis focuses were a key factor in the renewal of French popular music in the second half of the twentieth century.

Note

1   Space limitations do not allow for a discussion of this first wave of French rock music here. For more information on this subject and on the development of French rock in general, see Gérôme Guibert, *La production de la culture* (2006).

Bibliography

Berstein, Serge, and Pierre Milza. 1996. *Histoire du XXe siècle, tome 2, Le monde entre guerre et paix. 1945–1973.* Paris: Hatier.
———. 2010. *Histoire du XXe siècle, tome 3, La fin du monde bipolaire: 1973 aux années 1990.* Paris: Hatier.
Bourdieu, Pierre. 1979. *La distinction: Critique sociale du jugement.* Paris: Les Editions de Minuit.
Guibert, Gérôme. 2006. *La production de la culture: Le cas des musiques amplifiées en France.* Paris and St Amant Tallende: Irma/editions Seteun.
Klein, Jean-Claude. 1988. "Chanson et music-hall dans les années 20." In *La chanson française et son histoire*, edited by Dietmar Rieger, 299–305. Tübingen: Gunter Narr Verlag.
Mendras, Henri. 1994 [1988]. *La seconde révolution française: 1965–1984.* Paris: Gallimard.
Schlesser, Gilles. 2006. *Le cabaret "rive gauche." De la Rose Rouge au Bateau Ivre (1946–1974).* Paris: L'Archipel.
Vian, Boris. 1997 [1958]. *En avant la zizique . . . et par ici les gros sous.* Paris: Pauvert.

1

Yéyé Covers or the Keynote to a Societal Adaptation

Matthieu Saladin

"L'Amérique ça me fait rêver
Et pourtant je n'y suis jamais allée
Mais je connais tous les refrains
Tous les airs du folklore américain."[1]
Sheila, "Le folklore américain" ("American folk")

The success of copies, rather than any fetishism attaching to originals, is a sign of the autonomous expression of the aesthetic function of works.

Jean-Marie Schaeffer, "Originalité et expression de soi: Éléments pour une généalogie de la figure moderne de L'artiste," 83

The weekend edition of *Le Monde* of the 6th and 7th of July 1963 included its usual lot of news items, with both local and international stories taking up column inches in the financial, cultural and political sections. You could read about the inclusion of an armoured brigade in preparations for the Bastille Day procession and how social policy was providing Gaullism with its "second wind." Then there were reports on the festivities marking the first anniversary of Algerian independence, the arrest in Baltimore, on the other side of the Atlantic, of 300 "integrationist" protestors and attempts, behind the Iron Curtain, by Soviet and Chinese authorities to contain a diplomatic incident. The longest article of all, however, covered an entirely different subject, something French society seemed astonished to have become aware of, the "sudden" appearance of a "new age group": the teenager.

This article was written by Edgar Morin following the disturbances that took place during *La nuit de la Nation*, an event held at Place de la Nation in Paris on 22 June 1963 by Daniel Filipacchi and Frank Ténot, hosts of the Europe n° 1 radio show *Salut les Copains*.[2] It was put on to celebrate the first anniversary of the magazine of the same name and more than 150,000 young people—instead of the projected 30,000—gathered to see concerts given by *yéyé* stars, Johnny Hallyday, Sylvie Vartan, Eddy Mitchell and Richard Anthony. In his article, the sociologist portrayed a new generation with increased spending power and its own value system, the duality of which—comprising both conformity and opposition—had found its resolution in a nihilistic construct: "This construct may be said to be nihilistic in the sense that its overarching component is play itself" (Morin 1994, 403). Yet what Morin discerned in the *yéyé* phenomenon (the rise of mass culture and youth consumerism) was in fact none other than a more profound transformation of French society as a whole: "The arrival of the new teen class showed in microcosm what was happening to society as a whole. It already comported the values of consumerism and pleasure of what was an evolving civilisation, contributing its own specificity: youth" (Ibid. 404).

Figure 1.1 *Salut les Copains*, magazine, front cover, n° 89, January 1970.

The *yéyés* can thus be seen as symptomatic of something larger. A profound cultural mutation was to be expressed through them, or rather through the social phenomenon they embodied. This chapter aims to look more specifically at the nature of the songs which were so vital to the identity of the youth culture which provided the soundtrack to this social change. These songs, played repeatedly on the teen radio shows of the time, were in fact songs of a specific type: they were covers, or, more exactly, French adaptations of, often contemporaneous, English-language hits. Here we will look at the role of these covers in the transformation of French society at the beginning of the 1960s and what they show and tell us about underlying cultural developments.

An Onomatopoeic Transposition

While the rationale behind doing covers of popular songs is many and varied—comprising shameless plagiarism, local adaption of hits from abroad, *hommage*, parody, co-opting for commercial reasons, musical practice and identification with a certain tradition—it always consists of appropriating something that is already available, already there and has already been heard. Covers make use of a found object, a sort of off-the-peg musical item that is part of a more or less shared experience, reformulating it according to various deliberate changes. They are in this sense *derivative*, owing their make-up to something else in order to become something else themselves.

Many of the *yéyé* hits from the beginning of the 1960s were covers. They appeared on the French musical landscape having taken tunes, chords, instrumentation and, in certain cases, lyrics from rock 'n' roll, country and western and rhythm 'n' blues repertoires which topped the charts on the other side of the Atlantic or Channel. They were then adapted for local audiences, with, in particular, the specificities of the French language and French variety being taken into account. Thus, among the *yéyé* successes of the time were "L'idole des jeunes" (1962) performed by Johnny Hallyday and adapted by Ralph Bernet from "Teen Age Idol" (1962) sung by Ricky Nelson and Sylvie Vartan's "Le loco-motion" (1962) (Figure 1.2) and Richard Anthony's "On twiste sur le loco-motion" (1963), both derived from Little Eva's "The Loco-Motion" (1962). Frank Alamo's "Ma biche"[3] (1963) was a reworking of "Sweets for My Sweet" (1961), popularised by the group The Drifters, and Sheila's "Bang Bang" (1966) was an adaptation of Cher's "Bang Bang (My Baby Shot Me Down)" (1966), which was also covered by Nancy Sinatra that same year.

The term "adaptation," often used to refer to these covers, characterises their specificity rather well. It is also used in film production when, for example, a novel is "adapted" for the big screen without audiences necessarily having read or being aware of the novel. In this context, adaptation signifies the transference from one medium to another, from one art form to another, such that two works come to coexist, each with its own "autonomy." When it came to *yéyé* covers, the medium remained the same. They were still experienced as vinyl recordings or broadcast on the radio or played on stage. The process of adaptation involved rather their transition from one context to another, from one society to another, a cultural transposition through which a process of acculturation (Savev 2004, 6) and vernacular adjustment could take place, without the process of "stereophonic listening,"[4] which comes into play when a song is listened to as a cover, necessarily being in operation.

From this point of view, the expression *yéyé* itself conforms to the same register of adaptation. It is a double onomatopoeia of the interjection "yeah" that was so ubiquitous

Figure 1.2 Sylvie Vartan, "Le loco-motion," RCA Victor, 1962, EP front cover.

in American popular music at the time, phonetically translated using French spelling. As Johnny Hallyday clarified in the March 1964 issue of *Salut Les Copains*, it was "taken up as 'yé-yé' by French lyricists who wanted to retain the sound in their adaptations of American songs rather than translate it by the French language equivalent of 'ouais, ouais.'" The term therefore does not so much originate in a specific song as in recurrent phrasing from the choruses of many base songs. As David Looseley tells us,

> Contrary to what most accounts claim, the term *yéyé* could not have derived from the Beatles' single "She Loves You", since it was already in use before the song was released in August 1963. It is more likely to have originated in the common refrain "woah, woah, yeah, yeah" used by a variety of pre-Beatles singers from the Everly Brothers to Helen Shapiro.
> (2003, 35)

The "meaning" of the expression was nevertheless extended to suit its usage in reference to a wider phenomenon, whether as an "analytical category," as with Edgar Morin, a commonly held and somewhat deprecatory designation of contemporary French popular music as nothing more than a sanitised version of so-called original rock, or a set formula used to refer to the youth of the time (Sohn 2001, 273–374). While, as Morin tells us, "one meaning behind the term yé-yé was: 'we are young'" (1994, 402), that which seems to have rapidly imposed itself as definitive was rather closer to "you are young," in other words an expression taken up by adults struggling to understand the new phenomenon they were faced with.

On the Presumed Inauthenticity of Covers

One of the most prominent factors leading to the discrediting of *yéyé* is that many *yéyé* hits were covers. The shift towards alterity that characterises covers also knocks up against the preconception that they are nothing more than a devalued product of the act of copying. The distinction between song writing and the production of covers is in fact part of a deeper distinction, that between creativity and imitation. Thus, criticism of covers focuses on the fact that they are a pretence of creativity, the simple reiteration of something already in existence, not true, authentic works in their own right.

If we step back for a second and place our discussion in a wider temporal context, this common criticism finds its source in the emergence of the figure of the modern artist and more especially in the insistence on originality that became established in Western culture from the eighteenth century onwards (Schaeffer 1997, 79). Stepping in close again to look at the history of popular music, it resurfaces in the advent of the figure of the songwriter, or at least the new aura that was bestowed on singer-songwriters at the beginning of the 1960s, leading to a certain dialectic of authenticity (Cook 2006, 18) and a devaluing of the qualities of vocal artists who perform other people's songs (Cusic 2005, 177). According to this logic, covers have little aesthetic value precisely because they suffer from a deficit of authenticity, relying on the words, music and—the height of inauthenticity—feelings of others.

In its endless production of covers of English and American hits, *yéyé* could be said to be the paragon of creative inauthenticity in the history of French popular music. On one hand it cannot be compared to what is seen as the higher-quality tradition of French *chanson* by artists such as Brassens, Brel and Ferré, being "consigned [rather] to the status of non-art and the anti-humanism of poor quality industrial production" (Morin 1994, 304). On the other, *yéyé* stars were also to fall out of favour with the young as soon as the market developed in favour of the direct commercialisation of originals, pushing the category of adaptations to one side. In the manner of the early French rock groups (Guibert 2006, 132–133), *yéyé*'s principal virtue seems in the end to have been to get local audiences used to the sounds of the adopted idiom and prepare the ground for the arrival of the so-called originals. Michel Rose, journalist at *Rock & Folk*, recalls,

> What sticks in my mind from that much-talked-of time, is that French adaptations allowed us to discover the great American pioneers. I very quickly changed up my record collection so that "Eddie soit bon" by the Chaussettes Noires became "Johnny be good" by Chuck Berry; "Ma petite amie est vache" by the Chats Sauvages was transformed into "Mean woman blues" by Elvis Presley and "Elle est terrible" by [Johnny] Hallyday

metamorphosed into "Something else" by Eddie Cochran. All this took place through the supremely self-evident method of reading record covers on which, most of the time, the name of the original track and composer were to be found.

(Rose [1981], quoted by Guibert 2006, 132)

Looseley goes even further, suggesting that "it was with this triumph of *yéyé* [. . .] that a particularly tenacious Anglo-American representation of French pop was born: vacuous and embarrassingly inauthentic, a colonised music that eternally misses the point" (2003, 32). This mark of inauthenticity was to blight the careers of many *yéyé* stars like some persistent stain, in spite of the fact that some of them took the plunge and ventured into composition themselves: "Although Johnny Hallyday has become increasingly involved over the years in songwriting, he still tends more often to be identified as the singer of other people's songs, and therefore as lacking the supposed authenticity and skill of the singer-songwriter" (Tinker 2005, 946).

The Construction of a Generational Culture

Whether well founded or not, the persistent aesthetic discrediting of *yéyé* should not take anything away from the fact that it was a truly successful form in the 1960s. Indeed, the cult of authenticity was able to find expression within this so-called inauthentic musical genre, with its criteria going far beyond the mere composition of the tracks that were performed and founding itself within the construction of a collective identity specific to the young. The mark of authenticity became defined first and foremost as belonging to this identity.

The first issue of *Salut les Copains*, the magazine of the dazzlingly successful *yéyé* stars, appeared in 1962. By 1963 it was read by one in two teenagers (Sohn 2001, 91). Such fervour, however, obscured what was a much longer process with important ramifications for the whole youth media industry. In 1959, Lucien Morisse, then artistic director at the minor radio station Europe n° 1, was experimenting with the programming of this eponymous show, specifically targeted at young audiences, to the tune of one half-hour slot every Thursday. The show only really took off when Filipacchi, whose tone stood out from the style of other presenters of the time, was drafted in to host it in October of the same year. It then became a daily show, scheduled from 5–7 p.m. in order to pull teenagers in at the end of the school day.

Daniel Filipacchi and his co-host Frank Ténot already had a solid background in radio as the presenters of the programme *Pour ceux qui aiment le jazz* and also had a good knowledge of the recording industry, with Filipacchi, in particular, artistic director at Decca and RCA. Their passion for jazz led them to follow the latest developments in American popular music closely, watching as rock 'n' roll established itself on the other side of the Atlantic at the end of the 1950s and noting the enthusiasm it garnered in the young and its apparent market potential as an import to France. As Gérôme Guibert notes, "jazz was their passion but the media was their profession" (2006, 202).

The programme, *Salut les Copains*, followed the editorial line established by Morisse in 1956, which prioritised plugging a small number of songs. Thus, features such as "*banc d'essai*" (test bench) for hopefuls or the week's "*chouchou*" ("favourite") were established, hyping, for example, in 1962 Claude François's "Belles, belles, belles," a cover of "Made to Love" by The Everly Brothers. This programming policy, allied to the fact that there was little competition on the airwaves, meant the show had a direct impact on record sales (Sohn 2001, 81). It was in order to exploit this opportunity that the magazine version of the show was launched. Young readers could thus extend the experience of listening to *yéyé* hits, pore over reports on their idols—with Jean-Marie Périer's photos taking pride of place—follow the hit-parade and study the lyrics to songs in a series of articles adroitly interspersed with well-chosen adverts.

The success of the stars and the media that promoted them led to the creation of "the conditions for a generational media culture" (Guibert 2006, 106). One of the particularities of this culture, as Jean-Marie Périer highlights, was to focus on a relatively limited number of singers (Périer, in Verlant 2001, 11), who were also served by a small group of lyricists adapting songs from abroad.[5] The manufacture of this specific culture on the back of a musical genre and in opposition to that of the adult population allowed the young to affirm an identity of their own through their consumption of it (Sohn 2001, 66). Love, the principal theme of the songs, played a major role in the economics of feelings and the identification it promoted, having the status of both "the most marketable of commodities and the absolute zenith of modern individualism" (Morin 1994, 400). It was, however, an experience shared by both stars and their fans, by reason of the youthfulness of both. Thus, while covers are often dismissed, as we have seen, for their supposed deficit of authenticity, the choice of young artists was a guarantee of a certain authenticity in the performance of the songs and ensured that singers and audiences experienced shared feelings.[6] The feelings that the lyrics of the adapted hits called forth could easily be interpreted as true life experiences—and indeed no doubt were in some cases, such as in the relationship between Johnny and Sylvie. Any authenticity that might be missing from *yéyé* adaptations, which was nevertheless so essential for the process of identification to come into play, was thus re-established, or at least preserved. Projection was thus also permitted, and a further process, an extension of the covers themselves, was allowed to germinate and fuel the collective identity. Here we refer to the process of appropriation within which the individuation of young listeners took form, with a more or less fragmentary imitation of stars (themselves the result of other imitative relationships) emerging from an identification with their appearance and behaviour and manner of being mediatised. These two aspects were thus played out in the spheres of both the marketing and morals of *yéyé* and now found themselves to be complementary.

The first of these aspects, the imitation of the media image of stars, revealed the extent of the commercial dimension of the advent of this youth culture and also highlighted the role of the visual representations which accompanied the songs and contributed to the manufacture of role models. Thus the "ranch" style made a breakthrough in the wake of the film *D'où viens-tu Johnny?*, the choice of a pair of trainers worn on a record sleeve led to all the stock of this shoe being sold out a few months after its release and the hairstyles chosen by Françoise Hardy or Sylvie Vartan became a reference for young women (Sohn 2001, 73–75). Adverts, magazine covers and record sleeves were all put at the service of these representations and their plurality provided a panoply of images which anyone could identify with, each according to their singularity.[7] The commercial aspect of the phenomenon would seem to have been that much more efficient as the fashions disseminated essentially remained very traditional: "a tartan skirt for Sheila and a petty-bourgeois style for her clothing line, a bell-shaped dress for Sylvie Vartan, pencil skirt, roll neck sweater and pumps for Françoise Hardy" (Sohn 2001, 72).

While, according to Anne-Marie Sohn, the force of attraction that these stars exerted on teenagers was not "the fruit of shrewd media manipulation" but was rather due to the fact that "the singers, who were young themselves, were undergoing the same experiences as their audiences" (2001, 88) and therefore provided a tangible reality onto which the collective identity could project itself, it does nevertheless seem to be the case that such complicity could be boosted, or in any event maintained, both by means of the recruitment of young artists (Guibert 2006, 111–112) and the style changes that gave certain stars their longevity. The chameleon-like qualities of Johnny Hallyday would appear to be exemplary here, the singer moving from rock covers at the beginning of the 1960s to hippie hymns with "San Francisco" in 1967. As Christian Hermelin notes in his study on imitation dynamics at work in the *yéyé* phenomenon, "the singer became a role model, but of course in order to become a model, you first have to allow yourself to be modelled" (1965, 45). A virtuous circle of imitation thus came into being: while the first French rockers imitated American artists by covering their songs and attitudes on stage and taking up American-sounding stage names, the *yéyé* idols in turn exercised "influence as role models" on their fans "by means of a combination of attitudes experienced and described in their expressions and lyrics" (Hermelin 1965, 49), which could moreover develop according to fashions, contexts and cultural transformations and the imitative nature of which went far beyond mere music itself.

The second aspect to be taken into account is the moral dimension of identification with *yéyé* idols. Imitation cannot simply be reduced to such and such a haircut or item of clothing but also operates, perhaps more diffusely, through attitudes, views and opinions. Moreover, a rapid improvement in moral standards characterises the relatively short history of *yéyé*. While they certainly made their mark, the rabble-rousers of the Place de la Nation were an exception and actually later served as a guilty reminder used to maintain the moral order. *Salut les Copains* came out against the troublemakers and then against drug taking (Savev 2004, 8). Johnny Hallyday shed his black jacket, stopped rolling around on the floor at concerts and sent letters to the magazine during his military service. However, it was as much the song lyrics themselves that communicated the party line: "Their songs became moralising, like 'Le pénitencier' ('The penitentiary') [cover of 'The House of the Rising Sun' by The Animals] or 'Je me suis souvent demandé' ('I have often asked myself') [an adaptation of a Dutch song by Bobbejaan Schoepen]" (Hermelin 1965, 51). Here again, the consensus-based adaptation of cover lyrics speaks for itself: while Ray Charles endlessly repeats "Babe, shake that thing now" at the end of "What'd I Say," in conclusion to her twist cover "Est-ce que tu le sais?" ("Do you know?") Sylvie Vartan intones, "*Que faut-il faire dans la vie pour dénicher un gentil mari*" ("What's a girl got to do to catch herself a good husband?"). *Yéyé* singers weren't simply idols; they were also examples to be followed, showing young people the responsible route to a seemly adult life assimilated into society.[8] The generational conflict seen at the beginning of the phenomenon had found its resolution in a consensus on the appreciation of values, understood in all senses of the word.

Break—the Monadology of Covers

To gain a better grasp of the social intercourse at work in the *yéyé* phenomenon and its attachment to covers, we will here further detail the processes within which imitation and adaptation fall. The process of *reprise*, understood as operating towards both the discovery and recovery of something already there, is by no means a particularity of popular music: the history of ideas is also steeped in it. Thus in his essay "Monadologie et Sociologie" published in 1893, Gabriel Tarde proposes a *reprise* of—and thus transforms—Leibnizian monadology, in which, in its infinitesimal subdivision, "each portion of matter can be conceived as like a garden full of plants, or like a pond full of fish" (Leibniz 1995, § 67). For Tarde, social intercourse, characterised by heterogeneity, had to be apprehended first and foremost at a molecular level, taking as its starting point the multiplicity which unfurls from that which is infinitesimal.

Parting from Leibniz, Tarde's monads are characterised by their permeability to other monads and their environment. Each individual is understood as a singularity, but a singularity resulting from a network of influences. Social intercourse is constituted by "the realisation of a multitude of elementary virtualities, each with its own character and ambition, each carrying its distinct world within itself, its world as reality and dream" (Tarde 1999, 136–137). It is also a process whereby each of us "borrows, from a hundred, a thousand, ten thousand people (each of whom is considered noteworthy in some respect) elements of ideas and actions which we then combine ourselves" (Tarde 2001, 55–56). However, according to Tarde, imitation is only one aspect of social intercourse because it takes place within a "conceptual triptyque," which also includes opposition and adaptation, which is none other than the form that results from the coming together of a plurality of imitations:

> Adaptation does not spring *ex nihilo* into the realm of adaptations: it is the combination which, in the case in point, seems best to bring a lack of resolution to term, or in other words, resolve the opposition between two imitative currents.
>
> (Saquer 2007, 120)

Transposed to *yéyé*, these currents can basically be seen as comporting covers of American rock 'n' roll hits, on the one hand, and linking to the specificities of the French context (language, French "*music-hall*" forms, etc.), on the other.

Thus, multiple piecemeal borrowings constitute various molecular flows, composed of each other, slotting together, sitting astride and altering one another—in short, *adapting* to produce *difference*. Whatever the presumed aesthetic value of this difference, it does indeed exist. However, these imitative flows do not only concern social activities or musical creations. They are also constitutive of individuals themselves and are what their individuation is founded in: "The principal being to ape each other continually and repeatedly and, by means of varying combinations, come up with something original" (Tarde 1970, 470). Moreover, in his micro-sociology, Tarde highlights the remote interplay of emotional forces which constantly structure an individual's changing subjectivity. The individual is therefore in no sense an island but rather a network of influences. In this light, the opposition between creativity and imitation no longer necessarily applies. Quite the contrary! Imitation becomes one of the building blocks of creativity and individuation, understood as complex adaptations of imitative flows. Imitation is present everywhere in creativity and individuation, nourishing and enabling. In return, invention also becomes a launch pad for further imitations and new adaptations.

Covers as a Driver of Societal Adaptation

Although *yéyé* remains largely synonymous with covers, it shouldn't be forgotten that the place of covers in the history of French popular music extends far beyond *yéyé* alone. Firstly, and at the same moment, covers are just as common among so-called anti-*yéyés*, defined as an alternative to the well-meaning morality of the *Salut les Copains* icons (Eudeline 2006). Secondly, there's nothing new in the influence of American popular music on French "*music-hall*." We're talking a long-term love affair here. After being banished during Occupation, jazz returned in triumph with Liberation, colouring the songs of Mireille and Trenet. Yves Montand took up the uniform of the cowboy and Charles Aznavour adopted the crooner style (Looseley 2003, 22).

The Americanisation of French culture therefore preceded and to a certain extent gave license to the *yéyés*, just as the *yéyés* themselves, during the first half of the 1960s, contributed to a revolution in the tastes and functioning of cultural industries, resulting in an *engouement* for English and American groups themselves. As this itself became a major phenomenon, receiving the same sort of media exposure as *yéyé*, covers also became recognised as a form which, in the medium term, could cause aesthetic lines to move and contribute to wider cultural transformations by patiently acclimatising ears to an appreciation of new sounds. It was partly by means of covers that new instruments and aesthetic novelties, ways of singing and moving the body, moved into the mainstream (Cooper 2010, 45; Cusic 2005, 175).

However, acculturation alone is not sufficient to define the dynamics at work. Acculturation operated alongside the *absorption* of English and American music by French "*music-hall*." This wasn't a unilateral process nor can it simply be dismissed as an early sign of cultural globalisation. It is also one of local adaptation: "Just as it had been receptive to the influence of jazz in its musical arrangements at the end of the 1920s, French 'music-hall' would incorporate rock 'n' roll at the end of the 1950s" (Guibert 2006, 108). In the same way, the success of the *yéyés* would mainly be replaced during the "societal changes linked to the thirty-year post-war boom [. . .] increasing the aspirations of the young in what was a new, affluent French society" (Guibert 2006, 114). These *yéyé* cover adaptations, then, also bore witness to another adaptation, which was more widespread and borne out in the profound societal transformations of the 1960s. Morin already quite rightly remarked in his 1963 article that "necessary commotion aside, the young were being funnelled down a narrow channel towards *adaptation* to social intercourse" (Morin 1994, 407). However, the social intercourse to which the young adapt by listening to their idols is never simply the same as that which has existed before and which they are supposedly happy to reproduce. This social intercourse becomes itself the very difference that transpires through the adaptation of the young, as this intercourse, in turn, changes by means of this adaptation.

Notes

1   This can be loosely translated as "America makes me dream / Though I've never been / But I know all the choruses / To the songs of American folk."
2   Translator's note: This can be loosely translated as "Hi There, Buddies."
3   Translator's note: Here, a pet word loosely rendering "Honey" or "My Honey."
4   For Deena Weinstein, listening to a cover as a cover necessarily results in a dual experience, whereby the simultaneous presence of both the base song and cover in the mind of the listener creates meaning through a process of comparison (2010, 244–246).
5   Although all too often only the names of the stars are mentioned, the role of the lyricists adapting the songs from abroad should not be minimised in terms of the *music-hall* transformations that were part of the *yéyé* phenomenon. Here we particularly note the contributions of Georges Aber, Ralph Bernet, Fernand Bonnifay, Claude Carrère, Pierre Delanoë, Eddy Marnay, Jacques Plante, Jean Renard, Jacques Revaux and André Salvet.
6   In her study on French youth of the 1960s, Anne-Marie Sohn quotes the words of a young man who would seem to be exemplary of the time:

> I think that girls or boys who see themselves in songs sung by their "idols" feel somehow supported and can tell themselves: "I'm not alone." And this is really important when your morale is down as it can help you to pull yourself back up.
>
> (2001, 87)

7   For example, Dick Rivers and Eddy Mitchell incarnated the figure of the rocker, while Sheila and France Gall played high-school girls and Françoise Hardy represented the young romantic woman and so on. For more on the diversity of role models, see Sohn 2001, 88–89; Hermelin 1965, 47.
8   By means, for example, of the presentation of such stereotypes in *Salut les Copains*, see Tinker 2008.

Bibliography

Birgy, Philippe. 2012. "'Si cette histoire vous amuse, on peut la recommencer': Le *yéyé* et l'importation de la con-tre-culture américaine." *Volume! La revue des musiques populaires* 9(1):151–167.
Cook, Nicholas. 2006 [1998]. *Musique, une très brève introduction.* Paris: Allia.
Cooper, B. Lee. 2010. "Charting Cultural Change, 1953–1957: Song Assimilation Through Cover Recording." In *Play It Again: Cover Songs in Popular Music*, edited by George Plasketes, 43–76. Surrey: Ashgate.
Cusic, Don. 2005. "In Defense of Cover Songs." *Popular Music and Society* 28(2):171–177.
Eudeline, Christian. 2006. *Anti-yéyé: Une autre histoire des sixties.* Paris: Denoël.
Guibert, Gérôme. 2006. *La production de la culture: Le cas des musiques amplifiées en France.* Paris and St Amant Tallende: Irma/editions Seteun.
Hermelin, Christian. 1965. "L'interprète-modèle et 'Salut les Copains.'" *Communications* 6:43–53.
Leibniz, Gottfried Wilhelm. 1995 [1714]. *Monadologie.* Paris: Gallimard.
Looseley, David L. 2003. *Popular Music in Contemporary France: Authenticity, Politics, Debate.* Oxford and New York: Berg.
Morin, Edgar. 1994 [1984]. *Sociologie.* Paris: Seuil.
Plasketes, George, ed. 2010. *Play It Again: Cover Songs in Popular Music.* Surrey: Ashgate.
Saladin, Matthieu, ed. 2010a. "La Reprise BIS." *Volume! La revue des musiques populaires* 7(2).
Saladin, Matthieu, ed. 2010b. "La Reprise dans les musiques populaires." *Volume! La revue des musiques popu-laires* 7(1).
Saquer, Laurence. 2007. "Variation sur la grammaire différentielle de Gabriel Tarde." *Sociétés* 96(2):115–123.
Savev, Marc. 2004. "Deux exemples de presse musicale jeune en France, de 1966 à 1969: *Salut les Copains et Rock & Folk.*" *Volume! La revue des musiques populaires* 3(1):5–28.
Schaeffer, Jean-Marie. 2004 [1997]. "Originalité et expression de soi: Éléments pour une généalogie de la fig-ure moderne de l'artiste." In *Art, création, fiction: Entre sociologie et philosophie*, edited by Nathalie Heinich and Jean-Marie Schaeffer, 71–98. Nîmes: Editions Jacqueline Chambon.
Sohn, Anne-Marie. 2001. *Âge tendre et tête de bois: Histoire des jeunes des années 1960.* Paris: Hachette.
Tamagne, Florence. 2009. "'C'mon everybody.' Rock'n'roll et identités juvéniles en France (1956–1966)." In *Jeunesse oblige: Histoire des jeunes en France XIXe–XXe*, edited by Ludivine Bantigny and Ivan Jablonka, 199–212. Paris: PUF.
Tarde, Gabriel. 1970 [1896]. "Fragment d'histoire future." *Revue française de sociologie* 11(4):467–487.
———. 1999 [1898]. *Les lois sociales.* Paris: Les empêcheurs de penser en rond.
———. 2001 [1890]. *Les lois de L'imitation.* Paris: Les empêcheurs de penser en rond.

Tinker, Chris. 2005. "Johnny Hallyday: Mediated Masculinities." In *Proceedings IASPM 5*, edited by Geoff Stahl, 945–952. Rome: IASPM. www.iaspm.net/archive/IASPM05LIGHT.pdf.

———. 2008. "Salut les Copains et la (dé)mobilisation des stéréotypes de genre." In *Adolescences et cultures, pratiques, usages et réception à L'épreuve des genres*, edited by Patricia Caillé et Nassira Hedjerassi, 62–76. Strasbourg: IUT Robert Schuman.

Verlant, Gilles. 2001. "Les sensationnelles sixties de Jean-Marie Périer." In *40 ans de tubes, 1960–2000, les meilleures ventes de 45 tours et CD singles*, edited by Fabrice Ferment, 11–12. Paris: Snep/Larivière.

Weinstein, Deena. 2010. "Appreciating Cover Songs: Stereophony." In *Play It Again: Cover Songs in Popular Music*, edited by George Plasketes, 243–251. Surrey: Ashgate.

2

Juvenile Delinquency, Social Unrest and National Anxiety

French Debates and Controversies Over Rock 'n' Roll in the 1960s and 1970s

Florence Tamagne

Rock 'n' roll made its debut in France in 1956. From the beginning, it had a bad reputation. From 1959 until the mid-1960s, it was associated with the juvenile delinquency of the *"blousons noirs"* (black leather jackets); after May 1968, it was linked with the hippie and countercultural movement, particularly leftist organisations, although they maintained an ambivalent attitude towards pop culture.

Based on a collection of various sources (national and local archives, police reports, press articles, etc.), this chapter will discuss some of the issues raised by rock and pop music in 1960s and 1970s France.[1] Although some topics, such as the association of rock 'n' roll with violence and loose morals, were common features of its reception in most countries at the time, others should be read in light of a French context marked by the shadow of the dark years of the Vichy regime, the end of the Algerian war, the May 1968 protests and the lasting influence of the left-wing revolutionary spirit.[2]

The *"Blousons noirs"*: Rock 'n' Roll and Juvenile Delinquency

The triptych of *blousons noirs*, juvenile delinquency and rock 'n' roll emerged in the national press in 1959, with the arrest of the Saint-Lambert gang, which was named after a square in Paris where its members used to gather. According to the media, the youngsters spent the night at the police station, singing rock 'n' roll songs.[3] From 1959 to 1964, the *blousons noirs* regularly made the front page of daily newspapers: fights between gangs, attacks against passers-by, "riots" during rock 'n' roll concerts, each incident was reported and emphasised, sometimes even staged.[4]

Although some of the youth gangs wore leather jackets, which they often customised, as a sign of distinction, the phrase *blouson noir* was an invention of journalists, based on images borrowed from popular culture: movies like *The Wild One* (Laszlo Benedek 1953) or *Blackboard Jungle* (Richard Brooks 1955), as well as outfits worn by Elvis Presley, Gene Vincent or Vince Taylor. By focusing on a piece of clothing, the media artificially helped create a sense of unity between youth gangs and youth subcultures, which did not necessarily share the same purposes or philosophy. At first a phenomenon located in Paris's metropolitan area, the *blousons noirs* gangs were soon emulated in the provinces, although some incidents, like the ones that occurred in beach resorts on the Channel or the Mediterranean seaside, might have been committed by Parisian gangs on holiday.[5] By identifying the French *blousons noirs*, sometimes wrongly, with other foreign youth subcultures, such as the British Teddy Boys, Mods or Rockers, or the German *Halbstarken*, the media contributed to the illusion of a coherent international phenomenon.[6]

Fear of youth, especially when it came from the "*classes dangereuses*" ("dangerous classes," i.e., the proletariat), was of course nothing new.[7] Nevertheless, it had gained ground since the end of the Second World War, as juvenile delinquency was on the rise, a phenomenon which had also been observed in other countries, such as the United States, Britain or Germany, and was interpreted as a consequence of the war, poverty, sloth, heredity and the failure of the family unit. The *blousons noirs* phenomenon took place in a context where teenagers had more free time because of the lengthening of compulsory education and temporary exemptions from military service, something demographer Alfred Sauvy called "the rise of young people" (Sauvy 1959).

The association between music, dance and juvenile delinquency was also rather common. In the nineteenth century, the waltz, between the wars, the Charleston, and in the 1950s, swing dance, for example, had been associated with dubious morals, bohemianism, even violence. However, most articles dealing with the *blousons noirs* in the national press did *not* allude to rock 'n' roll, but simply to common delinquency. On the other side, the more detailed reports written by sociologists or street educators always tied juvenile delinquency to rock 'n' roll. In the same way, whenever the press covered a rock 'n' roll show where incidents occurred, *blousons noirs* were mentioned.

As a matter of fact, the *blousons noirs* did not hide their love for rock music, although they hated the soppy songs of the "*yéyés*"—that is, most of the French rock 'n' roll singers, except maybe Johnny Hallyday or Eddy Mitchell, the lead singer of the band Les Chaussettes Noires. Their heroes were the American pioneers, such as Elvis Presley and Gene Vincent and the British rocker Vince Taylor, who was their main idol. The Foire du Trône, Paris's main travelling fun fair and a favourite meeting place for youngsters, became, between 1958 and 1962, a battlefield for youth gangs. Among the various objects belonging to *blousons noirs* confiscated there by police forces, especially because they could be used as weapons, were, for example, leather studded belts, some of them engraved with the name of French or American rock stars like Johnny (Hallyday), Les Chaussettes Noires, Les Vautours or Elvis Presley.[8]

A symbol of the crisis of masculinity, too aggressive (he was an "animal"), or too feminine, with his long hair and tight-fitting trousers (he was called a "fag" [*pédé*]), the *blouson noir* was seen as a countermodel to the ideal of manliness, embodied, in official discourses, by the French soldier, who fought in Germany or Algeria (Tamagne 2008). In Rethel, in August 1962, soldiers shaved bald several *blousons noirs*, in front of a crowd who heartily applauded, a punishment whose gendered and political connotations were then obvious.[9] The military service, which lasted between eighteen and twenty-eight months, was the ultimate rite of passage: much as Elvis Presley, Johnny Hallyday achieved his redemption when he performed his service in Germany.

Although *blousons noirs* only represented a minority, all rock 'n' roll fans were treated with suspicion. Behaviours which were deemed contrary to the norms of the times—especially class and gender norms—such as unkempt appearances, sensual dancing and promiscuity of boys and girls within venues, were regarded with incomprehension. For the popular newspaper *Le Parisien libéré*, rock music did indeed "promote juvenile delinquency, even induce it deliberately. A certain Vince Taylor, clad from head to toe in black leather, swinging a golden chain, openly encouraged the thugs to brandish bicycle chains."[10]

The rise of juvenile delinquency was indeed a source of concern for the Paris municipal council, as well as for mayors in the provinces.[11] Nevertheless, there was no general policy. Some advocated the construction of *"maisons de jeunes"* (youth clubs), to offer them some kind of diversion; others took a hard-line approach. Parisian city counsellor Auguste Marboeuf, a conservative who was in charge of the Youth and Sports Commission, proposed to set a youth curfew.[12] André Roulland, a Gaullist member of parliament from the Parisian suburbs, advocated a ban on rock 'n' roll shows, after the incidents that occurred during Vince Taylor's November 1961 concert at the Palais des Sports[13] in Paris, inside and outside the venue. Several cities, such as Cannes, Biarritz, Bayonne or Strasbourg, had already decided to cancel Johnny Hallyday's summer shows after a string of incidents, the most spectacular having occurred in Paris, on 24 February 1961, during the first Festival International de Rock. The minister of the interior, Roger Frey, another Gaullist, flatly refused. The ban of shows was under the responsibility of mayors or, in Paris, the prefect of police, who had to assess, on a case-by-case basis, the opportunity for rock 'n' roll concerts. Although there were incidents, "the majority of these exhibitions [ran] smoothly. There [was] no ground for a general ban."[14]

La Nuit de la Nation: The Nation at Risk?

The controversy over rock 'n' roll reached its climax on 22 June 1963, with the "Nuit de la Nation" (The Night of the Nation), a free concert organised by youth magazine *Salut les Copains*, which featured all the French "idols" of the time and gathered 150,000 people together.[15] As the crowd had gone wild, the press derisively labelled the concert *"Salut les Voyous"* ("Hi There, Rascals") instead of *"Salut les Copains"* ("Hi There, Buddies").[16] However, the actual number of young fans who attended the concert made it impossible to dismiss the rock 'n' roll phenomenon as the temporary and marginal expression of a delinquent youth group.

Although it took place one year before the May 1964 Mods and Rockers riots in England, the Nuit de la Nation provoked what can be called a "moral panic" (Cohen 1972, Warne 2006). Indeed, we typically find an intensive media coverage, the naming of scapegoats and the intervention of experts posing as moral entrepreneurs: journalists, policemen, psychologists, sociologists, politicians. The threat seemed real: some media, such as the popular daily newspaper *France-Soir* or the socialist newspaper *Le Populaire*, interpreted the event as a "riot." If we read between the lines, such comments may have been meant to summon the ghost of the 6 February 1934 riots, when the fights between far-right leagues and the police in front of the parliament had been interpreted as an aborted attempt at a fascist coup.[17] Some commentators, such as Philippe Bouvard in the right-wing newspaper *Le Figaro*, did not hesitate to compare the young fans to the masses gathered in Nuremberg during NSDAP rallies.[18] The actual setting of the concert—once again, the Place de la Nation—was largely exploited: the very future of the nation seemed to be at stake that night.[19] The fact that the police asked the soldiers on leave who were attending the concert for help in maintaining order had some people believe that the authorities were going to proclaim a state of emergency. The day after the concert, some shopkeepers evoked the possibility of forming "defence committees," a phrase that recalled the Algerian war that had ended just a year before.

Part of the press, and first of all the youth press, which was directly called into question, tried to calm things down.[20] It seemed essential to distinguish the majority of young people from a minority of delinquents.[21] Nevertheless, prejudice was obvious, especially class and race prejudice. According to the police, the crowd was mostly composed of "rather uncouth young people," "coming from a modest background if one looked at their clothes" and looking "not very intellectual." Young people were animalized or racialised, compared to "barbarians" or "savages."[22] The most obvious proof of this dehumanisation was the rape perpetrated against a young girl, next to the stage, by about twenty *blousons noirs*, some of them Algerians, a fact that was regularly underlined, although its authenticity is dubious.[23]

As a matter of fact, the event challenged traditional gender norms. In the middle of the crowd, disregarding the traditional rules of modesty and decency, girls, who amounted to about one quarter of the audience, were in close contact with boys. They were not just a passive audience: they yelled, clapped or booed the artists they didn't like. Some tried to kiss Johnny Hallyday; others attempted to reach the stage in order to dance at his side. Some girls were particularly bold: although police reports mentioned only "young boys" who tried to climb on street furniture, press photographs reveal that there were also a few girls among them. For some commentators, there was the proof that this music made them lose control. The pathologisation of youth behaviour was connected to the power of amplified music, especially the electric guitar, which acted as a stimulant and put nerves on edge. Fascinated by idols they slavishly imitated, members of the audience would then give way to "scenes of collective or individual hysteria."[24]

The debates soon took a more political turn. The Nuit de la Nation gave de Gaulle's opponents the opportunity to criticise the government. The far-right newspaper *Minute* implied that the government had tried to get the affair hushed up and directly attacked Maurice Herzog, the minister of youth and sport.[25] The socialist newspaper *Le Populaire* remarked that the police forces mobilised for the evening were far less numerous than for demonstrations against the Algerian war.[26] For the left-wing newspaper *Libération*, the troublemakers of the nation were treated with far more indulgence than workers on strike.[27] According to Prefect of Police Maurice Papon, there were no reasons to ban the event. To forbid a gathering of young people, who "came here, not as enemies, but simply to have fun," would have been "inconceivable."[28]

Some tried to maintain some perspective. For left-wing newspaper *Combat*, the youths' excesses were to be understood in light of

the excesses of the Liberation, the colonial wars and their horrors, the FLN's bomb attacks in the streets of Paris, the torture accounts, the grenades, the assassinations, the OAS,[29] plastic explosives, and above all the constant justification of violence in the name of an ideology, of more or less just causes, and the intellectual licentiousness that it implied.

The violence that had erupted at Place de la Nation echoed the violence of the Algerian war. Young people, who had served in Algeria for twenty-eight months, had not forgotten their lessons there.[30] Starting from the same premise, far-right writer Lucien Rebatet drew very different conclusions: for him, the young twist fans conditioned by the media reflected "the people who had overwhelmingly supported the capitulation and liquidation of Algeria."[31]

It was, however, sociologist Edgar Morin, in *Le Monde*, who provided the most thorough analysis of the phenomenon.[32] According to him, the Nuit de la Nation revealed the teenagers' economic consciousness, who formed a new age class, the *yéyés*, in reference to the music they listened to (Tamagne 2009). Although this age class was not homogeneous, the *yéyés* shared some common features, which helped forge a sense of community and solidarity, like a common "outfit," the access to consumer goods, a specific vocabulary, "communion rites" and idols. Although most commentators shared Morin's analyses regarding the importance of consumption as a unifying factor, many considered that the media took advantage of the young people's naïvety for their own benefit. For city councillor and journalist Claude Bourdet, himself a former resistance fighter and anti-colonial activist, the Nuit de la Nation was a typical expression of the "depoliticisation of youth." The media, "organs of the capitalist society," tried to divert the people from the real questions of the time by promoting escapism.[33]

The most immediate result of this process was the loss of the sense of values, the best example being the fortune quickly accumulated by the young idols, who could buy properties and cars "that many adults could only dream to possess," a remark which shows the frustration and bitterness of the war generation facing a youth who enjoyed economic growth. For the left wing, the selling out of culture meant the abandonment of the old humanist dream; for the right wing, the cult of the idols was the sign of the "moral collapse of the elites."[34] The answer was in the definition of a new cultural policy, aimed at youth, and, more specifically, at working-class youth. Indeed "if so many young people came to Place de la Nation, it was because, whether in their family, at school, in sport clubs or anywhere else, there was nothing for them."[35]

Although it marked the climax of the *blousons noirs* phenomenon, the Nuit de la Nation also symbolized its end. From then on, rock 'n' roll, at least in its less subversive forms, would be seen as part of a commercialised youth culture, generally looked down on, but nonetheless legitimate. By ascribing the responsibility of the concert's troubles to a fringe of popular youth, commentators exonerated middle-class children and made possible the creation of a youth culture centred on music. It was then impossible to imagine that some of them would be throwing cobblestones in May 1968.

The Ban of Pop Festivals in the 1970s: Politics and Revolution

The Nuit de la Nation had other long-term consequences. In France, free open-air concerts were for a long time regarded with suspicion (Warne 2006). In the 1970s, in a very different social and political context, rock music came once again to the centre of public attention, when several French municipalities decided to ban pop festivals.

In France, as in other countries, the youth and music press had published detailed articles about the American and British festivals. In August 1970, *Woodstock*, directed by Michael

Wadleigh, was released on French screens, spurring new interest in those events. Nevertheless, if there was a demand for pop festivals in France, to set one up proved difficult.[36] In 1969, Jean-Luc Young and Jean Georgakarakos (known as Karakos), the creators of jazz label BYG Actuel, with Fernand Boruso and later Claude Delcloo, had tried to organise a pop festival in Paris, and then in the Parc de Saint-Cloud. After several refusals, the First Paris Music Festival took place in Amougies, in Belgium, from 24 to 28 October 1969. Another festival took place in Le Bourget, in March 1970, provided that the number of festival-goers be limited and that no reference be made to "pop music" (Deshayes and Grimaud 2008, 24).

In the post-1968 context, at a time when the press published many articles dealing with drugs, hippies and revolutionary groups, pop festivals seemed conducive to outbursts. Leftist groups, the countercultural press (*Actuel, Le Parapluie*, etc.) and rock bands, such as Komintern, Red Noise or Maajun, discussed at length the revolutionary power of pop music. If some of them intended to use pop music for their own political aims, others saw music as part of a cultural revolution: "to play the music of one's life and live one's life in music."[37] Raymond Marcellin, the minister of the interior, a Gaullist who had been nominated just after the May 1968 events, explicitly denounced pop festivals in a circular dated 27 June 1970 and sent to all prefects. He recalled that Maoist groups had claimed they would carry out a series of actions aimed at disturbing the tranquillity of holidaymakers. Pop festivals would be their favourite place for such disorders, as had already been the case in Britain and Belgium. Prefects had to evaluate the risks, alert the mayors and take measures as appropriate.[38]

The bans of the 1970s on festivals were therefore the consequence of administrative orders (*arrêtés*). The Saint-Raphaël pop music festival, which should have taken place on 8 and 9 August 1970, was cancelled following the prefectorial decree of 24 July, for "security reasons" as it put it. The Aix-en-Provence festival (1–3 August 1970), which had been described as a "leftist gathering," which could be used by far-left students, already present in Aix, to foment trouble,[39] was banned by the municipal order of 20 July 1970, also supposedly for security reasons and fire hazards. The festival took place nonetheless, but it lasted two days instead of three and only attracted between 5,000 and 12,000 people, about a tenth of what was expected. Although there was no significant incident, the police performed about 3,000 identity checks, 119 people were taken to the police station, 14 were arrested and 4 minors were returned to their parents. Six people were prosecuted for possession of anarchist pamphlets.[40] In Orange, although a pop festival had taken place in 1975 with no major incident, the 1976 edition, which was supposed to be held both in Orange and Nimes, was cancelled just a few days before the date of the event.[41] After the ban by Nîmes, the Orange municipality refused to welcome the festival for an extra two days, and cancelled the authorization given on 13 July 1976.

To many observers, festival bans were the sign of a generational conflict and helped draw the line between conservatives, "who hated young people," and liberals, who "were ready to let them express their opinion, although not without supervision."[42] Things were in fact not so one-sided, and local circumstances had to be taken into account. In Aix, the field was rented out by the Lord of Saint-Pons, and the organiser, General Clément, formerly the administrative director of the Festival International d'Art Lyrique of Aix and more surprisingly a proponent of French Algeria, whose far-right opinions were well known,[43] appeared as an improbable defender of pop music. If his discourse at the time could sound demagogic—he

Figure 2.1 Petition for a second Orange pop festival (extract), 1976. From the Archives municipales d'Orange, photo: F. Tamagne.

portrayed himself as a champion of freedom of assembly and a spokesman for the rights of youth—he was nonetheless an old jazz fan who had played in several bands. In his auto-biography, he appeared as a strong advocate for the hippie movement and an opponent to the Gaullist regime, which he deemed "incapable of change" (Clément 1971, 320). On the other side, the ban was issued by a socialist mayor, Félix Ciccolini, for mostly pre-electoral reasons. Many shopkeepers, as well as the municipal Casino, feared that the pop music fes-tival would deter the wealthier audience of the classical music festival, which took place almost at the same time, from coming to Aix.[44] His strategy clearly paid off, since he gained support from the centre right, who had refused to welcome "this wild crowd [*faune*]," who had "invaded" the city "in a debauchery of somewhat unhealthy exhibitionism,"[45] and he was re-elected mayor in 1971.[46] In Orange, another city where a classical music festival took place, the Gaullist mayor Jacques Bérard chose on the contrary to authorize the three-day pop festival (15–17 August 1975). Although part of the press described a "city under siege" and "panicked residents," most reviews were positive. A petition, asking for a new edition of the festival in 1976, was later signed by many residents and shopkeepers, especially barkeep-ers, something which tended to prove that a pop audience could be profitable (Figure 2.1).[47]

As a matter of fact, most observers, especially in the press, condemned the bans, even on the far right.[48] On the far left, positions were more mixed. The Communist Party and many leftist activists spoke out against the bans that exemplified "the reactionary politics of the government," while viewing pop festivals as capitalist enterprises, which pushed youth towards consumerism, and they denied that they could be the basis of a dissident move-ment.[49] In France, most pop festivals were indeed organised by promoters, sponsored by private radios (Europe n° 1 in Aix, Radio Luxembourg in Biot and Orange) and were not cheap.[50]

The French advocates for free (live) music were nevertheless numerous—and internation-ally famous. At the 1970 Isle of Wight Festival, French leftist groups had made themselves known by invading the field and the stage, alongside the White Panthers, in front of about 60,000 people.[51] They denounced not only ticket, food and drink prices but also the safety measures, which resulted in the building of fences, the exclusion of parts of the audience and sometimes violence from the security forces. In France, free riders and leftist activists were held responsible for most of the disturbances, either in open-air festivals or in concert halls—for example, at the Palais des Sports on 22 September 1970 and January 1971. In Biot, less than 4,000 out of the 30,000 festival-goers had paid for their tickets. An attempt to pass the hat round, as had been done in some American free festivals, resulted in a derisory sum. Unable to pay the artists—some of them, like Soft Machine, refused to play—the organiser Jean Karakos decided to end the festival on 6 August at 5 a.m. Things degenerated into a fist fight, with French Maoists denouncing the capitalist "exploiters."[52] In Aix, about half of the audience was made of free riders. French leftist band Komintern whipped up the crowd, claiming that "the bourgeoisie was right to fear youth gatherings, since they represented a new generation, ready to continue the fight of May 68."[53] In October 1970, the Front de Libération Internationale de la Pop (FLIP), close to the far left, published a manifesto claim-ing that they wanted "to draw lessons from the 1970 summer of pop." The failure of "com-mercial and bourgeois" pop festivals proved that, for youth, "pop music was something else than a market, it was a new way of life which implied a radical contestation of the bourgeois society, of its laws, of the alienation it produces and which—a thousand-headed hydra—threatened to smother us all [. . .]" (Deshayes and Grimaud 2008, 28–29).

Were pop festivals a new kind of political demonstration? Observers were divided on this issue (Drott 2011, 155–202), as was, for example, the editorial team of music magazine *Rock & Folk*: editor-in-chief Philippe Koechlin considered the "pop movement" as "apolitical," but for Paul Alessandrini, the summer of 1970

> was in some way the failure of those who refuse that pop music is a political fact, although we have to denounce those who, for militant reasons, exploit [these events], in the name of revolutionary infantilism and preach Socialist Realism.

François-René Christiani concluded, "Obsessed with Woodstock, organisers rushed [to deliver services]. Frightened by youngsters, leaders issued bans. Waving the threat of protest, the audience refused to pay."[54]

With its numerous bans on pop music, France seemed, at the beginning of the 1970s, an exception in Europe. Philippe Aubert, in *Combat*, did not hesitate to compare its situation with the Spanish and Portuguese dictatorships, or communist countries.[55] It was, of course, a gross exaggeration, but until the beginning of the 1980s, and the institutionalisation of a rock music policy under Minister of Culture Jack Lang, the relation between French public authorities, youth subcultures and rock music would remain ambivalent to say the least. Other musical genres would then fall under suspicion, such as rap and techno (Cannon and Dauncey 2003, Warne 2006).

Notes

1 Some parts of this chapter have already been published or will soon be. See Tamagne 2008, 2011, 2013.
2 Due to space constraints, I will not develop the question of the reception of rock 'n' roll as a "foreign" genre that threatened French national musical identity, exemplified by *chanson*. See Looseley 2003; Cannon and Dauncey 2003.
3 *France-Soir*, 24 July 1959. More than twenty-five youngsters were arrested.
4 See, for example, *Paris-Journal*, 25–26 July 1959.
5 *Le Parisien*, 5 August 1959.
6 See, for example, *Paris-Journal*, 25–26 July 1959.
7 See Sohn 2001; Galland 2002; Bantigny 2007; Jobs 2007; Tamagne 2009.
8 Archives de la Préfecture de Police, Boîte "Blousons noirs." One of the belts is engraved with the inscription "Elvis Presley fan club." Les Chaussettes Noires and Les Vautours were French rock 'n' roll bands.
9 *Le Parisien Libéré*, 3 August 1962. The Zazous, a youth subculture of jazz fans who opposed the Vichy regime, were the target of young fascists who wanted to "scalp" them. At the end of the Occupation, women who were said to have collaborated with the Germans were shaved bald.
10 *Le Parisien Libéré*, June 1965.
11 *Bulletin Municipal Officiel [BMO] de la Ville de Paris*, Thursday, 10 January 1963 session, 2–10.
12 *BMO de la Ville de Paris*, Séance du Vendredi 5 janvier 1962, 17.
13 See *Paris-Jour*, 20 November 1961, and *France-Soir*, 21 November 1961.
14 *Le Monde*, 26 July 1961.
15 APP-FD-Manifestation 22 juin 1963. I would like to thank Olivier Accarie-Pierson, who gave me access to this file.
16 *Paris-Presse*, 25 and 29 June 1963, and *Minute*, 28 June 1963. The damage was relatively limited and mostly unintentional (degradation of trees and street furniture, cafes, buildings and cars), although pickpocketing, car and motorbike thefts and the looting of a newspaper stand were mentioned. A policeman was assaulted, and his weapon was stolen; a girl was sexually abused. Seventy-three people were arrested, among them twenty-nine minors under 20; forty-six judiciary enquiries were opened, fourteen affecting minors under 20. *BMO, Conseil Municipal de Paris*, séance du jeudi 27 juin 1963.

17   *Le Populaire*, 25 June 1963, and *France-Soir*, 25 June 1963.
18   *Le Figaro*, 24 June 1963.
19   *Paris-Presse, L'Intransigeant*, 25 June 1963.
20   See *Le Parisien libéré*, 24 June 1963; *Paris-Jour*, 24 June 1963; and *Salut les Copains*, n° 13, August 1963.
21   See *Capri*, 7 August 1963.
22   *Carrefour*, 3 July 1963; *Minute*, 28 June 1963; and *Le Hérisson*, 18 July 1963.
23   APP-FD-Manifestation 22 juin 1963.
24   Ibid.
25   *Minute*, 28 June 1963.
26   *Le Populaire*, 25 June 1963. Maurice Papon had been nominated prefect of police of Paris in 1958. He was responsible for the bloody repression of the 17 October 1961 Front de Libération Nationale (FLN) demonstration and of the anti-Organisation Armée Secrete (OAS) 8 February 1962 demonstration.
27   *Libération*, 6 July 1963.
28   *BMO, Conseil Général de la Seine*, 3e session ordinaire de 1963.
29   The FLN fought for the independence of Algeria against France. The OAS was a paramilitary organization in favour of French Algeria.
30   *Combat*, 25 June 1963.
31   *Rivarol*, 4 July 1963.
32   *Le Monde*, 6 and 7–8 July 1963.
33   *BMO, Conseil Municipal de Paris*, séance du jeudi 27 juin 1963.
34   See *BMO, Conseil Municipal de Paris*, séance du jeudi 27 juin 1963, and *Minute*, 28 June 1963.
35   APP-FD-Manifestation 22 juin 1963. See also *Combat*, 24 June 1963.
36   However, pop and free jazz bands did play in a number of venues, notably in jazz and contemporary music festivals.
37   Front de Libération de la Rock Music, *Le Parapluie*, November 1972.
38   Archives départementales des Bouches-du-Rhône [ADBdR], 135 W 492.
39   ADBdR, 135 W 492.
40   Ibid.
41   Archives municipales d'Orange [AmO], R 3899.
42   *Combat*, 29 July 1970.
43   See *Le Figaro*, 3 August 1970, and *Combat*, 24, 27, 29, 30 and 31 July 1970.
44   ADBdR, 135 W 492.
45   *Le Monde*, 31 July 1970.
46   *Le Monde*, 19–20 July 1970, 31 July 1970 and 1 August 1970.
47   AmO, R 3899. *Le Dauphiné Libéré*, 18 August 1975, and *France Soir*, 14 August 1975.
48   See *Rivarol*, 6 August 1970.
49   *France-Nouvelle*, weekly newspaper of the French Communist Party, quoted in *Le Monde*, 9–10 August 1970. See also *Combat*, 28 July 1970, and Drott 2011.
50   The Bièvres festival (1972–1973), organised by Philippe Bone, the coordinator of the Underground Press Syndicate in Europe, was one of the few French free festivals (Deshayes and Grimaud 2008, 34).
51   *IT*, n° 87, 10 September 1970. The White Panther Party was an anti-racist, leftist organisation.
52   *Le Monde*, 8 August 1970
53   ADBdR, 135 W 492.
54   *Rock & Folk*, n° 44, September 1970.
55   *Combat*, 31 July 1970.

Bibliography

Bantigny, Ludivine. 2007. *Le plus bel âge? Jeunes et jeunesses en France de L'aube des Trente Glorieuses à la guerre d'Algérie*. Paris: Fayard.
Cannon, Steve, and Hugh Dauncey, eds. 2003. *Popular Music in France From Chanson to Techno*. Aldershot: Aldergate.
Clément, Claude (Général). 1971. *Faites l'amour et plus la guerre*. Paris: Fayard.
Cohen, Stanley. 1972. *Folk Devils and Moral Panics*. London: MacGibbon & Kee.
Deshayes, Eric, and Dominique Grimaud. 2008. *L'underground musical en France*. Paris: Le mot et le reste.
Drott, Eric. 2011. *Music and the Elusive Revolution: Cultural Politics and Political Culture in France, 1968–1981*. Berkeley: University of California Press.
Galland, Olivier. 2002. *Les jeunes*. Paris: La Découverte.
Jobs, Richard Ivan. 2007. *Riding the New Wave: Youth and the Rejuvenation of France After the Second World War*. Stanford: Stanford University Press.

Looseley, David L. 2003. *Popular Music in Contemporary France: Authenticity, Politics, Debate.* Oxford and New York: Berg.

Sauvy, Alfred. 1959. *La montée des jeunes.* Paris: Calmann Lévy.

Sohn, Anne-Marie. 2001. *Âge tendre et tête de bois: Histoire des jeunes des années 1960.* Paris: Hachette.

Tamagne, Florence. 2008. "Le 'blouson noir': codes vestimentaires, subcultures rock et sociabilités adolescentes dans la France des années 1950 et 1960." In *Paraître et apparences en Europe occidentale du Moyen-Age à nos jours,* edited by Isabelle Parésys, 99–114. Lille: Presses Universitaires du Septentrion.

———. 2009. "'C'mon everybody.' Rock'n'roll et identités juvéniles en France (1956–1966)." In *Jeunesse oblige: Histoire des jeunes en France XIXᵉ–XXᵉ,* edited by Ludivine Bantigny and Ivan Jablonka, 199–212. Paris: PUF.

———. 2011. "La Nuit de la Nation [The Night of the Nation] (22 June 1963): Youth Culture, Rock'n'Roll and Moral Panic in France in the 1960's." Paper presented at the Tagung PopHistory. Perspektiven einer Zeitgeschichte des Populären, Berlin, November 3–5.

———. 2013. "Les festivals 'pop' et 'rock' en Europe: débats et enjeux (fin des années 1960-début des années 1980)." In *Une histoire des festivals XXe–XXIe siècle,* edited by Anais Fléchet, Pascale Goetschel, Patricia Hidiroglou, Sophie Jacotot, Caroline Moine, and Julie Verlaine, 89–97. Paris: Publications de la Sorbonne.

Warne, Chris. 2006. "Music, Youth and Moral Panics in France, 1960 to Present." *Historia Actual Online* 11:51–64.

3

"Lost Song"

Serge Gainsbourg and the Transformation of French Popular Music

Olivier Julien

For decades, scholars with an interest in *chanson* insisted on what Antoine Hennion calls the "poetic ambition" of French "'artistic' singer-songwriters" (Hennion 1983, 179). This ambition did not escape Peter Hawkins when he wrote, in 2000, "For a long time, the genre has struggled to affirm its literary credentials" (Hawkins 2000, 10). It did not escape David Looseley either when he noted, drawing on sociologist Paul Yonnet's work on rock music and French *chanson*,

> Artistic legitimacy in France . . . was . . . identified with a national literary tradition; so it was natural for singer-songwriters to build their reputation and self-image by identifying themselves with a high-cultural form, namely poetry: setting established poets to music as Ferré, Brassens and Ferrat did, having their own lyrics published by Seghers in its "Poètes d'aujourd'hui" ("Poets of Today") series, or recited by famous stage actors.
>
> (Looseley 2003, 38)

Naturally, this is completely different from the usual approach to lyric writing in the English-speaking world, where, according to Allan Moore, "in everyday reality, the closest we come to the sung lyric is in the words of conversation" (Moore 2012, 109). Conversely, France nurtured what might be described as a "tradition . . . of regarding *chanson* as oral poetry" (Looseley 2013, 21).

As I have argued elsewhere (Julien 2010), this lyric-centered approach is one of the reasons why the shift from "popular music in the sense of folk music" to "popular music in the sense of industrial music," which has been described as taking place at the turn of the twentieth century in the English-speaking world (Middleton 1990; Scott 2008), did not occur in France. But it also accounts for what appears to be the most defining feature of this "hybrid form of popular culture which is French *chanson*" (Hawkins 2000, 4), as opposed to Anglo-American popular music as we have known it since the 1950s. Several theories have been advanced to try and explain how French songwriters came to develop this particular trait. In *Sounds of the Metropolis*, musicologist Derek Scott asserts it dates back to the golden age of Montmartre cabarets and early *chansonniers*:

> A *chanteur* simply sang songs; a *chansonnier* was a singer-poet, though this did not necessarily entail composing the music. The precursors of nineteenth-century *chanson* were the songs sung to existing tunes and disseminated by words alone.
>
> (Scott 2008, 197)

From a more literary and local perspective, Lucienne Cantaloube-Ferrieu presents Charles Trenet as a key figure, reminding us that poets "Max Jacob, Léon-Paul Fargue [and] Jean Cocteau insist[ed] repeatedly on [his] poetic gifts: this author, who chose an oral form to express himself, [was] truly one of theirs" (Cantaloube-Ferrieu 1981, 14). The idea that Trenet was the French songwriter who actually "brought poetry to the street" (Pessis 2003, 50) is indeed well spread among French *chanson* lovers. However, Cantaloube-Ferrieu goes on to observe that "before World War I, Max Jacob, Guillaume Apollinaire, André Salmon, Pierre Mac Orlan, Francis Carco, [and] Roland Dorgelès were regulars at the Lapin Agile" (15–16); she even goes so far as to trace the lineage back to Villon and Rabelais; to La Fontaine, Racine, and Boileau; then to Gérard de Nerval and Jean-Jacques Rousseau; and finally, to Chateaubriand, Théophile Gautier, Théodore de Banville, and Charles Baudelaire (18–19). Without necessarily going to such extremes, one can only agree that these "interaction[s] between *chanson* and its more prestigious literary cousin" (Hawkins 2000, 4) are deeply rooted in French culture and history. As Derek Scott hints, Montmartre cabarets made them all the more apparent in an era when "the popular [was] aspiring to something more than entertainment" (Scott 2008, 100); then, as *chanson* was, in fact, turning into a commercial product of the mass media industry, Trenet blurred the lines further before the blurring became almost complete with a generation of singer-songwriters who had grown up listening to his songs:

> A particular place, the cabaret, gave birth to a particular genre ("artistic *chanson*" ["*chanson à texte*"]) and a particular species (French singer-songwriters). Until [the 1950s], the world of *chanson* had been characterized by a division of labor: on the one hand, performers sang what others wrote for them; on the other hand, composers and authors wrote their own material. The cabaret bred this new "species," that of singer-songwriters, who sang what they wrote and composed. And this species had a father: Charles Trenet.
>
> (Calvet 2013, 117)

Given that most of these new cabarets were located on Paris's Left Bank, the type of *chanson* whose genesis is recalled here by Louis-Jean Calvet came to be known as "Left Bank *chanson*." Its practitioners not only made no secret of their debt to Trenet (as Jacques Brel famously remarked, "without him, we'd all be chartered accountants"—quoted in Hawkins 2000, 85) but also made clear their "desire to emulate the cultural prestige of the literary figure" (Hawkins 2000, 15). Still, strictly speaking, they did not only do so by singing what they wrote and composed. Following the example of Trenet, who set "Chanson d'automne" by Paul Verlaine to music in 1941, they developed new artistic ambitions, which showed through in their penchant for adapting the work of famous French poets. Léo Ferré, who devoted entire albums to Baudelaire, Aragon, Verlaine, and Rimbaud, was certainly the most well known in relation to this practice. He was not alone however: Georges Brassens adapted texts by François Villon, Victor Hugo, Paul Fort, Francis Jammes, and Jean Richepin; Guy Béart used lyrics by contemporary writers André Hardellet, Marcel Aymé, and Louise de Vilmorin; Jean Ferrat released several singles of Louis Aragon poems; and Barbara set Paul Eluard's "Printemps" to music.

"If People Call Me a Poet, I'm Happy With It"

Even though the younger generations would soon forget his beginnings as a *chanteur à texte*, Gainsbourg was, in the early days of his career, one of these Left Bank singer-songwriters. In many respects, he may even be regarded as a typical figure of the cabaret scene in 1950s Paris. First, he was born in 1928, which means he was only two years younger than Léo Ferré, seven years younger than Georges Brassens, and actually one year older than Jacques Brel. Second, when he began performing live in his late twenties, he was a regular act at clubs such as the Milord L'Arsouille (where he made his début in 1957, after it brought to fame singers like Brel, Béart, and Ferré) or Les Trois Baudets (a venue that also hosted shows by Brel, Béart, and especially Brassens on a regular basis). Third, and perhaps more importantly, from 1958 through 1962 (i.e., during the first five years of his recording career), he too set established French poets to music, namely Alfred de Musset ("La Nuit d'octobre"), Gérard de Nerval ("Le Rock de Nerval"), Charles Baudelaire ("Baudelaire"), Victor Hugo ("Chanson de Maglia"), and Félix Arvers ("Le Sonnet d'Arvers"). He even dared to record a modernized adaptation of Ronsard's famous "Ode à Cassandre" on his first album ("Ronsard 58"), while the short text he wrote for the back sleeve of his following record made his intentions even clearer in terms of how he perceived himself in his relationship to the world of high culture:

> Of the "Claqueur de Doigts," I would say he hangs around juke-boxes here and there; of "L'Amour à la Papa," that "I'm not interested"; of "Indifférente," that it is about a bad loser, and of "Adieu Créature," that it is about a "cheater."
>
> As for "La Nuit d'Octobre," I shall answer for it to Musset only, and I know he will forgive me.
>
> (Gainsbourg 1959)

In short, if a songwriter must almost apologize for setting a poet to music, Gainsbourg's relationship to poetry is such that he will answer for it to Musset only. And, naturally, he knows the poet will forgive him. It is striking to note that these few words contain the seeds of the ambiguity the songwriter maintained throughout his life when referring to *chanson* as an *art mineur* ("low art," i.e., an art form whose products are, in an Adornian perspective, "no longer also commodities, but . . . commodities through and through"; Adorno 1991, 100). On the one hand, he never missed a chance to draw a thick line between *chanson* and poetry, making hundreds of definite statements such as, "Don't talk so much about poetry in *chanson*, will you? . . . I believe poetry should be read with the eyes and in silence" (quoted in Gasquet 2003, 66). Yet, on the other hand, there was always a certain haziness as to which side of this line he wanted to be perceived as standing on. For even after he acknowledged he had turned his back on "*chanson* that's full of literary pretense" and "changed [his] tune" for a "tune [that] makes the same sound as a cash register" (quoted in Verlant 2012, 256), in the mid-1960s, he would never completely renounce his early Left Bank singer-song-writer poetic ambitions. To name but a few examples, one only need think of the final track on his 1971 album, *Histoire de Melody Nelson*, whose lyrics were structured as two genuine sonnets. Moreover, the Italian rhyming scheme and structure of those sonnets were, by his own admission, inspired by José Maria de Heredia's "Les Conquérants" (Szpirglas 2011, 28). On the same train of thought, two years later, he revamped Verlaine's "Chanson d'automne," deconstructing it and rearranging its most famous verses in "Je suis venu te dire que je m'en vais"—not to mention countless references to poets such as Arthur Rimbaud, Charles Baudelaire, Edgar Allan Poe, Apollinaire, Lautréamont, and even Stéphane Mallarmé, whose "Une négresse par le démon secouée" is cited word for word on his last album in 1987.

Inevitably, this most equivocal attitude helped, in turn, create a certain confusion in the minds of the great public and mass media as to Gainsbourg's actual status and ambitions. Was he merely a commercial songwriter in search of "*auteurist* legitimacy" (Harrison 2005, 54)? Was he, as journalist Denise Glaser once called him, "a master forger [with] an original talent" (quoted in Verlant 2012, 304)? Was he rather a "*poète maudit* born too late" (Anderson 2013, 86)? Or was he, to paraphrase the title of a compilation album released in the United Kingdom in 2010, an elusive character, "Part poet, part provocateur" (Gainsbourg 2010)? Whatever the answer, it should be pointed out that this type of strategy, in terms of cultural legitimation, was also a typical feature of the great figures of so-called *chanson à texte*. François René Cristiani and Jean-Pierre Leloir's 1969 triple interview with Georges Brassens, Jacques Brel, and Léo Ferré exemplifies this point. When asked by Cristiani if he considered himself a poet, Brassens replied, "Not really. I don't know whether I'm a poet, but it doesn't really matter. I merely mix words with music, then I sing them." Brel then interrupted, stating, with what might be viewed as typical false modesty, "I'm a *chansonnier*, that's what I am! I'm a little craftsman of *chanson*." Finally, Ferré concluded, claiming, "People who call themselves poets are the people who really aren't poets. People who like being described as poets are Sunday poets who published leaflets at their own expense." But he also added, "That said, if people call me a poet, I'm happy with it" (Cristiani and Leloir 1969).

This last sentence arguably sums up Gainsbourg's double-entendre attitude when referring to high culture. And, in this respect too, he would remain a typical Left Bank *chanteur à texte* until the end of his life, as attested by an infamous interview with journalist Bernard Pivot on the set of *Apostrophes*, on December 26, 1986. A mere four years before Gainsbourg's death, in March 1991, those who saw the show at the time no doubt remember how exhausted he looked. He was actually so drunk that he did not even remember the titles of songs he wrote himself when mentioning them. But even more startling was this feeling that, after decades of definite statements about *chanson* being an *art mineur*, he was finally revealing his true colors when Pivot got him to talk about poetry and asked him his opinion about his own lyrics.

Serge Gainsbourg, you consider all your songs to be minor things?
Absolutely.
Really?
Yes . . . Except for some, which . . . came close to Rimbaud . . .

Some?

Some, lately.

Which ones?

"Mélodie au-dessus du jardin," [*sic*] "Melody Nelson," "Sorry Angel" . . . my last songs for Charlotte [Gainsbourg], my last songs for Isabelle Adjani . . . and those for Jane Birkin.

(Léridon 1986)

To put it differently, "All songs are 'minor things,' including mine, but with the exception of several dozen amongst those I wrote since the early 1970s." To get back to the 1959 sleeve notes I already mentioned, "As for 'La Nuit d'Octobre,' I shall answer for it to Musset only, and I know he will forgive me."

"American Songs With Subtitles"

Following the importation of rock 'n' roll in France, the rise of *yéyés* signaled a turning point in the way local popular music had developed since the era of Montmartre cabarets. Just a few months after sociologist Edgar Morin first used this name to refer to French imitators of American rockers (Morin 1963), poet Louis Aragon observed, in an interview with Francis Crémieux, "there is, nowadays, a different impression of French *chanson*. One has the feeling that, in terms of audience, it is being demolished by what you might call the 'say-nothing,' that is, *yéyé*" (Aragon and Crémieux 2012, 129). Retrospectively, the turn of the 1960s was indeed a time when traditional French *chanson* was being swept away by the latest sounds from the English-speaking world while *chanteurs à texte* were losing out to local performers who used aliases such as "Johnny Hallyday," "Sheila," "Eddy Mitchell," or "Dick Rivers." Like his fellow Left Bank singer-songwriters, Gainsbourg suddenly seemed out of touch with this new generation of artists and their audience's expectations. As an example, when his third album, *L'Etonnant Serge Gainsbourg*, came out in April 1961, it was obvious that

[t]he majority of subscribers to French teenage magazines like *Spécial Pop* hadn't read the books necessary for comprehending . . . tracks like "La Chanson de Maglia" (from Victor Hugo) and "Le Rock de Nerval" . . . Serge [Gainsbourg]'s devotees—if that is the word— were still of a type more likely to browse in bookshops than be an Eddy Mitchell fan.

(Clayson 2005, 62)

But the younger generations keeping away from bookshops was not the sole reason for their lack of interest in Gainsbourg as a singer-songwriter. "With three years on Berry and not much younger than Bill Haley," he was, in the words of Alan Clayson, "never cut out to be an icon of *le yéyé.*"

Far removed from Berry, The [Big] Bopper . . . and . . . classic rock in general, [he] seemed, in one of the bilious clichés of music journalism, to have Grown Old With His Audience . . . Indeed, it was as if he'd always been old.

(Clayson 2005, 60–61)

One might add this was also the case with such singers as Brel, Ferré, and particularly Brassens. However, Gainsbourg faced another difficulty: even in the standards of *chanson à texte*, he was still a rather obscure artist. As a result, "if sales were never great for [him], *yéyé* made things worse" (Simmons 2002, 38).

Interestingly, his first reaction to the *yéyé* storm was typical of old-time *chanteurs à texte*: he insisted on *yéyés*' lack of maturity due to both their young age and that of the audience they were addressing, and he also pointed to their being in thrall to a so-called American model:

> I'm not going to add a "y" at the end of my first name. And I think that milky white teeth fall out quickly, while wisdom teeth come in only with pain . . . That stuff (the *yéyés*), that's American pop. American songs with subtitles . . . French *chanson* is not dead. It has to evolve and not hitch itself to America's wagon.
>
> (Verlant 2012, 223)

The latter part of the statement is surprising, to say the least, when one thinks of Gainsbourg's 1984 album, *Love on the Beat*, whose eight tracks would all have titles in English. And it is all the more surprising considering this very statement was just a few months before Gainsbourg announced, in the November 22, 1964, issue of *Le Journal de Genève*,

> [Left Bank] *chanson* style is over. I know because I watched it die when I closed the last of those kinds of clubs . . . I was a pianist, then a headliner, and then they closed . . . And those that are still around are old hat. What's more, it's a sorry sight to see someone who supposedly has nothing to say if he's accompanied by crappy music. He strums his guitar, maybe three chords . . . And still, people listen . . . What can you do? They've never been exposed to anything better.
>
> (Verlant 2012, 254)

As already mentioned, what happened between those two statements was Gainsbourg's "chang[ing] his tune" for a "tune [that] ma[de] the same sound as a cash register." When he came up with this now famous witty remark, he was actually referring to the fact that he had turned his back on serious *chanson* once realizing that he could write hits more or less on demand for *yéyé* icons like France Gall and other teenage idols. Beneath the surface, though, this change of tune meant more than embracing a new career as a commercial songwriter. And it meant even more than succeeding in "marrying commercially-successful (pop) music with serious *chanson*" (Harrison 2005, 115). In fact, this change of tune implied a change of focus in terms of song writing.

According to Jane Birkin, "[Serge Gainsbourg] was always very bright . . . he twigged onto things before anybody else, and he liked the English sound better" (quoted in Simmons 2002, 38). Combined with a will to emulate the Anglo-American style the *yéyés* were looking for, his ability to anticipate musical trends finally made him the first French artist to truly understand the importance of sound in the way popular music was evolving following the global success of rock 'n' roll. Foreshadowing 1960s French singer-songwriters like Michel Polnareff, he even got into the habit of going in search of that sound where it originated. As early as January 1963 (i.e., several months before the British press coined the term "Beatlemania"), he began recording in London, where he would work, over the years, with local producers and arrangers like

Harry Robinson, David Whitaker, Arthur Greenslade, and Alan Hawkshaw. In 1978–1979, as reggae was breaking into the mainstream on the international music scene, he was also the first white singer to record in Kingston, "showing the way to Dylan, Cocker, and quite a few others" (Brieu 2001, 2). He actually cut a couple of albums in the West Indies with Peter Tosh's rhythm section and the Wailers' female backing trio before the electro-funk sounds of "Rockit" and Arthur Baker's productions, which were then pervading British and American charts, led him to New Jersey and Southside Johnny and the Asbury Jukes' lead guitarist Billy Rush in 1984. In sum, having reviewed his early position on the *yéyé* approach, he spent the rest of his career endeavoring to produce "Anglo-American songs with original French-speaking lyrics."

With regard to the way the latter lyrics were affected by their being put to genuine British, Jamaican, or American playbacks, it is worth noting that the more Gainsbourg found himself immersed in those sonic trends from the English-speaking world, the less he was concerned with setting his words to melodies. This particularly struck bassist Robbie Shakespeare during the recording of his first reggae album, *Aux armes et caetera*: "It wasn't really singing. He was more like a poet doing French poems on top of popular rhythms at the time" (quoted in Simmons 2002, 88). The fact that Gainsbourg progressively gave up singing for "talk-over" certainly contributed to his being perceived as a "*poète maudit* of the modern age" (Anderson 2013, 89). As Peter Hawkins remarks, the publication of song texts in the "Poètes d'aujourd'hui" series by Seghers

> invited the reader to regard them as poems and to analyze them as such. [Still,] however poetic they may be, these are not poems, but song lyrics, designed to be sung and indissociable from the music and even the orchestration that accompanies them.
>
> (Hawkins 2000, 11)

But what about song lyrics that were designed to be *read* over music? Were they, as their author suggested, "so sophisticated in the prosody that they [couldn't] be put into a melody" (quoted in Verlant 2012, 432)? If so, then Sylvie Simmons hits the nail on the head when she notes that, "unlike the more modern French singer-songwriters like Jacques Brel and Georges Brassens, who essentially set poetry to music, Serge [Gainsbourg]'s words, uniquely, were welded to the music" (Simmons 2002, 28). Only the music in question was not, strictly speaking, francophone music: it was music from the English-speaking world. In this respect, considering that "a culture's . . . music reflects the prosody of its native language" (Patel 2008, 222), Gainsbourg's self-proclaimed sophisticated approach to prosody finally proceeded from his trying to weld French words to the English language's rhythm and melody.

Such an approach to lyric writing probably accounts for what biographer Alan Clayson describes as Gainsbourg's tendency for "stretching out vowels and splitting up words to ensure that lines ended with the required root syllable," the latter process allegedly indicating that, to him, "sound mattered more than meaning" (Clayson 2005, 63). It also sheds light on sound engineer Dominique Blanc-Francard's recollection of their many recording sessions together:

> he had a technique of cutting the words in the middle and replacing them with a rhythm and accent that was very English but with a meaning that was completely French. For him the sound of words [was] as important as the sense, and that was completely new in France.
>
> (Quoted in Simmons 2002, 137)

In any case, however innovative Gainsbourg's technique was as a lyricist, however hard he tried, as a composer, to override the influence of the French language's rhythm and melody on musical structure, it is revealing that, from his reggae period through his electro-funk period, his songs almost systematically combined spoken verses in French with English-speaking refrains that were sung by native backing vocalists (the I Threes, then the Simms Brothers, Brenda White King, and Curtis King, Jr.). All things considered, it was as if the more he succeeded in capturing the spirit of a culture where popular music scholars came up with provocative titles like "Why do songs have words?" (Frith 1988), the more his mother tongue reminded him that, in the world he came from, popular music scholars were more likely to ask, "Why do songs have music?"

"Now, I'm the Only One Left"

In one of the few passages from Gilles Verlant's classic biography that were omitted from the English version, one may read that, "[o]n the death of Brassens, on October 30, 1981, Gainsbourg told Jane [Birkin]: 'Now, I'm the only one left'" (Verlant 2000, 561). By then, Gainsbourg had

> already drifted . . . from the stylistic path of *chanson française* [due to] his penchant for provocation, his creative use of English, his taste for American symbols of modernity, and his flippant experimentation with non-French musical identities [that] set him apart from the [Brel-Brassens-Ferré] trinity.
>
> (Hill 2003, 120–121)

Still, he obviously had not forgotten his beginnings and early ambitions as a *chanteur à texte*. That very day, presenter Patrick Poivre d'Arvor broke the news on French television with the following headline: "Everyone's sad . . . whether 20, 40 or 60 years old, we all lost an uncle." People on the set all agreed that Brassens would "go down in history as a poet"; Poivre d'Arvor also reported a few official statements by French personalities, and then he played a recording of Brassens commenting on Jacques Brel's death, three years earlier: "A member of our family just passed away . . . I don't think Brel is actually dead—not with what he wrote . . . As a matter of fact, I believe he's more alive than he ever was" (Léridon 1981).

Three decades later, there would be almost a dozen Jacques Brel streets and as many Georges Brassens streets in France. And yet the emotion that followed those deaths was nothing compared to the stir caused by Gainsbourg's death, on March 2, 1991. As Sylvie Simmons puts it, "When he died . . . France went into mourning . . . President Mitterrand [called him] 'our Baudelaire, our Apollinaire,' [before adding] 'He elevated [*chanson*] to the level of *art*'" (Simmons 2002, ix). What is more, this time, the emotion seemed to traverse all categories of French society. To quote the words of Peter Hawkins again,

> Gainsbourg's reputation at his death in 1991 could not have been greater: he was the idol of French youth culture of the 1980s, a symbol of the nihilism of the *bof* ["so what"] generation, a model of cynical nonconformity to received values.
>
> (Hawkins 2000, 158)

Indeed, Gainsbourg's inclination toward nonconformity was a characteristic trait of his personality, and this showed through many aspects of his work, including his aim to "unit[e] French *chanson* with pop in a way alluded to by [other] artists . . . but never actually achieved by [them]" (Harrison 2005, 126). His ability to bridge the gap between French *chanson à texte* and popular music *à la française* is even reflected in the fact that he died as a youth culture idol over thirty years after starting out as a Left Bank singer-songwriter, embodying, in a way, the end of the former world and the rise of the latter. As for his much-vaunted "cynical" approach to his art, it has been said that his songs, being "simultaneously 'throw-away' pop numbers and intelligent, distanced commentary on 'throw-away' pop numbers, subvert[ed] the genre in which they [were] working" (Harrison 2005, 126). Unless, of course, they were

Figure 3.1 Serge Gainsbourg, *Love on the Beat*, Philips (Mercury), 1984, 33⅓ rpm front cover.

actually subverting *chanson* with the codes of popular music instead. As the Anglo-American band The Kills would sing in their 2006 adaptation of "La Chanson de Slogan,"

In the end, foe or friend, live apart
Call it hate, call it love, I call it art.

(The Kills 2006)

Bibliography

Adorno, Theodor W. 1991 [1938]. "On the fetish character in music and the regression of listening." In *The Culture Industry: Selected Essays on Mass Culture*, edited by Jay M. Bernstein, 98–106. London and New York: Routledge.
Anderson, Darran. 2013. *Histoire de Melody Nelson*. New York, London, New Delhi and Sydney: Bloomsbury.
Aragon, Louis, and Francis Crémieux. 2012. "La parole à la chanson: Louis Aragon." *La Nouvelle Revue française* 601:121–136.
Brieu, Jean-François. 2001. Liner notes to the *Gainsbourg . . . Forever* 18 CD box set compilation. Mercury/Universal Music France 548572-2.
Calvet, Louis-Jean. 2013. *Chansons: La bande son de notre histoire*. Paris: L'Archipel.
Cantaloube-Ferrieu, Lucienne. 1981. *Chanson et Poésie des années 30 aux années 60: Trenet, Brassens, Ferré . . . ou les "enfants naturels" du surréalisme*. Paris: A.G. Nizet.
Clayson, Alan. 2005. *Serge Gainsbourg: A View From the Exterior*. London: Sanctuary.
Cristiani, François-René, and Jean-Pierre Leloir. 1969. "Interview de Georges Brassens, Jacques Brel et Léo Ferré." Accessed July 6, 2014. http://brassensbrelferre.free.fr/.
Frith, Simon. 1988. "Why Do Songs Have Words?" In *Music for Pleasure: Essays in the Sociology of Pop*, 105–128. New York: Routledge.
Gainsbourg, Serge. 1959. Liner notes to the album *Serge Gainsbourg* No. 2. Phillips 840.903 BZ, 33 rpm.
Gainsbourg, Serge. 2010. *Poet and Provocateur*. El Records ACMEM180CD, compact disc.
Gasquet, Lisou. 2003. *Gainsbourg en vers et contre tout*. Paris: L'Harmattan.
Harrison, Kim Tracy. 2005. "The Self-Conscious Chanson: Creative Responses to the Art versus Commerce." PhD diss., University of Leeds.
Hawkins, Peter. 2000. *Chanson: The French Singer-Songwriter From Aristide Bruant to the Present Day*. Aldershot, Burlington, Singapore and Sydney: Ashgate.
Hennion, Antoine. 1983. "The Production of Success: An Anti-Musicology of the Pop Song." *Popular Music* 3:159–193.
Hill, Edwin C., Jr. 2003. "Aux Armes Et Caetera! Recovering Nation for Cultural Critique." *Volume! La revue des musiques populaires* 2(2):115–127.
Julien, Olivier. 2010. "'Musiques populaires': de L'exception culturelle à L'anglicisme." *Musurgia* 17(1):49–62.
The Kills. "I Call It Art." In *Monsieur Gainsbourg Revisited*, Barclay/Universal Music France LC 00126, 2006, compact disc.
Léridon, Jean-Luc. 1981. "October 30." *Journal: Edition 20H*. Antenne 2.
———, ed. 1986. "Apostrophes en chanson." *Apostrophes*. Antenne 2.
Looseley, David. 2003. *Popular Music in Contemporary France: Authenticity, Politics, Debate*. Oxford and New York: Berg.
———. 2013. "Outside Looking in: European Popular Musics, Language and Intercultural Dialogue." *Journal of European Popular Culture* 4(1):19–28.
Middleton, Richard. 1990. *Studying Popular Music*. Buckingham: Open University Press.
Moore, Allan F. 2012. *Song Means: Analysing and Interpreting Recorded Popular Song*. Farnham and Burlington: Ashgate.
Morin, Edgar. 1963. "Salut les copains." *Le Monde*, July 6: 1, 11.
Patel, Aniruddh A. 2008. *Music, Language, and the Brain*. Oxford: Oxford University Press.
Pessis, Jacques. 2003. *Chronique de la chanson française*. Trélissac: Editions Chronique.
Scott, Derek B. 2008. *Sounds of the Metropolis: The 19th-Century Popular Music Revolution in London, New York, Paris, and Vienna*. New York: Oxford University Press.
Simmons, Sylvie. 2002. *Serge Gainsbourg: A Fistful of Gitanes*. New York: Da Capo Press.
Szpirglas, Jérémie. 2011. Liner notes to the album *Histoire de Melody Nelson*. Mercury/Universal Music France LC 00268, compact disc.
Verlant, Gilles. 2000. *Gainsbourg*. Paris: Albin Michel.
———. 2012. *Gainsbourg: The Biography*. Translated by Paul Knobloch. New York: TamTam Books.

4

The Record Industry in the 1960–1970s
The Forgotten Story of French Popular Music

Marc Kaiser

Little has been written on the history of the recording industry in France, particularly concerning the period covering the arrival of rock 'n' roll and its development within variety
music.[1] This gap in scholarship is undoubtedly due to the fact that the study of French popular music is quite a recent phenomenon, resulting in limited data available for researchers.
Nevertheless, the recording industry was marked by a series of crises and developments,
which must be taken into account in order to contextualise its current situation, and thereby
understand that rock is not "a revolutionary form or moment, but an evolutionary one, the
climax of (or possibly footnote to) a story that began with Edison's phonograph" (Frith 1988,
12). When it comes to France, the first forms of rock 'n' roll were incorporated by the major
labels and large independent labels (especially Barclay and Vogue) into the modes of production and distribution, which had already been tested by variety music. The evolution of
the record industry into a mass market at this time was not only related to the development
of a new musical culture (*yéyé* music), which corresponded to the youth of the 1960s. Other
factors that must be taken account include new modes of consumption (related to the development of 45 rpm singles), the arrival of new intermediaries into the industry specialised
in the production of "hits" and, more generally, the economic and demographic prosperity of this period. The establishment of official "charts" in 1968 by the French recording
industry association[2] intensified the logics of production of "showbiz" (D'Angelo 1989) and
strengthened the divide of the French musical scene into French variety music on the one
side and Anglo-American pop on the other. As a result, little space was left for new musical
currents flourishing in the early 1970s, which had to evolve outside of established distribution and promotion channels. In terms of this chapter, the research carried out relies on various data obtained from unpublished archives held by the main French recording industry
association.[3]

From One Crisis to Another

Pathé played an important role in the industrialisation of French music at the beginning of
the twentieth century. It produced cylinders and 90 rpm sapphire records (by vertical cutting) in bulk at its factory in Chatou; it had a recording studio (with a catalogue of approximately 100 artists); and it had a shop in Paris, as well as numerous international subsidiaries
(London, Milan, Moscow, New York, Shanghai, Hong Kong, etc.). Pathé was the first major

French record label and had a leading position in the European market, particularly against its main competitor, the Gramophone Company, which produced needle records at their factory in Hanover.

However, with the electrification of modes of reproducing needle records in the mid-1920s—coupled with the electrification of recording methods (the microphone, the tube amplifier) and diffusion (speakers)—Pathé lost its monopoly within a few years. In fact, since it had a huge stock of matrix, Pathé wanted to improve its own material, but its engineers did not succeed in developing electric vertical cutting until 1927. It was already too late because the cylinders and their 90 rpm records were of poor quality compared to the competition's 78 rpm records (whose sound spectrum had increased from 100 to 5,000 Hz).

In 1928, the British record label Columbia seized Pathé's branch dedicated to the phonograph and imposed lateral cutting. Four years earlier, it had already bought Odéon and Parlophone. Following the merger between Columbia and Gramophone, the new British multinational Electric and Musical Industries (EMI) was established in 1931. The concentration of ownership on the French market was thus clearly visible: EMI brought together Pathé, Odéon, Parlophone, Columbia France and the General Gramophone Company.

The First Crisis to Overcome

Although French trade of "talking machines" only represented a few million dollars in the early 1920s, it reached more than 500 million in 1928 (Maisonneuve 2009). Nevertheless, the 78 rpm records did not represent an object of mass consumption. At the time, "*phonos*" were still associated with bicycle, haberdashery and electricity shops. But with the all-important diversification of repertoires (especially with the rise of jazz) and the democratisation of normative discourse on recorded music (thanks to the appearance of specialised journals and prizes), the record was no longer considered as an object of curiosity or as a simple means of selling phonographs. It was now viewed as a medium for recorded music in its own right, which depended upon a channel regrouping manufacturers of devices and materials, publishers, distributors and retail stores.

In the 1930s, the French record industry was hit hard by the economic crisis. While production at EMI's French branches was at 2,807,280 records in 1932, the French industry as a whole only produced 2.45 million units in 1938 (Masson-Forestier 1969). This was also the period when radio became a direct competitor: not only were the rates of equipment of French households and various public places increasing, but the program schedules were increasingly occupied by music programs, notably from the illegal broadcasting of commercially purchased records.

Faced with these difficulties, EMI defined a new strategy for Pathé: the company began to produce radios and by 1934, this activity represented 75% of its turnover (Tournès 2002). The group thus refocused its activities and developed "The Pathé Marconi Musical and Electrical Industries" (in 1936) after Columbia France and the General Gramophone Company had integrated Pathé. EMI, which also benefited from an association of repertoires with its main competitor at the international level (RCA Victor), was finally the undisputed leader on the French market.[4]

The Record Industry's Post-War Economic Boom

In the aftermath of the Second World War, new opportunities were available for French phonographic publishers thanks to the development of the album coupled with a favourable socio-economic context (Kaiser 2014). The first vinyl records were released[5] before the manufacturing process was imported. Alongside the major labels, two independent record labels succeeded in making a name for themselves on the French market, thanks in particular to the development of variety music: the French phonographic company created by Eddie Barclay in 1953 had up to 400 employees and would go on to have subsidiaries abroad, a recording studio and a team of artistic directors (Boris Vian, Léo Missir, Jacques Souplet) and musicians (including Quincy Jones). The society Vogue (founded in 1947) employed up to 700 people, had its own factory with twenty subsidiaries in France and abroad and had a team of artistic directors, a recording studio, a photo studio and a printing company.

In the 1960s, the market hit the jackpot when the 45 rpm EP became the preferred medium of variety music (D'Angelo 1989; Currien and Moreau 2006). The Figure 4.1 shows how the EP was the bestselling format at the beginning of the decade until the introduction of the 45 rpm single in 1967.

In 1960, 11.2 million 45 rpm EPs were sold or exported, compared to 3.3 million 30 cm albums and 2.3 million 25 cm albums. In 1967, the 30 cm record established itself over other 33 rpm formats (when the first "concept albums" appeared), while sales of 45 rpm EPs reached almost 22 million. From 1969 onwards, when the concept of producing "hits" took off, nearly twice as many "singles" were sold compared to "EPs" (26.2 million compared to 14 million). This was also the period when new intermediaries appeared in the industry (independent producers) and the distribution market was modernised (long-distance sales, multiplication of outlets, rack jobbing). At the beginning of the 1970s, popular music thus represented over 70% of sales.

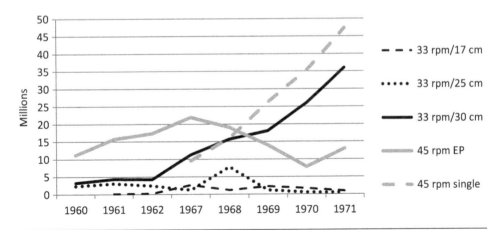

Figure 4.1 Numbers of records sold per year by type of format (France + exports) (1960–1971).

New Crises and New Developments

Figure 4.2 shows the evolution of sales of members belonging to the main French phonographic publishers' union.

The explosion of the record industry during the post-war economic boom is evident: 7 million units sold in 1948 compared to 154 million in 1978. The growth of the industry during this period was strong and relatively consistent, with an average of between 10% and 20% annual increase.[6] Figure 4.2 also shows how several economic crises (oil, monetary, etc.) impacted sales in France by the end of the 1970s. Sales were affected not only by the decline in purchasing power but also by the increase in production costs.

The 1980s were marked by the development of a global market for cultural goods related to new information and communication technologies and increased consolidation of cultural and media industries. The major labels developed new strategies (notably by buying labels and publishers) and introduced new formats that were of better quality and cheaper to produce (the videodisc and then the compact disc).[7] However, the CD had trouble establishing itself and did not help with the decline of sales: in 1982, the number of phonograms sold was down to 150 million units, which then fell to 104 million in 1987. Several economic factors thus contributed to reviving the music industry in France: the democratisation of laser turntables, the restructuring of the distribution market, reductions in VAT, advertising on TV and, significantly, the broadcasting of music videos. In 1988, CD sales surpassed those of vinyl records[8] and reached their highest level in 2002: 107 million CDs sold.

Since then, sales of physical formats have continued to fall with the increase in practices related to the digitisation of music. In 2012, the total number of units sold (physical and digital) was again growing. The entire music industry is working to find new ways of monetizing music, given the fact that the discography sector has always been confronted with many

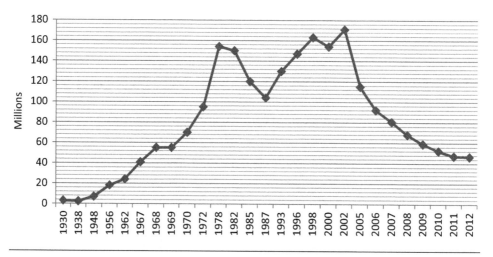

Figure 4.2 Numbers of physical formats sold per year by members of the main record industry union (SNICOP/SNEPA/SNEP) (1930–2012).

recurring problems when going through cycles of growth, crisis, innovation, obsolescence of goods and so on.

Rock 'n' Roll "*à la Française*" and the Variety Music Kingdom

Although rock 'n' roll had not yet reached France, the music industry was undergoing change during the 1950s. In a market dominated by the major labels (who still viewed radio as a direct competitor), it was the independent labels that first seized the promotional potential of commercial radios. Unlike official radios, which had abandoned popular programs, radio stations broadcasted from neighbouring countries[9] offered music programs that appealed to a large French audience. In 1956, Barclay thus associated itself with the radio station Europe n° 1 to get its young talent on stage at the Olympia during the broadcast of the *music-hall* program *Musicorama*. This new strategy would go on to launch many variety music stars: Gilbert Bécaud, Charles Aznavour, Jacques Brel, Dalida and so on.[10]

This burgeoning "showbiz" (D'Angelo 1989) or "*music-hall*" (Guibert 2006)—which brought together professionals from the recording industry, performing arts, radio and television—henceforth adopted new concepts of production and distribution: artistic directors made choices (both aesthetic and commercial) in order to introduce songs to commercial radios to be looped (using the technique of "plugging")[11] in the hopes of obtaining significant record sales, with live performance seen as just another promotional tool.

Yéyé Music: The Rock 'n' Roll of Variety Music

In 1959, when the first French show dedicated to rock 'n' roll (*Salut les Copains*) was broadcast on Europe n° 1, it almost instantly became one of the key vectors for new youth culture (Blandin 2013). Local bands formed and gathered in Golf Drouot's concert hall, which would become the epicentre of French rock 'n' roll (Guibert 2006).[12] While foreign productions of R&B, soul and rock 'n' roll were distributed under license,[13] the first rock 'n' roll musicians were hired,[14] mostly to perform French versions of the latest American and British hits.

But this idea of a "band" did not correspond to the standards of "showbiz." Artistic directors sought "recordings talents" (Hennion 1983) embodied solely by the singers of these bands, in line with the French tradition of cabaret and *music-hall* singing tours. What's more, this strategy helped to expel the subversive nature of rock 'n' roll, which had emerged after several public gatherings (most notably after the "Wild Night").[15]

French rock 'n' roll thus ascribed to the strategy previously developed for variety music by professionals in the recording, performing arts and media industries. They knew how to meet the expectations of French youth who were passionate about this new music and followed the actions of their new "idols."[16] These idols soon became the spokespeople of the *yéyé* movement (Morin 1963a, 1963b), a term that refers more broadly to the emergence of a "teenager moment" (Glevarec 2003) in which the media played an important role.

Figure 4.3 The *yéyé* "idol" France Gall on *Mademoiselle Age Tendre* magazine front cover, n° 33, July 1967.

The appropriation of rock 'n' roll by "showbiz" resulted in a "great divide" (Guibert 2006) between, on the one hand, an electric version of variety music targeted at the youth market and, on the other, a craze for English-speaking artists. The emergence of a "youth culture" coupled with a favourable economic and demographic climate finally allowed the record market to take off by becoming segmented.

The Arrival of Independent Producers

Faced with the success of the *yéyé* artists, it was primarily the artistic directors[17] and lyricists[18] who gradually freed themselves from the major labels to produce their own artists. Although these new intermediaries could record at lower costs (notably with the development of independent studios), they still remained dependent on the distribution and promotion channels of the recording labels. The major labels in turn relied increasingly on producers to find new talent.

Nevertheless, these early independent producers followed the concept of the "hit" because their productions could only exist within the established forms and channels of "showbiz." A year after the appearance of the single, a study conducted in 1968 on behalf of the Syndicat national de L'industrie et du commerce phonographiques (SNICOP) shows that over 80% of record dealers questioned felt that a "hit" had better chances to sell if it was available in 45 rpm single format and not exclusively in 45 rpm EP format (Masson-Forestier 1969).

While production of French variety music increased with these new intermediaries, new music from counterculture movements was emerging in France. New local scenes appeared (Mignon 1982; Mignon and Hennion 1991; Guibert 2006), related to leftist movements (Lagrée 1979; Guibert 2006), and labels were created,[19] sales made and tours organized.[20] In the early 1970s, producer Francis Dreyfus declared that "85% of all records are now produced independently and about 70 percent of those independent producers are publishers," since "it is not very interesting or exciting just competing for French cover versions of songs we sub-publish" (Hennessey 1971).

But these new forms of popular music remained on the margins of "showbiz" and were broadcast very little. This was even more so the case with the development of concept albums and multi-track consoles, with recording studios becoming veritable creative laboratories (arrangements, doubling of voices, etc.)—"thus enabling rock to develop as a 'serious' music in its own right" (Frith 1988, 22)—which went against the norms in place. Although the French music industry had "accommodated the hippie trend, just as it had accommodated rock 'n' roll in the early 1960s and jazz in the 1920s, it has not made place for French rock bands" (Guibert 2006, 140). One of the main reasons for this was the way in which the phonographic publishers' union imposed two musical genres on the market (French and international variety music) with the introduction of official "charts."

Variety Music and the Rest

In the late 1960s, the French phonographic publishers' union (the SNICOP) included around thirty companies[21] that provided 85% of sales and 90% of production. However, the arrival of many new players disrupted the organization of the sector. This is why the Centre for Information and Documentation on the Record ("Centre d'Information et de Documentation du Disque") (CIDD), directed by Jacques Masson-Forestier, was established in 1967, "to serve the public and the natural intermediaries—the record dealers—by keeping them informed; in other words, by helping them in their buying" (Masson-Forestier 1971). Four main areas were developed to achieve this goal: "General Public" (aimed at the public to provide a practical information service), "Record Dealers" (to provide information to help them with their orders),[22] "Press, Associations and Communities" (to provide basic information

Figure 4.4 SNEPA, "Hit Parade National du Disque." February 1975 single charts by the CIDD.

on records and tapes)[23] and a "National Chart." The objective of the National Charts (HPND: "Hit-Parade National du Disque") was twofold: on the one hand, they connected producers with record dealers (estimated at more than 3,000 at the time), and on the other hand, they informed the public and the retailers on a regular basis about the most requested songs in the country. The concept of rankings, established firstly from the number of sales and then from consumer opinions, was a popularity tactic, which would in turn increase the number of sales in places of distribution. The establishment of the HPND resulted in the segmentation of the popular music market around solely variety music (French and foreign), leaving aside music which did not correspond to these known genres (French rock, pop and folk bands).

French and International Variety Music Charts

In the case of variety music, several chart lists existed[24] or were offered at the time.[25] The establishment of a ranking by the publishers themselves was enforced specifically to "clean a market cluttered with charts that were too often trivial, which complicated the information and restocking of records" (Masson-Forestier 1968a). The first HPND of variety music, developed with the help of record dealers, covered all sales of singles without genre distinction from 24 September 1968 to 8 October 1968 (Masson-Forestier 1968b). When observing this ranking, it is noteworthy that very few Francophone artists are at the top of the charts.[26] Record dealers immediately had reservations about this situation because, according to them, the results grouped together two distinct genres, which could have negative impacts on sales. Thereafter, a "French" variety music chart (i.e., sung in French) was distinguished from a "foreign" variety music chart (sung in foreign languages) for sales of singles. It is interesting to note that this division did not apply to the charts of popular music albums, all grouped under the name "30 cm Variety Music."

Each month, the French public could now have access to these rankings by consulting the press,[27] by listening to the radio, which from then on resumed the official charts, or by looking at the listings in retail outlets. The HPND was also published in many foreign countries.[28] This also gave rise to new strategies by phonographic publishers: once a song entered in the charts, it was performed by various artists and in different languages to take maximum advantage of the "reputation" of the song.[29]

By the early 1970s, however, the functioning of the HPND seemed to have reached its limits: the amount of paperwork to be filled in by record dealers was too large (every fortnight), the listings were inaccurate (titles not yet received for sale, titles for which sales had ended, etc.), the figures were distorted (publishers deliberately inflated sales in order to submit more titles for judgment by retail outlets), sales were evaluated on memory and not on the actual figures and the majority of the record dealers who participated in the charts were recommended by the commercial services of the major labels with whom they had distribution agreements.

The CIDD therefore decided to use an accountant to check the rankings obtained and subsequently control the declared numbers directly with the accounting services of each publisher. Other special charts were developed: "30 cm Jazz," "Audiobooks for Children," "Children's Records," "Secular Vocal Music (30 cm Classical)," "Instrumental Music" and so on. But these were only annual and did not relate to other genres of popular music since they were meant to meet the expectations of other union members specialised in classical music and children's music.

From the HPND to the "Top 50"

When the union changed its status in 1974 (to become the SNEPA, Syndicat National de Édition Phonographique et Audiovisuelle), it was decided that consumers would be questioned directly in order to put an end to tensions connected with the HPND, which had become a real strategic issue. Representing the entire population, 11,560 households spread over the whole French territory were then questioned throughout the year about their record purchases. When consumers reported records published by non-member companies, research was conducted to determine the distributing member of the SNEPA. Some

Figure 4.5   Sheila B. Devotion, "Love Me Baby," Carrère, 1977, single front cover.

non-member companies thus benefited indirectly from the promotional tool implemented by the union. But with the increase in production costs and the decrease in sales related to the oil shock of 1973, the members decided to suspend CIDD activities at the end of December 1975.

Given the central role of the charts in the modes of production, distribution and promotion of French popular music, the HPND nonetheless continued to exist until the introduction of a "Top 50" in 1984. Survey companies established a computer system to retrieve sales data, from each shop in the panel, to determine a list of the fifty best physical sales of singles in France, all genres included.[30] Incidentally, this chart gave birth to many television programs specialised in broadcasting music videos that helped perpetuate the logic of "hits" (developed three decades earlier for variety music).

In order to understand the specificity of popular music "made in France," this chapter began by showing that a certain sense of linearity exists in the history of the French record industry (new technological advances, strategies by the various industry players to cope with market changes, new uses and modes of consumption). It then developed the fact that the music industry had already been restructured before the arrival of rock 'n' roll in France around the large independent labels specialised in the production of variety music on vinyl. The 1960s nevertheless marked an important step in the record history since it was during this decade that the market would take flight. The introduction of a new format met with new market expectations connected to the development of a "youth culture," and this in turn intensified the logics of the production of "hits" with the arrival of new intermediaries in the sector. And when new musical movements emerged, independent productions exploded without being integrated into the distribution and promotion networks, which remained firmly in the hands of "showbiz." The official charts further legitimised the division of the French scene between French variety music and English-language popular music while new local scenes were emerging in the 1970s in reaction to this hegemony. The latter included several musical styles, each possessing elements of its own culture—though punk and DIY constitute the main catalysts (Guibert 2006). But that is the story of another very specific point in history—the birth of French alternative music.

Notes

1   In French, the term "*variétés*" denotes popular music that arose from the tradition of cabaret and *music-hall*.
2   Then known as the SNICOP and later designated successively first as SNEPA and then as SNEP.
3   This included five linear metres of archives split into twelve boxes (containing correspondences, studies, reports, accounting documents, press cuttings, etc.).
4   In front of Decca, Ultraphone, Ducretet, Salabert, L'Oiseau Lyre and so on.
5   The first album published in France was the "Apothéose de Lully" by L'Oiseau-Lyre in 1949.
6   The 8-track tape and the cassette were introduced into the French market in 1969.
7   Videodiscs were introduced into the French market by the end of the 1970s; the CD arrived in 1983.
8   Large-scale production of albums stopped at the beginning of the 1990s, and that of the single in 1993. According to the SNEPA, vinyl records represented 0.4% of the total market in 2012.
9   To overturn the state monopoly, several commercial radios (called "*radios périphériques*") broadcasted from regions adjacent to France: Europe n° 1 (in Saarbrücken), Radio Luxembourg, Radio Monte-Carlo, Radio Andorra and so forth.
10 Dalida is the artist who sold the most vinyl records in France during the second half of the 1950s.
11 Lucien Morisse, at the time artistic director on Europe n° 1, explains that "'plugging'" ['*matraquage*'] [. . .] on the radio consisted of showing off—or rather imposing—the singer or the song that we liked and for which we sometimes had the exclusive rights" (Guibert 2006: 107–108).

12   This Parisian café was one of the first places in Paris to have a jukebox in 1955, before transforming the mini-golf on the first floor of the Café d'Angleterre into a concert hall. It rapidly became the French equivalent to the Cavern in Liverpool or the Club in Eindhoven.

13   Barclay: Atlantic, Baccarola, Bang, Buddah, Chess, Jubilee-Jaygee, Stax and so on; Vogue: Elektra, Pye, Red Bird and so on.

14   Johnny Hallyday, Richard Anthony, Lucky Blondo, Long Chris, Les Chaussettes Noires, Les Chats Sauvages, El Toro et les Cyclones, Les Vautours, Les Pirates and so on.

15   To celebrate the first year of the magazine *Salut les Copains*, inspired by the radio show, a free concert was organised at "Place de la Nation" in Paris on 22 June 1963. Instead of the expected 50,000 "friends," more than 150,000 young people turned out for the event. The few acts of misbehaviour recorded at the first event of this kind evoked a slight backlash in the national press the following day—Philippe Bouvard: "What's the difference between a twist at Vincennes and Hitler's discourse at the Reichstag?"; Pierre Charpy: "Hello hooligans!" De Gaulle made the following now-famous comment: "Those young people have energy that could be bottled. If only we could make them use it to build roads!"

16   Johnny Hallyday, Sylvie Vartan, Eddy Mitchell, Françoise Hardy, Sheila and so on.

17   Jacques Canetti, Jacques Plait, Claude Carrère and so on.

18   Frank Thomas, Jacques Revaux and so on.

19   Saravah (Jacques Higelin, Brigitte Fontaine, Catharsis, etc.), BYG Records (Gong, L'Âme son, etc.), Motors et Somethin'Else (Christophe, Pop Corn Orchestra, J.-M. Jarre, Silence Hears, Dynastie Crisis, etc.).

20   If the Olympia was the "holy grail" for variety music artists at the beginning of the 1970s and Bobino one of the so-called Left Bank singers, French pop groups (which was the term used at the time instead of rock) could only come about within certain cultural institutions ("*Maisons de la Culture*") and in the many places dedicated to popular education.

21   The major labels, the big independent labels and a few producers (Lucien Adès, Henri Salvador), but also pressing factories and recording studios.

22   Given the rapid increase in the number of producers and the reinforcement of distribution licences, a diversity of products was available on the French market. The CIDD released a directory (*Who Produces What?*), which provided an inventory of all the marks, labels, collections and series, both French and foreign, distributed in France by each phonographic publishing house (whether or not a member of the union).

23   Thanks most notably to the *ABC of Records* ("*L'A.B.C. du disque*"), which retraced the important steps in the history of the record, giving technical data about its fabrication, the status of the French market in the world, some practical maintenance suggestions and a list of SNICOP members.

24   In the journal *Music-Hall*, in the newspaper *Le Figaro* and so on.

25   In the radio show *Salut les Copains* on Europe n° 1 with the "Family Hits" and so on.

26   The first Francophone artist was J. Dassin, who came in seventh place (behind Mary Hopkin, Peter Holm, The Beatles, The Equals, The Aphrodite's Child and Arthur Brown).

27   In the professional press (*Le Métier, La Discographie de la France, Show-Business*), and in over fifty newspapers.

28   In the press (*Musikmarkt* in Germany; *Musica Dischi, Billboard Italia* and *Centro Italia Musica* in Italy; *Records Retailer, The Gramophone, Music Business Weekly* and *Record World* in the United Kingdom; *Billboard* and *Cash Box* in the United States, etc.) and on the radio (BBC, Radio Luxembourg, Radio Andorra, Radio Monte-Carlo, etc.)

29   For example, the song "Those Were the Days," which became "Le Temps des fleurs" in French, occupied five different spots—according to the different versions and performers—in the French and foreign variety music rankings of November 1968.

30   Since 2012, physical and digital sales are grouped together in the Top 200.

Bibliography

Blandin, Claire. 2013. "Radio et magazine: une offre plurimédia pour les jeunes des sixties." *Le Temps des médias* 2(21):134–142.

Currien, Nicolas, and François Moreau. 2006. *L'industrie du disque*. Paris: La Découverte.

D'Angelo, Mario. 1989. *La renaissance du disque*. Paris: La Documentation Française.

Frith, Simon. 1988. *Music for Pleasure*. London: Routledge.

Glevarec, Hervé. 2003. "Le moment radiophonique des adolescents: Rites de passage et nouveaux agents de socialisation." *Réseaux* 119:27–61.

Guibert, Gérôme. 2006. *La production de la culture: Le cas des musiques amplifiées en France*. Paris and St Amant Tallende: Irma/editions Seteun.

Hennessey, Mike. 1971. "French publishers are minding their P's–Publish, Produce, Promote!" *Billboard* 83(18):F-21.

Hennion, Antoine. 1983. "Une sociologie de L'intermédiaire: le cas du directeur artistique de variétés." *Sociologie du Travail* 4:459–474.

Kaiser, Marc. 2014. "De la constitution d'un patrimoine à partir d'artefacts éphémères: l'exemple du disque vinyle." *Hybrid* (1). http://www.hybrid.univ-paris8.fr/lodel/index.php?id=161.

Lagrée, Jean-Charles. 1979. "Production culturelle et mouvements sociaux, bandes, beatniks, hippies." In *Les cultures populaires*, edited by Geneviève Poujol and Raymond Labourie, 183–200. Toulouse: Privat.

Maisonneuve, Sophie. 2009. *L'invention du disque: 1877–1949*. Paris: Editions des archives contemporaines.

Masson-Forestier, Jacques. 1968a. Compte-rendu de la réunion du 19/9/69. Hit-Parade National. Memorandum, 20 September (unpublished archive).

———. 1968b. Hit-Parade National. Memorandum, 30 September (unpublished archive).

———. 1969. *L'industrie phonographique française: Faits et Chiffres*. Paris: C.I.D.D. (unpublished archive).

———. 1971. "The Role of the C.I.D.D." *Billboard*, May 1, 83(18):F-25.

Mignon, Patrick. 1982. "Rock la Galère: on revient toujours à Gisors." *Esprit* 1:168–173.

Mignon, Patrick, and Antoine Hennion, eds. 1991. *Rock: De l'histoire au mythe*. Paris: Anthropos.

Morin, Edgar. 1963a. "Salut les copains!, une nouvelle classe d'âge." *Le Monde*, July 6–7.

———. 1963b. "Salut les copains!, le yéyé." *Le Monde*, July 7–8.

Tournès, Ludovic. 2002. "Reproduire l'œuvre: la nouvelle économie musicale." In *La culture de masse en France, de la Belle Epoque à aujourd'hui*, edited by Jean-Pierre Rioux and Jean-François Sirinelli, 220–258. Paris: Fayard.

PART II

Politicising Popular Music

PREAMBLE

Gérôme Guibert and Catherine Rudent

Music, as a mode of cultural expression, presents a challenge in terms of meaning. In France, it has played and continues to play a political role from the point of view of production (producing music to make demands or offer support or opposition), reception (listening to music or declaring oneself to be a fan can be a way of recognising peers or finding one's place in society) and intermediaries (representing a musical genre or attitude as a record label or a specialised media, fulfilling a public service mission, broadening cultural appeal or supporting a local musical scene, e.g., by organising shows). As the general introduction to this book and many of the chapters presented here show, the political role of music, from a historical perspective, is played out on many levels, be it in terms of class, gender and race relationships or, more specifically, regional territorial identities.

True, these elements were little explored in France until the end of the 1990s, with this exploration only beginning with new research into the cultural history of the 1960s (Rioux and Sirinelli 2002) and work on the leisure and culture industries of the first part of the twentieth century (Kalifa 2001; Ory 1985). This work opened the way towards more complex analysis, which previously had tended to operate a clear separation between art (supposedly worthy of interest) and *entertainment* (supposedly uninteresting).

Previous approaches to sociology no doubt lie at the heart of why social sciences took such a late interest in popular music (Shusterman 1993). In France, before the work of the Frankfurt School met with any significant success (Adorno and Horkheimer 1947, first French translation in 1974), the sociology of the media was long dominated by critical theory, including the paradigm of cultural legitimacy proposed by Bourdieu (1979) and structuralist analysis influenced by Marxist materialism and the notion of superstructural ideology (Guibert and Quemener 2015). Drawing on cultural studies in Britain and particularly the Gramscian interpretations proposed by Stuart Hall, many young French researchers began intensively exploring the complexity of customs and hegemonic and counterhegemonic dynamics related to the asymmetry of power relations (Maigret 2003). This step allowed French works hitherto little used in research on popular music to be brought back to the fore. Among these were the work by Grignon and Passeron, *Le Savant et le populaire*[1] (1989); Michel de Certeau's works, particularly the first volume of *L'Invention du quotidien* (first published in 1980, translated into English under the title *The Practice of Everyday Life*); and even Edgar Morin's seminal work (1962).

Let us focus briefly on this last example, criticised and then rediscovered by a large number of French researchers. In the words of Eric Macé, who wrote the preface to the 2006 edition of *L'Esprit du Temps*,

Morin holds that mass culture [. . .] must be understood in anthropological terms as a specific form, typical of modernity, of production of collective imaginations with universal pretentions. [. . .] The modernity of mass culture comes from the fact that [. . .] a shared culture is not produced by institutions but by the dynamics, uncertainties and the transnational versatilities of the market.

(12)

In this mass culture, there is a tension between a logic of production, characterised as "industrial-bureaucratic-monopolistic-centralising-standardising" and a logic of creation, which is, on the contrary, "individualistic-inventive-competitive-autonomous-innovative." This tension exists between the majors and independents, but also within the majors. Thus, for Morin, mass culture constructs myths that are the expression of sociocultural tensions specific to every historical context. These myths help us understand how collective representations, which may be reversible, develop. Thus, for Macé, offering a reading of Morin's ideas and taking them further,

the early '60s were a time when individual happiness seemed a desirable and even transgressive prospect for those who did not yet possess the right to self-expression (youth, women), the '70s were the years of disenchantment, lasting until, it might be added, the new myths of performance and competition of the '80s, which appeared before a recurrence, if not of disenchantment, of the uncertainties of the second modernity.

(Ibid.)

We find these trends in many studies on popular music in France, even if their social and spatial contextualization leads to a more complex version of these readings, especially when looking at emerging subcultures on the margins or when the age spectrum or social milieus are broadened. In the first part of this book, we saw how, from the mid- to late 1950s, vinyl records became a mass product and almost the whole French population became equipped with radios. Popular music in France accompanied economic growth and structural social mobility. However, this movement was put into perspective by the events of 1968, which expressed a deeper desire to change society. Popular music, particularly rock music (but also jazz in its free form; protest songs in the tradition of Léo Ferré, Colette Magny or even Jean Ferrat; and a form of regionalist folk, whether it be, e.g., Breton, Basque or Corsican) was understood in opposing ways. Thus it could, in the context of an underlying struggle between communists and currents of the extreme left, be read, in turn, as a force for emancipation and as a tool for the propagation of US imperialism due to its standardised forms of marketing (Penasse 2008, 2011). Sklower's chapter, which opens this section of the book, offers a detailed analysis of the issues at work in the role of journalists in the jazz press: primarily, here, the leftist militants Michel Le Bris and Jean-Louis Comolli. Sklower then looks at the positioning of the musician Michel Portal in relation to his work. Through the Fou-cauldian concepts of "apparatus" and "governmentality," he demonstrates the importance of political challenges experienced by music activists who saw their work as a mission.

The next chapter, by G. Guibert, covers a period beginning ten years later, in the late 1970s. The two oil price shocks had already taken place. Unemployment, which was virtually non-existent at the beginning of the decade, was now higher than 1% of the active popula-tion. The crisis was relative, but at a time when periods of inflation and competitive deval-uations (currency wars) followed on one from the other, the pessimism hawked around by the group Trust got to the top of the charts, notably in the form of the hit "Antisocial," which made reference both to models from Anglo-American hard rock heavy metal and a rebel song tradition.[2] While punk was never a popular current in France, the positions Trust took up can be likened to it, although the group's heavy guitars made it the founder of a French brand of hard rock / heavy metal. Trust's career is studied and positioned in relation to polit-ical change: this allows the reasons why the group's popularity waned following the election of Mitterand in 1981 and the French government's move to the left to be brought into relief (Heurtebize 2010). Guibert puts forward the hypothesis that their song lyrics and the ideas they bombarded public space with no longer chimed with those who had previously been fans, at least in France. They nevertheless laid the foundations of the French heavy metal scene, perceptions of which were to remain mostly negative (Guibert and Sklower 2011).

With the transition to a policy of budgetary discipline at the end of 1983, variables other than relationships of social class exploded in the media. They concerned issues related to immigration and the post-colonial society (Dubet 1987). While the image of *banlieue* (urban ghetto) music was still linked with rock and rock rebellion in the late 1970s ("*les murs de la cité résonnent: AC/DC*"[3] ["the projects/estates echo with the words: AC/DC"], Trust was still declaiming in 1980), the riots of summer 1983 at Les Minguettes, near Lyon, as well as the March for Equality and Against Racism, dubbed "*les marches des beurs*"[4] by the French media, from October (Marseille) to December (Paris) 1983, highlighted the challenges of intercultural cohabitation and the limitations of the republican model of assimilation. Bar-bara Lebrun explains the issues related to this new social phenomenon through an analysis of two emblematic singers who have an immigrant identity in France. Rachid Taha, is known from the mid-1980s for his cover of the Charles Trenet classic "Douce France" ("Sweet France"), which he played at the time with his band, Carte de Séjour (Residence Card), and which can be understood in several ways. Taha then had an international career, built on the explosion of world music. The second figure, Magyd Cherfi, whose group Zebda, from Tou-louse, had an impact on French *variété* in the 1990s with several emblematic titles, including "Désolé" ("Sorry") (1998), with its emblematic chorus. With the commercial success of rap and R&B during the 1990s, artists from immigrant backgrounds fit African-American rhet-oric to their own situation in France (Ramdani 2011; Ervine 2011). The specifics of the situa-tion in France were soon studied by social scientists, although they remained few in number according to some analysts (Mathis-Moser 2003; Raibaud 2011). From this point of view, the fact that Lebrun, the author who discusses these questions here, teaches in Britain is probably not anodyne. At the present time, and with rare exceptions, the same observation could be made on gender issues (Tinker 2015) or on combined gender and postcolonial perspectives.

Notes

1   Translating to *Highbrow/Lowbrow* (our translation).
2   For example, in the 1981 Akai record guide, Trust singer Bernie Bonvoisin is compared to Jacques Brel because of the conviction with which he sings the group's songs.
3   In Trust, "Ton dernier Acte," *Marche ou Crève*, October 1981. In the English version, the title appears as "Your Last Gig," *Savatage*, October 1981.
4   "Arabe" in *verlan*, backslang where syllables are inversed.

Bibliography

Adorno, Theodor, and Max Horkheimer. 1974 [1947]. *La dialectique de la raison, Fragments Philosophiques*. Paris: Gallimard.
Bourdieu, Pierre. 1979. *La distinction: Critique sociale du jugement*. Paris: Les Editions de Minuit.
De Certeau, M., ed. 1990 [1980]. *L'invention du quotidien: Essai sur les nouvelles classes moyennes. 1. Arts de faire; 2. Habiter, cuisiner*. Paris: Gallimard.
Dorin, Stéphane, and Gérôme Guibert. 2008. "Le secteur des musiques actuelles: Les paradoxes de la professionnalisation." In *Les arts moyens aujourd'hui*, edited by Florent Gaudez, 67–78. Paris: L'Harmattan.
Dubet, François. 1987. *La galère: jeunes en survie*. Paris: Fayard.
Ervine, Jonathan. 2011. "Kamini's Rural Rap: A Study of Minority Identities, New Media, and Music." *Contemporary French Civilization* 36(1–2):127–140.
Grignon, Claude and Jean-Claude Passeron. 1989. *Le savant et le populaire. Misérabilisme et populisme en sociologie et en littérature*. Paris: Seuil.
Guibert, Gérôme, and Nelly Quemener. 2015. "Cultural Studies et Économie Politique de la Communication: Quel rapport au marxisme?" *Réseaux* 192:87–114.
Guibert, Gérôme, and Jedediah Sklower. 2012. "Hellfest: The Thing that Should Not Be? Local Perceptions and Catholic Discourses on Metal Culture in France." *Popular Music History* 6(2):100–115.
Heurtebize, Frédéric. 2010. "Washington face à l'Union de la gauche en France, 1971–1981." *Revue Française d'Éudes Américaines* 124:82–102.
Kalifa, Dominique. 2001. *La culture de masse en France. 1: 1860-1930*. Paris: La Découverte.
Lebrun, Barbara. 2002. "A Case Study of Zebda: Republicanism, Métissage and Authenticity in Contemporary France." *Volume! La revue des musiques populaires* 1(2):59–69.
Macé, Éric. 2006. "Actualité de *L'Esprit du temps*." In preamble to the new edition of *L'Esprit du temps*, edited by Edgar Morin, 1–7. Paris: Armand Colin.
Maigret, Eric. 2003. *Sociologie de la communication et des médias*. Paris: Armand Colin.
Martin, Denis-Constant, ed. 2010. *Quand le rap sort de sa bulle: Sociologie politique d'un succès populaire*. Bordeaux and Paris: Mélanie Seteun/Irma.
Mathis-Moser, Ursula. 2003. "L'image de 'l'Arabe' dans la chanson française contemporaine." *Volume! La revue des musiques populaires* 2(2):129–144.
Morin, Edgar. 1962. *L'Esprit du temps*. Paris: Grasset.
Ory, Pascal. 1985. "Notes sur l'acclimatation du jazz en France." *Vibrations* 1:93–102.
Penasse, Jean-Philippe. 2008. "Mick Jagger et les camarades." *Rue Descartes* 60:94–105.
———. 2011. "Le parti communiste et la pop." Interview With Guillaume Heuguet and Etienne Menu. *Vox Pop* 20:20–21.
Raibaud, Yves. 2011. "Armstrong, je ne suis pas noir . . ." *Volume! La revue des musiques populaires* 8(1):223–232.
Ramdani, Karima. 2011. "Bitch et Beurette, quand féminité rime avec liberté: Représentation du corps féminin noir et maghrébin dans la musique rap et le R'n'B." *Volume! La revue des musiques populaires* 8(2):13–39.
Rioux, Jean-Pierre, and Jean-François Sirinelli. 2002. *La culture de masse en France: De la Belle Époque à nos jours*. Paris: Fayard.
Shusterman, Richard. 1993. "Légitimer la légitimation de l'art populaire." *Politix* 24:153–167.
Sklower, Jedediah. 2006. *Free jazz, la catastrophe féconde*. Paris: L'Harmattan.
Sutcliffe, Ellie. 2011. "Managing the Media, the Musique and Metissage: Compromise in the Music of Faudel and Magyc Cherfi." *Contemporary French Civilization* 36(1–2):97–112.
Tinker, Chris. 2015. "Genre, Gender and the Republic: Televising the Annual Charity Concert Les Enfoirés." *French Cultural Studies* 26(3):343–353.

5

Aural Wars
Race, Class, Politics and the Dilemmas of Free Jazzmen in 1960s France

Jedediah Sklower

Musical Worlds, Apparatuses and the Government of Senses

Our ears often ignore the winding paths we follow when listening to music. The musical sense is a hybrid one, constantly hijacked by interventions of exogenous instances—other senses, ideas, environments, objects. Since Antoine Hennion's seminal work on musical passion (2007 [1993]),[1] French research on musical experience has changed perspectives, nuancing traditional reception theory by emphasizing not only the activity of the receiver (or how subjects appropriate a stable object in various ways) but also the performativity of the act of listening. Music lovers inform the shape of the music they listen to in order to appreciate it, they "dress it to taste it" (Ibid., 229) with ideas, representations, rituals, and within social interactions and environments. Form, reception and context mutually influence and design each other, in a circular, sequential co-production of the aesthetic experience.

In France, the history of listening to music is a new frontier in music studies. Sociologists, inspired by American pragmatism (John Dewey, William James), art world or field theory (Howard Becker vs. Pierre Bourdieu) and/or the new social history of art (Michael Baxandall, Francis Haskell, Svetlana Alpers)—among others—have published works on classical music, dealing with the nineteenth-century invention of Bach (Fauquet and Hennion 2000) and the baroque revival in France (Hennion 2007), as well as the birth of discographic practices (Maisonneuve 2009) and experiences of popular music (Pecqueux and Roueff 2009; Sklower 2013).[2] Similar approaches dealt with jazz in France. The history of its reception between the 1930s and late 1950s was treated by Ludovic Tournès (1999), who focused on Hugues Panassié and the Hot Clubs de France movement, and political scientist Denis-Constant Martin and sociologist Olivier Roueff (2002) tackled the first half of the twentieth century; a recent book by the latter (2013) offers a history of the successive jazz worlds, from the discovery of cakewalk in 1902 to examples of avant-garde improvisation clubs nowadays, and how they contributed in forming "apparatuses of appreciation."[3]

My aim here is to follow these leads and push them one notch further, using Michel Foucault's concepts of "apparatus" ("*dispositif*") and "governmentality" ("*gouvernementalité*") (2001; 2004; 2005). A "musical apparatus" shall refer here to an assemblage of heterogeneous elements—the musical object and how it is discursively identified, relatively stabilized and practiced within cultural (aesthetic, ideological), social (fan groups, subcultures, scenes), institutional (art worlds, the State, the market) and material (listening spaces and devices) frames—that work to produce, without any necessary internal coherence, a set of possibilities "arranged"[4] for the experience of music.[5] I call "government of the senses" the productive result of this apparatus in peoples' experiences, or the way in which various elements of this system both induce and are appropriated by music lovers and musicians when they engage with music, and that draw the silhouette of a "regime of listening" (Szendy 2001, 41) and of music making. These elements include, for example, the listener's career as a music lover or performer, whether individual or within a fandom or an art world, and thus all the procedures one deploys to ritualize the musical actions; one's heuristics, or how one selects the material that will constitute the basis for experience—albums, tracks, riffs, themes, choruses and musemes (Tagg 1982), as well as images, gestures, styles and so forth—and one's hermeneutics, or the tools and codes one uses to associate feelings and meanings to the information one has (i.e., pays attention to) on a performer, a performance, the production context and so on. The apparatus (the multilayered frame), the listener (the subjective configuration) and the nature of the experience (the individual or recurring event) obviously influence each other, in a systemic way. If portions of the musical apparatus can work "as one," its governmental effects are not the product of a unified, centralized source of power. The fact is, art worlds, fields or apparatuses function both as collaborative and antagonistic systems. The consequences are not necessary, universal or complete: there can be partial, fleeting or contradicting effects, or even none of them, as well as diversions or "tactical resistances" to the "strategic" frame,[6] as I shall illustrate later on.

France was one of the first countries in the world to revel in the wonders of Afro-American rhythms, with the cakewalk craze in the early twentieth century, followed by the invasion of "jazz-bands" on 1920s Parisian *music-hall* stages and the national dissemination of New Orleans jazz with the Hot Clubs de France movement in the 1930s and so forth. Free jazz was no exception to this trend. Also, French intellectuals and middlemen played a major role in its formal definition and, thus, of how it should be listened to, appreciated and what it should mean—racial elements being particularly important in the process, considering the specific relationship French society has had both to American culture and to racial, colonial and postcolonial issues. In France, the jazz world is the location of one of those iconic links between myths pertaining both to the United States and racial representations. I will thus use the aforementioned conceptual framework to understand the relationships between representations of race and class, ideology and musical listening that the French free jazz world established in the 1960s, and how these configurations set the stage for and eventually governed free jazzmen's discourses, practices and career choices. I will start with the political identification of free jazz and the ascetic ear sculpted by most militant critics in the second half of the 1960s, then examine the career path that one musician, Michel Portal, followed in function of his position within this apparatus and according to his evolving conceptions of the relationship between music, its experience and practice and his cultural representations of jazz, politics, class and race. The choice of this particular musician for this demonstration is justified by the fact that he is a particularly iconic example of the history of French free improvisers, as he was one of the leading figures in the French free jazz world (in terms of recordings, network and aura) and his career, from free jazz to "European improvised music," was emblematic of significant trends that French (and even European) jazz followed in the 1970s and beyond.

The Politics of the Ascetic Ear

I have described elsewhere (2006, 142–166) the birth of a free jazz world in France. I will only briefly recall here how the "New Thing" was politically identified, before focusing on how this discourse prescribed norms on how to listen to this music. From the mid-1960s on, free jazz was defended as a radical form, both aesthetically and politically. Formal elements of the new style were construed as a modernist rupture and the sign of a revolutionary agenda (see Drott 2011, 131–135; Lehman 2005). The specific political dimension of the objectification of free jazz was accepted jointly by its sycophants and denigrators: whatever the reality of the meaning of such new aesthetic practices and how the performers themselves interpreted them, the French jazz world collectively agreed to joust within the frame of this particular identification.[7] The polemics took place within a common, accepted binary frame, the defendants arguing for the historical necessity of free jazz with regards to the new political conjuncture (the radicalization of Black politics in the United States, the student and worker movements around the globe, decolonization and opposition to the American intervention in Vietnam), while the opponents denounced a mere rhetorical cloud used to camouflage musical nihilism. This is what I coined a "polemical collaboration," with regards to how Albert Ayler's music in particular was construed in France (Sklower 2008, 195, 213).

The critics, in many articles in the jazz press and most systematically in Philippe Carles and Jean-Louis Comolli's essay *Free Jazz/Black Power* (2000 [1971]), developed the idea that free jazz was the sign of a broader opposition than the one LeRoi Jones had set forth in *Blues People* (1963): not only the resistance of Black subjects against White oppression and commercial hijacking, but more globally of the oppressed against the oppressor, the colonized against the colonizer. Because of its historical, social and racial situation, free jazz could not be analyzed with the concepts of traditional idealist, universalist, bourgeois aesthetics. This interpretative frame thus broke with the project and structure of the previous generations of critics who had legitimized jazz by erecting a pantheon of outstanding individual performers, expressing their genius via improvisation, whether via Panassié's amateur and subjectivist praise of hot jazz heroes from the 1930s on, or Hodeir and Malson's avant-gardist defense of boppers from the mid-1940s on. The new generation of jazz journalists, often university students who were under the influence of various facets of the 1960s French intellectual field (linguistics, semiology, or structuralism for the method, Marxism and its political derivatives for the meaning), listened for something else in jazz and thus valued another experience of the music: not the charms of Black primitive joy and creativity,[8] but the oppressed's visceral rebellion against repression; not the universal art of the individual genius, but the collective political forces located in society: "It is jazz as a mirror of the established order that speaks through the musician, not the latter who expresses himself through jazz," as critic Michel Le Bris put it (1967, 18).[9] Jean-Louis Comolli wrote that to "analyze the forms without analyzing the forces would be a fraud," adding that "one cannot enjoy the form without taking up the cause" (1966a, 28). An aural ethos was thus prescribed: orthodox listening practices were the condition of ethics, knowledge and—if need be—pleasure.

This more intellectualist, distanced ear, which saw music as a decipherable sign more than a pleasurable performance, depended less on the listening environment than had the Panassié phonographic and pantomimic regime of listening (the "conférences-auditions" within the Hot Club de France network),[10] or the 1940–1950s tamed jazz-club formula. In this sense, the first presentation of free jazz in disciplined spaces such as elite concert halls or silenced jazz clubs was quite coherent with the project of the previous generation of jazz intermediaries (Charles Delaunay, André Hodeir, Lucien Malson and the like), whose goal of canonizing jazz came with the domestication of the audience—that is, the disqualification of the amateur, bodily experience and the valorization of the ascetic, expert ear (Roueff 2013, 185–187). In this case, the focus however no longer was "graphocentric" (the formalist listening with an eye on the musical score), but "semiocentric" (the political reading of the sign revealing a social structure). For the former generation, jazz was a legitimate, universal expression, best understood with musicological skills; for the latter, jazz was a revolutionary, situated reflection, best construed with the right ideological tools. Yet in both cases, intellectual knowledge was the key to understanding and appreciating it, and any form of pleasure associated with the body was discredited as inferior. They may have engaged in an esthetico-ideological controversy; in the end they both aimed at producing similar structures of auditory attention: this too is a form of "polemical collaboration."

Carles and Comolli thus degraded the idea of "simple" aesthetic pleasure. They, for example, asserted that the "purity of the idea," the location of the "unrestrained pursuit of pleasure"—one of the popular situationist slogans of those years, derided here—was a "capitalist fantasy" (2000, 389). Any element in jazz that could threaten to seduce the ear was considered a sign of a commercial colonization of jazz. Themes, for example, had become an object of "comfort and melodic security" before the birth of free jazz. With the new generation of musicians, the "commodity-theme" as an object of "aesthetic pleasure/consumption" was definitely ignored, in favor of dissolutions or ironic "mimicking" and "deconstructions" thereof (Carles and Comolli 2000, 347). To refuse or to freely work on themes, as Eric Dolphy, Albert Ayler or the Art Ensemble of Chicago did (Carles and Comolli 2000, 348–350) was to revolt against a whole ideological, aesthetic and commercial system. The contrary was to submit to the empire of the bourgeoisie by flattering its lazy, contemplative ear.

Indeed, according to Jean-Louis Comolli, contrarily to the "music of Miles Davis, Art Farmer or of John Coltrane" and "classic jazz," which could be considered as an "art of seduction," free jazz was one of "frustration," which, as it "never fulfills" his usual aural desires, "requires that the auditor be acutely attentive, present in each instant, that he never get carried away by a dream, nor look for a state of semi-sleep" (1966b, 33). As it looked to interpret the music more than feel it, to find the means by which free jazz would "provoke a realization" (Ibid.), this "aural logos" valued a formalist experience rather than one that could be influenced by other extrinsic factors associated with bodily experience, made up of collective reactions and how they defined the environment (an ardent militant atmosphere, for that matter). Many "neo"-purist[11] critics, for example, specifically dismissed hippie reactions to free jazz concerts they could observe as "petit bourgeois" jouissance[12]—they were supposed to remain within the confines of pop environments. Indeed, countercultural manifestations of emotional pleasure and pointless rêverie were considered as diametrically opposed to the aware, militant ear these critics associated to free jazz. Comolli did defend hippies in one article inasmuch as they were "beatniks, vietniks and [. . .] long-haired killjoys" (1966a, 28), but never the pop or psychedelic experience and its manifestations (drug-infused trance, noisy and fidgety demonstrations of ecstasy and the like). For, within this aural logos, immediate, emotional, choreographic experiences of free jazz were once again failed ones or a "fraud": the true message was not received nor understood when blurred by the senses. Such an ear for the enjoyable was almost the aural equivalent of the LeRoi Jones-inspired dialectic—another expropriation of the Afro-American's culture by White colonialist aesthetics, which reduced the musicians to their never-ending role as minstrels. Some Black performers, of course, were guilty of leniently adopting the blackface mask: for Michel Le Bris, "the time of the fool who rolls his eyes to amuse the audience is long gone, the revolution is coming" (1967, 17), and for Carles and Comolli, Sidney Bechet and Louis Armstrong "perpetuate the ideal image of the 'good Black man who has more than one trick up his sleeve'" (2000, 318). In the 1960s, decoding the ambiguities of tricksterism and signifyin' was not part of the intellectual game.[13]

Michel Portal and the Burden of Authenticity

To test my hypothesis on the "government of senses," I will now focus on the career of saxophonist Michel Portal: the types of choices he made, his perspective on the practice and the meaning of free jazz and how all of this relates to the French free jazz apparatus in the 1960s. An important member of the Parisian free jazz scene, Portal had started his career within the classical music world, and constantly kept a foot in it throughout his career, also playing works by contemporary composers such as Pierre Boulez, Karlheinz Stockhausen, Luciano Berio or Mauricio Kagel. He was joined in 1969 by Vinko Globokar, Carlos Alsina and Jean-Pierre Drouet to form "New Phonic Art," a formation dedicated to collective improvisation, sonic research and instantaneous creation (Marmande 1994, 948). His "Portal Unit" would shortly thereafter confirm his appeal for such musical crossovers between Afro-American idioms and European contemporary classical forms, which makes him one of the key figures in the evolution of French free jazz toward "European improvised music."

These cultural, aesthetic and professional elements are important to understand his ethical dilemmas within the free jazz scene, which I will look into now thanks to a few quotes from his interviews in the press. In 1968, he felt that French jazzmen were playing a "stolen music," which was "born in a specific context, in reaction to a specific political and ideological situation," a situation that "is not ours." White performers were both "rootless" (he dismissed French folklore—mentioning *"bourrée auvergnate"*—as "pitiful") and had no good reason to revolt: while Afro-American music had always been a "protest" music, their own adoption of it was inauthentic (1968, 15–16). Such comments, which weren't that unfamiliar among French musicians in those years (Sklower 2006, 203), clearly demonstrate the productiveness of the French jazz world's identification of jazz and its "distribution of the sensible"[14] according to which Afro-Americans, as they were oppressed both socially and racially, created authentically revolutionary music. Here, the politicized free jazz apparatus, by efficiently radicalizing social and racial assignations as we have demonstrated earlier, contributed in governing Portal's representations of music and thus his relationship to the jazz world. Combined with his prior musical training and career and his needs in terms of

Figure 5.1 Michel Portal, *Alors!!!*, Futura Records, 1970, 33⅓ rpm album front cover.

experimentation, these uncomfortable feelings of inauthenticity shed light on his commitments to projects linking free-form improvisation and contemporary classical music, with New Phonic Art from 1969 on (1971) and later with his Michel Portal Unit (1973). Indeed, to fulfill free jazz's emancipatory promise (aesthetic self-exploration through omnivorous free improvisation), many French musicians had to find aesthetic material unburdened by their mythologies of Afro-American creativity and thus look beyond that musical tradition.[15] This perceived inadequacy of the White, Western performer within the "jazzistic field"[16] is one of the factors that can explain the development in the Old Continent of "European improvised music"— that is, improvisatory experimentations that integrated contemporary classical music and the jazz tradition while socially and culturally establishing a certain musical and symbolic distance from the latter. This was a musical trend quite specific to 1970s Europe, which does not mean some Afro-American free jazz performers weren't influenced by contemporary classical music—Anthony Braxton was one, for example.

But paradoxically, in another interview five years later, he recanted his puzzled feelings and adopted an absolutely opposite stance:

> I believe there is a negritude of jazz, when I play this music, I am a negro. You might find this silly, but since I started playing jazz, I looked back into my genealogy to see if I didn't

Figure 5.2 Michel Portal Unit, *Chateauvallon: 23 août 1972*, recorded live by ORTF (Universal, 2003, compact disc new edition and cover, originally published by Le Chant du Monde in 1974).

belong to other races. Well, I found Moroccan blood. It makes me very happy. Although I feel perfectly fine within this music, I think its negro component is an absolutely essential element.

(Portal 1973, 9)

This racial conception of jazz goes back to the early twentieth century and beyond, yet the reference to "negritude"—an essentialist discourse on African culture too but from a Black, anticolonialist perspective—gives it a legitimizing Black and left-wing edge. So to feel authorized (and no longer uncomfortable) to play Black music, this White, classically trained performer locates a foreign racialized presence (the "Moroccan blood") within himself, which acts as a "factish," as Bruno Latour would have it (2009): a totem whose cultural efficiency depends on the faith invested in it. Finally, although the political and class elements are less important here, in an ideological context marked by decolonization and Third-Worldism, the blood's "nationality" is also significant. Indeed, Morocco was a former French (and Spanish) protectorate: this self-orientalization thus plays the double function of "negritude" as a less distant, more relevant racial and a political myth.

Conclusion

The discovery and reception/appropriation of free jazz in France offered musicians the classic tools for a politicized, modernist agenda in cultural production. On the one hand, it enabled them to position themselves as aesthetic revolutionaries and to try and conquer a space of their own within the highly competitive, bop-dominated French jazz scene; on the other hand, within the political context of the 1960s, they could also posit themselves as militants who challenged the French cultural and political system as a whole. They thus adopted a symbolic, discursive bias to express and feel solidarity for a people whose social, political and ethnocultural background they did not share materially. But that balance did not resist beyond the Afro-American free jazzmen's stay in Paris, the radicalization of Black politics in the United States and the intense political phase in France, in the late 1960s. In a career sequence typical of artistic empowerment, they used the libertarian aesthetico-ethic resources of free jazz to experiment with other possibilities offered by the surrounding cultural landscape. For some, to depart from jazz while acknowledging its input in their musical practices meant they also had to justify severing the ties to the symbols associated to Afro-American avant-garde performers—lest their appropriation be interpreted as another example of cultural "colonization." Michel Portal's felt political inauthenticity and racial irrelevancy within the free jazz idiom, as well his and others' later search for other forms of political commitment and (ethno) cultural roots (Sklower 2006, 200–230) hint at the validity of my introductory hypotheses.

As philosopher Christian Béthune wrote, with jazz, "*double consciousness*[17] covertly became the common fate of Blacks and Whites" (2008, 320). Indeed, the career paths taken by Portal, as well as by others (e.g., François Tusques's departure from the free jazz world to play popular protest music), demonstrate the relative efficiency of the politicized and racialized 1960s apparatus within the free jazz world, not so much in terms of musical experience (from what the archives tell us), but of musical ethics and evaluations of the experience. The best clues to the active existence of a "government of the senses" are the musical and simultaneously ethical interrogations these musicians felt they had to confront in order to make aesthetic, and thus professional choices—and for musicians, these are also often existential ones. Behind the variety of paths, there is a common set of aesthetico-ethic norms, and injunctions they had to consider when making such aesthetic and career choices. Tacit, difficult and ambiguous questions on musical practice such as "Am I capable of playing free jazz?" "Am I entitled to doing so?" "How can I relate to someone else's experience?" "What should I play?" "Is my music serving the right cause?" "What does it mean?" "Where does it come from?" and so forth—self-reflexive musical hermeneutics—were decisive in how these musicians practiced music, and thus lived their lives.

Notes

1 For an overview of his research on listening, in English, see 2001.
2 For a review of works on the history of listening in the English-speaking world, see Weber (1997); see also Maisonneuve (2002).

3   Jean-Louis Fabiani had already considered a few trends concerning the links between discourses and musical practices in an early article (1986). For a musicological approach to European free jazz, see Jost (1987), and to its French scene, see Cotro (1999).
4   The French verb "*disposer*" is richer here, as its polysemic nuances include the idea of an external agent "arranging" certain elements, "inducing" someone into accepting them as they are, as well as the subject's own means of "disposing of" them.
5   Olivier Roueff used a similar definition of this concept ("*dispositif musical*") when analyzing the objectivation of jazz in France in the 1920s (2001, 240–241).
6   Concerning the diverting of signs, I refer, of course, to classic cultural studies themes (Hall and Jefferson 1976; Hebdige 1979); on the strategies/tactics dichotomy, see de Certeau (2011 [1990], 59–63).
7   As was the case also in the United States (see Anderson 2007, 132).
8   For a nuanced critical discussion of Panassié's primitivism, see Guibert (2006, 188–195) and Perchard (2011).
9   For Michel Le Bris's role at *Jazz Hot* during the "Mao" phase, see Sklower (2006, 187–190). This particular article refers in its footnotes (a practice significantly inaugurated by this new generation of critics) to Roland Barthes, Ferdinand de Saussure and Roman Jakobson (as well as to Edgar Morin and Jean-Paul Sartre): a typical cocktail of structural linguistics, semiotics and existentialism.
10 For an analysis of how Hugues Panassié developed his own brand of such a government of the ear in the 1930s, thanks to conferences during which, while playing records, he would mime the instruments and stress the musical elements or moments one should pay attention to, in order to understand what authentic hot jazz was, see Tournès (1999, 44–45) and Perchard (2012, 384–386).
11 The first purists were Hugues Panassié and his followers.
12 There are many continuities in the history of French jazz criticism: the same type of exclusion had hit the "zazous" during the Second World War—the hot jazz amateurs (among which were Charles Delaunay, Boris Vian and André Hodeir) despised their extravagant, uncivilized behavior during concerts, a sign of their lack of culture. See Régnier (2009, 137–140) and Legrand (2009, 149–150).
13 Here, Carles and Comolli share LeRoi Jones's disdain for mainstream jazz and its entertainers. For a debate in the United States between the latter and Ralph Ellison concerning blues and jazz, and specifically the meaning of "Armstrong's smile," see Parent (2007, 144–146).
14 Jacques Rancière uses this concept to refer both to the "sharing" of common spaces, times and activities and the discriminations the definition of such a common ground imply (see Rancière 2000, 12–13; 2008). In French, the term "*partage*" is both a "sharing" and a "division/distribution."
15 Many musicians started digging into other traditions and fields to nourish their practice of improvisation: Indian or African influences, for example, with Barney Wilen (Schoof et al. 1967; Wilen 1972), and experimental music or *musique concrete* with Bernard Vitet (1971) and Barney Wilen (1968) again. Contemporary classical was a common feature of the French (see Cotro 1999), as well as the German, the Italian or the British scenes (see Jost 1987; Saladin 2014). And rock music, of course, was yet another creative source.
16 Concept developed by ethnologist Alexandre Pierrepont (2002), to expand the sources of Afro-American musical creation beyond "jazz" and to consider the social dynamics that underpin it.
17 In English in the text.

Bibliography

Anderson, Iain. 2007. *This is Our Music: Free Jazz, the Sixties, and American Culture*. Philadelphia: University of Pennsylvania Press.
Béthune, Christian. 2008. *Le Jazz et l'Occident*. Paris: Klincksieck.
Cotro, Vincent. 1999. *Chants libres: Le free jazz en France, 1960–1975*. Paris: Outre Mesure.
De Certeau, Michel. 2011 [1990]. *The Practice of Everyday Life*. Translated by Steven F. Rendall. Berkeley: University of California Press.
Drott, Eric. 2011. *Music and the Elusive Revolution: Cultural Politics and Political Culture in France, 1968–1981*. Berkeley: University of California Press.
Fabiani, Jean-Louis. 1986. "Carrières improvisées: théories et pratiques de la musique de jazz en France." In *Sociologie de l'Art*, edited by Raymonde Moulin, 231–245. Paris: L'Harmattan.
Fauquet, Joël-Marie, and Antoine Hennion. 2000. *La Grandeur de Bach: L'amour de la musique en France au XIXe siècle*. Paris: Fayard.
Foucault, Michel. 2001 [1975]. *Surveiller et punir: Naissance de la prison*. Paris: Gallimard.
———. 2004. *Sécurité, Territoire, Population: Cours au Collège de France (1977–1978)*. Paris: Seuil.
———. 2005 [1976]. *Histoire de la sexualité, Vol. 1: La volonté de savoir*. Paris: Gallimard.
Guibert, Gérôme. 2006. *La Production de la culture: Le cas des musiques amplifiées en France. Genèse, structurations, industries, alternatives*. Paris and St Amant Tallende: Irma/editions Seteun.
Hall, Stuart, and Tony Jefferson, eds. 1976. *Resistance Through Rituals: Youth Subcultures in Post-War Britain*. London: Hutchinson.

Hebdige, Dick. 1979. *Subculture: The Meaning of Style.* London: Routledge.

Hennion, Antoine. 2001. "Music Lovers. Taste as Performance." *Theory, Culture & Society* 18(5):1–22. Thousand Oaks: Sage Publications.

———. 2007 [1993]. *La Passion musicale: Une sociologie de la médiation.* Paris: Métailié.

Jost, Ekkehard. 1987. *Europas Jazz: 1960–1980.* Frankfurt am Main: Fischer Taschenbuch Verlag.

Latour, Bruno. 2009. *Sur le culte moderne des dieux faitiches.* Paris: Les Empêcheurs de Penser en Rond/La Découverte.

Legrand, Anne. 2009. *Charles Delaunay et le jazz en France dans les années 30 et 40.* Paris: Éditions du Layeur.

Lehman, Steve. 2005. "I Love You With an Asterisk: African-American Experimental Music and the French Jazz Press, 1970–1980." *Critical Studies in Improvisation*: 1–2. Accessed November 2, 2013. www.criticalimprov.com/article/view/18/49.

Maisonneuve, Sophie. 2002. "Du concert à L'écoute: tendances récentes de l'histoire sociale de la musique." *Revue de Musicologie* 88(1):171–186. Paris: Société Française de Musicologie.

———. 2009. *L'invention du disque, 1877–1949: Genèse de l'usage des médias musicaux contemporains.* Paris: Éditions des Archives Contemporaines.

Marmande, Francis. 1994. "Michel Portal." In *Dictionnaire du jazz*, edited by Philippe Carles, André Clergeat and Jean-Louis Comolli, 947–948. Paris: Robert Laffont.

Martin, Denis-Constant, and Olivier Roueff. 2002. *La France du jazz: Musique, modernité et identité dans la première moitié du XXe siècle.* Marseille: Parenthèses.

Parent, Emmanuel. 2007. "Ralph Ellison, critique de LeRoi Jones." *L'Homme* 181:131–150. Paris: Éditions de L'EHESS.

Pecqueux, Anthony, and Olivier Roueff, eds. 2009. *Écologie sociale de l'oreille: Enquêtes sur L'expérience musicale.* Paris: Éditions de L'EHESS.

Perchard, Tom. 2011. "Tradition, Modernity and the Supernatural Swing: Re-reading 'Primitivism' in Hugues Panassié's Writing on Jazz." *Popular Music* 30(1):24–45. Cambridge: Cambridge University Press.

———. 2012. "Hugues Panassié contra Walter Benjamin: Bodies, Masses, and the Iconic Jazz Recording in Mid-Century France." *Popular Music and Society* 35(3):375–398. London: Routledge.

Pierrepont, Alexandre. 2002. *Le Champ jazzistique.* Marseille: Parenthèses.

Rancière, Jacques. 2000. *Le Partage du sensible: Esthétique et politique.* Paris: La Fabrique.

———. 2008. *Le Spectateur émancipé.* Paris: La Fabrique.

Régnier, Gérard. 2009. *Jazz et société sous l'Occupation.* Paris: L'Harmattan.

Roueff, Olivier. 2001. "Les Mots du jazz: Retour sur *Le Jazz* d'André Schaeffner et André Cœuroy." *L'Homme* 2001 (2–3):239–259. Paris: Éditions de L'EHESS.

———. 2013. *Jazz, les échelles du plaisir.* Paris: La Dispute.

Saladin, Matthieu. 2014. *Esthétique de l'improvisation libre: Expérimentation musicale et politique.* Dijon: Les Presses du Réel.

Sklower, Jedediah. 2006. *Free jazz, la catastrophe féconde: Une histoire du monde éclaté du jazz en France (1960–1982).* Paris: L'Harmattan.

———. 2008. "Rebel With the Wrong Cause: Albert Ayler et la Signification du free jazz en France (1959–1971)." *La revue des musiques populaires* 6(1–2):193–219.

———, ed. 2013. "Écoutes. Discours, pratiques, médiations." *Volume! La revue des musiques populaires:* 10–11.

Szendy, Peter. 2001. *Écoute: Une histoire de nos oreilles.* Paris: Éditions de Minuit.

Tagg, Philip. 1982. "Analyzing Popular Music: Theory, Method, and Practice." *Popular Music* 2:37–65.

Tournès, Ludovic. 1999. *New Orleans sur Seine: Histoire du jazz en France.* Paris: Fayard.

Weber, William. 1997. "Did People Listen in the 18th Century?" *Early Music* 25(4):678–691. Oxford: Oxford University Press.

Whiteley, Sheila, and Jedediah Sklower, eds. 2014. *Countercultures and Popular Music.* Farnham: Ashgate.

Recordings

Barney Wilen. *Moshi.* Paris: Saravah SH 10028, 1972, 33⅓ rpm.

Bernard Vitet. *La Guêpe.* Paris: Futura Son 05, 1971, 33⅓ rpm.

Manfred Schoof, Irene Schweitzer, and Barney Wilen. *Jazz Meets India.* Paris: Saba 15142, 1967, 33⅓ rpm.

Michel Portal Unit. *À Châteauvallon/No, No But It May Be.* Paris: Le Chant du Monde LDX 74526, 1973, 33⅓ rpm.

New Phonic Art. *Begegnung in Baden-Baden.* Mainz: Wergo WER 60060, 1971, 33⅓ rpm.

Sources

Carles, Philippe, Daniel Caux, Jean-Louis Comolli, Pierre Lattès, Jacques Réda, and François Tusques. 1971. "Un soir autour d'Ayler . . ." *Jazz Magazine* 193:5–6.

Carles, Philippe, and Jean-Louis Comolli. 2000 [1971]. *Free Jazz/Black Power*. Paris: Gallimard.

Comolli, Jean Louis. 1966a. "Voyage au bout de la new thing." *Jazz Magazine* 129:24–29.

———. 1966b. "Les conquérants d'un nouveau monde." *Jazz Magazine* 131:30–35.

Jones, LeRoi [Amiri Baraka]. 1963. *Blues People: Negro Music in White America*. New York: William Morrow & Company.

Le Bris, Michel. 1967. "L'artiste volé par son art." *Jazz Hot* 229:16–19.

Portal, Michel. 1968. "Entretien." *Jazz Hot* 241:15–16.

———. 1973. "Portal en long, Portal en travers." *Jazz Hot* 296:9–11, 21.

6

Marche ou Crève
The Band Trust and the Singular Case of the Birth of French Heavy Metal

Gérôme Guibert

As in many other countries, the rise of heavy metal in France was notable in the 1970s, both in economic and in cultural terms (Picard and Legras 1982; Guibert 1998; Hein 2003). After the English precursors at the beginning of the decade and popular success of stadium rock in the United States that followed in the mid-1970s (Straw 1983; Waksman 2009), the spread of the New Wave of British Heavy Metal made heavy metal a dominant genre, first in Britain, in part as a reaction to the 1977 English punk movement (Bayer 2009), then in other European countries, in particular in Germany and France (Hein 2003). But even circa 1983, before specialized media and independent labels appeared in France, Trust, a singular band, whose success was as massive as it was ephemeral, would play a decisive role (Abraham 1984).

We'll begin by presenting the band, contextualizing its birth and development. We will show that Trust, from its early days, was in contact with players of the world of metal, while setting itself apart with some singular characteristics. We will then analyze why the public positioning of Trust, as reflected in the lyrics of their songs and confirmed by the statements made by their singer in the press, was first an asset for the band, before becoming a burden. Can we attribute the break between the band and its fans to the artistic direction taken by Trust, or by changes in French society between the end of the 1970s and the mid-1980s? We will show that these two factors worked together, distancing Trust from the French heavy metal community developing at the time.

Massive Success From 1979 to 1981

Trust is a French band that began in 1977. It had a pair of leaders, the guitarist Norbert Krief, known as Nono, born in 1956 in Tunisia, and the singer Bernard Bonvoisin, known as Bernie. Bernie was also born in 1956 and was raised in Nanterre in the Paris suburbs. Nono, a guitarist with very strong technique, was influenced by the guitar heroes of the 1970s. He earned a living as a guitarist for dances in the Paris area, then at the Club Med in Morocco, before founding Trust on his return to France at the end of 1976, when he met Bernie Bonvoisin, who was working as a technician at the Olympia music hall. The band began to rehearse, then to play in small venues in Paris and nearby suburbs.

At the end of the 1970s, after twenty years without real policies aimed at signing "local" bands other than for *variété* music, the French recording industry took its first shaky steps toward French rock bands. Trust took advantage of this effervescence to sign with EMI. But the record label preferred to invest in another rock group it had also just signed, Téléphone (Durieux 1988). It offered no support for Trust, which recorded its one and only 45 rpm for them in 1978, at the Pathé Studios in Boulogne-Billancourt, of which only 3,000 copies were produced. Despite this, this studio experience would serve Trust in several ways, in particular because it was their first attempt to sing in French. Their choice to continue to sing in French would greatly contribute to their success (Abraham 1984). In addition, Bernie met Bon Scott, the singer from AC/DC who had come to see his guitarist friend Ron Wood (the Rolling Stones were recording in the neighboring studio). Bernie befriended Bon Scott, who a few months later would propose that Trust open for AC/DC at the Stadium de Paris in October 1978. In the meantime, Trust had played a great deal and perfected its original repertoire. Opening for the Australian band was the big break for Trust, allowing them to sign with CBS in November, with this label making Trust a priority, thanks to CBS's new boss, Eric Levy (Durieux 1988), who greatly appreciated the band. They recorded their first album at Scorpio Studios in England. The album came out in May 1979 with a now stable lineup including bassist Yves Brusco (Vivi) and drummer Jean Emile (Jeannot). This first album led to success for the band, in particular thanks to the single "L'Elite," with its very New Wave of British Heavy Metal sound. The demand of the public for Trust surprised even the record company. The success of the band was amplified by its live performances, which everyone agrees were very effective. The band sold out venues throughout France, in particular during a forty-one-show tour produced by their manager Bobby Bruno in October and November 1979 (Durieux 1988).

Trust then began a European career. In December 1979, they signed with an English agent with international scope, Cobwell, who managed in particular Iron Maiden and AC/DC. They opened for Motörhead and Iron Maiden in the United Kingdom and Germany before doing their own UK tour in 1980 and headlining at the Reading Festival in 1981 and 1982.

In October 1980, while the band's first album was not yet out in Britain, their song "L'Elite," released in the United Kingdom that year on the hard rock album *Killer Watts* (a compilation album bringing together the new heavy metal releases from CBS), hit number one according to the English rock charts in UK magazine *Sounds*. The second album, *Repression* (1980), also recorded in England, included the hit "Antisocial." Given the warm reception of the group (Lenquette 1981), an English version was recorded for the international market.[1] In France, the band was ranked first in a 1980 vote of readers of *Best*[2] and performed on the leading *variété* music shows on TV, in particular on those hosted by Guy Lux and Michel Drucker, as well as the commercial "*radios périphériques*." In France in 1980, only AC/DC sold more than Trust in hard rock and heavy metal.

Although the band had opportunities to tour the United States thanks to their tour agent (opening for Judas Priest, Iron Maiden, and finally Def Leppard), they preferred to focus on the French market and invested heavily for a new French tour. But their third album, which came out in October 1981, did not perform as well in France, despite the growing success of the band's performances in the United Kingdom and Germany.[3] It was the beginning of the end for Trust, whose fourth and fifth albums (*Idéal*, 1983, and *Rock'n'roll*, 1984) were flops.

Figure 6.1 The band Trust on *Best* magazine's front cover, n° 133, February 1980.

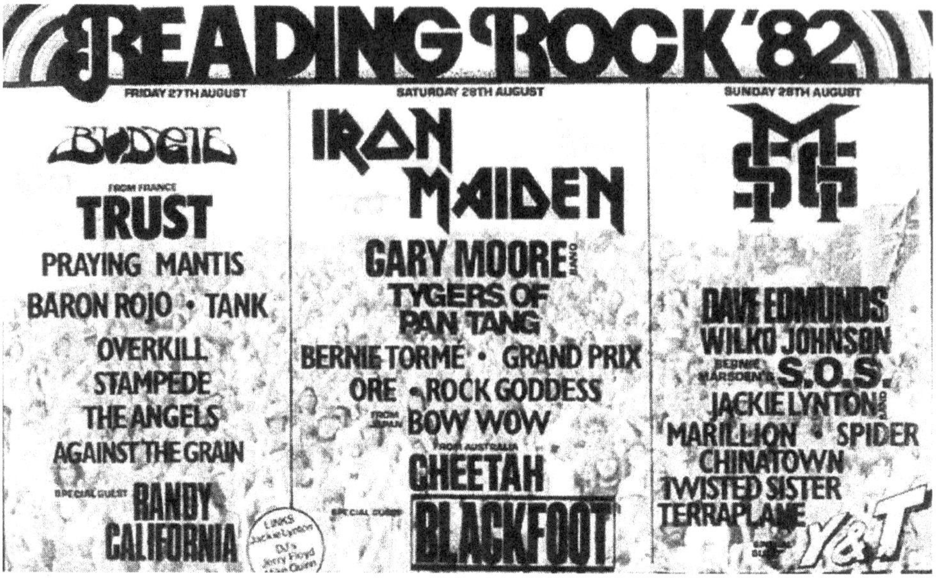

Figure 6.2 Reading Festival program, 1982.

Along with tours that attracted fewer spectators than in the period 1979–1981, these lower sales would lead to the end of the band. At the time of the end of the band, at the beginning of 1982, Trust had nonetheless sold more than 1.5 million albums and had had a strong impact on French music production.

Trust, a Unique Heavy Metal Band

Trust is the first French band to have a truly heavy metal sound. They benefited from production values equal to the British bands of the time (in terms of technology, audio equipment, and sound engineers) for their recordings, if we consider Les Variations and Shakin' Street[4] as precursors to the genre. Nono's guitar solos move from powerful riffs to guitar virtuosity. The musicians had long hair and wore leather and jeans as required by the codes of hard rock of the time. In 1977, their repertoire was made up of many covers of AC/DC,[5] supported by all band members.

But Trust, from its earliest days, had a singularity, its front man, who was marked by punk rock. During their first concerts, in particular when they opened for Bijou at the Olympia in December 1977, Bernie's look was influenced by the Sex Pistols and the punk movement, with a graffiti-covered bodysuit and bright red high-top shoes.[6] Interviewed by *Hard Rock Magazine* in April 1985, Nono the guitar player recalls this period (our translation):

At first, Bernie was really into punk [. . .]. He had me listen to the Sex Pistols, Sham 69, Damned . . . At the time, I wasn't really into it . . . And I was just coming out of an experience at Club Mediterranée, where I was playing Stevie Wonder, Santana [. . .]. But my roots were

Led Zep, Deep Purple, Clapton, Hendrix. [. . .] Bernie was into AC/DC at the time, and I liked that stuff. But the Pistols, for me at first . . . over time he explained it to me and got me to understand lots of stuff, and in the end, there was good stuff there.

Question: So it was the shock of these influences that made Trust special?

Answer: Yes, it's that mixture, it was sort of magic [. . .] we sold half a million of the first album.

When Trust was building their repertoire, the first wave of UK punk was in fashion. The media talked about the currents of hard rock and heavy metal as a developing culture that was underreported in the mainstream press and in particular in rock magazines (Quillien 2006). The affirmation of the New Wave of British Heavy Metal can be seen as a reaction to punk rock (Waksman 2009). At the time, the two movements were often in conflict, in particular in regard to their relationship with instrumental technique (essential for heavy metal, secondary for punk).[7] It's thus interesting to note that in October 1978, when Bon Scott proposed to Bernie and his managers that Trust open for AC/DC, it was under one condition: "the band must in no case have a punk look or attitude. Bernie will get rid of the last badges and other Pistols brand elements that he had left" (Durieux 1988, 17). And yet, during the first period of Trust (until 1981), if journalists described the band as "punk-hard," it was not only because of Bernie's appearance but also because of his lyrics.

At the time, hard rock and heavy metal largely used lyrics tied to the triptych of "sex, drugs and rock and roll," or themes tied to the world of imagination, in particular heroic fantasy (Weinstein 2000). Contemporary political and social issues and critiques are tied more to punk rock.

But Trust took on these issues. The band's lyrics were particularly aggressive. They were often libertarian in tone, denouncing restrictions on freedoms and everything Bernie perceived as injustices, written by someone who identified himself as coming from a working-class suburb. The first album opens with a sequence of a bass drum played with a double-kick pedal (a technique that would become common in heavy metal in the 1980s), and the song "Préfabriqués" continues with lyrics by Bernie (our translation), "I spit in the face of the system," before hitting, "I go where I want, I think like I want [. . .]. Your ideas are based on an overdose of TV, I can only preach unreason, destruction."

In his *Anthologie du hard rock* published in 1982, Hervé Picard, a music writer from the magazine *Best*, wrote,

With Nono we discovered our first French guitar hero [. . .]. As for Bernie's angry singing, it was surprising at first. We weren't used to hearing the language of [French poet] Ronsard sound like that [. . .]. There was the rebellious message of Trust that was shocking. Labor unions, the police, psychiatry, fashion, all the everyday scandals that fill the newspapers were excuses for the biting fury of the quartet [. . .]. Clearly Trust was a problem, its force made others afraid. In any case, Trust was not one of those groups that the media impose on the public. They grew from their base: they earned the beautiful title of a popular band.

(1982, 114, our translation)

Figure 6.3 A look between punk rock and heavy metal. *Repression*, CBS, 1980, 33⅓ rpm album back cover.

In March 1980, Trust played at the prison of Fleury-Mérogis, acclaimed by prisoners shouting "*Police, milice*" ("Police, [fascist] militia"), the title of one of their songs. *Répression*, the second album, which came out in May of the same year, denounced the conditions of the murder of Jacques Mesrine (a famous terrorist killed by the police after escaping) and even included on the album a text written by Mesrine that they set to music ("Le Mitard"), which raised a good deal of controversy in the media (Dordor 1983). Despite this, the album included a song that would become a hit, "Antisocial," from whose lyrics come this extract (our translation):

> You work your whole life just to pay for your tombstone
> You hide your face behind your newspapers
> You walk like a robot in the corridors of the subway [. . .]
> Antisocial, you're losing your cool . . .[8]

In 1984, Mychèle Abraham tried to analyze in real time what Trust represented at the start of the decade, based on the repertoire of these two first albums:

France of Giscard d'Estaing was experiencing a rather nervous end of reign. Bernie spoke of politics with harsh and simple words, and proved his authenticity daily by giving his all on stage [. . .]. They [Trust] spoke up strongly and represented a sort of symbol: revenge of kids of the suburbs, condemned before even having lived.

(1984, 123 and 125, our translation)

Trust encountered difficulties with several town councils that canceled scheduled concerts. The concert at the Pavillon de Paris in December 1979 only began at 10:45 p.m. after negotiations between the promoter KCP and the police department, with 10,000 overheated fans waiting impatiently. The sometimes-nihilistic lyrics of Trust, along with the perceived violence of the music, generated a lack of understanding between generations. The same issue arose with the song "Bosser huit heures" ("Work eight hours"), which was a critique of the CGT, a labor union close to the working class, historically tied to the Left, and in particular to the Communist Party. In this song from the first album, Bernie sings,

The union doesn't give a shit about you
It's all about who will fuck you over the best
When it comes to demonstrations, you're right:
They're making a fool of you
You're just a pawn in this cop country [. . .]
The day will come where you'll think back and realize
They really got me, those bastards
I can see my father, they took advantage of him
For them, he's just a future retiree.[9]

Bernie believed that the band just needed to deal with any incidents during their concerts:

We played this concert for this factory on strike [. . .]. It was in Joigny with people from the CGT [. . .]. The CGT told us "long live democracy, comrades, but don't play 'Bosser huit heures'!" We played the concert, there were 1,500 people in the audience, we left the stage and the audience started calling for us to play "Bosser huit heures." We went back on stage and played it [. . .]. But then there were thirty guys who came up, furious, aggressive, big talkers [. . .]. We don't bother anyone, but if you come looking for trouble, we won't hesitate to defend ourselves.

(Perrin, Jean-Eric. 1983. *Rock & Folk* 161, 54, our translation)

At the time, for Bernie,

It's not like because we spit on the union and we write a song about them that we're telling people that they have to think just like us. But we talk about things that touch us and we speak the same language as the guys who come and see us. [. . .] At the Pavillon de Paris when I realized there were 10,000 guys singing the words and dancing to the music, I said, "Wow, what's happening?" The big idea from that is that the guys don't want us to change.

(Ibid. 56)

The arguments of Trust are in phase with the times. What would change to create a lack of understanding between Trust and their audience that had appeared so devoted?

Political Changes in France: The Point of View of Trust

It appears that a first important change arose from a variable from outside the career of Trust, the election of François Mitterrand as president of France in May 1981. For many people, in particular in the middle and working classes, this period was seen as a utopian moment, open to change (Sirinelli 2007), with the first left-wing majority elected in the Fifth Republic.

Figure 6.4 Tribute to Bon Scott from AC/DC. *Marche ou Crève*, CBS, 1981, 33⅓ rpm album insert.

In September, when their third album, *Marche ou Crève*, came out, Trust kept up the same message, as if nothing had changed.

The band was far from the events taking place in France, locked up in Polar Sound studios in Stockholm with Tony Platt (a sound engineer who had worked with AC/DC and Foreigner), but that does not explain everything. From the first song, "La grande illusion," through the end of the French presidential election, the atmosphere is set with a questioning of the "democratic objectivity" of the election:

> You who talk about new liberty
> Proud of the money your father left you
> You'll spit out your hate on our poor manuals
> While spreading our ghettos you call public housing
> You want me to vote to reassure you
> You want me to vote to reassure me . . .
> I'm only a ballot you poison
> And slip into a ballot box.[10]

With regard to this moment, Abraham (1984) writes in her work on Trust that, "while France was passionately clinging to the elation following the change of government in May 1981, Bernie was not giving an inch in his desire to point out shit wherever he saw it" (127), which would allow her to affirm that "Trust was only speaking of essential things, and had known since the beginning that left and right mean nothing for the 'concrete' generations" (162).

Interviewed by H. Picard in 1982, Bernie said that

> [t]hroughout the *Répression* tour there were towns that were looking to create problems for us, that would cancel our concerts at the last minute. And I have to say that this came more often from the left than from the right. It was hard to take, but we managed to deal with it.
> (116)

Trust began to appear out of touch with a French fanbase that was no longer able to situate Bernie. This divergence of opinion was most strongly present in the band's own country. On the contrary, the band was welcomed on stage in Germany for *The Number of the Beast* tour, with Iron Maiden,[11] which would allow Trust to be chosen to perform in a prestigious concert in Cologne on June 5, 1982. The concert would be broadcast live during the program *Rockpalast*, seen in many European countries, but not in France, despite the fact that *Rockpalast* was at times shown during the French TV show *Les Enfants du Rock*.[12]

In the interviews and albums that followed, Bernie would recall both his disappointment in the policies following the victory of the Left in 1981, and more broadly his lack of understanding of the attitude of French people. Thus, in June 1983 he said in regard to the socialist experiment in France, "you're talking to someone who is disappointed" (Dordor 1983, 41), and about the song "Jack le Vaillant" ("Valiant Jack"),[13] which dealt with the efforts of the first culture minister of the period,

> Jack Lang should sell deli meat or shoes, but not handle culture. What right does he have to impose on people a certain cinema, a way of reading, a way of speaking? There are words you're not allowed to use. This country makes me afraid.
> (Ibid.)

Another example was in 1985, shortly after the release of the album *Rock'n'roll*, at a time when the heavy metal press finally existed:

> What's too bad today, and it's what I explain in the song "Mongolo's Land," is this collective apathy, this lack of combativeness among French people for some time now. Since May 1981, there've been various laws, various decrees, and everything has been passed without any protests. I don't get it. . . .
>
> (Touchard, Philippe. 1985. *Enfer* 21:14)

From Lack of Understanding to a Divorce

In the band's third album, *Marche ou Crève*, at the end of the year 1981, Bernie again denounces dictatorships, rejecting both the Far Right ("the junta") and the Soviet communist regime ("the brutes"), following a tradition that began with "L'Elite" on their first album.

Figure 6.5 Trust, *Ideal*, CBS, 1983, 33⅓ rpm album front cover.

But at the end of the band, he tended to add to this denunciation a critique of France (as in "Varsovie"), or even a pro-US position.

> I support the "America first" thing. It's missing here, the flag thing [. . .]. We lack a sort of faith in what we do, a shared hope. You get the idea that in France nobody cares about anything. Look at how lax things are socially, publicly, culturally? You get the impression that everything's going to hell [. . .]. Lots of people have no memory. At the end of WWII people would kiss the American soldiers, in 1970 they would spit in their face [. . .]. What risks happening is that one day if we call on them for help—because it's certain that it's the Americans who we'd call—they won't come.
>
> (op. cit., 10, our translation)

Bernie would go as far as associating the socialist French government (which included a few communists as of June 1981) to Eastern-bloc countries with respect to their critical attitude toward the United States.

Thus, with regard to "I Shall Return" (1984), a pro-American song that sought to point out the lack of recognition by France of the United States, "It was one of the songs we thought about for a single, and then we thought about it and figured that a pro-American song in a Socialist regime risked shocking too many people" (Ibid.).

He even thought that leftist dictatorships are the most dangerous. With respect to the rise of Jean-Marie Le Pen's National Front, he said in 1985:

> Yes, it's serious, a dictatorship of the right or of the left, the effects are the same. The difference is that you can leave a fascist country like Chile or Argentina, whereas in a socialist dictatorship, everything is done under the table, power is parceled out, divided, so that you're always stuck and can't flee.
>
> (Ibid.)

From the earliest days of the band, Bernie attributed his hatred of communism to the municipal policies of the town where he grew up, Nanterre, and more broadly of the so-called red belt of communist municipalities around Paris.[14]

> Well, I come from Nanterre. It's one of the last, well no, one of the main communist strongholds, where, I mean, if you're 15 and you want a place to rehearse, and you don't belong to the party, you're not getting a place. Where you have a small number of people who join the party by conviction and a large majority who join because of brainwashing or pressure. [. . .] It's a city where you take so many blows that you soon learn to fight back.
>
> (Schmock, Bill. 1980. *Best* 139, February, 39)

Beyond this anti-communism, this revolt against restriction on liberty, Bernie recalls his position, that of a young person of proletarian origin who was raised in a public housing project: "Being a rebel for me, it's an interior phenomenon. It's your baggage, it's your background. For me, the notion of a rebel, it's doing what I want when I want" (Dumatret and Lamet 1988).

But when the Left took power, Bernie's head-on attitude lost its relevance, all the more so because Bernie's own social status changed by earning a great deal of money with the first albums. Bernie's observations on the amount of tax he had to pay did not please his fans: "Shit, I made a 140,000-franc tax payment last month. I pay 76% income tax [. . .] there're limits, I'm not going to bust my ass to pay for a Maserati for [first socialist budget minister Laurent] Fabius!" (Dordor 1983).

The same went for his understanding of success and the status of the music industry, at a time when dynamic independent record labels were arising in resistance to the oligopoly of the major record companies (Guibert 2006), in contradiction with his own goals:

> There's no point hiding it: I want to sell millions of albums and earn millions of dollars. We're all in the same situation, the American dream still exists for us. [. . .] For us, it's normal to work very hard and to earn dough in return.
>
> (Dumatray and Lamet 1988, 14)

The same kind of idea is expressed here:

> There's always this idea of suspicion behind success. We can't imagine that men earn money without there being something up. It's like the people who told me, when we signed with CBS, that we were part of the system [. . .]. We need the system to do a poster, to present decent shows [. . .]. It's this analysis that is needed rather than saying, there they go, they've signed with a multinational.
>
> (Sabouret, Jean-Pierre. 1997. *Hard'n'Heavy* 31, 41)

Conclusion

In just a few years, Trust went from unknown band to the voice of a generation in France, then disappeared.[15] Trust revealed the existence of heavy metal to a large portion of working-class youth, and after accompanying the success of AC/DC in the early 1980s, they were a catalyst for the development of this musical genre, FM "pirate" radio programs, magazines, record stores, and T-shirt and accessory vendors, as well as heavy metal nights at discos (Hein 2003; Guibert 2006), and they spurred vocations among many bands. Yet at the very moment a heavy metal community was rising, they were distancing themselves from it.

First, the musicians of Trust distanced themselves from the heavy metal community beginning with *Idéal*. Whereas they had previously seemed close to bands like Rose Tattoo, Iron Maiden, or AC/DC, they began speaking more about rock 'n' roll or blues. While promoting *Idéal*, Bernie said, "I know nothing about hard rock" (*Best*, 1983). He no longer wore black leather or band T-shirts, no wristbands or bullet belts as he did in 1979 or 1980. He rarely spoke of hard rock or heavy metal bands after 1981 and went as far on several occasions as to praise Johnny Hallyday and "the professions of show business" (Bernie would be at times associated with the tradition of *chanson française*, and would attempt a solo career in *variété* music as of 1985, while Nono would become a guitarist for Johnny Hallyday).

In hindsight, the message of Trust appears out of synch with the evolution of the heavy metal scene that was then working to become more autonomous. For example,

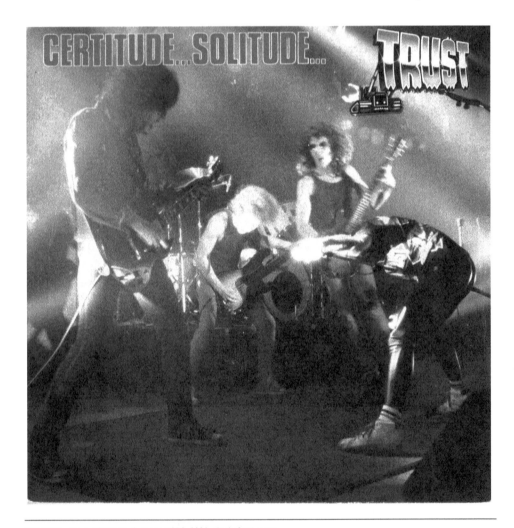

Figure 6.6 Trust, "Certitude Solitude," CBS, 1981, single front cover.

Enfer Magazine, the first French monthly magazine, published from April 1983, declared *Kill 'Em All*, Metallica's first album, as 1983's album of the year. The album was considered radical, and described as speed metal or thrash metal after being released in the United States on an independent label.

Second, the members of Trust rose in social class by selling so many albums. They changed their lifestyle, which critics of the band would link to the changes in Bernie's lyrics as of the third album. He abandoned telling stories based on his life to adopt the role of a voice above the fray, of a political commentator often described as a preacher giving lessons (Sabouret 1997). In 1983, in the magazine *Best*, Francis Dordor asked him, "Why is it that you always talk about big topics and never about individuals?" There seems to have been a loss of references to their potential audience in France.

The members of Trust would thus remain pioneers, the big brothers. In the middle of the 1980s, one could find legacies and ties among the first wave of heavy metal bands (for music) and alt rock (for the anarchist positioning and militant demands), with these two waves having each taken on the principle of independent production. We can also call back to Trust at the time of the explosion of rap music that would in the 1990s become the favorite music of many teens from the working class. Trust would remain known for its first period, in particular for its best-known song, "Antisocial."[16] But with the arrival of rap, no one would say, as Trust did in 1981, "The walls of the projects resound with AC/DC."[17]

Notes

1 *Répression, Marche ou Crève*, and *Idéal* had English versions, with an English version of "Préfabriqué" included on the international compilation *Heavy Metal* (October 1981, CBS), which came out with the Canadian animated film *Heavy Metal*.
2 Trust would be ranked second French artist the following year, with AC/DC voted best foreign band by *Best* in the same two years, 1980 and 1981.
3 But their records were not readily available in these countries because, at the time, the major labels lacked an international strategy for local bands outside the Western, English-speaking world (Guibert 2006).
4 We should note that in the second half of the 1970s, the bass player of Les Variations played with several members of Trust, and that the guitarist of Shakin' Street spent time playing with Trust.
5 They performed seven covers of AC/DC at their start, according to Durieux (1988), including one used on their first single ("Love at First Feel," with new lyrics, under the title "Paris by Night"), and another ("Ride Out") on their first album in 1978 and 1979.
6 Photos of him appear in Abraham 1984.
7 Thus at their beginning, Iron Maiden claimed the legacy of Deep Purple and clearly positioned themselves as a reaction to the punk rock movement (*Hard-Rock* Iron Maiden special issue, 1985, 8–9).
8 *Tu bosses toute ta vie pour payer ta pierre tombale / Tu masques ton visage en lisant ton journal / Tu marches tel un robot dans les couloirs du métro [. . .] / Antisocial tu perds ton sang froid . . .*
9 *Le syndicat se moque de toi / C'est à celui qui te baisera le mieux / Quant aux manifs t'a bien raison / Là ils te font passer pour un con / Tu n'es qu'un pion dans ce régime de flics [. . .] / Un jour viendra où tu repenseras / Ils m'ont bien eu ces enfoirés / Moi j'vois mon père ils l'ont roulé / Pour eux ce n'est qu'un futur retraité.*
10 *Toi qui parles de nouvelle liberté / Fier de l'argent que ton père t'a laissé / Tu cracheras ta haine sur nos pauvres manuels / En répandant nos ghettos que tu nommes HLM / Tu veux que je vote pour te rassurer / Tu veux que je vote pour me sécuriser. . . / Je ne suis qu'un bulletin qu'on intoxique / Et qu'on glisse dans une urne.*
11 It was following this tour that Nicko McBrain, Trust's drummer at the time, joined Iron Maiden, with Trust recruiting in exchange, but on a temporary basis, Clive Burr, the lead drummer of Iron Maiden.
12 Trust's third album would be the most successful in Germany.
13 It would not end up on the album *Idéal* and would instead be released on *Backsides* (1997).
14 Expression used to describe the postwar cities of the Paris suburbs with communist majorities in the city council.
15 Beyond France, Germany, and the United Kingdom, one could see in 1987, with the cover of "Antisocial," produced by the New York thrash metal band Anthrax, that Trust was also known to American heavy metal fans.
16 They're regularly mentioned as having had an impact on the history of popular music in France, even by mainstream magazines like *Les Inrockuptibles* (see, e.g., "Pop en France," *Les Inrocks* 2, 2001, 98, or "Made in France," *Les Inrockuptibles* 206, July 1999, 80).
17 In "Ton dernier Acte," the homage to AC/DC singer Bon Scott on the album *Marche ou Crève*.

Bibliography

Abraham, Mychèle. 1984. *Trust*. Paris: R&F/Albin Michel.
Bayer, Gerd. 2009. *Heavy Metal in Britain*. London: Ashgate.
Dordor, Françis. 1983. "Liberté provisoire." *Best* 179:41–45.
Dumatray, Henri, and Christian Lamet. 1988. "Relève toi et marche." *Hard-Force* 23:12–16.
Durieux, Arnaud. 1988. "Trust Story Part I." *Hard-Force* 23:16–19.

Guibert, Gérôme. 1998. *Les nouveaux courants musicaux: Simples produits des industries culturelles?* Nantes: Mélanie Seteun.

Guibert, Gérôme. 2006. *La production de la culture, le cas des musiques amplifiées en France.* Paris and St Amant Tallende: Irma/editions Seteun.

Hein, Fabien. 2003. *Hard Rock, Heavy Metal, Metal.* Paris: Irma/Seteun.

Lenquette, Youri. 1981. "Version anglaise." *Best* 153:44–49.

Perrin, Jean-Eric. 1980. "Le hard sauvage." *Rock & Folk* 161:53–56.

Petit, James. 1985. "Trust. Sept ans de réflexions." *Hard Rock magazine* 8:34–39.

Picard, Hervé, and Jean-Yves Legras. 1982. *The Hard-Rock. Tome 2.* Paris: Jacques Grancher.

Quillien, Christophe. 2006. *Génération Rock&Folk.* Paris: Flammarion.

Sabouret, Jean-Pierre. 1997. "And Justice for All." *Hard'n'Heavy* 31:36–41.

Schmock, Bill. 1980. "Brain Trust." *Best* 139:34–39.

Sirinelli, Jean-François. 2007. *Les vingt décisives: 1965–1985, le passé proche de notre avenir.* Paris: Fayard.

Straw, Will. 1983. "Characterizing Rock Music Culture: The Case of Heavy Metal." In *On Record*, edited by Simon Frith and Andrew Goodwin, 97–110. New York and London: Routledge.

Touchard, Philippe. 1985. "Bernie plus ni moins." *Enfer* 21:8–14.

Waksman, Steve. 2009. *This Ain't the Summer of Love: Conflict and Crossover in Heavy Metal and Punk.* Berkeley: University of California Press.

Weinstein, Deena. 2000. *Heavy Metal: The Music and Its Culture.* New York: Da Capo.

7

Rock, Race and the Republic
Musical Identities in Post-Colonial France

Barbara Lebrun

France is Europe's most multi-ethnic state, yet the republic has consistently rejected the concepts of "race" and "ethnicity" as categories of identification, insisting instead on colour-blind universalism for fear that acknowledging cultural differences will fragment the nation (Hargreaves 2007:14). Consequently, while the experience of "difference" is a daily reality for many French citizens, this is ignored by official discourse and, to a large extent, by mainstream society. This chapter examines the presence of this paradox in popular music, an art form that both reflects society and shapes it, through a comparison of the careers and outputs of two French-Algerian artists who gained fame in late twentieth-century France, Rachid Taha and Magyd Cherfi.

This focus on singers with a post-colonial background builds upon existing research on the place on Maghrebi musicians in France (Moser 2003; Gastaut 2006), and examines the meaning of "race" in French music culture more generally, questioning the widespread conceptualisation of French-Maghrebi music in terms of *métissage*. However, because Taha and Cherfi also self-define as "rockers," at least in their role as members of the groups Carte de Séjour (1982–1989) and Zebda (1988–2003 and 2011–present), this chapter also takes research on post-coloniality and popular music beyond rap, deconstructing certain assumptions about the relations between music genres and ethnicity.[1] By reading "rock" as a metaphor for the majority taste, it argues that symbolic values (commercial success, prestige) also contribute to shaping the ethnicity of musical identities.

"Identity," "Race" and "Ethnicity" in France

Since the late 1970s, the notion of "identity" has become central to academic debates in the humanities, under the leadership of cultural studies theorists like the late Stuart Hall. Hall (2010, 2) explains that an identity is the result of an individual's "recognition of some common origin or shared characteristics" with a group, arising from a fluctuating "process of articulation" (Hall 2010, 3) between the individual and a perceived authority, political or social. Identities are thus elaborated dialogically through the perception of difference and sameness, difference being at once needed and rejected for the purpose of self-identification. Cultural theorists have moved away, then, from the Cartesian understanding of the subject as essence, considering that "identities" are constructed within society rather than fixed in nature, a process and not a truth. For this reason, identities are unstable performances, whereby the thinking subject is endlessly fashioned through negotiation, accommodation or confrontation with the perception of difference—whether through a regulatory system, social conventions or an imaginary Other. As discourses of self-position, as the "narrativization of the self" (Hall 2010, 4), identities are fundamentally contingent, unstable and determined by the material and symbolic conditions of existence.

Ethnic and racial identities are only two aspects of identity, but defining them requires laying down the specific historical and ideological circumstances that mould contemporary France. France's official ideology is universal republicanism, a citizen-centred conception of national cohesion aimed at abolishing group privileges based on "origins." Devoted to egalitarianism, republicanism demands that the "public sphere" of identity, controlled by and representative of the state, remain neutral, the sole expression of a common Frenchness, and that individual differences, which are inevitable, be contained within the so-called private sphere (Gildea 1996). This principle is irreproachable. Yet it is largely utopian since "private" and "public" spheres of identity are rarely watertight. Indeed, the supposedly neutral parameters of "Frenchness" were themselves fixed by educated, White, French-speaking, heterosexual men of Christian heritage, who privileged these same characteristics in their understanding of citizenship (Silverman 1995). Throughout republicanism's history, various interest groups falling outside these parameters have defended their "private" particularisms, and the state has occasionally demonstrated its ability to recognize their specificity through differential legislation, whether granting working mothers the right to maternity leave, gays the right to marry or disabled people a minimum income.

Aside from gender, sexuality and disability, the area of identity where the state has stayed firm in its dedication to universalism is "race," a category of (self-)identification that is virtually taboo today (Hargreaves 2007, 9). "Race," of course, is a construct, not a biological category, but it is socially unavoidable due to the empirical observation that humans have distinct somatic appearances, notably their skin colour. Race is an "organizing discursive category" (Hall 2000, 222), which can be yielded to generate power and hierarchies by generalizing, dividing and excluding individuals from an implied norm. Indeed, throughout the French colonial period, the White majority claimed their racial superiority and right to "civilize" non-Whites. Since decolonisation, however, the state has reiterated its dedication to universalism, with Article 1 of the 1958 Constitution declaring that French citizens are equal before the law, "regardless of origin, race or religion."[2]

The post-war context of post-colonial immigration, however, saw the mass settlement of non-White, non-Christian individuals hailing chiefly from Algeria and Morocco (Hargreaves 2007, 21), which created a challenge for French universalism. While the state ignores physical variations between humans, social interactions (messy by definition) have continued to be influenced by the awareness of "race," triggering inequalities. French Maghrebis, known as *beurs* in the 1980s and 1990s, are the least economically privileged in France today (Hargreaves 2007, 10), "the most visible, the most stigmatised" ethnic minority (Tarr 2005, 3). In early twenty-first-century France, the CVs of job applicants with Arab-sounding names are regularly rejected by French employers (Amadieu 2004), and the Paris police checks individuals thought to be "Arab" at least seven times more than those deemed "White" (Jobard et al. 2013).

This discrimination has its roots in the violence and legacy of resentment of the Algeria War, the economic downturn that coincided with the end of legal migration in the 1970s and the sadly commonplace practice of stereotyping (Hargreaves 2007, 35). Yet it demonstrates that "race" and "ethnicity" matter socially, since the visible appearance of French Maghrebis (brown skin, dark hair) and their common culture (including Arabic language and Islam) facilitates their amalgamation and rejection as "different." Thus, while the term "ethnicity" is now preferred to that of "race," encompassing as it does shared cultural practices such as language, faith or customs (reaching beyond the merely somatic), it remains analytically insufficient. "Race" continues to shape social interactions, pointing to a gap between republican ideals of equality, and lived practices of exclusion.

These tensions are at the heart of the musical expression of Rachid Taha and Magyd Cherfi, two successful singers who happen to have personal Algerian backgrounds and who privilege, in their performance, an ethnically marked French-Maghrebi persona. The fact that the social reality "outside" of music and the discourse "within" converge here is arbitrary, the result of an artistic decision, for not all French-Maghrebi artists are similarly concerned with exploring their ethnicity in their work. But for these two at least, the various publicly available outputs of their songs (lyrics, music, performance) and declarations in books and interviews, which collectively constitute their "star text" (Dyer 1998, 63), are ethnicized.[3] As we shall see, however, this ethnic nexus is not finite and fixed, but elastic and slippery, and only one aspect of the artists' broader musical identities.

Rachid Taha and Magyd Cherfi

Taha and Cherfi are hardly comparable artists given their different nationalities, musical influences and levels of fame. Taha was born in 1958 in Oran, Algeria, and extols his Algerian citizenship despite having lived in France since he was 10. He became famous in 1986 with the funk-rock group Carte de Séjour and has, as a solo artist, become a regular on the international circuit with his oriental-rock-electro fusion, mainly singing in Arabic. His solo albums sell around 300,000 copies each (Kershaw 2005, 13), and he is known in the United Kingdom as a "cult artist" (Denselow 2001), a bestselling "Algerian rocker" (Spencer 2013). By contrast, Cherfi is squarely "French": born in Toulouse in 1962, he sings in French, champions republicanism, and has experienced limited international success. Cherfi is the front man of Zebda, a ragga-rock group with left-wing credentials whose greatest commercial success was in 1999 with the number one single "Tomber la chemise" ("Shirts off"). Since 2003, Cherfi has pursued a low-key solo career in parallel and written melancholy *mémoires*. By contrast, Taha is an exuberant showman with self-aggrandizing tendencies (Pascaud 2007).

Nevertheless, the two men were born only four years apart, have Algerian parents and have lived in France virtually all their lives. They both reached adulthood in the early 1980s, and belong to the first *beur* generation. They became professional musicians in that period and have released numerous albums since.[4] Both are recognized as important national artists through regular press reviews and entries in popular music encyclopaedias (Saka and Plougastel 1999; Dicale 2006). Taha and Cherfi also share the distinction of having become academic objects of study (Gross, McMurray and Swedenburg 2001; Seery 2001; Marx-Scouras 2004 and 2006; Oscherwitz 2004; Ervine 2008; Nemer 2008; Lebrun 2007, 2009 and 2012; Sutcliffe 2011; Stratton 2013). What most academics perceive as noteworthy in their work relates to their Maghrebi origins, and both artists' contribution to the national

Figure 7.1 Carte de Séjour, *Rhorhomanie*, CBS, 1984, 33⅓ rpm front cover.

soundscape is predominantly conceptualised in terms of *métissage*, or cultural hybridity. *Métissage*, a term referring to miscegenation in the nineteenth century (Yee 2003), has since the late 1970s identified multi-ethnic mixing in the cultural sphere, especially in music and sports, and always with positive undertones. *Métissage* is certainly an apt descriptor for the music of Taha and Cherfi, whose compositions incorporate elements of rock, funk, reggae, *chanson* and North African music, sometimes with multi-lingual lyrics. The term is also used to imply a protest position against racism, so that the musical hybridity of Taha and Cherfi, which appears to cross-fertilize the French national soundscape, is also understood as "a discursive space of resistance" (on Zebda see Ervine 2008, 202), with the potential to "overturn the power of the colonizer" (on Taha see Stratton 2013, 10). *Métissage*, then, works as an attractive metaphor for musical multiculturalism and its implied power to resist exclusion and conservatism. This proposition has attracted large numbers of White, left-leaning and educated audiences (Lebrun 2009), and accounts for the popularity and lucrative nature of any music perceived to be "oriental" or "hybrid" in France (Kiwan 2005).

However, conceptualizing the music of French Maghrebis in terms of *métissage* is limited. Firstly, it implies that French popular music only became hybrid when post-colonial artists joined the ranks of music practitioners, which denies centuries of non-colonial migration and its impact on creativity. Secondly, it privileges optimistic narratives that contrast with the rather more nuanced *chanteur* position of these artists, who also perform sentiments of rejection and bitterness. Finally, *métissage* is a conceptually fraught term in the sense that, as Jennifer Yee (2003, 415) explains, it extols racial categories only if they can offer a new universal ideal of tolerance—a utopian message that only returns to a republican denial of race as socially constructive. Thus, mobilizing *métissage* with reference to post-colonial minorities not only glosses over the multiple, contradictory expressions that artists from similar backgrounds necessarily produce but also idealistically implies the end of racial conflict. For this reason, foregrounding the narrower, anti-republican notions of "race" and "ethnicity" might account more comprehensively for the actual type of musical identities that minority artists project in their "star text."

French and Algerian: One Ethnicity, Several Identities

Over the last thirty years, Taha and Cherfi have located themselves ethnically as French Algerians, French Maghrebis and "Arabs" more generally, building on their direct and proxy experience of post-colonial immigration to expose their sensitivity to matters of "race." For instance, in interviews and autobiographies, both tell youth anecdotes involving hammams, tajine stews and Muslim clothing (Taha 2008; Cherfi 2007). Both insist on their support for the 1983 Marche des Beurs, a nationwide demonstration that mediatized the specificity of a French "Arab" generation in France (Moreira 1987, 49; Taha 2008, 108; Green 2012, 57), thus expressing their belonging to a common *beur* community, ethnically and racially different from the White majority. Both denounce racial discrimination and confront republican values by repeatedly mentioning race categories such as "Whites," "non-Whites," "Arabs" and "Blacks" alongside provocatively racist terms like "*bougnoules*" ("towel-heads") (Taha 2008, 160–161; Cherfi 2007, 144–148). They explicitly target institutional racism, the failings of France's integration policy, and the French taboo surrounding these issues (Taha in Pascaud 2007, 14; Cherfi 2007, 146). Furthermore, Taha and Cherfi are extremely lucid about the interconnectedness of ethnicity and class and the racially subordinated position of migrant labourers (see Gilroy 1991, 115). They frequently acknowledge their own working-class roots by sharing stories of poverty and employment discrimination (Taha 2008; Cherfi 2007), insisting that they narrowly escaped the cultural determinism of their ethnic group by meeting members of the White middle class, who gave them access to "culture" (Taha 2008, 78; Marx-Scouras 2004, 66). By talking publicly about their personal experience as French Algerians, both artists "narrativize" themselves as ethnic minorities and critics of the republic's egalitarian rhetoric, and shape a particularist framework for their musical identities.[5]

In their lyrics, both pass for French Algerian *chanteurs* humiliated by an implicitly oppressive majority. "Désolé" ("Sorry") (*Carte de Sejour* 1984) and "Je crois que ça va pas être possible" ("That won't be possible") (Zebda 1998) stage the rejection of Arab-looking men in socioprofessional settings, with choruses mocking racist apologies. With "En enfer" ("In hell") (Cherfi 2004), a plaintive voice over a slow, melancholy tune evokes a lack of fit, while musical evocations of North Africa make the Maghrebi identity of the *chanteur* clear. Elsewhere, they use irony to challenge racist discourse: Carte de Séjour's cover of "Douce France" ("Sweet France") was "an antiphrasis" (Taha 2008, 129), intended to show that post-colonial immigration is nothing but sweet; Cherfi scorned the racism of the president of the republic in "Le bruit et l'odeur" ("The noise and the smell") (Zebda 1995). Taha and Cherfi thus perform, at the twin levels of personal statements and song products, a common French "Arab" ethnicity, yet its varied expression and foregrounding of vulnerability and anger prevent us from identifying it as *métissage*.

The two artists also ethnicize their performance musically by incorporating "Maghrebi" sounds and instruments, and do so in a multi-purpose fashion that simultaneously invokes and rejects stereotypes. For instance, they frequently reference North Africa through techniques deemed typical of this region, including the double harmonic major scale and singing with elongated vowels (melisma), also using the oud, *derbouki* percussions and string sections. Yet while Western composers have traditionally incorporated the "Orient" to invoke sexual fantasies (Stokes 1994, 4), Taha and Cherfi reject such exoticism, whether by ignoring it and favouring songs with a political subtext (Cherfi), or by inverting its heterosexual convention and dancing languorously himself (Taha).

Their use of language also reveals that there are multiple ways to perform a French Maghrebi identity, as Taha and Cherfi use Arabic in different proportions and with different effects. Cherfi only sings in French with the occasional inclusion of Arabic in choruses ("Oulalaradime," 1998; "Sheitan," 2002). These accents give a linguistic coherence to his ethnically marked persona, but French remains the vehicle of choice for songs primarily intended for a Francophone audience. Taha, by contrast, is primarily an Arabic-language singer, who first writes his lyrics in French and translates them in *darja*, the Algerian vernacular (Meouak and Aguadé 1996); he also sings Oranese covers. He has consequently attracted a large Arabophone diasporic audience, even if some have expressed their distaste at his excessively guttural pronunciation (Moreira 1987, 36–37). In France, rock critics have praised the "rough-sounding" credentials of his Arabic-speaking persona (Hakem 1999, 40), but Taha consciously chose to sing in Arabic in order to confront the French stereotype of the non-integrated migrant (Lebrun 2012, 333), treading a fine line between reproducing and undermining exoticism. Cherfi is less confrontational than Taha in his performance of ethnicity, but taken together, their distinct approaches reveal the unstable nature of ethnicity itself.

From Maghrebi Victim to Rock Rebel?

If ethnicity is certainly central to both artists' musical identities, their musical identities cannot be reduced to it. Indeed, Taha and Cherfi both refuse to be pigeonholed as "ethnic" artists, disparaging the two music genres usually associated with North Africans in France, *raï* with its excessive sentimentality, and rap with its stereotypical violence (Taha 2008, 143, 201–203, 246, 250; Lebrun 2007). Instead, both self-define as rockers (Moreira 1987, 32;

Marx-Scouras 2005, 76), their songs being sustained rhythmically by electric bass guitars and drums, often copying the offbeat rhythm of reggae ("L'adjectif" ["The adjective"], Cherfi 2004; "Ecoute-moi camarade" ["Listen comrade"], Taha 2006). This rock identity greatly expands the potential narrowness of their ethnicity, however "authentically" they perform it. Indeed, as an international music idiom, rock reaches beyond race, and audiences frequently suspend their awareness of race during a performance, proving that "anti-essentialism is a necessary part of the musical experience" (Frith 1996, 122).

Yet, if both artists offer a complex definition of race, and cannot be reduced to their race anyway, race continues to influence their music identities sometimes despite their best efforts. For, as ethnic minority artists, the ways in which they "define themselves in music have to take into account the power relations which pertain between the groups defining and being defined" (Stokes 1994, 20). This means that Taha and Cherfi's identities are also dependent on the opinions and perceptions of France's cultural gatekeepers, in particular music critics. In France, like elsewhere in the West, critics have, since the late 1960s, ascribed the highest degree of prestige to rock music, for its ability to project the figure of the challenger or "social marginal" (Frith 1996, 122; Teillet 2003). Ethnic minorities often threaten the national regulatory system, and their "Otherness" is often perceived by the dominant culture as "potentially problematic" (Stokes 1994, 18–20). Thus, in an ideal process of convergence, Taha and Cherfi not only perform a minority ethnicity that is verifiably based on personal experience, and thus perceived as "authentic," but also fit into the broad conventions of rock music thanks to that projected ethnicity, which matches the imperative of anti-establishment and non-conventionality.

Commenting on the trans-Atlantic movement of African music, Paul Gilroy (2004, 61) noted that Blackness was used to "bleed risk, pleasure and excitement" in Western culture. Refocusing on trans-Mediterranean crossings, it seems here that the "Arabness" of Taha and Cherfi conveys threat and satisfaction in equal measure in France, the artists' performance of minority ethnicity legitimizing their position as underdogs. On the one hand, then, and like most ethnic minority musicians in the West, their Maghrebi ethnicity challenges ideologically, and re-dynamises musically, the national (French) 'order that is perceived to be discriminatory or culturally stale (Stokes 1994, 17). This is the positive side of *métissage*, the optimistic celebration of their contribution to French popular music. Put differently, Taha and Cherfi's performance of "Arabness" provides them with a platform from which to scrutinize social injustice, including racial discrimination; this in turn gives them credentials as protest artists, a cultural tradition benefiting from high prestige.

On the other hand, however, their prestige remains partly dependent on the public knowledge of their Algerian origin, so that their artistic expression never fully reaches beyond race. So, while they certainly cannot be reduced to their ethnicity, and perform this ethnicity in multiple ways, they still cannot escape it. To nuance Frith's aforementioned comment, then, perhaps racial essentialism never entirely disappears from the musical experience when the artists are ethnic minorities themselves, especially post-colonial ones.

Taha and Cherfi both faced this conundrum at the time of their biggest success. In 1986, Taha's group Carte de Séjour had a hit with "Douce France." This song was first and foremost a parody of Charles Trenet's original, aiming to debunk his authority as France's greatest *chanson* poet, but it was co-opted by the Parti Socialiste to enhance their own anti-racist agenda, and by Trenet to enhance his own prestige. Taha never forgave them, and the mainstream media that publicized his cover, for limiting his intentions to the performance of a *beur* identity (Lebrun 2012). In summer 1999, Zebda became France's bestselling group with a festive song that contrasted with their habitual leftist activism. Reflecting on its huge commercial success, Cherfi was adamant that "Tomber la chemise" only comforted mainstream audiences with an Orientalist stereotype of bodily display, sweat and passion (Leclère 1999). In both cases, then, although for diametrically opposed reasons, both artists' relationships with the media were fraught because of racial expectations. Taha wanted to be taken seriously as an ironic rock performer, but for the Parti Socialiste and the press, his ethnicity could only involve anti-racist activism. Cherfi wanted to be taken seriously as a protest artist, but only his blandest, least intellectual song was widely successful. Both, then, extol a complex notion of Maghrebi ethnicity that includes ignoring that very notion, yet both have been

Figure 7.2 Magyd Cherfi, *Cité des étoiles*, LKP, 2004, front cover.

simplistically reduced to their ethnicity by the media. If identity formation is complex and paradoxical, that complexity is rarely apprehended as such by the mainstream or dominant discourse.

Conclusion

Taha and Cherfi have common Maghrebi roots, and their "star texts" are importantly influenced by that ethnic experience, but this commonality is performed musically in plural ways. It is at once nostalgic and modern, defensive and inclusive, parodic and sincere, celebratory and despondent. It is also paradoxical in seeking to reconcile opposites, the republican aspiration to universalism (which rock music somehow provides, uniting audiences beyond race), and the particularism of post-colonial ethnicity—the desire to have full creative agency, and the fact that musical meanings are dependent on sociocultural conventions.

Their full identities as music artists, moreover, cannot be reduced to race, as the artists themselves insist, and if this chapter focused on singers with a post-colonial background, it did not imply that only subaltern groups produce valid, coherent or productive ethnic identities. Indeed, the place and meanings of race in French music culture can also be studied with reference to "majority" artists. Moreover, Taha and Cherfi are seen, from outside the national boundaries, as particularly "French," which constitutes another level of ethnic specificity, albeit not a sub-national one. Indeed, they are French ideologically in negotiating their Maghrebi identity in relation to France's republican codes. They are French historically when connecting their performance to the heritage of France's Algerian colonisation. They are French sociologically in their aspiration to be understood by the French elite. And they are French musically with their Euro-Arab fusion sound that the British, among others, don't really do. Thanks to the quantity and quality of academic works now delving into French popular music, there is no doubt that the important concepts of race, identity and ethnicity, and the important artists who work with them, will continue to be apprehended with the sophistication and complexity that they imply, and which they deserve.

Notes

1   For sophisticated accounts of that relationship, see Béru (2007) and Hammou (2012).
2   Extract from the Constitution of the French Fifth Republic, which may be accessed on www.assemblee-natio nale.fr/connaissance/constitution.asp#titre_1.
3   The conceptualisation of identity is incomplete without acknowledging audience experiences (Frith 2010, 123), but this cannot be developed here; Lebrun (2009, chapter 5) partly surveys Zebda's audiences.
4   Full discographies can be found on the artists' official websites: www.rachidtahaofficial.com/biography and www.magydcherfi.com/index2.php.
5   Ethnicity is only one facet of their performance. Their gay-friendliness as straight men and reverence towards the work of older women constitute two fascinating, gender-related areas for further study (Cherfi in Anon 2004; Taha 2008, 57, 87–88).

Bibliography

Amadieu, Jean-François. 2004. "Enquête 'Testing' sur CV." http://cergors.univ-paris1.fr/docsatelecharger/pr%E9sen tation%20du%20testing%20mai%202004.pdf.
Anon. 2004. "Les parents homosexuels et Zebda." 29 May. Reproduced in *Libération Hors-Série*, "Chanson française 1973–2006," Spring 2006, 78.
Béru, Laurent. 2007. "Le rap français, un produit musical postcolonial?" *Volume! La revue des musiques populaires* 6(2):61–79.

Cherfi, Magyd. 2007. *La Trempe*. Paris: Actes Sud.

Denselow, Robin. 2001. "Nuclear Fusion." *The Guardian*, May 28. https://www.theguardian.com/culture/2001/may/28/artsfeatures1

Dicale Bertrand. 2006. *La Chanson française pour les nuls*. Paris: First Éditions.

Dyer, Richard. 1998 [1979]. *Stars*. London: British Film Institute.

Ervine, Jonathan. 2008. "Citizenship and Belonging in Suburban France: The Music of Zebda." *ACME, An International E-journal of Critical Geographies* 7(2):199–213.

Frith, Simon. 2010 [1996]. "Music and Identity." In *Questions of Cultural Identity*, edited by Stuart Hall and Paul du Gay, 108–127. London, Thousand Oaks, New Delhi and Singapore: Sage.

Gastaut, Yvan. 2006. "Chansons et chanteurs maghrébins en France (1920–1986)." *Migrations Société* 18(103):105–115.

Gildea, Robert. 1996. *France Since 1945*. Oxford: Oxford University Press.

Gilroy, Paul. 2004. *After Empire: Melancholia or Convivial Culture?* Oxford: Routledge.

Green, Milo. 2012. "Zebda." *Music: La bande-son des sociétés* 1:56–58.

Gross, Joan, David McMurray, and Ted Swedenburg. 2001 [1996]. "Arab Noise and Ramadan Nights: Rai, Rap and Franco-Maghrebi Identities." In *Displacement, Diaspora, and Geographies of Identity*, edited by Smadar Lavie and Ted Swedenburg, 119–156. Durham and London: Duke University Press.

Hakem, Tewfik. 1999. "Métèque et mat." *Les Inrockuptibles* 206, July 7:40–41.

Hall, Stuart. 2000. "Conclusion: The Multicultural Question." In *Un/Settled Multiculturalisms: Diasporas, Entanglements, "Transruptions,"* edited by Barnor Hesse, 209–241. London and New York: Zed Books.

———. 2010 [1996]. "Who Needs Identity?" In *Questions of Cultural Identity*, edited by Stuart Hall and Paul du Gay, 1–7. London, Thousand Oaks, New Delhi and Singapore: Sage.

Hammou, Karim. 2012. *Une histoire du rap en France*. Paris: La Découverte.

Hargreaves, Alec. 2007. *Multi-Ethnic France*. New York and London: Routledge.

Jobard, Fabien, René Lévy, John Lamberth, and Sophie Névanen. 2013. "Mesurer les discriminations selon L'apparence: Une analyse des contrôles d'identité à Paris." *HAL-Archives Ouvertes*. https://hal.archives-ouvertes.fr/hal-00781605.

Kershaw, Andy. 2005. "Africans Not Included." *The Independent*, June 4, 12–13.

Kiwan, Nadia. 2005. "'Maghrebi Music' in and Beyond the Post-Colonial City." In *Urban Generations: Post-Colonial Cites*, edited by David Richards, Taoufik Belghazi, Taieb Belghazi, 345–354. Rabat: Faculty of Letters.

Lebrun, Barbara. 2007. "Le bruit et l'odeur . . . du succès? Contestation et contradictions dans le rock métis de Zebda." *Modern and Contemporary France* 15(3):325–337.

———. 2009. *Protest Music in France: Production, Identity and Audiences*. Farnham and Burlington: Ashgate.

———. 2012. "Carte de Séjour: Re-Visiting 'Arabness' and Anti-Racism in 1980s French Culture." *Popular Music* 31(3):331–346.

Leclère, Thierry. 1999. "Zebda, les chanteurs de la contestation festive." *Télérama* 2566, March 17:32.

Marx-Scouras, Danielle. 2004. "Rock the Hexagon." *Contemporary French and Francophone Studies*, January, 8(1):51–61.

———. 2006. *La France de Zebda*. Paris: Autrement.

Mathis-Moser, Ursula. 2003. "L'image de 'l'Arabe' dans la chanson française contemporaine." *Volume! La revue des musiques populaires* 2(2): 29–43.

Meouak, Mohamed, and Jordi Aguadé. 1996. "La Rhorhomanie et les Beurs: L'exemple de deux langues en contact." *Estudios de dialectología Norteafricana y Andalusí* 1:157–166.

Moreira, Paul. 1987. *Rock métis en France*. Paris: Souffles.

Nemer, Noha. 2008. "Kent, Zebda et Cali: pour un lyrisme du politique." In *La chanson politique en Europe*, edited by Céline Cecchetto and Michel Prat, 137–148. Bordeaux: Presses Universitaires de Bordeaux.

Oscherwitz, Dayna. 2004. "Pop Goes the Banlieue: Musical Métissage and the Articulation of a Multiculturalist Vision." *Contemporary French and Francophone Cultural Studies* 8(1):43–50.

Pascaud, Fabienne. 2007. "Rachid Taha." *Télérama* 2977, January 31, 14–18.

Rosello, Mireille. 1998. *Declining the Stereotype: Ethnicity and Representation in French Cultures*. Hanover, NH, and London: University Press of New England.

Saka, Pierre and Yann Plougastel (ed.). 1999. *La chanson française et francophone*. Paris: Larousse.

Seery, Mairéad. 2001. "*Essence ordinaire* de Zebda: carburant pour une 'République en panne'?" *The Irish Journal of French Studies* 1:15–24.

Silverman, Max. 1995. "Rights and Difference: Questions of Citizenship in France." In *Racism, Ethnicity and Politics in Contemporary Europe*, edited by Alec Hargreaves and Jeremy Leaman, 256–264. Aldershot: Edward Elgar.

Spencer, Neil. 2013. "Rachid Taha." *The Guardian*, March 10. www.theguardian.com/music/2013/mar/10/rachid-taha-zoom-review.

Stokes, Martin. 1994. "Introduction: Ethnicity, Identity and Music." In *Ethnicity, Identity and Music: The Musical Construction of Place*, edited by Stokes, 1–28. Oxford and Providence: Berg.

Stratton, Jon. 2013. "Rachid Taha and the Postcolonial Presence in French Popular Music." *Performing Islam* 1(2):185–206.

Sutcliffe, Ellie. 2011. "Managing the Media, the Music and 'métissage': Compromise in the Music of Faudel and Magyd Cherfi." *Contemporary French Civilization* 36(1–2):97–111.

Taha, Rachid and Dominique Lacout. 2008. *Rock la Casbah*. Paris: Flammarion.

Tarr, Carrie. 2005. *Reframing Difference: Beur and Banlieue Film-Making in France*. Manchester: Manchester University Press.

Teillet, Philippe. 2003. "Rock and Culture in France: Ways, Processes and Ambitions." In *Popular Music in France from Chanson to Techno: Culture, Identity and Society*, edited by Hugh Dauncey and Steve Cannon, 171–190. Aldershot: Ashgate.

Yee, Jennifer. 2003. "*Métissage* in France: A Postmodern Fantasy and Its Forgotten Precedents." *Modern and Contemporary France* 11(4):411–426.

PART III

Assimilation, Appropriation, French Specificity

Gérôme Guibert and Catherine Rudent

The history of French popular music in the second half of the twentieth century has not always experienced such cultural tensions between the local and the global that are inherent in our contemporary world. Until the 1980s, the polar opposites were, on the one hand, the music practices thought of as national and, on the other, the soon-to-be hegemonic influence of popular music from the English-speaking world, especially the United States and the United Kingdom. How then has France managed to develop specific kinds of popular music—that is, different kinds of music that share a number of common characteristics, and that stand as different from the models from which they are inspired?

Both French artists and French audiences experience the influence of American and British popular music in a manner of different ways. In some cases, there is a certain form of resistance to this cultural "Other," to what some may see as a form of alienation coupled with a loss of identity and of cultural wealth. Some will simply opt for basic assimilation by following *to the letter* these "other" musical styles. We can also identify active forms of appropriation or, to borrow from Laplantine, forms of *métissage*, of musical hybridisation (Laplantine and Nouss 2014, 10). These forms differ from their model and the resultant musical output is unpredictable and creative, giving way to new musical styles.

Though cultural blends in France—a former colonial power—are studied on both a general and political level (see, e.g., Amselle 2011 and 2012), it is less the case for the resultant cultural output. A few authors have written about these blends in popular music, notably Borowice (2007) and Lebrun (2012a and 2012b). In 2013, a study day held at the Bibliothèque nationale de France (BnF), the French national library, titled "*Avec ma gueule de métèque . . .*" ("*What with my Dago mug . . .*") also dealt with these questions, as have some recent doctoral students (see Armelle Gaulier's work on Zebda, under Denis-Constant Martin's direction). These musical manifestations, however, equate to musicians in migration. Here, "*le métissage suppose la mobilité, le voyage*," hybridisation presupposes mobility and travel (Laplantine and Nouss 2014, 15).

It is our contention, however, that the musical blends in France influenced by the United States and the United Kingdom should be looked at differently, not as the result of the movement of people, but as that of the movement of the recordings themselves—in other words, the movement of devices (*dipositifs*) or of objects (*objets*) if one is to borrow from the vocabulary of actor-network theory (Latour 1991). It is the musical processes that move around and not the musicians or the audience. This has come to characterise the second half of the twentieth century where distribution methods have become increasingly efficient, from the development of the micro-groove vinyl record in the 1950s to the CD and the spread of digital formats in the 1980s, and, since the turn of the century, the advent of highly compressed digital files. Over the past few years, online music sharing has become more and more flexible and more and more massive through downloading and streaming.

The modes and results of these encounters are often examined through the prism of language: do we sing in English or in French (see Guibert 2004, Escoubet 2013, or the ongoing thesis work of Michael Spanu)? Though little work has been done on the appropriation of musical styles, however, it is worth mentioning such authors as Catherine Rudent (Rudent 2006, 2011a, 2011b, 2013) and Matthieu Saladin, who wrote the chapter on the aesthetics of *yéyé* for this book.

In this third section, the question of resistance and musical appropriation is discussed in relation to different musical genres: *chanson française*, rap and punk.

The first two chapters of this section deal with *chanson française*, and there is no other genre of popular French music that so firmly deals with the opposition between French identity and the Otherness of music from the English-speaking world. The term *chanson française* was used as early as 1963 on the French television programme *Discorama*. Serge Gainsbourg and the programme's presenter, Denise Glaser, use it in opposition to the songs of the "*nouvelle vague*" ("new wave") (Gainsbourg 1963). A few weeks later, the French sociologist Edgar Morin would coin the term *yéyé* to designate this new wave of American influence. In the early 1960s, Gainsbourg was still a cabaret act and he took a firm stand against the idea that *chanson française* should "tag along behind America." Thus, in that influential music television programme and in the words of two leading experts on the subject, *chanson française* becomes deeply entwined with national belonging and must reject the trappings of the United States. A few years later, the media used the label "*rock anglo-saxon*," a catchall phrase that could encompass, though somewhat indiscreetly, all music coming out of the United States and the United Kingdom.

Of course, during the early part of the twentieth century, French song had absorbed musical idioms from elsewhere without this being perceived as a threat to French culture. That is what happened with jazz: jazz was in France connected, during the 1930s, with the scene of Paris cabaret and, a few years earlier, with the music hall, and actually with every aspect of French music industry. Thus, jazz-inspired songs were composed or sung by Tranchant, Sablon, Mireille and Charles Trenet and were performed in the *music-hall* revues from the 1920s onwards, as well as in such cabarets as *Le Bœuf sur le Toit*. But the cultural context on the whole was undergoing a major upheaval, and come the 1960s French culture was no longer a dominant force on the world stage. Over the past decades, songs written and performed by French artists, as well as *chanson française* in its strictest sense, have always had a complicated and unsettled relationship with the music made by English-speaking artists that have come to produce the canon of international hits. The relationship between them has been characterised by varying degrees of closeness and distance, of musical integration and refusal, and this still holds true today.

It is possible to consider *chanson française* from the angle of "French national identity," from the viewpoint of a certain style of song. In this part of the book, Cécile Prévost-Thomas explains that *chanson française* "was a perfectly identifiable genre until the 1980s," and that it remains a musical and aesthetic style that reaches beyond the mere stereotype of being "out-dated" and "old-fashioned." Catherine Rudent, however, considers *chanson française* as an entity that is inclusive, the borders of which cannot be fixed down. According to Rudent, *chanson française* lacks a constant and identifiable stylistic unity. Rudent understands *chanson française* as a musical whole that cannot be defined no matter the musical criteria one chooses to apply.

Regardless of *chanson française*, it is possible to say that the assimilation of rock music in France was kept in check, especially in the 1960s and the 1970s. It took until the 1980s for the French music industry to start producing locally made rock music in any significant way, but even then record releases were far and few between. And yet, numerous French musicians, as well as large swaths of the audience, were turning towards rock music right from the beginning of the 1960s. Testament to this is the dense history of French-produced rock during the second half of the twentieth century (Guibert 2006) and the birth and rapid growth of two monthly French rock magazines, *Rock & Folk* and *Best* (Rudent 2000a). This historic shift in French musical taste, however, does not manage to establish itself for two whole decades (from the beginning of the 1960s till the end of the 1970s) on radio, television or, indeed, amongst record companies.

The second half of the 1970s is thus dotted with manifestations of rock and then of punk, forming what Guibert, following on from Greil Marcus, has called a "secret history" (Guibert 2006, 245). Indeed, as punk bursts onto the London scene in the summer of 1976 (Hebdige 1979), at the same time the Mont-de-Marsan Festival in France includes punk acts and groups close to the punk genre in its line-up, amongst which are such French bands as Marie et les Garçons, Asphalt Jungle, Little Bob Story and Bijou. Much research has been done on French punk, the issues it raised, its developments and its DIY ethic (Hein 2012)—one need only consider the works of Fabien Hein, the *La scène punk en France, 1976–2016* project directed by Solveig Serre and Luc Robène, or the March 2015 conference organised by Paul Schor, at Université Paris-Diderot, titled *Disorder: Histoire sociale des mouvements punk/post-punk*, which included a panel on French punk.

Just as France had positioned itself as the "second home of jazz" and had proven itself to be ahead of its time and open-minded when it came to punk, so it showed itself extremely welcoming towards rap. Stéphanie Molinero's chapter deals with rap and how "France has once again appropriated, as with jazz and rock music, a musical genre which originated in the USA." In fact, the sheer number of publications on rap demonstrates that France has taken the genre seriously for quite some time—the works of Lapassade and Rousselot (1990); of Christian Béthune (1999, 2004) and of Manuel Boucher (1999); the academic publications of Prévos and of Jacono; the special hip hop edition of *Volume!* in 2004; and the debate held between Anthony Pecqueux and Christophe Rubin on the ties between rap and *chanson française*; as well as the writings of such journalists as Olivier Cachin (1996), Fred Hanak and Thomas Blondeau (2007) and Mehdi Maizi (2015), are just a few examples. More recently we can turn to the academic writings of Marc-Martinez (2008), Déon, Karim Hammou (2012), Marie Sonnette (2013), the H-Herc mailing list and the rap seminar *La plume et le bitume* organised at the École Normale Supérieure in 2015 by Emmanuelle Carinos and Benoît Dufau, to which were regularly invited contemporary French rappers.

Chanson française, punk and rap are quite different musical genres emanating from areas of production and thought that are to a large extent relatively distinct. Facts of assimilation, creative appropriation and resistance, however, must be analysed through the same phenomena and gauged in the same manner, as is the case in the chapters that make up this part of this book. To begin with, there is the question of style—that is to say, the recognisable and identifiable musical features that serve as musical markers and reveal stylistic belonging (Rudent 2000b). In a world of cultural hybridisation, it is through these musical features that we perceive similarities and differences between different music genres. It is these features that trigger different levels of rejection or appropriation; it is these features that reveal how musicians position themselves between the two. The question of stylistic differences is addressed in the chapters by Prévost-Thomas and Rudent, as well as Stéphanie Molinero, who discusses how American rap is often perceived as more "creative," more musically inventive and better produced, but also perceived by some as more "formulaic" than French rap. One could perhaps contend that in contrast to "formulaic" music, it is the singularity of the various artists with regards to each other that comes to define the different expressions of French popular music. This singularity exists in *chanson française* and manifests itself, though more discreetly, in the chapters on French rap and punk.

Then, there is language. Of course, language plays a central role in the way influences from the English-speaking world are assimilated. Preconceived notions of the musical qualities of English underpin the relationship that French artists and audiences hold with the language. For instance, the amateur rappers in Molinero's chapter find it easier to get a good flow going in English than in French. If singing in French suffers from widespread negative representations in France, the objective validity of these representations still remains to be demonstrated through examining questions relating to phonology, vocal physiology and so on. Fabien Hein considers the language of French punk and notes that not only is French prevalent but also that a certain number of groups that choose to sing in English do so with a strong French accent. With regards to *chanson française*, the authors here remind us that the French language plays a fundamental role. As a result, there is a tendency in France today to see the use of the French language as the defining criterion of belonging to *chanson française*, more so than such matters as nationality, sensibility or even musical style.

The value of words, at both the political and poetical levels, is thirdly an inherent specificity of French musical appropriations. Indeed, fans of *chanson française* often draw attention to the poetic quality of the lyrics, a characteristic also put forward in books dealing with the genre. In the same way, in his chapter, Christian Béthune examines rap through the poetry of the lyrics—the "perspectives of expression" of the genre must be "analysed" through the prism of "a poetic expression" rather than through a "socially inevitable linguistic handicap." According to Béthune, rap is poetic because it bears the scars of transgression, of having transgressed the linguistic codes and rules of the French language, which is itself a contestation of social order.

The five authors of this part of the book also consider the complex and multifaceted filter that is the media. The nuances and practices of media coverage are a clue to the degree of musical assimilation, as well as the modalities of assimilation. The relationship a musical genre has with the mass media (television, radio, national press) rather than with specialty media reveals both its media profile and social position. Prévost-Thomas notes how the media profile of *chanson française* has weakened. Béthune reminds us how the media reinforce the negative stereotypes of rap, and Molinero confronts audiences that only come into contact with rap through the mass media with audiences that read specialty magazines, go to rap concerts and rap as a hobby. As Molinero points out, these are two very different rap audiences.

The authors also deal with the varying degrees of legitimation and institutionalization of the music genres they are studying. According to Béthune, rap holds little legitimacy and faces various forms of resistance, in particular from schools. For Molinero, however, rap is entering "into a process of social and cultural legitimisation." As an indication of this new phase, Molinero points to the diversification and the heterogeneousness of newly acquired rap audiences. Fabien Hein writes about the contradictions of French punk acts that benefit from public money (government grants, state funding) but then refuse to play the game and refuse to officially disclose such sources of income so as to preserve at least superficially their DIY ideal, their subversive state of mind and what they call the "anti-institutional mood" of the punk scene. Prévost-Thomas deals with the rather fraught relationship *chanson française* has with national institutions. All of these authors, therefore, demonstrate how research into popular music in France must necessarily consider the importance of public policy, which plays an important role in the development of musical practices, all the while being taken to task by the very people directly implicated in the different musical trends (Teillet 2003).

Musical style, language, poetic pursuit, media coverage, institutionalisation and legitimation: these parameters allow us to measure and analyse to what extent a music genre has been assimilated by France, by its musicians and by its audiences. In this manner, appropriation must not be studied in a quantitative and one-dimensional manner—for example, extent of media coverage or record sales—but must be understood as a complex matrix structure. One must not stop at knowing if the media has picked up a particular genre, but one must look closely at the manner of how the genre has been picked up and by which media exactly. One must not stop at knowing if a genre has a wide audience, but one must look closely at the different members of the audience and how they express their musical taste. One must not stop at knowing if there exists *a chanson française, a* French punk or *a* French rap, but one must look closely at how these specific genres come about and who produces them. Only then will we be able to understand the specificities of the different kinds of French popular music. For the moment, they seem to be driven by poetic sensibility and pursuit of artistic singularity.

Bibliography

Amselle, Jean-Loup. 2001. *Vers un multiculturalisme français.* Paris: Flammarion.
———. 2011. *L'ethnicisation de la France.* Paris: Lignes.
Béthune, Christian. 1999. *Le rap: une esthétique hors la loi.* Paris: Autrement.
———. 2004. *Pour une esthétique du rap.* Paris: Klincksieck.
Blondeau, Thomas and Fred Hanak. 2007. *Combat rap. 25 ans de hip-hop. Entretiens.* Bordeaux: Le Castor Astral.
Borowice, Yves. 2007. "La chanson française: un art de métèques?" *Amnis* 7. http://amnis.revues.org/804. doi: 10.4000/amnis.804.
Boucher, Manuel. 1999. *Rap, expression des lascars: significations et enjeux du rap dans la société française.* Paris: L'Harmattan.
Cachin, Olivier. 1996. *L'offensive rap.* Paris: Gallimard.
Escoubet, Stéphane. 2013. "French Pop Bands of the 2000s Singing in English." Paper presented at 17th IASPM biennial conference, Gijon, June.

Gainsbourg, Serge. 1963. "Serge Gainsbourg . . . et la nouvelle vague" (interview by Denise Glaser). *Discorama* (3DVD): INA, 2008.

Gaulier, Armelle. 2014. "Zebda, Tactikolectif, Origines Contrôlées: la musique au service de l'action sociale et politique à Toulouse." PhD diss., Université de Bordeaux.

Guibert, Gérôme. 2004. "Chantez-vous en français ou en anglais? Le choix de la langue dans le rock en France." *Volume! La revue des musiques populaires* 2(2):83–98.

———. 2006. *La Production de la culture*. Paris and St Amant Tallende: Irma/editions Seteun.

Hebdige, Dick. 1979. *Subculture: The Meaning of Style*. New York: Routledge.

Hammou, Karim. 2012. *Une histoire du rap en France*. Paris: La Découverte.

Hein, Fabien. 2012. *Do It Yourself! Autodétermination et culture punk*. Paris: Le passager clandestin.

Lapassade, Georges, and Philippe Rousselot. 1990. *Le rap ou la fureur de dire*. Paris: Loris Talmont.

Laplantine, François, and Alexis Nouss. 2014. *Le métissage*. Paris: Téraèdre (1977, Paris, Flammarion).

Latour, Bruno. 1991. *Nous n'avons jamais été modernes: Essai d'anthropologie symétrique*. Paris: La Découverte.

Lebrun, Barbara. 2012a. "Carte de Sejour: Re-visiting 'Arabness' and Anti-Racism in 1980s France." *Popular Music* 31(3):331–346.

———. 2012b. "Hybridity, Arabness and Cultural Legitimacy in Rock Metis." In *Music and Protest*, edited by Ian Peddie, 473–499. Farnham: Ashgate.

Maizi, Mehdi. 2015. *Rap français. Une exploration en 100 albums*. Marseille: Le Mot et le Reste.

Marc-Martinez, Isabelle. 2008. *Le rap français, esthétique et poétique des textes (1990–1995)*. Bern: Peter Lang.

Rudent, Catherine. 2000a. *Le discours sur la musique dans la presse française: l'exemple des périodiques spécialisés en 1993*. www.theses.paris-sorbonne.fr/these-%20Rudent.pdf.

———. 2000b. "L'analyse du cliché dans les chansons à success." In *Musique et sociologie: Enjeux méthodologiques et approches empiriques*, edited by Anne-Marie Green, 95–121. Paris: L'Harmattan.

———. 2006. "La télévision française et les 'voix québécoises' populaires: le trompe-L'œil d'un étiquetage médiatique." *Intersections: Canadian Journal of Music/Revue canadienne de musique* 27(1):75–99.

———. 2011a. *L'album de chansons entre processus social et œuvre musicale: Juliette Gréco, Bruno Joubrel, Mademoiselle K*. Paris: Honoré Champion.

———. 2011b. "Une intimité très médiatisée: les paradoxes de 'J'ai dix ans' (Souchon—Voulzy)." *Contemporary French Civilization* 36(1–2):81–96.

———. 2013. "Anglo-American Mermaids: The Troubled 'anglo-saxon' Fantasy in French Pop Song." Paper presented at 17th IASPM biennial conference, Gijon, June.

Sonnette, Marie. 2013. "Des manières critiques de faire du rap: pratiques artistiques, pratiques politiques. Contribution à une sociologie de l'engagement des artistes." PhD diss., Université Sorbonne-Nouvelle.

Teillet, Philippe. 2003. "Publics et politiques des musiques actuelles." In *Le(s) Public(s) de la culture*, edited by Olivier Donnat and Paul Tolila, 155–180. Paris: Presses de Sciences Po.

8

Chanson Française
Between Musical Realities and Social Representations

Cécile Prévost-Thomas

If the 1950s were the golden age of *chanson française*, what is its place today in the 2010s, in the cultural, economic, and media landscape of France and beyond? Now in the early twenty-first century, what is the meaning of the expression *chanson française*? To which musical realities does it refer? To which social representations is it associated? This chapter will attempt to answer these questions from the point of view of a sociologist.

Chanson Française or Popular Songs?

French became the official language of France in 1539 during the reign of Francis I and the ordinance of Villers-Cotterêts, but it was not until the mid-nineteenth century that 60% of the population was literate, and not until the end of the nineteenth century that there was free, public, and mandatory education.[1] This historical context favored the development of song as the leading means of expression of the people, passed on by the mode of oral transmission. The heritage of these songs, each of which can have many versions, and some of which remain present in the collective memory—"La complainte du Roi Renaud" ("The Lament of King Renaud"), "À la claire fontaine" ("In the Clear Fountain"), "Au clair de la lune" ("By the Light of the Moon"), and so forth—constitute what Claude Roy[2] would call the "Trésor de la poésie populaire française" ("the treasure of French popular poetry") (Roy 1954). These works illustrate "traditional" song, most of whose authors are unknown, and exemplify the first meaning of the term "popular": songs from the people, shared by the people.

From another category of what's known as "popular song" are the "workers' songs" found from the nineteenth century in the line of a long tradition of work songs and protest songs: anonymous songs, songs with authors—Pierre Dupont "Le chant des ouvriers" ("The Workers' Song"), 1846; Jules Jouy, "Filles d'ouvriers" ("Workers' Daughters"), 1887; Aristide Bruant, "Les Canuts" ("The Silk Workers"), 1894; Montéhus, "Ils ont les mains blanches" ("They Have White Hands"), 1910—can all be found in this category.

Lastly, two other similar meanings refer to the contemporary use of this expression. First, "pop songs" are those liked by a majority of listeners, spectators, and television viewers. Second, they are songs that are played on mass media and performed at concert venues.

In both cases, more often than not it's the fame of the singers that is the proof of their popularity; ever since the advent of phonographic recording, interest in song has moved from the work to the performer. Thus, at the annual Marché International du Disque et de l'Edition Musicale (MIDEM), a music industry trade show,[3] the traditional publication of the revenue of the best-paid singers in France is a precious indicator of the popularity of performers. For example, in 2013, Mylène Farmer (€4.7 million), Maître Gims (€3.1 million), Johnny Hallyday (€3 million), and Zaz (€2.9 million) were the performers who sold the most records or whose songs were played the most. We'll also note that, while in 2013 "the share of French productions reached its highest level in ten years with 70% of sales of *variété* music,"[45] this increase is due in part to the huge success of Belgian singer Stromae, who sold nearly 1.5 million albums in France.

"*Chanson*" or "*Variété*"?

As these statistics show, *chanson française* is often designated as *variété* in the singular, *variétés* in the plural, or *variété française* or *variété nationale* to distinguish it from *variété internationale*. But this expression "*variété*" is ambiguous because it also refers to forms of writing, performance, and musical composition that are less ambitious and less demanding than other forms, whether in terms of the words of songs or their music. With regard to the lyrics, *variété* contrasts with the works of writers, with music also known as *chanson à texte* or poetic songs. With regard to music, it is opposed to folk, rock, pop, or electro, whose esthetic concerns are clearer. Consequently, and particular to France, the expression *variété*, used more than that of *chanson* to refer to songs from France, can also imply a deprecated musical genre that is the product of the music and entertainment industry alone, and that does not have a place in the world of art. At best, *chanson française* is usually considered a "minor art," as described by one of its ambassadors, Serge Gainsbourg, on a TV program in 1986: "The major arts like painting, architecture, classical music, literature, and poetry require an initiation. Popular music [*chanson*] doesn't; it's a minor art."[6] Gainsbourg said this to provoke the defenders of the *chanson poétique* present in the studio with him, Guy Béart, Pierre Perret, and Anne Sylvestre, adding that in *chanson française* "it's the words that carry the ideas, and not the other way round." But the author of "Melody Nelson"[7] added his authority from within the world of *chanson française* to the idea already present in and spread by the intelligentsia: *chanson française* is an outdated genre, and those who like it, whether performers or fans, are uneducated and not "with it."

But this viewpoint is not held by all; if we focus on the extremities of a line defining song practices, we can see on one end high ratings for TV shows aimed at entertaining the masses, such as *La fête de la chanson française*[8] or *La chanson de l'année* (*The Song of the Year*)[9] and on the other, the creation and enduring and growing popularity of bistros,[10] various venues,[11] or festivals catering to niche interests, such as "Ta Parole"[12] or "Chansons de parole."[13]

"*Chanson Française*": An Expression with Multiple Meanings

In France, the term *chanson française* refers to various concepts determined among other criteria by social origin, age, cultural heritage, musical practice, or listening habits. On a broader scale, that of educational programs, cultural policies, record labels, places where music is played, and musical prerogatives, the representations of *chanson française* are also diverse, some favorable to its development, others indifferent or even hostile to its existence. This observation was at the start of my sociological questioning of the place given by our society to *chanson française* since the mid-twentieth century (Prévost-Thomas 1998). Why is *chanson française* on some occasions adulated and appreciated, and on others denigrated and despised? Why are so many of the artists who are recognized within the profession partially or totally ignored by the media that have the greatest influence on musical taste? Lastly, why does the term "*chanson française*" too often designate the esthetics of a bygone era where the only names and songs worthy of airplay or a place in our collective memory or social recognition would be those of Charles Aznavour, Jacques Brel, Édith Piaf, or Barbara, of "La bohème," "Ne me quitte pas," "La vie en rose,"[14] or "L'aigle noir"?

"*Chanson à Texte*"?

Twenty years ago, Charles Aznavour, perhaps the world's best-known living singer of *chanson française*, declared that "*chanson française* is first and foremost a matter of lyrics. At least that's what gives it its particular personality" (Aznavour 1994, 145). He added,

> I'm not saying that the music isn't important, but from the tango to jazz, and Afro-Cuban and rock in between, people have set *chanson française* to all sorts of rhythms without having it lose what makes for its profound originality.
>
> (Aznavour 1994, 145)

Thus, when designating a work or a broader esthetic with the expression "*chanson à texte*," still very present in common usage, we mean that the lyrics of the song predominate over the music. The lyrics are featured by using technical methods (careful articulation, vocals recorded before the accompaniment, attention to vocabulary, a form close to poetic language). The words are chosen and ordered so as to attract the attention of the listener with a strong poetic effect, a clear political message, and so on.

This tradition of *chanson française* imposed itself in the postwar period, in the "Left Bank" cabarets[15] where the first texts recited or sung by performers such as Pia Colombo, Juliette Gréco, Renée Lebas, Hélène Martin, Catherine Sauvage, Christine Sèvres, Francesca Solleville, or Cora Vaucaire were the poems of Louis Aragon, Pierre Mac Orlan, Jacques Prévert, Raymond Queneau, or Jean-Paul Sartre, the words of which it was agreed the greatest attention must be paid. In the early 1950s, under the influence of Félix Leclerc who came from Canada to Paris thanks to Jacques Canetti, singer-songwriters[16] continued with a style made of poetic and political texts that asserted a certain artistic commitment, of vocals, or of a particular stage performance, with a favored instrument (the guitar for Félix Leclerc, Georges Brassens, Anne Sylvestre; the piano for Léo Ferré and Serge Gainsbourg) to accompany oneself and support the lyrics.

Made in France

In the 1950s the singer-songwriter style was a sign of *chanson française*, but beginning with the *yéyé* wave of the 1960s, the influence of pop, rock, and reggae sounds encouraged many younger artists to turn away from this tradition by favoring rhythm and dance to lyrics and melodies. In addition, *chanson française* is now less heard in its diversity and less transmitted between generations than it was thirty years ago because, as Josée Boileau, a journalist at *Le Devoir*,[17] explained with regard to the results of the twenty-fifth Victoires de la Musique awards: "In Paris, it's English that is favored and performed" (Boileau 2010). This trend had already been observed in the songs themselves, often with humor, by French artists: "La langue française" by Léo Ferré in 1962 and "It is not because you are" by Renaud in 1980. The trend has been confirmed by the great success of *The Voice*, a musical competition broadcast on leading free-to-air broadcaster TF1 since 2012, and that presents contestants who perform for the most part in English. The full title of the show is "*The Voice—La plus belle voix* [*sic*],"[18] and in it one hears the hosts systematically use English expressions such as "battle," "coach," "prime," "replay," "ring," "show," or "standing ovation." The importance given by the people of Quebec to the protection of the French language in Canada is much more explicit and perceptible, if only when we observe the number of contemporary songs dedicated to this cause, the most famous of which are "Les gens de mon pays" ("The People of My Country") by Gilles Vigneault, 1965; "Le cœur de ma vie" ("The Heart of My Life") by Michel Rivard, 1989; "Malamalangue" by Loco Locass, 2000; and "La langue" ("The Language"), lyrics by Yvon Deschamps, with music by Daniel Boucher, who performed the song at the Quebec national holiday celebration in Montreal on June 24, 2014. In France, more and more young artists sing in English, and only a very few, like Mokaiesh, identify themselves as belonging to a tradition of *chanson française* written in the French language.

While the argument of wider understanding of English than French often used by young artists doesn't really hold up, their preference demonstrates their attraction for a pop/rock esthetic of the English-language culture, and assimilates it directly and almost exclusively to English-language singers and bands. This hypothesis leads us to observe more closely the share of music performed in French.

Musical Diversity With a Melodic Turn

It is impossible to separate words from music while fully appreciating a song. Here, too, a "French song" (the work) or "*chanson française*" (a genre) can be recognized by its music or the thoroughly original style of its performer(s). "Take someone like Higelin, Francis Cabrel, Renaud, Souchon or Michel Berger: They found a typically French tone, beyond the influences they were subjected to," says Charles Aznavour (Aznavour 1994). To this is added the musical specificity of *chanson française*—that is to say, its diversity and eclecticism (Rudent 2000, 372). In its musical composition, *chanson française* dips into all styles and currents of music: melody, *java*, swing, tango, jazz, rock, pop, disco, rap, electro, and more. Moreover, while most creators[19] often follow the musical fashions and trends of each generation when composing their songs, others favor a mix of styles and sounds, ever since Mireille brought swing into *chanson française* in the 1930s. Thus, over the last fifteen years we've heard rap/*musette* with the band Java; rock/*musette* with the bands Têtes Raides and La Rue Ketanou; mixtures of melodic music and electro with Alain Klingler, Bertrand Louis, and Emilie Simon; Romani swing with Sanseverino and Thomas Dutronc; and so on.

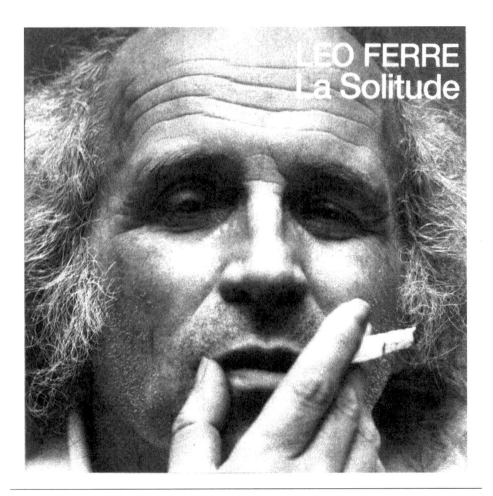

Figure 8.1 Léo Ferré, *La Solitude*, Barclay, 1971, LP front cover.

"Nouvelle Scène Française"?

Several of these artists are associated with what the media began calling in the early 2000s *"la nouvelle chanson française,"*[20] then soon after *"la nouvelle scène française"* ("the new French stage"). This second expression raises new esthetic stakes: *chanson française* finds itself diluted in other musical currents produced by French artists (in the "French Touch")[21] but who often perform in English. This is confirmed when we look closer at the programming of French artists in English-speaking countries. Recently we have seen new festivals created to export the performers of *"la nouvelle scène française."* These events confirm the porosity of musical boundaries and blur the outline of *"chanson française."*

"OohLaLA! Le Festival,"[22] held for its first editions in Los Angeles, San Francisco, Montreal, and New York, came to London for its 2013 edition, presenting from October 21 to 24 to the UK public performers, such as Rover, Mélissa Laveaux, and Tomorrow's World, who sang in English. We can see the same since 2012 in Australia for the festival

"So Frenchy, So Chic" in Melbourne and Sydney, with artists like Asa, Nadeah, or Lilly Wood and the Prick.

According to BureauExport, the partner for international promotion of French music, in 2012, the top export sellers for albums "made in France" were those of Feist (of Canadian origin) and Selah Sue (of Belgian origin), both of whom also sing in English.[23] Today, being a French artist no longer means being part of *chanson française*, although singers such as Aznavour, as already mentioned among the elders, and Zaz, among the younger artists, remain ambassadors of French quality abroad. To give just one example, Zaz, now 34 years old, has attracted an audience in Russia, Japan, Germany, Spain, Belgium, and Quebec with her two albums, *Zaz*, which came out in 2010, and her 2013 *Recto Verso*. But considering all esthetics and all generations, hundreds of French artists, recognized by their profession in France, remain totally unknown and invisible to the rest of the world.

Multiple Varieties of *Chanson Française*

Beyond the social representations according to which *chanson française* is an outdated genre, this diversity calls on the coexistence of several artistic families that correspond to different social realities. An interesting indicator allows for the measurement of the disparity that exists within the music industry: national music awards. Among these, the best known are the Prix de l'Académie Charles Cros and the Victoires de la Musique. The Académie Charles Cros, founded in 1947, brings together many independent music industry specialists, and announces the winners of its awards in a small circle of professionals at the Maison de Radio France (headquarters of the French public radio network) in a 220-seat auditorium. As for the Victoires de la Musique, they offer a bigger showcase, since they're supported by the record companies, broadcast on television since 1985, and watched by an average of three million TV viewers each year. In this logic, during the ceremony, recognition goes to top-selling artists like Stromae, who in 2014 won the awards for best male artist, best song album for *Racine carrée*, and best music video for his song "Formidable." The Académie Charles Cros in the last three years has recognized artists like Melissmell, L, and Damien Saez among younger performers, and Louis Chédid, Julos Beaucarne, and Jacques Higelin, who have each received a lifetime achievement award. To support these artists who have less media exposure than those nominated to the Victoires de la Musique, the Fédération des Festivals de Chanson Francophone (FFCF, or Federation of French-Language Music Festivals)[24] has tried since 2009 to offer them greater visibility by bringing together festivals specifically dedicated to *chanson française*. In addition, national structures like the Centre de la Chanson[25] and the Hall de la Chanson,[26] which have existed for twenty-five years, despite limited visibility due to limited public funding, encourage projects of young artists and lead to the discovery and enhancement of the legacy of *chanson française*.

Chanson Française as National Heritage

In recent years, we've seen renewed interest in the emblematic figures of *chanson française* in a series of exhibitions from 2007 to 2013 about Dalida,[27] Gainsbourg,[28] Brassens,[29] Trenet,[30] and Barbara.[31] In France these artists have given their name to many streets, squares, performance spaces, schools, and parks. These official honors place these singers at the same level of literary lights: national symbols. Yet, Charles Trenet, considered as the father of the modern *chanson française*, never obtained a seat as a member of the Académie Française, nor did he receive a national memorial service, unlike Pierre-Jean de Béranger, honored during his lifetime by Chateaubriand, Goethe, and George Sand, and recognized in the

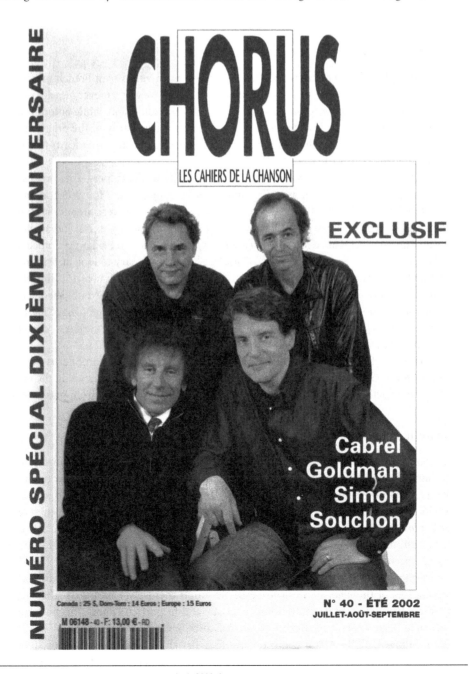

Figure 8.2 *Chorus. Les cahiers de la chanson*, n° 40, 2002, front cover.

nineteenth century as a "national poet," equal to Victor Hugo, and as the first author of "engaged" songs. Recognizing songs and their creators as works and artists that are part of the country's artistic and cultural heritage remains in France an isolated act[32] or an obstinate one[33] because *chanson française* is first and foremost considered, in practice, like the media uses of radio and television, as a consumer good that is flimsy, disposable, or recyclable.

Limited Media Coverage

Although it applies to other genres, too, the place of *chanson française* in French mass-market broadcasting continues to shrink. Since the early 2000s, we've seen ever less airtime for programs dedicated to *chanson française* on both radio and television, while entertainment programs such as *La Fête de la chanson française* mentioned previously, or the programming policies of radio stations like Chante France or Nostalgie offer nonstop broadcasts of the hits of *variété* performers from 1970 to 1990.

Thus, whereas until the 1990s one could listen to daily in-depth programs on *chanson française* on Radio France, such as *Pollen* and *Bonjour, bonjours les hirondelles*, at various times of the day, in 2014 only three programs on *chanson française* were broadcast on three evenings of the week on three different networks, but each at midnight: *Des nuits noires de monde* on Thursday on France Musique, *Regarde un peu la France* on Friday on France Inter, and *Chanson Boum* on Sunday on France Culture. It's thus necessary to look at print media to measure the status of *chanson française* from France and abroad. But here, too, the leading magazines like *Paroles et Musique* or *Chorus* (Figure 8.2) are no longer published, leaving only *Francofans*, an independent bimonthly on current French-language song,[34] *Platine, le magazine de la variété*,[35] or *Je Chante!*,[36] a magazine dedicated to the heritage of *chanson française*, but with limited circulation.

It's thus on the Internet that the diversity of the music and esthetics on offer is the most interesting. As an example, a website like *Nos enchanteurs*[37] offers regular news on the vitality and diversity of activities tied to *chanson française* that are totally absent from mass media.

A Hidden Identity

While *chanson française* was a perfectly identifiable genre until the 1980s, the change of generations, the profusion and diversity of new musical esthetics within popular music, the growing hegemony of English-speaking culture, and the political choices made by institutions with regard to music are specific factors that have reoriented the vision of the French toward *chanson française*. Thus, politicians, media outlets, and audiences have left aside *chanson française* in the diversity of its expressions in favor of other musical trends. Public policy has preferred expressions such as "youth music" in the second half of the 1980s and "current music" from the end of the 1990s to designate popular music from which representatives of the *chanson française* esthetic found themselves excluded. This lack of recognition affected several generations of artists, and in particular the singer-songwriters (Michèle Bernard, Jacques Bertin, Romain Didier, Philippe Forcioli, Rémo Gary, Jean Guidoni, Gilbert Lafaille, Allain Leprest, Véronique Pestel, etc.) who at the age of 30 or 40, decided in the same way as their elders (Barbara, Brassens, Ferré, or Sylvestre) to express themselves in a language that unites poetic or political language and classical melodies and arrangements.

Today, in the public space, often reduced to the space of media, the most visible artists expressing their engagement to French, those at the forefront of music, are associated to the esthetics of rap and slam, considered less old-fashioned and worn-out than those of *chanson française*. This evaluation, arising from lack of knowledge or consideration for a *chanson française* that is increasingly innovative (Bizzoni, Prévost-Thomas 2008), removes the players of contemporary *chanson française* from discussions of artistic engagement.

And yet if we just look at anti-Front national songs (songs opposing France's far-right National Front party) written between 2002 and 2014, they are for the most part created by artists who are the heirs of protest song heritage of *chanson française*, whatever their musical framing: from Damien Saez with "Fils de France" ("Sons of France") in 2002, written right after the first round of the presidential elections, which were favorable to the National Front,[38] to Benjamin Biolay with "Le vol noir" ("The Black Flight"), written after the European Parliament elections of May 2014, which were also favorable to the Far Right[39] and whose first lines of the chorus use the words and music of "Le Chant des Partisans" ("The Song of the Partisans"),[40] and along the way, Katerine with "Le 20–04–2005" (a song about Marine Le Pen, current president of the National Front and daughter of its founder, Jean-Marie Le Pen); Tryo with "Marine est là" ("Marine Is Here") (2012), and Melissmell with "Bleu Marine" (a play on "navy blue" and "Marine Blue") (2012).

These songs rarely become popular because they are not taken up by the media, with some journalists demonstrating their deepest disdain for them: "It seems that the National Front generates only the most deplorable ditties," wrote a journalist in a May 30, 2014, article published in Le Figaro and titled "Benjamin Biolay et les chiants des partisans" (the play on words relies on the similarity of the words "chant," or song, and "chiant," a vulgar term for "boring").

Mediation of *Chanson Française*

Thus, while despite these observations, *chanson française* remains the favorite musical genre of the French,[41] it is losing steam with the arrival of new generations and the lack of interest of influential media and public policies. Despite this, over the last fifteen years, French writers[42] and academics[43] have shown increasing interest in *chanson française* and have developed, in the interest of mediation, teachings to transmit the literary, musicological, and sociological knowledge that allow for understanding and measuring, far from ordinary representations, just how much *chanson française* is a central artistic and cultural object for our shared history.

Notes

1 "Jules Ferry" laws of June 16, 1881, and March 28, 1882.
2 French poet, writer, and journalist Claude Roy (1915–1997).
3 The MIDEM is held each winter since 1967 in Cannes.
4 The term *variétés* refers here to French mainstream popular music (*variété nationale*) and its foreign equivalent (*variété internationale*). The other 30% here are foreign *variété*.

5   Our translation, from Guillaume Leblanc, ed. 2014. *L'économie de la production musicale. Édition 2014*, 11, www.snepmusique.com/actualites-du-snep/economie-de-la-production-musicale-edition-2014.
6   Our translation. Serge Gainsbourg said this on the program *Apostrophes en chansons*, broadcast on public television network Antenne 2 on December 26, 1986.
7   This song is from the Serge Gainsbourg concept album *L'histoire de Melody Nelson* (*The Story of Melody Nelson*) from March 24, 1971. This cult album influenced many musicians, including Beck, Placebo, Portishead, and others.
8   On Friday, November 29, 2013, public television network France 2 broadcast the tenth *Fête de la chanson française*, which had 3,437,000 viewers.
9   Saturday June 14, 2014, *La chanson de L'année* (*The Song of the Year*) on TF1 (the leading broadcast television network in France) had 3,700,000 viewers.
10 Au Limonaire, Bistrot à vins et à chansons, Paris 9th arrondissement, http://limonaire.free.fr.
11 Le Forum Léo Ferré in Ivry-sur-Seine, www.forumleoferre.org.
12 This festival was created in eastern Paris in 2003 and moved to Montreuil (just outside the eastern limits of Paris) from 2005 and had its twelfth edition in June 2014. See www.festivaltaparole.org.
13 Founded in 1992, "Chansons de parole" is a festival that takes place in the town of Barjac in the Gard départe-ment in the south of France. Over the years it has become *the* summer destination for fans of "*chanson à texte.*" See www.chansonsdeparole.com.
14 With words by Édith Piaf and music by Louiguy, the emblematic song "La vie en rose," first sung by Piaf in 1947, gave its title to the international versions of the Piaf biopic directed by Olivier Dahan, known in France as *La Môme*.
15 To better understand this period in the history of *chanson française*, see Chevalier (1987) and Schlesser (2005).
16 This "quality label" was invented by Jacques Canetti, the artistic director of Philips and of the Théâtre des Trois Baudets, where singers such as Jacques Brel, Georges Brassens, Serge Gainsbourg, and Anne Sylvestre began their public careers.
17 The daily newspaper *Le Devoir* is the Quebec equivalent of *Le Monde* in France or the *New York Times* in the United States.
18 In Quebec, Canada's majority-French-speaking province, the same show simply has the title *La Voix*.
19 By "creator" we refer to any of the roles of lyricist, composer, performer, arranger, and so forth.
20 To be precise, in the early 2000s, this term designated a new generation of singers, such as Vincent Delerm, Bénabar, and Jeanne Cherhal, who all gave importance to the lyrics of their songs, which they performed in French.
21 The French branch of house music born in the 1990s and represented by artists such as Air, Laurent Garnier, Saint Germain, or Daft Punk.
22 Its slogan is "The best of current French music in London."
23 Press kit 2013, "Les succès export 2012: meilleures ventes," www.french-music.org/publications.html.
24 See the official website of the FFCF: www.ffcf.fr.
25 See the official website of the Centre de la Chanson: www.centredelachanson.com.
26 See the official website of the Hall de la Chanson: www.lehall.com.
27 "Dalida, une vie . . .," Paris city hall, May 11 to September 8, 2007.
28 "Gainsbourg 2008," Cité de la Musique, Paris, October 21, 2008, to March 1, 2009.
29 "Brassens ou la liberté," Cité de la Musique, Paris, March 16 to August 20, 2011.
30 "Trenet, le fou chantant de Narbonne à Paris," April 12 to June 30, 2013, in Paris and July 20 to October 20, 2013, in Narbonne.
31 "Barbara, la chanteuse et le photographe," Mairie du 17e arrondissement de Paris, November 4 to Decem-ber 31, 2013.
32 The artist Jacques Bertin has worked for more than ten years for a "restoration of the sung heritage" by means of courses in the performance of major works of contemporary *chanson française* unknown to the general public because of their lack of visibility. See http://velen.chez-alice.fr/bertin/atelier.htm.
33 The activities of the Hall de la Chanson, founded by Serge Hureau in 1988 with the support of the Ministry of Culture, to make *chanson française* part of French national heritage were visible almost only online until 2013. For the last year, this organization has had access to a small performance venue (140 seats) in the Parc de la Villette in Paris.
34 See their website: www.francofans.fr.
35 See their website: www.platine-mag.com.
36 See their website: www.jechantemagazine.com.
37 See their website: www.nosenchanteurs.eu.
38 The National Front candidate Jean-Marie Le Pen took 16.86% of the vote on April 21, 2002.
39 The list of the Front National headed by Marine Le Pen received 24.85% of the vote on May 25, 2014.
40 "Le chant des partisans," music by Anna Marly (1941), words by Joseph Kessel and Maurice Druon (1943), is considered *the* song of the Liberation and the French Resistance.

41 According to the latest survey of cultural practices of the French, the genres "*chansons françaises*" (13%) and "*variétés françaises*" (20%) are named as the favorite genres of French people, with classical music at 8%, rock at 7%, and jazz at 3%. In Donnat, Olivier. 2009. *Les pratiques culturelles des Français à L'ère numérique*, Enquête 2008. Paris: La Découverte/Ministère de la Culture et de la Communication, Département des études, de la prospective et des statistiques.

42 Including Annie Ernaux, Philippe Forest, Philippe Grimbert, Erik Orsenna, and Antoine Sénanque.

43 Including Bruno Blanckeman, Brigitte Buffard-Moret, Céline Cecchetto, Joëlle Deniot, Catherine Dutheil, Stéphane Hirschi, Joël July, Pascal Pistone, Catherine Rudent, and myself.

Bibliography

Aznavour, Charles. 1994. "Prends le Chorus." *Chorus, Les cahiers de la chanson* 7, Spring, 142–149. Interview with Marc Robine.

Bizzoni, Lise, and Cécile Prévost-Thomas, eds. 2008. *La chanson francophone contemporaine engagée*. Montréal: Triptyque.

Blanckeman, Bruno, and Sabine Loucif, eds. 2012. *Revue critique de fixxion française contemporaine* 5. www.revue-critique-de-fixxion-francaise-contemporaine.org.

Boileau, Josée. 2010. "Chanson française—Made in France." *Le Devoir*, March 9.

Bonnet, Gilles, ed. 2013. *La chanson populittéraire*. Paris: Kimé, Les Cahiers de Marge.

Chevalier, Marc. 1987. *Mémoires d'un cabaret, l'Écluse*. Paris: La Découverte.

Prévost-Thomas, Cécile. 1998. "La chanson francophone contemporaine: Structure, pratiques, fonctions." *Sociologie des Faits Musicaux et Modèles Culturels* 6. Paris: OMF.

Roy, Claude. 1954. *Trésor de la poésie populaire française*. Paris: Seghers.

Rudent, Catherine. 2000. "Le discours sur la musique dans la presse française: L'exemple des périodiques spécialisés en 1993." PhD diss., Université Paris-Sorbonne.

Schlesser, Gilles. 2005. *Le Cabaret "rive gauche," De la Rose Rouge au Bateau Ivre (1946–1974)*. Paris: l'Archipel.

9

Chanson Française
A Genre Without Musical Identity

Catherine Rudent

The concept of genre has received a great deal of attention in popular music studies, often from highly recognised researchers, the most prominent of whom are Fabbri (1982, 2012, 2014), Frith (1996), Moore (2001) and Brackett (2002). After more than thirty years of work in this area, Fabbri (2014, 12) has come up with a particularly concise definition of musical genre as "a set of music events regulated by conventions accepted by community." He thus settles on a very broad concept, in which the only fundamental criterion is the recognition of genre as such by a community. It may therefore come about that a genre is not evaluated in terms of its sound: "Not all musical genres are characterized by the same type of descriptors. Some genres may be characterized by some musical features, while others are determined by the calendar (e.g., Christmas music in Western cultures), or other industrial criteria" (Fabbri 2014, 16). His point is that sounds are amongst the primary criteria, but not the only ones, and sometimes not the most relevant.

If the question of genre is so central in popular music studies, this is surely because the categorisation of music plays a central role in popular music (Fabbri 1982; Frith 1996) and, probably, music in general (Fabbri 2014; Holt 2007). The proliferation of genre tags and labels is also a feature of common practice in the field of popular music. However, these designations and the reality of genres cannot be said to correlate exactly: Fabbri (2014, 10–11) points out the frequent and sometimes lengthy time lag (decades) between the practice of a genre and its sanction through the act of naming. The fact nevertheless remains that genre tags and genre labels are closely correlated to the definition and practical determination of musical genres. They can be regarded as ambiguous designations, but ones that are nevertheless used in a habitual and straightforward fashion, reflecting and enabling a process of categorisation with multiple objectives. Their primary function is one of recognition, related to the act of naming and the reflexive process to which this act belongs (Fabbri 2012, 10; 2014, 10–12). Indeed, like any designation, genres allow the grouping together of different works through classification, at the same time distinguishing these works, as a set, from other classifications, other sets and other music.

However, the fundamental epistemological function of genre names is combined with other ends, which may even hinder this primary one. Thus, a social function can be discerned, which may be ideological or political (Fabbri 1982), industrial and commercial (Frith 1996, 75–84) or linked in a more complex way to the configuration of social groups and the dynamics of their power relationships (Hamilton 2007). Among the most fascinating writings on this subject are those which show how a category and its denomination differ from musical practices (Tagg 1989) and may mask deliberate manipulation that is in conflict with the sup-posed authenticity of the genre in question (Peterson 1997; Hamilton 2007). These various studies show that designations not only do not relate to fixed entities but also are themselves of the order of process. In Fabbri's words (2012, 19), "categorization processes [. . .] are actually functioning in every moment of our interaction with music. [. . .] Musical life is a continuous process of categorization, production and recognition of the occurrences of types."

In a more diffuse but very effective way, tags take on signifiers that are less musical than symbolic, through representations that are attached to them in everyday life (Brackett 2002, 66), especially in the media, and that can in particular be located in formalised and often stereotyped formulations in the press (Rudent 2000; Escoubet 2015).

With such an accumulation of possibly divergent functions—epistemological, social, symbolic and so forth—it is easy to see how a musical tag can sometimes end up losing its relationship to musical characteristics in its designation of a set of works (Fabbri 2014, 16).

Nevertheless, it seems useful to distinguish genre tags that are partly based on sound characteristics and those that escape the criterion of sound likenesses altogether. Thus, one of the problems posed by the question of "musical genre" is understanding the extent to which this "genre" is determined by sound characteristics. Here I will look into where *chanson française* stands in this regard: if one does not know a piece of music, one cannot simply say from listening whether or not it is *chanson française*, even where one is familiar with the genre. Conversely, we cannot, when listening to a song, say that the music was influenced by *chanson*'s musical norms: in fact, it would seem that *chanson* is not associated with particular musical norms. Thus, if it is a genre (as defined by Fabbri), it would seem to be one of those genres for which musical characteristics are irrelevant.

To this first series of remarks, I would add that the meaning of the term *chanson française* can seem simple enough at first glance, compared with terms that are a priori somewhat obscure, such as *rock*, *jazz* or *reggae*: that is, a song, a short, simple vocal work, made in France,[1] should by definition be a *chanson française*. Yet this is not the case: not all songs made in France are considered to be *chanson*. This terminological oddity makes the defini-tion "*chanson française*" all the more elusive.

In this chapter I will examine three aspects of this musicological and terminological dif-ficulty. First, the semantic instability of the expression *chanson française*; next, the hetero-geneity of the music it refers to; finally, the musical diversity of *chanson* artists. Therefore, while there seems to be a consensus, in practice, on what is meant by *chanson*, this consensus very much depends on context (location, time, cultural affiliations of the person making the reference; see Fabbri 2014, 5–6) and, in addition, the genre's "canon" is extremely fluid.

Semantic Instability

The words "*chanson française*" designate a very different set of songs depending on the posi-tion of the speaker. Despite this ambiguity, the label is common, as our bibliography shows, with various works aimed at a diverse audience using them in their title. What music can be found in these books?

First, there are songs from Brassens, Brel, Ferré, Trenet and Piaf, with a somewhat lesser role for a few women artists (Gréco [Figure 9.1], Barbara, Sylvestre). While the "Left Bank

Figure 9.1   Juliette Gréco on *Music Hall*, n° 29, 1958, back cover.

cabaret" culture of Paris (Schlesser 2006) has a certain prestige, its performers are not the ones the most thoroughly presented (Mouloudji, Patachou, Frères Jacques, Catherine Sauvage, etc.). The group of "Canetti artists," corresponding in part to the previous group, is significant. Jacques Canetti, owner of Les Trois Baudets, an important venue for *chanson française*, was a figure from radio and an artistic director at Philips, and played a great role in *chanson française* during the 1950s. The artists he launched or accompanied to success include Brassens, Vian, Brel, Gréco, Guy Béart, Boby Lapointe and more. A bit of a special case, Serge Gainsbourg also belongs to a degree to these first worlds of *chanson française*, since he played and composed music, then sang, in the Parisian cabarets, and was signed on by Canetti to perform at the Trois Baudets.

Chronologically, the key period for *chanson française* is the 1950s and 1960s. The political values of the Left are very present among the performers of this time (Ferrat, Montand until 1968, Brigitte Fontaine, Reggiani, Higelin, Béranger, Barbara, etc.). The poetic ambition of the texts is also a recurring feature. The close ties between poetry and song can be found in poet-singers such as Caussimon, Ferré, Brassens and Nougaro, or poet-songwriters (Mac Orlan, Carco, Prévert, Queneau, etc.).

Other artistic families play an important role in writing on *chanson française*: the stars of the *music-hall* in the interwar period (Chevalier, Mistinguett, Baker, Sablon), those whose career extends before and after the Second World War (Mireille, Trenet, Piaf, Tino Rossi, Salvador) or right after it (Montand, Aznavour, Bécaud, Dalida). We can add the stars of the operetta through the 1950s (Luis Mariano, Georges Guétary), historic figures from the early days of the Parisian cabaret (Bruant, Jules Jouy, Mac-Nab, Xanrof, etc.), of the *café-concert* (Yvette Guilbert, Dranem, Mayol, etc.), of the *chanson réaliste* (Damia, Fréhel, Berthe Sylva, etc.), or of the cinema of the 1930s and 1940s (Jean Gabin, Suzy Delair, etc.).

Yet over time, the boundaries of *chanson française* have varied. A first break can be found in the 1960s. The trigger was the shock wave of rock 'n' roll, particularly acute in France beginning in 1960. From this time on, a chasm opens between *chanson française* and pop music from the United Kingdom and the United States. From that time on, rock becomes a pole of opposition to *chanson* and rock has often henceforth been understood, from the point of view of *chanson*, as the "Other." Because of this, the positioning of French artists with respect to musical currents in the United Kingdom and the United States, and their choice to integrate them a little, a lot or not at all, complicates their connection to *chanson française*.

Yéyé music, which emerged as of 1960, often appears as a rupture in the history of French popular music. *Yéyé* artists such as Hallyday, Gall, Hardy, Vartan, Claude François, Sheila and Mitchell were first seen as foreign to *chanson française* and symptomatic of a crisis in this music (Gainsbourg 1963). When the *yéyés* are mentioned in works dealing with *chanson française*, they are presented in works from the 1970s as middle rate or ridiculous (Calvet, Klein, Grimm 1972; Vernillat and Charpentreau 1977). That said, a new step is taken with artists such as Polnareff, Ferrer or Dutronc: they're already "post-*yéyé*," for they emerged around 1965–1966 in the wake of *yéyé* music, while practicing their profession in a different fashion, in particular due to the coherence of their musical choices. At the end of the 1960s, they begin to produce a mix of rock, pop, folk and Canetti-style *chanson française*, and are clearly included in *chanson française* in works dealing with it.

Later, during the 1970s, the terms "*rock anglo-saxon*," "*pop*" or "*rock*" would be opposed to the term "*chanson française*" (Musique en jeu 1971; Le Marcis 2001). But a new step in the musical integration of rock and *chanson* was taken between 1972 and 1980: various artists proposed a musical oeuvre even more coherent than before, by mixing the customs of France and those of the English-language "Other." Among these artists we can count Sanson, Berger, Souchon, Cabrel, Renaud and Goldman.

As a consequence of this bipolar situation, there have existed since the 1960s many French works and artists who can be found somewhere between *chanson française* and French rock: Higelin, Ribeiro, Manset, Thiéfaine, Bashung, Les Rita Mitsouko and Dominique A (as we move through the decades), cited both in *L'encyclopédie du rock français* (a work for the general public by Verlant 2000) and in the special issue "Chanson française" of the prestigious daily newspaper *Libération* (2006; Figure 9.2). There are also recognised French acts who are "even less *chanson française*" than those cited, because they appear to be "even more rock" (actually, they are bands and not individuals). But they are nonetheless found in works on *chanson française*: for example, Bijou, Starshooter, Trust, Téléphone, Niagara, Mano Negra, Bérurier Noir, Les VRP, Pigalle, Les Garçons Bouchers or Noir Désir, to speak only of the 1980s.

More recently, in the 1990s and 2000s, *chanson française* often refers to "*chanson néo-réaliste*" (neo-realistic *chanson*) (Lebrun 2009). Then, at the turn of the century, the term became closely tied to the very diverse "*nouvelle scène française*" (Delerm, Keren Ann, Biolay, Bénabar, etc.). At the same time, other forms of popular music in France, originating in the United States, are dissociated from *chanson*: rap; "*techno*" (French designation for EDM, in the 1990s), and a fuzzy grouping in rock, pop and folk music, whose artists sing more and more often in English (Moriarty, Revolver and Izia, to give only current examples).

Today, the term "*chanson française*" can be, on the musical level, an inclusive label, having assimilated rock. Or it can be a restrictive label, thus implying that the songs produced and listened to in France are no longer, since about 1960, only *chanson française*. In the first case, *chanson française* designates a huge set of works, including first the *chanson réaliste* of the 1930s and its more recent heirs; second, the verbal play and the pared-down musical resources of cabarets in the Left Bank spirit, the ideals of Canetti and their successors (in the post-war period); third, the various forms of music deeply impregnated by English-language rock and pop music (since 1960); and lastly, *variété* music[2] that benefited from intense media coverage and that reached its height in the 1970s (Joe Dassin, Aznavour, Bécaud, Claude François, Sardou, Mireille Mathieu, etc.). In the second case, it designates essentially the first two of these four trends.

Seen from other countries, these limits disappear, leaving a shapeless blob: for example, in his album *Après* (2012), Iggy Pop covers five *chanson française* works of radically divergent contexts and musical contents: "Et si tu n'existais pas" (Delanoë and Lemesle, Dassin 1975), "La Javanaise" (Gainsbourg for Gréco 1963), "La Vie en rose" (Piaf 1946), "Les Passantes" (poem by Antoine Pol set to music by Brassens in 1972) and "Syracuse" (Dimey and Salvador 1962). These pieces have nothing in common other than the cultural aura of France and the French language, already found in his album *Préliminaires* (2009), which included "Les feuilles mortes" by Prévert and Kosma.

Figure 9.2 *"Chanson française,"* special issue of *Libération*, 2006.

As we can see, the term "*chanson française*" changes meaning over the decades and depending on one's point of view. It does not designate a stable set of works, and it makes it difficult to study.

Use of the French language is one of the criteria applied since the 1990s for belonging to *chanson française*: there would thus be an equivalence between *chanson "française"* and *chanson "en français"* ("in French"), a characteristic that is becoming less and less dominant in overall music production in France. Yet we must consider the limits of this criterion: why should so many songs produced in France by French artists or by artists living in France not be considered *chanson française*? We'll see that this cannot be for reasons of musical style, since the musical diversity of the designation is very broad.

Stylistic Diversity

The second half of the twentieth century is marked by an extreme dispersion of musical styles of *chanson française*. A synthetic description will give some idea of the diversity of these works.

There is the spare style, centred on the pairing of a voice (a single voice, recorded close up and highlighted in the mix) and a piano or acoustic guitar (recorded at a distance, and mixed at a lower level), with the discreet support of one or two other instruments, also acoustic. This is the style of the recordings of Brassens (two acoustic guitars and a double bass), or of many songs by Barbara, close to simple piano and voice renditions, including "Nantes," "Attendez que ma joie revienne," "A mourir pour mourir," "Le bel âge," "La solitude" and so on: these songs are accompanied by a piano, a pizzicato double bass[3] and often an accordion, and sometimes with the rhythmic complement of a ride cymbal or a melodic touch from Michel Portal's saxophone.

This discreet presence of instruments, found in many other recordings from many other artists, is a sign of musical "distinction"—Bourdieu's surveys for *La Distinction* were in fact carried out in the 1960s—and of the refusal of facile seduction. This type of instrumentation is also an attribute closely associated with the singer (Brassens accompanies himself on the guitar, Barbara sings at the piano). Finally, it refers to their status, itself full of "distinction," that of singer-songwriter: these artists compose the piece on the instrument, then keep it at the heart of their performances on stage and in the recording studio. This pared-down style also recalls the tiny stages and the "Left Bank" cabarets in which there simply was no room for more musicians.

But this sobriety is not inevitable in this repertoire, since recording studios offered plenty of space: sophisticated arrangements could be, and often were, produced when the repertoire was recorded. Brel, Ferré, Lapointe, Gréco and many other "Left Bank" cabaret performers offered on their recordings from the 1950s and 1960s the refined orchestrations of Goraguer (Vian, Gainsbourg), Popp, Rauber (Brel), Defaye (Ferré) and so on. Here is a second style, very present in the 1960s. It can be recognised by its frequent use of woodwinds (clarinet, oboe, flute, bassoon, etc.), of percussion instruments rarely found in other styles (e.g., the glockenspiel for Rauber), but with a total rejection of the standard drumset. This style also refined the use of brass instruments: observe the backing melody of bugle over a basis of string instruments holding notes and slow piano arpeggios by Jean-Michel Defaye for Léo

Ferré's "Avec le temps." The lead vocal is often set to a lot of rich and inventive melodic additional elements: see the unending enrichment of nursery rhyme melodies by Rauber in Anne Sylvestre's *Fabulettes* albums. In this style, the musical language is close to high Western art, tinged with a certain modernism, when it borrows the modal colour of French composers from the early twentieth century like Ravel or Debussy.

In addition, we can find from the 1960s to 1970s more conventional orchestrations and recordings, very different from those discussed previously: I would call that second kind of orchestration "classical *variété*." This music dominated media and the music industry, and is well represented by Aznavour, Salvador, Bécaud, Dalida, Mireille Mathieu, Sardou, Claude François ("Comme d'habitude," "Le téléphone pleure") or Serge Lama ("Je suis malade").[4] It gives a sensation of undifferentiated music, of standardised arrangements, texts and tempos—for example, with drums oddly overlaid on a *java* in "Viens dans ma rue" (Mireille Mathieu), or the indistinct use of an invasive reverb. From the point of view of instruments, this style gives the leading melodic role to violins and uses a fairly loud electric bass and drums playing terribly flat formulas; it systematically rejects the electric guitar, uses brass instruments for punctuations and occasional martial tones, erases woodwinds and ties everything together with the formulaic use of the piano.

As for the voice, the performer of "classical *variété*" sings with an open throat: a homogenous range, with an expressive use of the upper end of the range, many long notes, with plenty of vibrato and generously held at the end of the musical phrase. This type of singing goes with a position free from the irony or humour so common in the previous two styles discussed. The singer, emotional and invested in the song, sings on the surface, whether it be Aznavour, Bécaud, Claude François, Mireille Mathieu, Sardou or Johnny Hallyday after his *yéyé* phase. The melodic curves offer the singers opportunities to show off a beautiful voice: they complacently repeat full and long musical phrases (the *discursive repetition* described by Middleton 1983), which intensively use "sequences" and symmetry. Sequence consists of immediately repeating the same melody transposed higher or lower in a staircase mode (chorus of "Chanson populaire," verse of "Comme d'habitude," two hits from Claude François); symmetry often consists in an "antecedent-consequent" structure, which means that the melody is sung twice, but ends with suspense the first time and concludes the second time, as in Aznavour's "La Bohème," verse and chorus.

This melodic sentimentality is supported with classical harmony, in the sense that the chords used belong to the vocabulary of Western written music from the eighteenth century on, without any update from the twentieth century. Furthermore, this style avoids "Americanisms" like binary backbeat rhythms, blue notes, rock or blues or jazz harmonies. No melodies broken up by riffs, no vocal contrast between chest voice and head voice or falsetto (as in rock or soul music). No phonographic effects (chorus, delay, movements through panning, etc.): this classical *variété* limits itself to a natural mixing of instruments, places the voice up front and applies to it a very audible reverb.

Lastly, while most of the songs in this style are in four-four time, the use of three-four time remains possible (Aznavour's "La Bohème," Mireille Mathieu's "Viens dans ma rue"). This rhythm allows for the recycling of the song styles of the 1930s, particularly waltz and *java*. Thus in the heart of a radically transformed France of the 1970s (Mendras 1994), this three-four rhythm, anachronistic, and totally absent from the English-language hits of the time, survives the changes in the music industry and affirms a form of Frenchness, of *francité*, following the recommendation of Barthes to name myths with neologisms ending in *-té* (1957, 206).

From all these musical habits, there comes for French "classical *variété*" a timelessness, sometimes an old-fashioned quality, reinforced by the presence of a symphonic orchestra and an immemorial harmony. This is yet another characteristic of mythological constructions: "Myth is constituted by the loss of the historical quality of things: Things lose the memory that they once were made" (original French in Barthes 1957, 230). The lyrics of these songs, very often, are outside of time, sometimes in no identifiable place other than a stereotypical celebration of a Paris that has no more reality than postcards of Montmartre or the Eiffel Tower.

Another stylistic colour of *chanson française* is jazz. But the uses of jazz are divergent. Important in the *chanson française* from the 1930s (compositions of Trenet or Mireille), it served as an engine for musical renewal: jazz songs were at this time the cutting edge of modernity. Later, in the *chanson française* of the 1950s, the presence of a jazz colour has already become more conformist: calling up images of Broadway or Django Reinhardt, certain repertoires of *chanson française* coloured by jazz adopt the musical habits already well established in musical entertainment for two decades. A good example is the repertoire of Yves Montand, at the height of his first success as a singer in the 1950s. "Du soleil plein la tête," "C'est si bon" or "Sanguine" borrow the musical colours of jazz, and the musicians who play with him are often jazz artists. Among them, Hubert Rostaing, an arranger who played clarinet and sax; pianist and composer Bob Castella; and guitarist Henri Crolla. Later still, singers turn to a jazz of the past to offer risk-free texture to *variété*: "Je m'voyais déjà" (1960) and "For me formidable" (1963) (Aznavour), "Dimanche à Orly" (Bécaud, 1963), "J'aime les filles" (Dutronc, 1967), and so on. At the same time, jazz sounds allowed for the Left Bank *chanson française* to open up and escape the sober settings of the cabaret and gain in scope and sophistication: embodied by Vian, a connoisseur of jazz and a jazz musician himself ("J'suis snob," "Je bois"), in the 1950s, this trend could be found in Gainsbourg in his first period (roughly from 1958 to 1964, in particular *Gainsbourg confidentiel*), Barbara ("Pierre," "Ni belle ni bonne," "Toi L'homme"), and Nougaro in almost all his songs. Even more recently, jazz tends, in songs like those of Biolay, to be used as a sound of the past ("La mélodie du bonheur," 2001, "La toxicomanie," 2009) and to become an auxiliary to signify nostalgia.

Thus, jazz in *chanson française*, first the sound of modernity, then a label for musical competency (Vian 1958, 82), progressively becomes the classical language of *chanson française*. Closely bound for ninety years to *chanson française*, jazz changes meaning over the years.

The stylistic diversity of *chanson française* also comes from the fact that it seems to be blown hither and thither with the winds of musical fashion. It is caught up by all the musical changes from the Anglo-American scene, unable to defend itself, one could say. This fascinated absorption of trends takes place with the twist in the *yéyé* years and continues with the series of hits by Ferrer in 1966 and 1967, successful imitations of the Stax sound; the evolution of Gainsbourg, from his pop period in the 1960s to his reggae album in 1979, and of course his concept albums of the 1970s that play with the codes of prog rock; with the jazz-rock of Zoo accompanying two Ferré albums in 1971; the disco-funk of the last two hits

Figure 9.3 Les Têtes Raides, *Gratte Poil*, Tôt Ou Tard, 2000, compact disc back and front cover.

of Claude François, "Magnolias for ever" and "Alexandrie Alexandra" (1977); the imitations of new-wave or post-punk sounds in Bashung's "Gaby oh Gaby" in 1980, or in the hits of Indochine from 1982 on.

In contrast, the redundant processes of the *chanson néo-réaliste* of the 1990s and 2000s (Les Têtes Raides [Figure 9.3], La Tordue, Les Ogres de Barback, Les Hurlements d'Léo, Les Fils de Teuhpu, Debout sur le Zinc, La Rue Kétanou) come to embody a certain stability, a musical identity proper to France: the bands often have many members, tied to street performance and the circus on one hand, and on the other, the punk and *rock alternatif* scene of the 1980s. They multiply the number of instruments, sometimes improvised instruments, and favour multi-instrumentalists. Their musical style, arising from the fast and brutal rhythms of punk, adds trends perceived as belonging to *chanson française* (accordion,[5] waltzes) and others perceived as Roma (sometimes with a reference to Goran Bregovic and his use of traditional music of the Balkans), as well as allusions to ska and reggae. These diverse sources take distance from Anglo-American influence, offering rapid tempos, systematic offbeats hammered on the acoustic guitar or brass, a rudimentary harmony (perfect chords) and rustic melodies, sung by rough male voices, heterogeneous, without vibrato, off key or with a limited range.

Fickleness

In connection with this diversity of styles, the performers are musically versatile. They change musical style as if changing a costume:[6] Vian, Ferré, Gréco, Gainsbourg, Higelin, Les Rita Mitsouko and more recently Biolay, Camille or Damien Saez are not identified by a musical style. At the same time, their vocal style is constant. Change almost never affects their voices, which are often quite distinctive. A few exceptional talents may change their vocal style depending on the song (see Juliette Noureddine, known as Juliette), but with limits. We can therefore consider that the musical identity of *chanson française* performers concerns first and foremost their voice. It's quite remarkable in the case of Gainsbourg, a veritable musical chameleon, but who remains constant in his use of a voice that is weak in timbre, low in dynamic range and insufficiently supported, combined with a frequent use of (non-rhythmic) speech rather than singing.

We can distinguish among these chameleon performers between the opportunistic followers and the ironic strategists: Hallyday, Claude François, Sardou and Dalida greatly change their musical style over the years, conforming to musical trends that have reached greatest international market penetration at a given time. Although they're singers who don't write their own music, the choice is theirs: at their level of fame, the composers and arrangers working for them follow the singers' artistic direction, as can be seen in the biographies of a Claude François or a Pierre Delanoë. This permeability to profitable trends allows them to be qualified as followers. Less pejoratively, we could invent the term "musical transigence" (as opposed to "intransigence"), which means accepting the changes in musical styles as they come, rather than attempting to lead these changes.

The case is different when, in the 1960s and 1970s, Gainsbourg moves from a jazzy cabaret style to perverted *yéyé* (songs for France Gall from 1964 to 1967), to a falsely superficial pop (songs for or with Brigitte Bardot, 1967–1968), to concept albums with inventive musical arrangements, like those of Jean-Claude Vannier in *Histoire de Melody Nelson* in 1971, to the reggae of *Aux armes et caetera* (1979). It's true that he chose musical styles of the day, but this choice was not made with an eye on the US charts. For Gainsbourg, the point was to perceive what at a given moment was musically pertinent, even if this meant abandoning the aesthetically purist ideals of his first creative period. Similarly, Higelin adopts in *BBH 75* tones from rock, blues and funk which had not been his before. Gréco sings on electro loops in her 2004 album. What is most important, for Gainsbourg, is that these changes of style are made with ironic strategies. "Aux armes et cætera" is particularly enlightening. The text of "La Marseillaise" (the national anthem of France), with its eighteenth-century-flavored language and its typically heroic accents, is most strangely carried by a reggae music, with its transgressive casualness. The dignified spirit of the national anthem is thus deeply perverted. The song is effectively derided without a single word being changed, aside for the disrespectful truncation of the chorus: this internal contradiction between the letter and the spirit of the message is the very essence of irony.

The humourous, ironic, and detached use of musical styles, preferably incongruous with respect to the lyrics, can also be found in Boris Vian ("La java des bombes atomiques"), Brel ("La valse à mille temps"), Léo Ferré ("Monsieur Barclay"), Gotainer ("Le mambo du décalco," "Capitaine hard rock"), Katerine (*Robots après tout*) and so on. It turns a power struggle on its head: in a context where some musical styles impose their hegemony on the cultural space, invading it with an almost irresistible force, these songs adopt processes and musical colours that are almost obligatory, but turning them to create meanings that are often subtle, pushing them beyond their obvious use. Stylistic humour is here a means of musical "resistance."

With other artists, music is a functional support, relatively indifferent, for the presentation of voice and lyrics. For Ferré, Leprest and Damien Saez, it sometimes seems to be just a basic setting for the text of the song. In this case, changes in musical style can be seen as a sort of indifference to style. It is not impossible that this is the legacy of an attitude like that of *chansonniers* (Vernillat and Charpentreau 1977, 22–40) who would place their voice and texts on pre-existing melodies. This hypothesis is attractive because it establishes a sort of coherence in the history of *chanson française*. But a genuine demonstration of this connection would be a huge musicological endeavour that no one has imagined undertaking so far.

Conclusion

Instability, heterogeneity and change are various aspects of the fundamental musical dispersion of *chanson française*. A fourth aspect will be mentioned here as a hypothesis—that of artistic singularities without heirs.

We might expect that the great innovators like Ferré, Brassens, Barbara or Gainsbourg would have followers, but this is not the case. From the Second World War on, with the exception of *yéyé*, *rock alternatif* and *chanson néo-réaliste*, there is hardly anything like a collective style in *chanson française*. For example, the music included in the name "*nouvelle scène française*" at the turn of the millennium in fact covers a wide range of musical styles. Actually, in the forefront of French popular music we find first and foremost personal styles that cannot be described by their resemblance to their predecessors, and which do not have, in a musical sense, successors. The worldwide musical domination of the United States and the United Kingdom that marked the second half of the twentieth century perhaps acted in France as a strong external current, creating the perception of a French "self" as marginal, and making it hard for a style shared by French artists to take root with performers recognising value independent of English-language music.

Whatever the case, *chanson française* is not defined musically. It is rather a collection of singularities, with its major performers, its evocative locations and its key works, unconnected by any musical throughline.

Yet many in France love this hard-to-grasp collection. They savour the unique artistic density of Brassens, Gréco, Brel, Barbara, Ferré, Juliette and so on. Others, in France and abroad, are fond of a profoundly different music under the same title of "*chanson française*": the music sung by a Bécaud, Aznavour or Piaf. We cannot assign to these cultural objects, so famous but so varied, a musical identity that would summarize their *francité*. Doing so would prevent us from seeing "what kind of music" is actually there—diverse and without any stable sonic identity.

Notes

1   We must distinguish it, therefore, from songs that are "in French"—that is, French-language songs, as referred to in work by Cécile Prévost-Thomas (e.g., Prévost-Thomas and Bizzoni 2008).
2   In this chapter, we will use "*variété*" in French for this type of very commercial popular music that dominates recorded music and music broadcasts.
3   That is to say, played by plucking the strings.
4   Among the musicians who master these musical "tricks": Franck Pourcel, Paul Mauriat, Raymond Lefèvre, Gabriel Yared, Christian Gaubert and so forth.
5   The accordion is at the heart of *chansons réalistes* of the 1930s ("La guinguette a fermé ses volets"), that were continued by Piaf ("L'accordéoniste," 1940), and that would become a symbol of "*francité*" ever since ("L'accordéon" by Gainsbourg for Gréco, albums of Barbara in the 1960s). See the discussion of Guibert (2006, 259–262), on the diversification of cultural references at the end of the 1980s, in the "second wave of alternative groups" and the emergence of a "new *chanson réaliste*."

6   There are also songs that change, that voluntarily use in each section different musical styles: "Il a fallu," "Le chef d'orchestre est amoureux" (Yves Montand), "Le jazz et la java" (Nougaro), "Les plaisirs démodés" (Aznavour) and so on.

Bibliography

Barthes, Roland. 1957. "Le mythe aujourd'hui." In *Mythologies*, 191–247. Paris: Editions du Seuil.

Bonnieux, Bertrand, Pascal Cordereix, and Élizabeth Giuliani. 2004. *Souvenirs, souvenirs . . . Cent ans de chanson française*. Paris: Gallimard/Bibliothèque nationale de France.

Bourdieu, Pierre. 1979. *La Distinction*. Paris: Les Editions de Minuit.

Brackett, David. 2002. "(In Search of) Musical Meaning: Genres, Categories, and Crossover." In *Popular Music Studies*, edited by David Hesmondhalgh and Keith Negus, 65–83. London: Arnold.

Brunschwig, Chantal, Louis-Jean Calvet, and Jean-Claude Klein. 1972. *Cent ans de Chanson française*. Paris: Editions du Seuil.

Canetti, Jacques. 2008. *Mes 50 ans de chansons françaises*. Paris: Flammarion.

Dicale, Bertrand. 2006. *La Chanson française pour les nuls*. Paris: Editions Générales First.

Escoubet, Stéphane. 2015. "La légitimation d'une pop 'indépendante' en France: The Divine Comedy d'après *Les Inrockuptibles*, une étude de cas." PhD diss., Université de Paris-Sorbonne.

Fabbri, Franco. 1982. "What Kind of Music." *Popular Music* 2:131–144.

———. 2012. *Genre Theories and Their Applications in the Historical and Analytical Study of Popular Music: A Commentary on My Publications*. Huddersfields: University of Huddersfield.

———. 2014. "Music Taxonomies: An Overview." www.academia.edu/14384292/Music_Taxonomies_an_Overview.

Frith, Simon. 1996. *Performing Rites*. Cambridge: Harvard University Press.

Gainsbourg, Serge. 1963. "Serge Gainsbourg . . . et la nouvelle vague" (interview by Denise Glaser), *Discorama* (3DVD), INA 2008.

Guibert, Gérôme. 2006. *La Production de la culture*. Paris and St Amant Tallende: Irma/editions Seteun.

Hamilton, Marybeth. 2007. *In Search of the Blues: Black Voices, White Visions*. London: Jonathan Cape.

Holt, Fabian. 2007. *Genre in Popular Music*. Chicago and London: The University of Chicago Press.

July, Joël. 2007. *Esthétique de la chanson française contemporaine*. Paris: L'Harmattan.

Lebrun, Barbara. 2009. *Protest Music in France*. Farnham: Ashgate.

Le Marcis, Monique. 2001. "Les années 70 ou l'âge d'or de RTL avec Monique Le Marcis" (interview by Gilles Verlant). In *40 ans de tubes*, edited by Fabrice Ferment and le SNEP, 61. Clichy: Editions Larivière.

Libération Hors-série. 2006. "Chanson française 1973–2006. Paroles, musiques & polémiques." Special issue. Paris: SARL Libération.

Mendras, Henri. 1994 [1988]. *La Seconde Révolution française, 1965–1984*. Paris: Gallimard.

Middleton, Richard. 1983. "Play It Again, Sam." *Popular music* 3:235–270.

Moore, Allan F. 2001. "Categorical Conventions in Music Discourse: Style and Genre." *Music & Letters* 82(3):432–442.

Musique en jeu. 1971. Section "La pop music" 2:66–110.

Peterson, Richard A. 1997. *Creating Country Music: Fabricating Authenticity*. Chicago and London: The University of Chicago Press.

Prévost-Thomas, Cécile, and Lise Bizzoni, eds. 2008. *La chanson francophone contemporaine engagée*. Montréal: Triptyque.

Reger, Dietmar, ed. 1988. *La Chanson française et son histoire*. Tübingen: Gunter Narr Verlag.

Robine, Marc. 2004. *Il était une fois la chanson française des origines à nos jours*. Paris: Librairie Arthème Fayard/Editions du Verbe (Chorus).

Rudent, Catherine. 2000. "Le discours sur la musique dans la presse spécialisée grand public." PhD diss., Université de Paris-Sorbonne.

Schlesser, Gilles. 2006. *Le Cabaret "rive gauche." De la Rose rouge au Bateau ivre (1946–1974)*. Paris: L'Archipel.

Tagg, Philip. 1989. "Open Letter: 'Black Music', 'Afro-American Music' and 'European Music.'" *Popular Music* 8(3):285–298.

Verlant, Gilles, ed. 2000. *L'Encyclopédie du rock français*. Paris: Éditions Hors Collection.

Vernillat, France, and Jacques Charpentreau. 1977 [1971]. *La Chanson française*. Paris: Presses Universitaires de France.

Vian, Boris. 1997 [1958]. *En avant la zizique*. Paris: Pauvert.

10

Rap Audiences in France
The Diversification and Heterogenisation of the Appeal of Rap Music?

Stéphanie Molinero

Understood as "the half-spoken, half-sung delivery of complex, rhyming and rhythmical texts, set over a musical backing composed of music samples and other sound effects" (Lapassade and Rousselot 1990, 9), rap music very quickly caught the attention of French sociology.[1] Studies initially focussed on the (professional and amateur) producers of rap music and not on its recipients.[2] Specifically, the first sociologists to conduct research into rap music concentrated on the production of rap music as a means of social integration: both integration into French society as a whole (Green and Desverité 1997, 169–213), and integration into smaller social groups such as the hip hop community (Bazin 1995), a community which places itself or which aims to place itself, according to Manuel Boucher (1998) and Béatrice Sberna (2001), in symbolic opposition to wider French society.

Rap music has thus been seen essentially as a "response from the *banlieues*" (Calio 1998), or at least as a response to a situation of social domination. More recently, but still within the field of sociology, research perspectives have been extended through studies on rap artists as "professionals," with investigations being led into the population of rap artists (Jouvenet 2006), public policies relating to hip hop (Lafargue de Grangeneuve 2008), the economics of rap music (Guibert 2000, 56; Hammou 2008, 127–141) and even the social "world" of professional rap artists (Hammou 2012). The only research to raise the issue of rap music reception has been Anthony Pecqueux's analysis of the various types of rap music, investigating as it did the different listening experiences provoked by each musical type (Pecqueux 2007).

My contribution to the field will tackle this question of audiences. It is based for the most part on a doctoral thesis which undertook a quantitative and qualitative study in 2003 and 2004 on the subject of the recipients of rap music (members of the rap music audience who have actively chosen to listen to rap). This chapter will first present the understanding of rap music on which this research is based, before broaching the question of audiences as described in the results of statistical studies. It will then set out, using the findings of a survey, the profile of several categories of rap music recipients and the manner in which the audience of this music is structured in France today.[3] In this way, this chapter will contribute towards a better understanding of the manner in which France has once again appropriated, as with jazz and rock music, a musical genre which originated in the United States, and the status of rap music in the processes of cultural legitimisation that jazz[4] and rock[5] underwent before it.

Positioning of the Researcher

In contrast to earlier studies by French sociologists, I have decided not to identify rap music solely with the "problem neighbourhoods" of France, but to consider it as a form of music which, whilst holding strong ties with life in these neighbourhoods, has spread across the whole of French society. Guided by previous research into rap music, I have also decided not to consider rap as a form of music which should be treated from a perspective which might look into the migrant status or the cultural, and perhaps ethnic, origins of its recipients; this is contrary to the perspectives which dominate English-language literature on rap music. I have done this for several reasons. First, the social reality of France is not the same as that of the United States: if it seems obvious to make the link between hip hop culture and the African-American community, the diversity of origins among French citizens coming from migrant backgrounds makes it impossible to extricate one particular "ethnic" community which might be particularly involved in the reception (and even in the production) of rap music in France. The only link that can be made, albeit only in a partial way, concerns rap music and *banlieue* culture. It was for this reason that this research project did not support a conceptualisation of rap as a type of music which can be linked, in some way or another, to a specific group, defined by its cultural origins or ethnicity, but instead considered it a form of popular music, more easily understood in terms of the social background of its producers and recipients than by their belonging to a particular ethnic community. In this way, this research project might appear very French in that it places more emphasis on analysis based on social context (most notably, on social class) than on ethnic, or racial, origins.[6]

Conceptualised in this way as popular music, rap has been considered here both as a music of mass appeal, and as a variety of music which has been produced for a narrower audience via the "underground" scene. It has also been considered as an example of popular art, with all the complexities that this term brings with it: as a form of music whose words reveal feelings of oppression, but also as a form of music that has succeeded in achieving a certain level of symbolic autonomy.

Working with such a definition, it is difficult to imagine that French rap music might be received by a socially homogenous audience, whose members all share the same point of view on every instance of rap music, and it is with this purpose of understanding how the audiences of rap music are structured in France that this project has been undertaken. The field research therefore gave priority to the "classic" tools of sociology (the questionnaire and the interview) rather than to a more ethnological approach as is most often used in France when analysing popular cultures.

The Audience of Rap Music in 1997 and 2008

Based on the results of a statistical study conducted on a much larger scale into the audience of rap music in France (Donnat 1998 & 2009), we notice that the recipients of rap music are mainly men, "young people" and members of the working classes, but that they are socially more and more diversified. We present here two snapshots of the rap audiences, from 1997 and 2008, whilst highlighting the evolutions in the population of rap music recipients during the period.[7]

First, rap music is enjoyed by nearly three times as many French people in 2008 as in 1997: 5% of French people report that they listen to rap music in 1997, compared with 14% in 2008.

If, between 1997 and 2008, the proportion of men listening regularly to rap music has multiplied by a factor of 2.4 (passing from 7% to 17%), that of women has more than tripled (from 3% to 11%). If rap music remains most often listened to by men, women are thus shown to be appreciating it more and more.

In the same way, the penetration rates of this activity, considered here with respect to age group, have all increased over the period. Nevertheless, the growth is higher as age increases. Whilst the penetration rate of listening to rap music grew, between 1997 and 2008, by a factor of 1.5 amongst 15- to 19-year-olds (passing from 28% to 42%), it quadrupled amongst 20- to 24-year-olds (passing from 10% to 43%), grew by a factor of 7 amongst 25- to 34-year-olds (passing from 3% to 21%) and by a factor of 10 amongst 35- to 44-year-olds (passing from 1% to 10%). We see a similar progression in the reception of rap amongst those aged 55 and over: not one participant from this age bracket reported that they listened to rap in 1997; in 2008, however, 2% of 55- to 64-year-olds and 1% of those aged 65 years and over answered that they listened regularly to rap music. We can conclude therefore that rap music continues to appeal most to "the youth," but that, as the years pass, and as "the youth" of the 1980s and 1990s grows older whilst continuing to enjoy this type of music, or as they begin to enjoy it, the popularity of rap music is tending to spread across all age groups. We can thus assume that, as with rock music, the audience for rap music will develop over the years into an older audience, whether it succeeds in renewing its appeal amongst younger people or not (a feat that it has achieved so far, at least until 2008). To summarise, we can state that the audience of rap music is a relatively young audience, but that it is less and less so.

In the same way, the proportion of individuals listening regularly to rap music is higher amongst those individuals who have qualifications below baccalaureate level[8] (more than 10% for those holding any qualification level lower than the baccalaureate in 2008) than amongst those who hold qualifications at a higher level (between 8% and 10% according to the level considered). Nevertheless, we notice that the proportion of participants holding a qualification from a higher education institution grew by a factor of almost three between 1997 and 2008, which is not the case for other levels of qualification (except for one), for whom the increase is less. We can conclude from this that if rap music is still most often enjoyed by individuals with a relatively low level of education, the level of education of the general rap music audience has tended to increase with time.

A similar conclusion can be drawn by observing the professional status of rap music recipients (or that of the head of their household when they are not yet in employment). In 2008, rap music is listened to most by labourers (18%) and employees (15%) than by associate professionals (12%), middle managers and other similar professionals (9%), or tradesmen and business owners (9%). The increase in people listening to rap music amongst the working classes is greater than that found in the middle classes, but it should nonetheless be noted that the popularity of rap music in these middle classes also grew significantly between 1997 and 2008.

A final observation comes from the comparison of the figures from 2003 and 1997 (those from 2008 having not yet been published): the penetration rate of the appeal of rap music remained generally the same in Paris as in other urban areas, whatever their size, between 1997 and 2003, but it nearly doubled in rural communities. We also have seen that in 2003, the proportion of people living in rural zones within the wider audience of rap music is the same as that of people living in these same zones within the national population. In addition, it should be noted that if the proportion of farm workers (or of the children of farm workers) listening to rap music was non-existent in 1997, it grew to 9% in 2008. Rap music has thus succeeded in establishing itself right across France, and is no longer the preserve of urban areas (nor indeed of deprived neighbourhoods in major urban areas).

In summary, the analysis of the statistical study results concerning the popularity of rap music brings us to the following conclusions: rap music is listened to most in France by men, but more and more women are beginning to enjoy it; it is most popular amongst people aged 25 and under, but its popularity is now spreading into other age categories; less well-educated people form the majority of the rap music audience, but the proportion of higher education graduates within this audience is growing; and finally, if rap music is listened to noticeably more by labourers and employees than by managers, the recipients of rap music are increasingly drawn from the middle and upper classes of society. We can thus conceptualise the audience of rap music as an audience which is undergoing a process of growth and diversification.

It is this question of the diversity of rap music audiences that motivated our field research. This was complemented by other sources of information: most notably, for what will be presented in this chapter, by an analysis of the textual and musical content of thirty-three rap albums as released by the twenty French artists most often cited during the survey.[9]

The Recipient Categories

Several factors contribute towards the structuring of the population formed by rap music recipients:

- the social background, age category and gender of the recipient
- the level of the recipient's interest in rap music, an interest which allows them to expand their musical capital and especially their "rapological" capital, understood as the collection of resources, knowledge, listening experiences and social experiences that relate to rap music
- the values associated with rap music and hip hop culture
- the distribution methods by which the music is accessed.

As a result, four categories of rap music recipients have emerged.

The "Consumers" of Rap Music

Individuals belonging to this category listen to rap music frequently and regularly via mass media outlets, and prefer artists and groups such as Rohff, Sniper, 113, Booba and, to a lesser extent, Kery James and La Fonky Family. Within this group, members of the youngest age category, as well as women and the working classes,[10] are over-represented. The "consumers" appreciation of rap music is not motivated by ethical or aesthetic considerations. They prefer "mass market" rap music, and their tastes are guided by fluctuations in the media exposure given to different artists. In this way, their preferences follow the latest trends and depend on the musical recommendations of the mass media, particularly the radio station "Skyrock."

The artists that are particularly enjoyed by rap music "consumers" frame their discourse within the context of the deprived neighbourhoods, describing the situation there with reference to the issue of immigration in particular. They demonstrate a firm rejection of political life, adhere to an established religion (Catholicism or Islam)[11] and express an ambivalent relationship with money (they criticise it as an indicator of social inequalities whilst desiring it nevertheless). The two artists that distance themselves most from this image are the group La Fonky Family, who maintain their adherence to hip hop culture, and Kery James, who, in contrast to the six other groups and artists, voices a strong criticism of certain young people living in these deprived neighbourhoods. This could in part explain why these two artists are less popular than Booba, Rohff, Sniper and 113.

More than the other rap artists frequently cited by the other survey participants, these artists generally construct their backing tracks from upbeat African-American music such as funk and disco (113), non-Western traditional music (Booba and Kery James), and pop music (Rohff, Figure 10.1).

The music of this last rapper, Rohff, as well as that of the group Sniper, is characterised, in contrast with other artists, by the prominence of violent sounds made by weapons, or, in the case of Rohff, of animal noises, particularly those of strong or dangerous animals (lion, wolf, horse).

The "General Public" of Rap Music

Individuals belonging to this group are less regular listeners to rap music than those belonging to the "consumers" group, although, as with this previous category, their tastes are still conditioned by the choices made by mass media outlets. As a result, they prefer "headline" acts, such as NTM, IAM, MC Solaar and, to a lesser extent, Oxmo Puccino. It is useful to note here that an appreciation for the female rapper Diam's can be considered as the characteristic that links the rap "consumers" and "general public" categories, given that Diam's is popular both with individuals belonging to the "general public" group (and particularly with women belonging to the "general public" group) and with individuals belonging to the rap "consumers" group (and again particularly with women belonging to the rap "consumers" group). The "general public" category is not defined by any specific social groupings when compared with the wider rap audience.

The "Fans" of Rap Music

Members of this category have a strong interest in rap music and their appreciation of the genre is governed both by ethical and aesthetic considerations (such as the vocal and rhythmic prowess of the rappers, the energy contained within their music or even the inventiveness of their backing track). They are particularly attracted to independent artists and groups (Sages Poètes de la Rue, La Rumeur, Assassin, Fabe, X Men). They are spread across all social classes, but differ from other recipients, in addition to what has already been noted, by the

Figure 10.1 Rohff, *La fierté des nôtres*, EMI, 2004, compact disc front cover.

fact that they are generally older and more often men. Links can be made between the "fans" and the "general public" by means of their common appreciation of the music of Oxmo Puccino (Figure 10.2) and NTM, this artist and this group being enjoyed more by these two categories of recipients than by the others.

More than any other group of recipients, the "fans" associate adherence to hip hop culture with a system of values and attitudes: non-violence; the adoption of positive, laid-back, friendly and tolerant attitudes; self-respect and respect of others; honesty; unity; creativity. Furthermore, the "fans" make much less than other recipients (and above all than the "consumers") of the link between adherence to hip hop culture and wearing particular clothes (street wear) or simply listening to rap music. Rather than associating adherence to hip hop culture with a specific social practice (listening to rap music or wearing a particular type of clothing), therefore, the "fans" define their belonging to this subculture by a general state of mind and a particular attitude towards rap music.

Figure 10.2 Oxmo Puccino, *Le cactus de Sibérie*, Delabel, 2004, compact disc front cover.

The music of the ten artists most frequently cited by members of both the "general public" and the "fans" categories is varied: these artists adopt a wide range of different musical styles in more or less equal measure, and they do not present any particularities as striking as those artists which were preferred by the "consumers." Their lyrics often formulate some kind of social and political critique which goes beyond the description of everyday life for the inhabitants of deprived neighbourhoods.

Survey participants frequently comment on the lyrics or *flow* of these artists, and these features are more systematically mentioned in reference to these artists than the other ten most frequently cited artists. The interview data shows that the music and lyrics of these artists is enjoyed for any of a number of reasons: from the themes that they rap about and their lyrics to their *flow* and their music. Their musical output offers a wider range, wider than that of the other artists, of appreciable qualities. In this way, the plurality of different ways of enjoying their music explains how they have managed, more than the other artists, to diversify their audience.

The "Discerning Public" of Rap Music

This category could also be named, more colloquially, the "indie crowd," representing as it does those recipients who, like the members of the "general public" audience, are less regular listeners to rap music than the "consumers" or the "fans," but whose preferences are not guided by the mass media. Membership of this category is determined above all by the social background of the recipient, rather than by gender or age group. Some of the artists favoured by this audience are similar to the preferences of the "fans" (TTC [Figure 10.3], Triptik, La Caution), but an appreciation of the music of the group Svinkels places the recipient much more within this category. Three of the groups that are most frequently cited (TTC, Svinkels

Figure 10.3 TTC, *Ceci n'est pas un disque*, Big Dada, 2002, compact disc front cover.

and Triptik) neither frame their discourse within the context of the deprived neighbour-hoods, nor evoke the issue of immigration. These artists generally hold strong and critical opinions with respect to politics, accord little importance to money, reject all religion and foreground their adherence to hip hop culture. In terms of their music, we observe that alternating verse-chorus structures are less common than in the music of those artists that were favoured by the "consumers." Furthermore, their backing tracks and instrumentals are inspired more by rock music (La Caution, Svinkels), electro (TTC) and African-American music, or by a mix of all musical styles (Triptik). If we consider non-instrumental sources of music too, electronic and percussive body sounds are used comparatively more by these artists than by the others. They also use major, or in the case of TTC, indeterminate musical keys more frequently. Finally, they are characterised by a more frequent use of the English language during spoken passages.

These are of course only typological categories. In keeping with Max Weber who under-lined that typologised social activities were only rarely found in so clear a form in the social reality, these four categories of recipients never really fit the facts. One recipient might well present attitudes and behavioural traits similar to those belonging to two and even, but more rarely, three of these categories. There are more links between the "consumers" and the "gen-eral public" of rap music, or even between the "general public" and the "fans," and the "fans" and the "discerning public" than between the "fans" and the "consumers," or between the "discerning public" and the "consumers." Furthermore, without being able to ensure how representative the survey sample is, it is impossible to give any real weight to these different categories dividing the population of rap music recipients. Nevertheless, based on the results of surveys and album sales for rap music in France, we can state without any doubt that more individuals belong to the "consumers" and "general public" categories than to the "fans" or to the "discerning public."

To finish, let us take a final look at the "fans" category so as to present how this group of recipients considers American rap music.

A Closer Look at the "Fans"

The "fans" of rap music surveyed highlight the fact that they "know" about rap and that they possess the knowledge-based resources required to form critical opinions about rap music. These resources are acquired gradually over time, through a set of defined social practices (like amateur music making, reading specialised magazines and attending concerts).

These "fans" do not all hold the same attitude with respect to American rap music: some of them listen to it regularly, preferring it even sometimes to French rap, whilst others main-tain a much more distant relationship with rap from the United States.

Those who listen to American rap music foreground its formal qualities. When they dis-cuss the message of American rap, it is generally to underline the fact that it is often difficult to relate this message to the social reality of France. The participants who listen to Ameri-can rap music consider it to be more diverse than French rap. More precisely, they cite the differences in terms of *flow* and backing tracks. The "fans" surveyed state that, first of all, it is easier to have a good *flow* rapping in English than in French, but also that rap music is more creative there than in France. Those who are unable to understand the meaning of the lyrics see an advantage in this: it allows them to make an abstraction of the words and to concentrate on the music. As a consequence, American music is enjoyed because, by placing a social distance between the music's producers and its recipients, it leaves more space to the imagination of the latter.

Those "fans" who listen to American rap music justify their choices with reasons pertaining to the artistic quality of American productions and, in particular, the musical inventiveness and quality of the *flow* of these rappers. Most of the time it is those "fans" who belong to more privileged social backgrounds who belong to this category.

Those who do not listen to American rap music because they find its style to be too formulaic generally belong to the middle and upper classes, whilst those who do not listen to it because of their inability to understand the lyrics belong more often to the working classes. Thus, whilst these do not listen to it because they are unable to access its meaning, those "fans" belonging to the middle and higher classes, whether they understand the lyrics or not, appreciate it because of what they see as its aesthetic qualities.

The Question of Ethnicity

In 1995, Hugues Bazin wrote that "if France was not already a multi-cultural society, hip hop made it so" (Bazin 1995, 111).

As stated previously, our questionnaire did not take into account the cultural origin of rap music recipients (for which we would have required some kind of reliable indicator besides). Nevertheless, results relating to this issue did appear indirectly throughout the interview stage of our study. We use the word "indirectly" here because if in effect the rap music recipients did raise this issue during the interviews, they broached it, or to be precise evoked it, in order to demonstrate that it did not appear to be a major factor for them in determining their musical preferences. In other words, the issue of the cultural or "ethnic" origins of the rap recipients did not appear in their discourse as a fundamental explanatory factor for the structure of rap audiences in France. What is more, the results of the questionnaire reinforce this finding, their analysis not leading us to consider that the cultural origin of rap artists might be the cause of their being preferred by any particular category: the artists favoured by the "consumers," "fans" or even of the "general public" cannot be grouped according to their cultural origins, this being varied across the group. Nevertheless, we can observe that the artists who are most preferred by the "discerning public" are more often Caucasian (White) than the other artists (by which we may explain the link made by one "fan" between rap music "for White people" and "bourgeois" rap).

We can consider therefore that cultural origin is an explanatory factor in preferences *for* rap but not *in* rap. That is to say, the appeal of rap music as a whole, as opposed to other musical genres, could be linked to a foreign cultural origin. This hypothesis remains to be tested by taking into consideration all recipients of rap music in their entirety, and by comparing them with the recipients of other types of music. If, in contrast to other types of music, rap succeeds in bringing together individuals from a variety of cultural backgrounds, we could therefore conclude that rap is indeed a vector of communication between cultures, but such research remains to be realised so that we might know to what extent, more than the other types of music, rap fulfils this function. Here we can simply note that, based on our study, rap unites individuals coming from a range of different backgrounds, whilst not being able to claim here that this is a specificity of rap music.

Conclusion

When discussing rap music, it seems necessary to apply the term "musical genre." As with cinema, literature, art and theatre, rap has been adopted on multiple levels of society, from the most "learned" to the most "popular": it has reached, in its various forms and in many different ways, the whole of the French population. The audience of rap music in France is structured not only by the social class of its members but also by their level of interest in rap and individual involvement in this type of music: this has resulted in the development of a range of musical tastes distinguishable from those sustained by the mass media industries. Furthermore, the differences in attitudes observed between the youngest rap music recipients and the oldest leads us to note the emergence of generational factors in the structure of the rap music audience, whose effects we can speculate will be all the more significant and decisive as time goes on. But beyond this issue of the diversity of rap music recipients in France lies that of their heterogeneity, a development that we can observe occurring from the moment a "popular" form of music succeeds in establishing itself firmly within the culture and in diversifying its audience, from the moment it enters into a process of social and cultural legitimisation.

Notes

1 The first study produced in France was that realised by Georges Lapassade and Philippe Rousselot (1990).
2 We will use the term "recipients" here, rather than that of listener or of fan, because the former could include people who listen to rap without choosing to, while the latter is deemed too restrictive. The term "recipient," on the other hand, has the advantage of containing in itself the idea that he or she who listens to rap music does so as the result of a deliberate action.
3 For a full presentation of the results of this research, see Molinero (2009).
4 See, for example, Coulangeon (2003, 3–33).
5 See, for example, Donnat (2009).
6 In this regard, see the note regarding the author (Raibaud 2010, 233–236).
7 Our initial research, conducted in 2007, was based on the comparison of figures from 1997 and 2003, as provided by the French National Institute for Statistics and Economic Research (INSEE), but we present here the figures from 2008 rather than those from 2004. These were chosen because they are more recent and they have been produced by the same organisation that conducted the study according to the same procedures in 1997 as in 2008 (which was not the case with the figures from 2004).
8 The baccalaureate is a qualification which marks the end of secondary education in France and which is required (or its equivalent) in order to be able to pass on to higher education.
9 For reasons linked to the defined geographic scope of the study, as well as the feasibility of treating the responses received, it was decided that the questionnaire should ask the participants only about the French artists that they most preferred.
10 The social class of participants is taken here by means of their socioprofessional status or that of their parents.
11 For a more detailed analysis of religion in French rap music, see Molinero (2011, 105–123).

Bibliography

Bazin, Hugues. 1995. *La Culture Hip Hop*. Paris: Desclée de Brouwer.
Boucher, Manuel. 1998. *Rap, Expression des lascars: Significations et enjeux du Rap dans la société française*. Paris: L'Harmattan.
Calio, Jean. 1998. *Le rap, une réponse des banlieues*. Lyon: ENTPE-ALEAS.
Coulangeon, Philippe. 2003. "La stratification sociale des goûts musicaux: Le modèle de la légitimité culturelle en question." *Revue française de sociologie* 44(1):3–33.

Donnat, Olivier. 1998. *Les pratiques culturelles des français: Enquête 1997*. Paris: La Documentation Française.

———. 2009. *Les pratiques culturelles des Français à l'ère du numérique: Enquête 2008*. Paris: La Documentation Française.

Green, Anne-Marie, and Jean-Raphaël Desverité. 1997. "Le Rap comme pratique et moteur d'une trajectoire sociale." In *Des jeunes et des musiques: Rock, rap, techno*, edited by Anne-Marie Green, 169–213. Paris: L'Harmattan.

Guibert, Gérôme. 2000. "L'éthique Hip Hop et L'esprit du capitalisme." *Mouvements: Hip Hop: les pratiques, le marché, la politique* 11:54–59.

Hammou, Karim. 2008. "L'économie du rap en France." In *La musique, une industrie, des pratiques*, edited by Pierre François, 127–141. Paris: La Documentation Française.

———. 2102. *Une histoire du rap en France*. Paris: La Découverte.

Jouvenet, Morgan. 2006. *Rap, Techno, Électro: Le musicien entre travail artistique et critique sociale*. Paris: Éditions de la Maison des sciences de l'homme.

Lafargue de Grangeneuve, Loïc. 2008. *Politique du hip hop: Action publique et cultures urbaines*. Toulouse: Presses Universitaires du Mirail.

Lapassade, Georges, and Philippe Rousselot. 1990. *Le rap ou la fureur de dire*. Paris: Loris Talmart.

Molinero, Stéphanie. 2009. *Les publics du rap: Enquête sociologique*. Paris: L'Harmattan.

———. 2011. "The Meanings of the Religious Talk in French Rap Music." In *Popular Music and Religion in Europe*, edited by Thomas Bossius, 105–123. London: I.B.Tauris.

Pecqueux, Anthony. 2007. *Voix du rap: Essai de sociologie de l'action musicale*. Paris: L'Harmattan.

Raibaud, Yves. 2010. "Note to the Reader." *Volume! La revue des musiques populaires* 7(2):233–236.

Sberna, Béatrice. 2001. *Une sociologie du rap à Marseille: Identité marginale et immigrée*. Paris: L'Harmattan.

11

Towards a Greater Appreciation of the Poetry of French Rap

Christian Béthune

Rap is generally viewed rather negatively by French educational establishments (Béthune 2004; Pecqueux 2008), and this is true across all levels of the school system (from primary through to secondary and *lycée*). Only the universities it seems, unable perhaps to ignore dissertations and theses written on the subject of hip hop culture, appear to have accorded it some little merit. As a general rule, the educational authorities discourage teachers from using examples drawn from this form of cultural expression in their lessons, especially in so-called problem neighbourhoods and other areas of educational priority (Zones d'Éducation Prioritaires, or ZEP). The reasoning is simple and its pertinence at least is clear: according to educational policy makers, the students living in these neighbourhoods, coyly categorised as "underprivileged," already (and all too often) tend to employ the substandard dialect of the problem estates, to misuse the French language, to express themselves, in short, like rappers, both in their spoken and their written language. As a consequence, any attempt to base French-language teaching on rap texts would have the result of shutting students within a limited cultural horizon, rather than opening them up to new perspectives of expression.

Effectively, many consider that the language of rap texts should be analysed as representative of a socially inevitable linguistic handicap, rather than as a form of poetic expression. Far from containing any aesthetic value, the words used by rap artists are limited to a sort of social symptom in which societal failures and linguistic deficiencies are exposed. This view is summed up in a statement made by Alain Bentolila, author of a number of noteworthy works (Bentolila 1996) on combatting illiteracy and a scientific advisor for the ANLCI,[1] in an interview for the French weekly news magazine *L'Express*: "We should stop being so astonished by rap groups, stop lauding them as the new Baudelaires" (Simonet 2002).

A Poetry of Transgression

In response to those who would criticise rappers as illiterate, let us remember for a start that these individuals are often able to manipulate several different linguistic codes. The majority of rappers indeed are not only capable of expressing themselves in standard French but also can also speak one or two foreign languages (African languages, Arabic, Creole, Berber, Spanish, etc.). Furthermore, some of them have even shown themselves able to translate the lyrics of American rap music and to comprehend the subtleties contained within them in much more precise a way than even their English-language teachers.

Thus, when critics of rap artists pass judgement on their linguistic competence, we could counter with lyrics by MC Seyfu: "I can speak in French, then switch to Soninke, sink into Arabic before speeding through with Japanese."[2]

For many young people living in France's most deprived neighbourhoods, rap music represents a way of liberating the language that they have felt banned from using by the educational institutions they attend, a way of reclaiming their right to free speech. This point is made clear by the female rap artist Casey:

> Until then, school had taught us that writing was reserved for the elite. It wasn't for us. But with rap, this restriction was blown apart. Suddenly young people had the right to write, without Victor Hugo's ugly mug sneering down over our shoulders.[3]

Irrespective of the potential linguistic competence of its creators or of their ability to master the correct syntactical forms, rap is not unaware of the fact that it often breaks both a taboo and a consensus with regards to language use. Indeed, the rappers of the group 113 openly declare themselves as "textual wrongdoers," whilst the rap artist Kery James has asserted, "This year, we've been rapping so dirtily, so wrongly, that people think we're rapping in German."[4] Little does it matter what proportion of the "errors" come as the result of deliberate manipulation and which as the result of a social handicap, the rapper knows perfectly well he stands at the periphery of the linguistic canon, of generally accepted and legitimised (grammatical, lexical and phonetic) forms of expression. Rappers are proud of the verbal disrespect they show. What is important in this approach is the rappers' desire to reclaim language through their poetry. While most people might consider the language of rap texts to be substandard and believe that the users of this language should assimilate the norm of the dominant discourse, rap culture encourages artists to take up a pen and make themselves heard by asserting their difference. Even if they have not necessarily read Deleuze and Guattari, rap artists have the unvoiced "gut feeling" that "a grammatical rule is more an indicator of power than one of syntax" (Deleuze and Guattari 1980, 96). Considered "radically minor"—in the Deleuzian sense of the term[5]—the language of rap artists is laden with an ideology that refuses to enshrine the "words of the master"—perhaps those of the "school master"[6]—as "master words." The lyrics of the rappers belonging to the group La Rumeur concur, not without lucidity, nor elegance: "Master words and words of the master, master words to follow to the letter, word order and words of order, ordering words specially trained to bite."[7]

One of the major problems directly linked with understanding rap texts is that rappers have an essentially performative conceptualisation of language. In other words, the physical act of delivering their texts and the illocutionary effects of their speech take precedence over the syntactic organisation of each individual utterance and its strictly semantic significance. As a consequence, every time there is a potential conflict between the syntactic norm associated with a phrase and its illocutionary effectiveness, it is the influence of the latter that will dominate the organisation of the utterance.

What is more, in order to be interpreted correctly, a speech act assumes a certain amount of implicit shared knowledge between interlocutors. Thus, whilst some commentators tend to consider the difficulty in understanding what rappers are saying as the consequence of a linguistic deficiency on the part of the author of those texts, in many cases, this comprehension difficulty results from the fact that the listener neither possesses the knowledge its producer has assumed to be shared, nor understands the rules which govern the use of this assumed knowledge as contained within the speech of the rap artist. In addition, some of the vocabulary used by rappers may be unknown to the listener. According to William Labov, in the language of inner-city ghettos, the comprehension of the overall meaning of an utterance often hinges on whether the interlocutor has understood a clause which is implied but not explicitly expressed within it (Labov 1972, 269–272). This implicit clause is drawn from the local culture and "*lore*" of the ghetto. Similarly, we can note a range of shared knowledges within French rap music which give structure to utterances and which instil a sense of

Figure 11.1 Casey, *Libérez la bête*, Ladilafé, 2010, compact disc front cover.

complicity between the rapper and their audience by making the words spoken make sense. It is by means of this shared culture that a word's connotations often take priority over its literal meaning (its denotation).[8] Furthermore, this knowledge or *lore* which is contained implicitly within rap texts remains completely foreign to the majority of researchers, and to linguisticians in particular. Ultimately therefore, it proves much easier to decree incompetence and to evoke notions of linguistic failure than to go investigate, over the course of several months of fieldwork, the full particulars of this discourse and to proceed with a detailed review of a large number of rap texts.

Rap culture offers writers a guilt-free approach to the French language which is likely to incite those young people who feel at odds with the school system to reclaim language for themselves and to learn to express themselves successfully in writing. In questioning the linguistic competence of the producers of rap texts from the very start, we discount the aesthetic and poetic qualities of such texts, regarding them instead as a symptom, and thus reduce the expression of hip hop culture merely to the social conditions of its development and circulation, limiting ourselves to a reductive sociological conceptualisation of failure and deficiency.

Instead, we should take into account the pressing desire shown by rap artists to make themselves heard by means of a reclaimed language whose mastery is indispensable for success: "Away from all judgements, I sharpen my lines, because words can undo/the knots lodged in the soul."[9]

This desire goes hand in hand with the real, and often difficult, labour of writing: "Learn to write or learn to keep quiet," recommends the rapper Casey (Figure 11.1),[10] a point on which the group A Tribe Called Quest agree, denouncing those "Phoney rappers who do not write."[11]

Rap as a Form of Written Expression

There is a tendency to view rap only in terms of its oral dimension. And yet, this is to forget that, except in instances of freestyle (a largely marginal practice in hip hop culture), before it is recited, most rap texts must first be composed in writing. The aggressive imagery of rap artists is not alone in considering the pen just as powerful a weapon as the microphone, but MCs take great pains in the crafting of their texts. Even more so than in American rap, it is unusual for a French-speaking MC to recite a segment of which he cannot be proud. This is why the composition of a rap text demands particular care. In an interview dedicated to the release of his first, aptly titled, album *My Manuscript*,[12] the MC MOH from Marseille makes particular note of the meticulous effort required throughout the writing process, discussing it in all its difficulty:

> I sweated over it! I stopped my academic education at the age of eighteen and everything I know I owe to rap. I worked myself hard to succeed, I spent sleepless nights going through pages and pages of dictionaries, books and newspapers to improve my vocabulary, to find the exact wording. As someone who always hated reading, I finally ended up writing everything.[13]

As Christophe Rubin highlights, rap is first and foremost "a form of writing for the voice."[14] It is for this reason, before setting out to battle against other MCs under the glare of the spotlights, one must first fight with the blank page. In their own way, French rap artists can thus be defined as men and women of letters, as Sami Zégami (2004) has suggested, and even if they try to distance themselves from it, literary culture often leaves its trace on their texts.

We hardly need mention for instance Descartes's much quoted adage, "I think therefore I am," a phrase which has led to a number of recent variations along the lines of "I rap therefore I am."

Ménélik (whose stage name is borrowed from the king to whom Rimbaud sold weapons in Abyssinia) frequently cites Baudelaire: "*Quand le ciel bas et lourd comme un couvercle*" ("When the low, heavy sky weighs like a lid")[15] and speaks about the strong influence French literature has had on his work. Oxmo Puccino's song "Mourir mille fois," on the other hand, references a little known play by Molière, *Le Dépit amoureux* ("The Love-Tiff").[16] The reference to Molière is twofold since Molière makes his character say, "*on ne meurt qu'une fois, et c'est pour si longtemps*" ("We only die once and it is for such a long time").[17] The subject matter of La Rumeur's "La meilleure des polices" ("The best of police forces")[18] is based on a Nietzchean vision (*The Dawn*, Book III, §. 173) which denounces the constraints of social norms as "the best of police forces." We could also cite the heavily Sartre-influenced song title "L'enfer c'est les autres" ("Hell is other people") featured on the album *Noir Désir*[19] by Youssoufa. Indeed, this rap text ends with an allusion to the notion of "*mauvaise foi*" ("bad faith"), one of the central features of Sartre's philosophy. By linking a now rather clichéd citation to a key concept of the philosopher's work, Youssoufa opens the way for a much more profound interpretation of Sartre's phrase than that most commonly circulated.

While there is not enough space here to list the stylistic processes employed by rap artists, we must note that in this respect as well it has in part been by drawing from the forgotten cultural heritage of the French language and combining this with contemporary urban dialects that rap artists have been able to develop their own original poetry. Rap artists have not only endeavoured to bring up-to-date terms and expressions borrowed from the slang of the turn of the nineteenth and twentieth centuries—"*blaze*" ("name"), "*surin*" ("knife"), "*daron/daronne*" ("father/mother"), "*frelot*" ("brother") and even "*cambuter*" ("to cheat or swindle")—but also rediscovered verse forms that had previously fallen into disuse. The following verse forms have rarely been employed since the *Grand Rhetoriqueur* poets of the fifteenth and sixteenth centuries:

- "Internal rhymes" ("*rimes batelées*") which rhyme the end of the line with the end of the first hemistich of either the following or the preceding line: "En moi la hargne *gronde* quand la nuit *tombe* / Une lueur d'espoir si nos rêves se con*fondent*" ("My aggression rumbles inside of me as night falls / a glint of hope if our dreams begin to merge"), Mafia Trece, "Toutes peines confondues."
- "Chained rhymes" ("*rimes enchaînées*") in which the last word of a line rhymes with the first of the next line: "Des intrigues sur mes cahiers, crée l'école du tourne*vis* / *vice* en poche, hisse la bannière" ("[I write] stories in my notebooks, create the school of the screwdriver / all my vices in my pocket, I raise the flag"), Arsenik, "Un monde parfait."

- "Ambiguous rhymes" ("*rimes équivoquées*") based on a play on words or a pun: "C'est pas du rap de fêtard / Mais d'la musique *meurtrière*, parce qu'il y a eu un *meurtre hier* / Le crime tourne dans ma rue, parce que le *meurtre y est hier*" ("It's not upbeat rap / but murderous music, because there was a murder yesterday / Crime is everywhere in my street, because the murder was there yesterday"), Rohff, "Sensation brave." Given the tendency of rap artists to add as many formal features to their texts as they can, this example could also be said to demonstrate a form of internal rhyme ("*rimes batelées*").

Other examples abound: alternative forms of internal rhyme, "broken rhymes," "double rhymes" and so on.

We must also note rap artists' predilection for stylistic features which foreground the phonetic aspects of language: alliteration, assonance, echo and, above all, paronomasia (linking similar sounding nouns and other syntactic units to achieve a particularly striking effect):

Nos textes *sont des toiles* que dévoilent nos mal-êtres
des destins *sans étoiles*
(Our texts are canvases which our discontent unfurls
destinies without stars).

(Kery James, "A l'ombre du showbizness")

Here, the paronomasia between "*des toiles*" and "*étoiles*" is reinforced by the echo found in "*dévoile*."

Finally, rap artists have become adept at foregrounding the relationship between composition and performance, thus demonstrating a particularly advanced level of complexity in the content of their texts. In this respect French rappers seem to exploit a particularity of the French language which relates to the links between oral and written language, a particularity which the psychoanalyst Guy Rosolato has explored: "We can assert that the French language maintains a separation between its spoken and written forms" (Rosolato 1969, 290).[20]

Rappers do this by manipulating many of the numerous homonyms that can be found in the French language. When, for example, Rocca titles one of his tracks "Sang Pitié,"[21] his aim of highlighting the relationship between spoken and written language is clearly demonstrated. Effectively, one must read the title aloud in order to appreciate the play on words "*sans pitié / sang pitié*" ("without pity / blood to be pitied").

An even more significant instance of this strategy can be found in the ambiguities developed by the group La Rumeur in the following two lines:

Jette-moi 8 mesures à souiller comme 8 murs
assaillis d'enflures sur des aires de raclures.
(Give me eight [musical] bars to defile like eight walls
scrawled over by scum-heads in some shitty city park.)[22]

It should be noted that these lyrics have not simply been collected at random from some Internet-based fan site. Rather, they come from the booklet which accompanies the CD. We can legitimately assume therefore that the authors (Hamé, Ecoué, Mourad and Philippe) have not only carefully checked that their lyrics have been transcribed correctly, but that they specifically wished for the words of their lyrics to be printed, in order that, in addition to simply being listened to, they can be read by their audience. Indeed, the full impact of the homonymy of the word "*aire*" ("area") / "*air*" ("tune") can only really be recognised when reading the text. Both meanings of the word are united by themes of subversive transgression: while the "*aires*" refer principally to the "areas" or "city parks" in which the eight graffitied walls stand, the phrase also provides a powerful echo to the abrasive (musical) "air" or "tune" referred to by the "*8 mesures*" ("eight bars") for which the rapper asks. (The length of eight bars is the most common length of a musical segment to be "sampled" in the creation of a backing track, a technique which, although dismissed as musical pollution by purists, has been fully embraced by rap artists.) In the audience's ears and then before their eyes, "airs" and "*aires*" condense with elegant efficiency all the transgressive power of hip hop culture.

We have seen therefore that one must read the text of the song "A nous le bruit" closely in order to take full measure of the poetry of its eminently subversive and disruptive intent: one must appreciate the subtlety of the wordplay both in terms of how it sounds and in terms of how it is written in order to appreciate the way in which rap has revitalised the relationships between writing and speaking, and between performing and reading.[23] In any case, the elaboration of rap texts has been shown to be a process involving meticulous linguistic craftsmanship whose pertinence and richness as a form of expression should not be ignored.

Conclusion

Rap texts enact multiple linguistic transgressions compared with the lexical, grammatical and prosodic norms proscribed by the Académie Française.[24] This way of mistreating the language, of behaving as "textual wrongdoers" seems particularly striking given the way these transgressions are often based on complex literary forms, a technique more usually reserved for the most sophisticated of written texts: rap artists have brought back verse forms that had previously fallen into disuse, demonstrated their ability to conduct advanced research in terms of vocabulary, worked with extreme precision on the prosody and rhythm of their texts and experimented with the relationship between meter and rhyme, spoken and written language.

In order to understand rap texts, the listener is generally required to make a perhaps unexpected interpretative effort, but many still tend to refuse to take such a step, following instead their negative preconceptions. This is perhaps all the truer given that the effort required to critique the lyrics should be complemented by additional efforts in order to understand the music: for example, there is the art of sampling, an area of study which surely represents a deep mine of possibilities to be explored by the musicologist. As such, the production requires effort, time, analysis and critical reflection which undoubtedly explains why so many rap artists usually need several years in order to create their work.

The composition of rap texts can thus be seen as a kind of textual gymnastics: in the same way as basketball players or boxers must train in their sports, rappers must train to juggle words (as DJs do with sounds thanks to their skills on the turntables), and this training process is often difficult. The sequence of words in rap lyrics is comparable to the sequence of punches, sidesteps, feints, parries and counterattacks delivered by a pair of competing boxers, or to the sequence of dribbles, passes, bounces and dummies enacted by basketball players before successfully "slam-dunking." And as with these sporting encounters, there is a certain amount of automatic reflex involved in the writing (and the delivery) of rap texts: learnt over the course of many years, this automatic linguistic reflex is achieved through a process of interiorising aspects of a vernacular culture and through training. It is dominated by the priority of rhythm and the sounds of words. The beat becomes a source of inspiration and invention: words call to each other phonetically, rhythmically, and respond to each other with a kind of subconscious reciprocity, an automatic reflex which reaches back to the very roots of the language. In doing so, rappers force us to consider a whole new aspect of the French language of which we are not necessarily aware in the course of our everyday speech.

Notes

1 Agence Nationale de Lutte Contre l'Illettrisme, the organisation tasked with combatting illiteracy in France.
2 "Je peux parler le français, puis enchaîner en soninké, mettre un crochet en arabe pour accélérer en japonais." "Sans Plomb 93." In *Suis-je le gardien de mon frère?*, Bec-5772326, 2008.
3 "*Jusque-là, L'école nous avais appris que l'écrit c'était réservé à l'élite. Ce n'était pas pour nous. Avec le rap cet interdit a sauté. Soudain les jeunes ont eu le droit de toucher aux mots, sans avoir la tronche de Victor Hugo juste derrière leur épaule à ricaner.*" Interview: Aeno Leo in *Longueur d'Ondes* magazine, June 2010.
4 "*Cette année on rappe salement tellement malment qu'ils croient qu'on on rappe en allemand.*" "Foolek." In *A l'ombre du Show Business*, Warner, 2008.
5 For further discussion of hip hop as a "minor" culture, see Béthune (2011a).
6 "It wasn't school that taught us our ways of speaking" ("*C'est pas l'école qui nous a dicté nos codes*") Diam's, "La boulette."
7 "*Maîtres mots et mots de maître, maîtres mots à suivre à la lettre, ordre des mots et mots de L'ordre, ordre des mots dressés pour mordre.*" "Maitre mot, mots du maître." In *Regain de Tensions*, 2004.
8 It should be made clear that the nature and quantity of implicit knowledge needed to understand a rap text varies between groups. Rappers such as Lim, Larsen and Alibi Montana who can be categorised as "local" artists and whose speech is very close to that of the neighbourhoods in which they live, make more reference to local forms of knowledge than those groups that target a more national audience. To be able to understand fully the lyrics of a rap text by Lim, it is desirable to be up to date with the events in and around the "Cité du Pont de Sèvres" (Boulogne-Billancourt, 92); similarly, when the group 113 was making its first records, being in touch with life in the "Cité Camille Groult" (Vitry-sur-Seine, 94) was useful, if not essential, in order to be able to appreciate the texts of songs such as "Truc de ouf" and "Ouais, gros!"
9 Keny Arkana. "A l'ombre des jugements." In *L'Esquisse 2*, Because Music, 2012.
10 Casey. "Apprends à t'aire." In *Libérez la bête*, Ladilafé Productions, 2010.
11 A Tribe Called Quest. "Phony Rappers." In *Beats, Rhymes and Life*, Jive Records, 1996.
12 Soli Muzik/Musicast, April 2012.
13 "*J'ai sué pour y arriver! J'ai arrêté L'école après le bac, et toute ma culture générale, je la dois au rap lui-même. J'ai énormément travaillé pour réussir, j'ai passé des nuits blanches à parcourir des pages et des pages de dictionnaires, des livres, des journaux pour enrichir mon vocabulaire, trouver les formules exactes. Moi qui ai toujours eu horreur de lire, j'ai finalement tout écrit.*" www.marsactu.fr/culture-2013/moh-lartiste-de-la-soli-rappe-son-man uscrit-27671.html (last accessed 7 May 2012).
14 2002. "Le texte de rap: une écriture de la voix." In *Actes du 22e Colloque d'Albi: Langages et Significations: "L'oralité dans L'écrit et réciproquement"* (9, 10, 11, 12, July 2001), 267–276. C.A.L.S./C.P.S.T.
15 The citation appeared in "Il est parti." In *Phénoménélik*, Sony, 1995, and is drawn from the poem "Spleen" in *Les fleurs du mal*.
16 Album *Opera Puccino*, Time Bomb/Delabel, April 1998.
17 *Le dépit amoureux*: Act 5, scene 3.
18 La Rumeur. *Du Cœur à l'Outrage*, ADAMI/SCPP/FCM, 2007.
19 Youssoufa. *Noir Désir*. EMI, 2012.
20 "*On pourrait donc dire que le français assure un écart entre le code parlé et le code graphique.*" It should be noted here that the voice is understood by the psychoanalyst at least as much in terms of its impact as its sound.
21 Album: *Rocca*, Barclay/Universal, 2001.
22 La Rumeur. "A nous le bruit." In *Regain de Tension*, La Rumeur Records/EMI, 2004.
23 For more on this relationship between spoken and written language, see Béthune (2001b, 185–201).
24 The Académie Française is France's official authority on French language use.

Bibliography

Bentolila, Alain. 1996. *De l'illettrisme en général et de L'école en particulier*. Paris: Plon.

Béthune, Christian. 2004. *Pour une esthétique du rap*. Paris: Klincksieck.

———. 2011a. "Le Hip Hop: Une expression mineure." *Volume! La revue des musiques populaires* 8(2):161–185.

———. 2011b. "Sur les traces du rap." *Poétique* 166:185–201.

Deleuze, Gilles, and Félix Guattari. 1980. *Mille plateaux*. Paris: Minuit.

Labov, William. 1972. "Rules for Ritual Insults." In *Rappin' & Stylin' Out*, edited by Thomas Kochman, 268–269. Urbana: University of Illinois Press.

Pecqueux, Anthony. 2008. *Voix du rap: essai de sociologie de l'action musicale*. Paris: L'Harmattan.

Rosolato, Guy. 1969. "La Voix." In *Essais sur le symbolique*, 290. Paris: Gallimard/Tel.

Simonet, Dominique. 2002. "Il existe une inégalité linguistique en France." l'Express February_17.

Zégami, Sami. 2004. "Le rap comme activité scripturale: l'émergence d'un groupe illégitime de lettrés." *Langage et Société* 110. Accessed May 15, 2012. www.cairn.info/revue-langage-et-societe-2004-4-pa.

12
Punk Rock Entrepreneurship in France

Fabien Hein

This chapter,[1] which is based on an ethnographic enquiry[2] on the French punk rock scene, aims at examining the way punk entrepreneurship works in France. This scene adopted "do it yourself" (DIY) as a core value in the same way other punk rock scenes around the globe had (O'Hara 1999; Calmbach 2007; O'Connor 2008; Dale 2012; Hein 2012). *To undertake* is its key phrase. This dynamic guided the emergence of a profusion of very small punk businesses, which usually have very limited economic resources. This constrains them to get by as best as they can (self-production) and leads them to tirelessly resort to cooperation (co-production). It so happens that these two dimensions precisely enabled, symmetrically and at different levels, the development of this punk rock scene. To account for this, after a presentation of punk rock action frames in France, this contribution will focus on conventional entrepreneurial resources, with the typical example of the local punk recording economy. It will then concentrate on a set of clearly less conventional—specifically French—resources, which have to do with the numerous systems public authorities implement in order to support cultural production, youth or even employment.

The Action Frames of Punk Rock

The punk rock scene is globally based on a network of artistic and cultural operators[3] who share common musical tastes. This shared attachment is objectively structuring, as it leads these operators to produce music, release records, organize concerts, publish fanzines, strengthen distribution circuits and endlessly exchange about the punk rock scene. In France just as elsewhere, the punk experience generally relies on the strong engagement of its operators (Rollins 1994; Sinker 2001; Hein 2011). For many of them, being punk is a real existential concern, which results in an intense entrepreneurial dynamic, based on the permanence of the DIY vulgate. This vulgate, which is deeply rooted in the history of the punk movement, is one of its main cultural features (Guibert 2006, 236–247; Reynolds 2007, 131–150; Hebdige 2008, 118; Savage 2012; Hein 2012). It even founds its interpretive frame[4] by supplying it with a principle of orientation. This frame will translate into specific regimes of commitment. Theoretically, the DIY vulgate is thus a relationship to the world—an invitation or even an injunction to take control of one's own affairs. To get by as best as one can—concretely, without putting things off, without anyone's approval, through commitment and action, with autonomy and independence as a horizon. As an attitude, DIY appears as a top resource. However, we must also acknowledge that it is a constraint, and for a good reason: to accomplish things by one's own means is very costly in terms of time and energy. To work with a limited number of intermediaries and scarce means forces one to do a lot on one's own—to go through with one's possibilities, creativity, resources. This "organization of experience" (Goffman 1974, 19) imposed itself very early as a fundamental criterion of authenticity within the punk rock scene.[5]

Punk Rock Cooperation

The French punk rock scene appears as a vast productive system based on a constellation of local punk scenes, scattered over the territory—local scenes that are more or less linked to one another and that, when necessary, mutualize their resources thanks to a multiplicity of small punk enterprises. To illustrate this, it is useful to examine the most widespread practices within the French punk rock scene, particularly the ones that have to do with the recording process.

Producing Punk Rock Records in France

In order to present this process, I will essentially focus on the band Flying Donuts,[6] which I wrote a monograph about (Hein 2011). The vinyl edition of *Until the Morning Comes*—the band's third EP (2009, Figure 12.1)—indeed appears to be paradigmatic of the DIY action frame and of the specificity of the punk recording economy in France. Its financial structure is particularly clarifying, especially owing to the distribution of the production costs between several structures. Table 12.1 charts its significant elements.

First of all, we must consider that the reproduction of a recording on vinyl is subject to the recording's actual achievement. In this case, the cost of this operation was taken in charge by the producer—José Records (the band's own label), which owns the master tapes (€4,000). The transfer of the master to the vinyl medium, with 500 copies printed, cost €1,950. This amount was financed by five of the associated structures. The main ones (José Records and Kicking Records) took on €525. The secondary structures (GPS Prod, Oni Red Chords and Bad Mood Records) each invested €300. A third structure, Chanmax Records, invested not money but work: the making of the vinyl's sleeve. In this case, the return on investment is mainly symbolic. For the other financiers, each structure was meant to receive a number

Table 12.1 Distribution of production costs of the vinyl album *Until the Morning Comes* (2009)

Production costs		Associated structures	Financing of pressing	Other investment	Return on investment	Monetary return on investment
Pressing	€1,600	José Records	€525	Master (€4,000)	200 units	€2,000
SDRM*	€350	Kicking Records	€525		150 units	€1,000
		GPS Prod	€300		50 units	€500
		Oni Red Chords	€300		50 units	€500
		Bad Mood Records	€300		50 units	€500
		Chanmax Records	–	Record sleeve and layout	Logo on booklet	Symbolic
Total	**€1,950**	**Six structures**	**€1,950**		**500 units**	**€4,500**

* Société pour l'administration du droit de reproduction mécanique (society for the administration of mechanical reproduction rights), the civil society in charge of the administration and perception of reproduction rights stemming from physical devices.

Figure 12.1 Flying Donuts, *Until the Morning Comes*, José Records/Kicking Records, 2009, compact disc front cover.

of copies equal to their investment. Thus, the primary investors (José Records and Kicking Records) each got 150 to 200 of them, while the secondary ones got 50 each. Based on this distribution of the goods, each structure was supposed to recover its initial stake through sales. This mechanism shows that in theory, such an operation is meant to generate profits, and thus future investments.

This cooperative phonographic production process sheds light on the relative weakness of French punk rock companies. The production costs make cooperation necessary on a daily basis. Without it, there are no recordings, and even less networks. In other words, it is cooperation that guarantees the punk rock scene's sustainability. In the same way, the multiplication of stakeholders reduces the risk inherent to any cultural production by dividing it among several participants. This is why each album is released in CD and vinyl formats, with the participation of one or several labels for each type of format. This operating mode illustrates a particularly efficient strategy, which enables the sharing both of costs and workload. And the plurality of stakeholders is all the more efficient because it activates and reinforces the punk rock network. From this perspective, we can say that punk companies thrive thanks to the punk rock scene and, symmetrically, the other way around. To my knowledge, this circular process seems to determine the concrete practical conditions of a majority of punk entrepreneurs, throughout the world.[7] However, the French punk rock scene still has a certain number of local features.

Specificities of the French Punk Rock Scene

In the second half of the 1970s, the emerging French punk rock scene[8] (Guibert 2006, 242–247; Rudeboy 2007; Pépin 2007) was essentially made up of bands singing in French (Métal Urbain, Asphalt Jungle, Starshooter, Olivensteins, etc.). This tradition carries on and is still dominant as of today (e.g., we can mention the famous, late bands Bérurier Noir, OTH, Les Cadavres, Ludwig Von 88 and other bands that remain active, such as Les Shériff, Charge 69, Tagada Jones, Les Sales Majestés, La Fraction, Guerilla Poubelle, Justin[e], Verdun, etc.). A less important set of bands use English,[9] with an accent that sometimes hardly dissimulates their nationality (Dogs, Les Thugs, Burning Heads, Sixpack, Seven Hate, Dead Pop Club, Dead End, Flying Donuts, etc.). In both cases, this double linguistic specificity (the use of French and the use of English with a French accent) seems to constitute a distinctive feature of this scene. At another level, it also stands out by its singular social, political and cultural environment. For example, the way the French administration is organized authorizes legal persons (particularly in their associative form) to solicit public institutions, such as ministries (culture or youth and sports), regional authorities (regions and departments), as well as local authorities (municipalities) for subsidies. In the same way, the Ministry of Labor can offer help for occupational integration to certain categories of population, with subsidized work contracts (the employer receiving a financial contribution, which reduces the cost of labor). In this composite context, public authorities potentially constitute real resources (but also a sum of constraints) for French cultural entrepreneurs. We will now see how some agents of our scene evolve within this environment, by pointing how these resources are most commonly perceived, justified and used.

Supporting Youth

A look at the career of the band Flying Donuts reveals that it has gradually become quite competent in identifying and activating levers useful for its development. For example, it never relinquished the idea of requesting support from a certain number of public institutions. Thus, as soon as 2001, the band applied for the Défi Jeunes (Youth Challenge) plan that was implemented by the Ministry of Youth and Sports. This plan aims at encouraging youth initiatives within many fields: cultural, social, humanitarian, ecological, sports, scientific, economic and so forth. The procedure is rather simple. It first consists of applying. Then, after a first selection, the remaining candidates defend their projects in front of a board of evaluation. There are plenty of projects, and certain punks will try—often with success—and land credits in order to create fanzines, labels, festivals and so on. The Flying Donuts thus got 12,000 francs (€1,830), a sum of money that enabled them to start the production of their first album, *Last Straight Line* (2002, Figure 12.2).[10] The album was immediately recorded at the studio Pôle Nord in Blois, by Fred Gramage, who was back then the star sound engineer of the French punk rock scene. This first practical success comforted the band in the choice

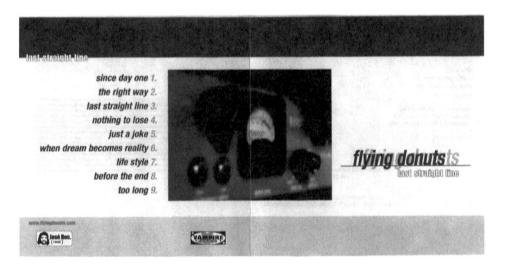

Figure 12.2 Flying Donuts, *Last Straight Line*, José Records/Vampire Records, 2002, compact disc back and front cover.

they had made to set up projects that could justify regularly soliciting institutions endowed with funds devoted to supporting cultural production.

Supporting Cultural Production

In France, support for cultural production is implemented in the name of cultural democracy. Broadly, the idea is to support cultural diversity, the professionalization of its agents and the development of economic sectors linked to culture (Teillet 2003). It is based on the idea that, in order to flourish, entrepreneurial dynamics stemming from the cultural sector have to rely on human (creative) and economic resources. Now, the cultural sector is characterized by a very strong imbalance between human resources, usually overabundant, and rather anemic economic resources. The resulting insolvency could theoretically be compensated by public action. Very clearly, French cultural democracy translates itself into the potential distribution of subsidies to agents of the art or cultural worlds, including the punk culture, as long as they are able to defend their application for subsidies, demonstrating their project is useful for society. This sometimes enables musical entrepreneurs to finance the production of an album, the organization of a tour or the making of communication material (posters, flyers). To give an example, Flying Donuts applied for funds from the Vosges Departmental Council's (*Conseil Général*) association for music, dance and theater, at the time of the release of their second album (2006, Figure 12.3).

Of course, the recipient of public funding must meet obligations: when, in France, a regional authority subsidizes a cultural enterprise, it usually expects its logo to be associated with the result. It is a principle of mutual gratitude: fair's fair. Yet, artists grudgingly play the game, as shown in the following conversation (Hein 2011, 95):

> [Flying Donuts] The Departmental Council helped us out two or three times. We asked them to support a release or a tour. Usually, it's for the release.

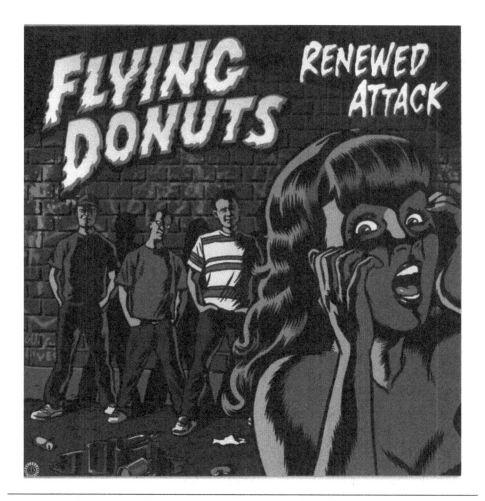

Figure 12.3 Flying Donuts, *Renewed Attack*, José Records, 2006, compact disc front cover.

[**Fabien Hein**] Yeah! And they never asked you to include their logo?

[**Flying Donuts**] They did, but we didn't do it, that's why they won't give us any more money . . . I was surprised that they refused to help us out on our latest album. I think they were pretty upset at us, because they gave several reasons to justify their refusal. The first had to do with the crisis. Less dough, which meant they had to make choices. The second was that we had never put their logo on the posters and the other material, when we were supposed to . . .

[**Fabien Hein**] And they still supported you several times?

[**Flying Donuts**] Yes, we were bastards. It's not that we didn't want to accept it, we just didn't want to have a logo . . . I mean the logo was a pain in the ass. I think I even went to the

Departmental Council once or twice, to give them the record. I had added the logo on the sleeve. I had printed it myself and I gave them that copy. Something kind of dishonest . . .

In fact, the logos of public authorities usually badly blend into punk rock sleeves. This leads artists to exert strategies of avoidance that are always unmasked one day or the other. Indeed, eight months after my book on Flying Donuts was published,[11] the person in charge of the Vosges Departmental Council's association for music, dance and theater sent the band an inflammatory message:

> I read the book *Ma petite entreprise* . . . , I have to tell you very clearly that the things you said on your relationship/position/attitude towards the Vosges Departmental Council are scandalous. I was shocked, both on a professional and a personal level. And I'm not the only one.
>
> (Thierry Szabo, email message to Flying Donuts, March 8, 2012)

This event will most probably terminate all relationships between the band and public authorities. By revealing its methods, Flying Donuts obviously exposed itself to strong moral reprobation, from an institutional point of view. Yet, in the end, the risk was quite small, since, at the time the band publicly exposed its views, it knew fairly well that it had exhausted all available institutional resources.[12] The band also perfectly knows that most subsidized artists (or artists looking for public support) deploy strategies identical to theirs, in order to avoid institutional labeling norms. This eventually makes the project grow in stature within the artistic community (whichever the form of art), which often considers public action as a resource one should make the most out of. As one fierce and very pragmatic punk entrepreneur, who had obtained the Défi Jeunes subsidy, told me,[13] "you have to suck up the cash where you find it."

In fact, it seems that the French punk rock scene constantly wavers between subversion and subsidy (Brandl 2009). This ambivalence can probably be even better understood in the light of "SMAC" labeled venues,[14] that in a certain way grant an indirect subsidy to certain artists. Indeed, these venues are subsidized as well, and are the rare places to offer the possibility of performing within good technical conditions (per diems, fees). Few artists, including those most critical of the institutions, can afford to refuse such opportunities. Besides, these venues also propose a certain number of development support funds, which especially support the professionalization of local artists. To take only one example, L'Autre Canal[15] set up a breeding ground for a handful of artists it had spotted beforehand, Flying Donuts being one of them. This system enabled the band to cover, every now and then, a certain number of overhead expenses that it could not have otherwise financed. These include studio recording sessions, run-throughs allowing the band to test and perfect a set in real conditions (with sound and light engineers) without the presence of the audience and, finally, to finance a promotional campaign (with press agents) and their album *Until the Morning Comes* (2009).

However, despite the quality of such plans, public action never totally resolves the solvency problems cultural enterprises face. Nor does it answer on the long term the professionalization stakes that are inseparable from it. At best, public action can help a band temporarily and partially overcome the uncertain sustainability of cultural activities. This frequently leads the more perseverant cultural entrepreneurs to resort to a multiplicity of support help plans.[16]

Supporting Employment

In France, access to the unemployment insurance regime for freelance entertainment workers (*intermittents du spectacle*)[17] usually is a good indicator of the professionalization of musicians. At the peak of their career, and despite a high number of concerts every year, Flying Donuts' band members were never able to justify 507 hours of declared work, the minimum amount to enter the regime. Failing that, the band thus turned to the Ministry of Labor, Employment and Vocational Training and the measures it implemented for occupational integration, thanks to which their label, José Records, was able to employ three musicians for two years.[18] These measures aimed at supporting employment[19] are also extended to nonmusicians. Each agent of the punk rock scene can thus potentially apply for them, in function of a certain number of criteria. The example of the "youth employments" (*emplois-jeunes*) system is a good illustration of this. Launched in 1997 and suspended in 2002, this program aimed at proposing five-year-long employment contracts for young people aged under 26, within the public or associative sectors.[20] To give a few details, the fanzines *Worst* and *Kérosène*, major players within the 1990s–2000s French punk rock scene, each could create one job. The label and distributor Overcome Records, which is specialized in punk rock, hardcore and metal, was able to employ five people for a while, thanks to subsidized employments. However, despite the beneficiaries' strong commitment and undisputable upscaling competences, the systems are rarely more than a reprieve. Within punk rock, those who manage to make their jobs perennial are rare.

Field workers generally know this. It is almost impossible to sustainably live off punk rock in France, on a full-time basis. There are no concrete exceptions to demonstrate the contrary. This is why DIY is so predominant in France. Key figures of French punk rock like the Burning Heads—who were on a contract with Epitaph Records, then Yelen, a French subsidiary of Sony—modestly came back to self-production. International references such as Bérurier Noir or Les Thugs never could (or wanted to) make any lasting income off their musical activities.[21] As for the economic situation of French punk labels (Bondage Records, Crash Disques, Spliff Records, Combat Rock, Guerilla Asso, Mass Prod, Kicking Records, Enragé Production, etc.), it never was very strong, with the result that, in the absence of sustainable (and thus prosperous) punk rock structures, nothing seems to indicate today any true inversion of the trend. Not to mention the fact that, for certain agents of this scene, the idea that their musical activity might someday evolve into a full-time job is out of the question:

So we wanna bust the market? / We ain't down to earth? Not ready to ask for 15 Euros for a concert / I'm ready to slave away with a side-job to stick to this deal, this fucking freedom / I'm not even gonna try to explain why / Why we're here and why we do this / If there's "Guerilla" in our name, it ain't to make a job out of it.

(Excerpt from "Punk-Rock Is Not a Job," Guerilla Poubelle, 2007)

The Punk Rock Biotope in France

In France, the institutionalization of rock, and then of contemporary popular music (*musiques actuelles*), leads many informed citizens to deeply interiorize the mechanisms of public intervention. Subsidies are part of the cultural sector's biotope. Almost everything is subsidized, so much so that the fact of resorting to the systems implemented by the public authorities is rarely debated, including within the punk scene, despite its anti-institutional mood. As an example, the Independent Musical Initiatives Day (Journée des Initiatives Musicales Indépendantes, or JIMI), which has been taking place every year since 2007, is subsidized by the Île-de-France Region and the Departmental Council of the Val-de-Marne, without this ever causing any stir. Of course, a handful of punk agents resolutely oppose any form of institutionalization:

> The money comes from my personal bank account. Everyone lives his life as he wishes, but for nothing in the world would I have asked for subsidies.
> (Stéphane, Lollipop Records label manager, *DaN* 1998, 44–45)

> We learn how to live / Without anyone giving us anything / We learn how to live / Without anyone giving us anything.
> (Excerpt from "Sirènes" ["Mermaids"], by the band La Fraction, 2006)

> That's the thing, that's the spirit. [. . .] You have to say "fuck off"* to all of that. Fuck off to all the problems relating to money, to advertising, to institutions, to all of that. We gotta stop. We gotta get back to something that pisses everyone off. We're gonna do our own thing and fuck you!
> (Excerpt from the DVD *Come on People!* by the band Les Thugs, 2012)

The idea of independence is part of the scene's common rhetoric. However, most punk entrepreneurs seem not to see any incompatibility between subsidy and independence, as the following quote illustrates:

> Let me be clear: in over ten years, we never touched a single penny of subsidy. Ideologically, if getting money imposes constraints on you and obliges you to submit to certain things, then it's out of the question. On the contrary, to get subsidies would be very useful. In fact, we didn't really look in that direction. If one day we get some, all the better, but I don't want to spend my time running after each public subsidy to get something done. It's the problem confronted by certain associations that only live thanks to them. If they enable you to go further, that's OK, but to choose State handouts is stupid.
> (Caps, Combat rock label manager and bass player for Charge 69, as quoted in Guite 2000, 74–79)

Such sentiments, which are shared by many French punk entrepreneurs, indicate that subsidies (whether direct or indirect) are indeed widely "naturalized" by the members of the scene. They are conceivable provided that they don't infringe upon the punk entrepreneur's independence of action, which means that subsidies are acceptable as long as they are considered a gift—a position difficulty defendable, inasmuch as gifts, according to Marcel Mauss, imply reciprocity in the form of countergifts. Thus, the awarding of public grants always engages the beneficiaries. This obviously strongly questions the relationship French punks have to DIY that, in a certain way—to put things exaggeratedly—could simply mean filling up the forms on their own. Within this configuration, there is absolutely no contradiction between the fact that a French punk entrepreneur will pretend to live according to the DIY ethics, on the one hand, while benefiting from public money, support for employment or other forms of public aid via subsidized establishments, on the other, especially as he can always deploy, with more or less skill, a certain number of strategies of avoidance, on a declarative or performative mode.

Conclusion: Punk Rock Authenticity

In France, punk authenticity linked to DIY practices generally relies upon three main types of antagonistic or complementary positions:

- An ideological position (in minority, essentially held by the anarcho-punk scene), which refuses any form of compromise with public authorities.
- A pragmatic position (dominant), which consists in resorting to public aids, while using cunning to avoid the obligations required by public authorities.
- A theoretical position (dominant), which denigrates public authorities without renouncing the resources its numerous systems offer.

Seen from the outside, the French punk rock scene could give the impression that it endlessly writhes about, or worse: that it bites the hand that feeds it. But on the substance, is this paradox specific to the French scene? With a few exceptions, it seems that a vast majority of the global punk scene has to deal with a similar paradox. Indeed, entangled in the toils of contemporary capitalism, its agents have to exploit the resources made available by their environment, in order to exist. In France, principles of cultural democracy, solidarity and innovation precisely offer a certain number of such resources. Elsewhere, commercial enterprises such as Vans or Eastpak are the ones that, inasmuch as they provide resources to the punk rock scene, are severely criticized within this scene. Consequently, the resources of the French punk rock scene can seem relatively original to the exterior observer. The necessity to obtain resources is a feature common to all punk entrepreneurs around the globe. In the end, the dialectics between DIY and independence are always a question of degrees, of a transaction between oneself and oneself, between oneself and one's environment.

Notes

1 I wish to thank Gérôme Guibert and Catherine Rudent for their comments on the first draft of this chapter.
2 The enquiry, which took place between September 2007 and June 2010, extended to the whole national territory, with a particular focus on northeastern France. It combined a certain number of methods: qualitative (participant observation and interviews), quantitative (questionnaire, tally, cartography) and documentary

(the exploitation of various types of archives, such as discography, photography, videos, specialist publications, accounts books and preliminary budgets).

3   This network, whose density and amplitude are variable, links human beings (producers, music lovers), objects (records, instruments, fanzines, etc.) and apparatuses (festivals, labels, distribution circuits, etc.).

4   That is, "the instance that organizes the person's behavior [and] organizes the coherence of action" (Karpik 2007, 104–105).

5   Most studies dealing with the punk scene show that punk authenticity generally develops itself within a dialectic opposing "commercial" punk and "DIY" punk (O'Connor 2008; Baulch 2002). The French punk scene is no exception to the rule (Hein 2012).

6   Flying Donuts is a punk rock trio from the French department of the Vosges. Since its inception in 1996, the band player over 500 concerts throughout Europe and Quebec. It also recorded three albums and three EPs (two of which split albums), released in CD, vinyl and 45 rpm formats. Additionally, the band managed to have tracks on approximately fifteen compilations. During its career, Flying Donuts self-produced or co-produced its own recordings via its associative structure, José Records. Since 2009, the band has been closely tied to the label Kicking Records, one of the leaders in the French punk market. Its way of functioning is typical of most French punk bands. It belongs to the category of experienced, stable and long-lasting bands. Its media coverage is intermediate: at the national level, it is neither a big nor a small band. Its commercial capacity spans between 1,000 and 3,000 copies per release (a figure that seems to be close to average at a national level and hints at the proportions of the French punk rock market).

7   A quick look at *Maximumrocknroll*, the most influent punk rock fanzine, suffices to confirm this fact.

8   Paris, Rouen, Le Havre and Lyon then being the most visible creative hubs.

9   To give a rough idea of the proportions, out of 280 French punk bands who have a page on Wikipedia, 235 sing in French.

10 The total budget amounted to €4,100.

11 I must state that everything the Flying Donuts said was validated by the band members before the publication of the book. The band members were thus perfectly conscious of the risks they were taking by being so outspoken.

12 On principle, support for cultural production is aimed at facilitating professionalization, and thus autonomy. Thus, support cannot be long lasting nor systematic. Roughly, the institutions try to avoid artists repeatedly capturing the subsidies, so as to enable newcomers to profit from them.

13 This young man, who has the gift of the gab, got 44,000 francs (€6,700) to start a magazine, without the board of evaluation ever asking him if he knew how to use a computer, or if he actually even had one.

14 Scènes de Musiques Actuelles (Contemporary Popular Music Venues). Since 1998, this institutional label tallies with the Ministry of Culture's program to support the diffusion of contemporary popular music. It designates a specific multiparty agreement, elaborated by venues and their public partners: state and regional authorities. As of today, France has seventy SMACs, and plans to have one per department by 2015 (i.e., forty-five more).

15 L'Autre Canal is a Cultural Cooperation Public Establishment (Établissement Public de Coopération Culturelle), managed by the town of Nancy, the Lorraine region and the Ministry of Culture, Regional Direction of Lorraine Cultural Affairs. This structure, which is labeled as a SMAC, is mostly known for being a concert venue dedicated to contemporary popular music.

16 These plans thus not only represent resources but also strategic stakes.

17 This unique regime offers a right to compensation (unemployment insurance) for artists and technicians temporarily working in the entertainment business (live performance, cinema, radio and television) who can justify a workload of at least 507 hours within a ten-month period; 100,000 people benefit from this regime in France.

18 These subsidized jobs were made of degressive public aids, as well as exemptions from employers' contributions. In broad outline, the state covered 90% of the wages during the six first months, 75% the following six months and 50% the second year.

19 These measures, which are characteristic of periods of crisis, are usually launched after government changes. For example, following the April 2012 presidential elections, the government decided to create a new plan of action called "jobs with prospects" (*emplois d'avenir*).

20 The state financed 80% of the contractual wages.

21 The rare French punk artists who are determined to live exclusively off their music usually struggle to achieve such a goal. In the best-case scenario, when they are freelance entertainment workers, they are often obliged to find fees in activities peripheral to punk rock (they often are technicians or teachers). In the end, the only French punk rock artists who managed to gain musical success seem to be Manu Chao (ex-Hot Pants, Mano Negra), Sergent Garcia (ex-Ludwig von 88) and Jean-Yves Prieur, a.k.a. Kid Loco (the creator of Bondage Records): in each one of these cases success was obtained after giving up punk rock. The example of the

Wampas is particular. Although the band has been on contract with majors since 1993 (BMG, then Atmosphériques, a subsidiary of Universal), its lead singer, Didier Wampas, held on to his job as an electrician for the RATP (the state-owned public transport operator for Paris and its suburbs), until he retired in 2012.

* Translator's note: In English in the text.

Bibliography

Baulch, Emma. 2002. "Creating a Scene: Balinese Punk's Beginnings." *International Journal of Cultural Studies* 5(2):153–177.

Brandl, Emmanuel. 2009. *L'ambivalence du rock: entre subversion et subvention. Une enquête sur l'institutionnalisation des musiques populaires.* Paris: L'Harmattan.

Calmbach, Marc. 2007. *More than Music: Einblicke in die Jugendkultur.* Bielefeld: Transcript.

Dale, Pete. 2012. *Anyone Can Do It: Empowerment, Tradition and the Punk Underground.* Aldershot: Ashgate.

DaN. 1998. "Lollipop Records." *Kérosène* 6.

Goffman, Erving. 1974. *Les rites d'interaction.* Paris: Minuit.

Guibert, Gérôme. 2006. *La production de la culture: Le cas des musiques amplifiées en France. Genèse, structurations, industries, alternatives.* Paris and St Amant Tallende: Irma/éditions Seteun.

Guite. 2000. "10 ans de Combat Rock." *Kérosène* 11.

Hebdige, Dick. 2008. *Sous-Culture: Le sens du style.* Paris: Zones.

Hein, Fabien. 2011. *Ma petite entreprise punk: Sociologie du système D.* Toulouse: Kicking Books.

———. 2012. *Do It Yourself! Autodétermination et culture punk.* Paris: Le passager clandestin.

Karpik, Lucien. 2007. *L'économie des singularités.* Paris: Gallimard, coll. "Bibliothèque des sciences humaines."

O'Connor, Alan. 2008. *Punk Record Labels and the Struggle for Autonomy: The Emergence of DIY.* Lanham: Lexington Books.

O'Hara, Craig. 1999. *The Philosophy of Punk: More Than Noise.* San Francisco: AK Press.

Pépin, Rémi. 2007. *Rebelles: Une histoire de rock alternatif.* Paris: Hugo and Compagnie.

Reynolds, Simon. 2007. *Rip It Up and Start Again: Postpunk 1978–1984.* Paris: Allia.

Rollins, Henry. 1994. *Get in the Van: On the Road With Black Flag.* Los Angeles: 2.13.61.

Rudeboy, Arno. 2007. *Nyark nyark! Fragments des scènes punk et rock alternatif en France. 1976–1989.* Paris: La Découverte.

Savage, Jon. 2012. "Esthétique du punk." In *Punk: Une esthétique,* edited by Johan Kugelberg and Jon Savage, 146–149. New York: Rizzoli.

Sinker, Daniel. 2001. *We Owe You Nothing: Punk Planet: The Collected Interviews.* New York: Akashic Books.

Teillet, Philippe. 2003. "Publics et politiques des musiques actuelles." In *Le(s) public(s) de la culture,* edited by Olivier Donnat and Paul Tolila, 155–180. Paris: Presses de Sciences Po.

PART IV

From Digital Stakes to Cultural Heritage
French Contemporary Topics

Gérôme Guibert and Catherine Rudent

From the standpoint of creation, where is French musical production today? And, conversely, how does the national population now see popular music? Has the place of music in society changed, and, if so, are these changes specific to France? Through four situated studies and an introduction, this section aims to review some of the more revealing debates currently surrounding music in France and thus also pick up on local research published in popular music studies.

Anyone taking an interest in the general trends affecting the music industry in France in the early twenty-first century cannot ignore the extent to which many of them are related to the international context. With the rise of the power of the Internet, the music market entered a crisis in France in the early twenty-first century. According to the Syndicat National de l'Édition Phonographique,[1] the sales turnover for recorded music in the country (both physical and digital media) more than halved between 2002 and 2010, from an annual €1.3 billion (2002) to €500 million in 2010. According to the Centre National de la chanson, des Variétés et du jazz,[2] live performance revenues, calculated via ticket sales, have however been rising steadily, equalling sales of recorded music at €500 million in 2010 (Guibert and Sagot-Duvauroux 2013), before exceeding them over the following years. These changes (rise of the Internet and changing sources of income) have led to a transformation in music production (Lizé et al. 2014) and the business models of companies involved in the sector as they seek to adapt (Moreau 2014).

The rise of digital has obviously had an impact at all levels of social life, and popular music has not been spared, whether in terms of the work of musicians (Rudent 2008), music's mediation (Hennion et al. 2000; Ribac 2004) or listening practices (Pecqueux and Roueff 2009; Sklower 2013). Some researchers, who hypothesise a profound change in practices and production methods, even go as far as considering most of the work constituting popular music research as irrelevant (Le Guern 2012), neglecting in particular the *material turn* and a return to things (Nowak 2013).

The higher stakes surrounding intellectual property rights and the move towards what in France is termed "cognitive capitalism" (Moulier Boutang 2007) have translated into original cultural consequences in the national context. We can mention two. The first concerns public policy. Following the confrontation between professional lobbyists and peer-to-peer sites in respect to the recognition of rights holders, the French state established a raft of measures to fight against illegal downloading including the HADOPI Law in 2009. An account of the background to these developments is given in this book in the chapter by Raphael Suire and Sylvain Dejean.[3] The French authorities initially reacted to repress peer-to-peer sites because, even in the current global context, the state is traditionally perceived as the guarantor of collective standards, including those from a cultural perspective.[4] Studying the impact of the measures of this law, and comparing them with the actual practices of French people, Suire and Dejean's work emphasises once again how the timing of decisions can be out of step with practices. It also reminds us of the extent to which the law is indicative of power relations between stakeholders, property rights being synonymous with potential earnings for those able to get themselves recognised as owners but with the potential restriction of freedoms for those who see themselves as resisting this position (De Certeau 1980). Focusing on a different group, French musicians,[5] Maya Bacache-Beauvallet et al. (2011) also shows how the position of musicians within the production chain has an influence on attitudes towards respect for intellectual property rights. When their incomes depend largely on the sale of recorded music or when they have produced or co-produced their recordings, they become rather legalistic. However, the more their income depends on performance (live music), the more favourable they appear to allowing their music to circulate, without it being paid for and even illegally circulated.

If, depending on context, consumers have made use of tactics to circumvent the law, producers and broadcasters have used strategies to accommodate accessibility to music (price, scarcity, accessibility), depending on the reputation of artists and the image they seek to produce. Thus, they have taken action on subscription pricing or the sale of files of recorded music. They have even, downstream, and according to strategic opportunities, placed more or less drastic controls on the circulation of sound files or videos on sites offering amateur content (Beuscart 2007; Bouquillion 2012; Constantini 2015). A radical case is described in the chapter in this book by Anne Petiau, whereby the name Tecktonik, used to describe a musical genre that developed in Île-de-France nightclubs around 2005, was bought by two entrepreneurs who made a brand out of it, limiting de facto the use of the term by enthusiasts of this emerging subculture and thereby bringing about its decline, even after certain proponents had renamed it electro dance.

The detailed analysis of this current in electronic music allows Petiau to shed light on new production configurations at work today, since, here, musical compositions that resulted from the work of self-produced musicians working at home (Jouvenet 2006) were put online on specialised platforms and circulated on social networks (Beuscart and Couronné 2009) before being acquired by larger companies that commercialised and promoted this content (Petiau 2011).

From an aesthetic point of view, the role played by electronic music in the revival of the landscape of French popular music must also be emphasised, especially music falling under the French Touch appellation and particularly the perception of it in the English-speaking world (Julien 2002; Guibert 2009). We can mention artists like Daft Punk, Air and Dimitri from Paris from the end of the last decade of the twentieth century, and then a few years later, at the dawn of the new millennium, others such as Phoenix, Justice and David Guetta. The success of these artists has also come about alongside the structuring of French cultural policy around export, notably through the BureauExport (established in 1993), an organisation receiving funds both from public sources and private companies in the world of music. If, despite popular international success, French Touch as such no longer constitutes a teeming musical genre in France, many musicians of the groups that once recognised themselves as being part of it (Gastaut 2012) continue today in careers as producers and musicians. The group Air, for example, after working on the soundtrack to Sofia Coppola's *The Virgin Suicides* (1999), were behind singer Charlotte Gainsbourg's album *5:55* (Because Music, 2006), and its musicians are now pursuing solo careers. For Nicolas Godin, one of the members of Air who is now a solo artist,

> At the beginning of the twentieth century,[6] the first "French Touch" wave, that of Ravel, Messiaen, Dutilleux and Schaeffer had a true worldwide aura, which got a bit lost with the triumph of rock. I wanted to reconnect with that musical history.
>
> (*Le Monde*, 27 September 2015, 21)

Indeed, it could be said that French electronic music provided an original rereading of the genesis of French music. Godin frequently puts centre stage composers considered to be art music composers (from Ravel to Dutilleux through Messiaen), film music composers (François de Roubaix, Michel Magne, Francis Lai, Michel Colombier, André Popp) and French musicians who were precursors of electronic music, especially GRM[7] members Pierre Schaeffer and Pierre Henry, but also, for example, Jean-Michel Jarre, who worked under Pierre Schaeffer before turning to pop formats.

The individualisation of social time is another great contemporary global trend in the evolution of music, as sound studies underlines. Music can now fit into the smallest nooks and crannies in cities (Rouzé 2005). In this book, Vincent Rouzé shows the multiplicity of possible derivations of musical recordings based on their social use. Whether as background music, music broadcast in public areas (commercial or otherwise) or thematic compilations dedicated to specific spaces or sporting activities or meditation, the history of this invisible music can inform us on the French context and its evolution. It also underlines, beyond new musical habits in part determined by economic developments and conditions of employment, the role of new technologies (Rouzé 2010) in the subjective appropriation of music. One of the most important results of Rouzé's work is indeed to show us how musical content can be re-interpreted according to the context in which it is played, "mood music" thus happily grouping together "French- and English-language works, pop and classical music," the importance being the broadcast context and the unobtrusive aspect of the selected recordings.

In France, as elsewhere, the profusion of the musical offering made possible by the Internet has led to selection strategies to cope with the "diet of abundance" (Auray 2011), inverting the traditional problem of scarcity (Baudrillard 1970). One response to the globalisation of the cultural offering is a return to proximity (Warnier 1999), to that which takes place close to home, locally (Guibert and Parent 2015). In addition to a renewed interest in local artists and events, both from residents and public policy in search of a positive image for municipalities (Guibert 2012; Saez 2014), there has been a multiplication of local initiatives, firstly in terms of archival collections and exhibitions that seek to preserve the memory of events and objects related to local popular music (Touché 2007). More broadly, we see popular music "becoming part of the focus for museums" (Touché 2012; Guibert 2013). Love of music, a desire for the recognition or legitimisation of popular music, nostalgia and identity construction are all part of the multiple and sometimes contradictory motivations behind this. Although recent, this phenomenon would seem to be far-reaching and is occurring at a time when museums are themselves in crisis. Juliette Dalbavie, who in her doctoral thesis in 2008 was a precursor in France in terms of these questions, deals with the case of the relationship between heritage and *chanson* through the figure of Georges Brassens, the museum dedicated to him in Sète, the town he came from, and the role of his grave, located near the museum (Espace Georges Brassens), echoing one of his most famous songs, "Supplique pour être enterré à la plage de Sète" ("Plea to be buried on the beach at Sète"). It thus seems that, by bringing a group of people together through common spatial-temporal components, collective memory research (Halbwachs 1997) facilitates the production of meaning and resources that sometimes need to be strengthened in a context of cultural globalisation. We are witnessing in France, as elsewhere, an "emotional turning point" and a rediscovery of the importance of materiality in daily living (Warnier 1994).

Notes

1 The SNEP is the French phonographic industry's national representative body.
2 Generally called CNV, the Centre National de la chanson, des variétés et du jazz is a French public body created in 2002 in support of live performance of jazz, *chanson* and pop.
3 These authors carried out several quantitative studies on perception and the impact of HADOPI, which can be found on m@rsouin.org
4 According to a logic many foreigners see as a restriction of freedoms, the HADOPI law is sometimes compared to the law on radio broadcasting quotas for French language titles that was enacted on 1 February 1994, these laws sometimes being associated with issues surrounding cultural exception or cultural diversity (Poirrier 2006).
5 From the ADAMI (French copyright clearance agency for artists and performers) members database.
6 The composers mentioned were in fact active at the beginning (Ravel), middle (Messiaen, Schaeffer) and then in the second half (Dutilleux) of the twentieth century. The division here is not chronological, as Dutilleux's work was contemporaneous to rock, but rather cultural, between music legitimised by institutions and music unfolding outside of them for a long time, until the 1980s.
7 Groupe de recherches musicales (a centre for musical research in the domain of sound and electronic music set up in 1958 by sound engineers working at the RTF—Radio Télévision Française).

Bibliography

Auray, Nicolas. 2011. "La consommation en régime d'abondance: La confrontation aux offres culturelles dites illimitées." *Revue Française de Socio-Économie* 8(2):85–102.
Bacache-Beauvallet, Maya, Marc Bourreau, and François Moreau. 2011. *Portrait des musiciens à l'heure du numérique*. Paris: Rue d'Ulm.
Baudrillard, Jean. 1970. *La société de consommation*. Paris: Denoël.
Beuscart, Jean-Samuel. 2007. "Les transformations de l'intermédiation musicale La construction de l'offre commerciale de musique en ligne en France." *Réseaux* 25(141–142):143–176.
Beuscart, Jean-Samuel, and Thomas Couronné. 2009. "La distribution de la notoriété en ligne. Une analyse quantitative de MySpace." *Terrains & Travaux* 15:147–170.
Bouquillion, Philippe. 2012. "Mutation des industries musicales et actualité des industries culturelles." In *Sound Factory*, edited by Stéphane Dorin, 125–140. Saffré: Mélanie Seteun.
Constantini, Stéphane. 2015. "De la scène musicale aux réseaux musicalisés. Les inscriptions territoriales et socio-économiques de l'activité artistique." *Réseaux* 4(192):143–167.
Dalbavie, Juliette. 2003. "Exposer des objets sonores: le cas des chansons de Brassens." *Volume! La revue des musiques populaires* 2(2):145–161.
De Certeau, Michel. 1990 [1980]. *L'invention du quotidien, I: Arts de faire*. Paris: Gallimard.
Dejean, Sylvain, Thierry Pénard, and Raphaël Suire. 2010. "La gratuité est-elle une fatalité sur les marchés numériques? Une étude sur le consentement à payer pour des offres de contenus audiovisuels sur internet." *Économie et Prévision* 194(3):15–32.

Flichy, Patrice. 2009. "Comment Internet est devenu un marché." In *Traité de Sociologie Économique*, edited by Steiner Philippe and François Vatin, 451–492. Paris: Puf.

Gastaut, Amélie, ed. 2012. *French Touch: Graphisme, Video, Electro*. Paris: Les Arts Décoratifs.

Gayou, Evelyne. 2007. *GRM. Groupe de recherches musicales: Cinquante ans d'histoire*. Paris: Fayard.

Guibert, Gérôme. 2009. "Versailles and the French Touch: When a Virtual Local Scene Becomes Real." IASPM biennale conference paper, Liverpool.

———. 2012. "'La classe rémoise': À propos du traitement médiatique des musiques populaires émergentes en France." *Contemporary French Civilization* 36(1–2):97–112.

———. 2013. "The sound of the city: À propos du colloque 'Pop music, Pop musée. Un nouveau défi patrimonial.'" *Musée et Collections Publiques de France* 268:28–33.

Guibert, Gérôme, and Emmanuel Parent. 2015. "When Folk Meets Pop: DIY Archives in the Making of a Punk Rock DIY Community in Western France." In *Preserving Popular Music Heritage: Do-It-Yourself, Do-It-Together*, edited by Sarah Baker, 104–113. New York: Routledge.

Guibert, Gérôme, and Dominique Sagot-Duvauroux. 2013. *Musiques actuelles: ça part en live. Analyse économique d'une filière culturelle*. Paris: Irma/DEPS.

Halbwachs, Maurice. 1997 [1950]. *La mémoire collective*. Paris: Albin Michel.

Hennion, Antoine, Sophie Maisonneuve, and Émilie Gomart. 2000. *Figures de L'amateur: Formes, objets, pratiques de l'amour de la musique aujourd'hui*. Paris: La Documentation Française.

Heuguet, Guillaume. 2014. "Le smartphone et le concert." *Esprit* 11:125–127.

Jouvenet, Morgan. 2006. *Rap, techno, électro . . . Le musicien entre travail artistique et critique sociale*. Paris: Éditions de la Maison des Sciences de l'Homme.

Julien, Olivier. 2002. "La technologie de la French Touch: Les Paul ou Pierre Schaeffer?" *Musurgia* 9(2):71–84.

Le Guern, Philippe. 2012. "Irréversible? Musique et technologies en régime numérique." *Réseaux* 172:29–64.

Lizé, Wenceslas, Delphine Naudier, and Séverine Sofio, eds. 2014. *Les stratèges de la notoriété: Intermédiaires et consécration dans les univers artistiques*. Paris: Éditions des Archives Contemporaines.

Moreau, François. 2014. "L'industrie de la musique aujourd'hui." *Cahiers Français* 382:39–45.

Moulier-Boutang, Yann. 2007. *Le capitalisme cognitif: La nouvelle grande transformation*. Paris: Éditions Amsterdam.

Nowak, Raphaël. 2013. "Consommer la musique à L'ère du numérique: vers une analyse des environnements sonores." *Volume! La revue des musiques populaires* 10(1):227–228.

Pecqueux, Anthony, and Olivier Roueff, eds. 2009. *Écologie sociale de l'oreille: Enquêtes sur L'expérience musicale*. Paris: Éditions de l'EHESS.

Petiau, Anne. 2006. "Marginalité et musiques électroniques." *Agora: Débats, Jeunesse* 42(1):128–137.

———. 2011. *Technomedia*. Saffré: Mélanie Seteun.

Poirrier, Philippe. 2006. *L'État et la culture en France au XXe siècle*. Paris: Le Livre de Poche.

Ribac, François. 2004. *L'avaleur de rock*. Paris: La Dispute.

Rouzé, Vincent. 2005. "Musicaliser le quotidien: analyse et enjeux de mises en scène particulières." *Volume! La revue des musiques populaires* 4(2):41–50.

———. 2010. *Mythologie de l'ipod*. Paris: Le Cavalier Bleu.

Rudent, Catherine. 2008. "Le premier album de mademoiselle K. Entre création individuelle et coopérations négociées." *Ethnologie Française* 38(1):69–78.

Saez, Guy. 2014. "La métropolisation de la culture." *Cahier Français* 382:10–15.

Sklower, Jedediah. 2013. "Audiologies." *Volume! La revue des musiques populaires* 10(1):7–20.

Touché, Marc. 2007. "Muséographier les musiques amplifiées: Pour une socio-histoire du sonore." *Réseaux* 25(141–142):297–325.

———. 2012. "Les musiques amplifiées s'exposent . . . et s'invitent dans les musées." *Questions de Communication* 22:57–86.

Warnier, Jean-Pierre, ed. 1994. *Le paradoxe de la marchandise authentique*. Paris: L'Harmattan.

———. 1999. *La Mondialisation de la culture*. Paris: La Découverte.

13

Incorporating *Chanson* Into Heritage, a Shared Process Between Museums and Collective Memory

The Case Study of Georges Brassens in Sète

Juliette Dalbavie

Does the *chanson de variétés*[1] become part of the national heritage as easily as a major work of art? The expression "to become part of heritage" shows how important it is to describe the process whereby cultural objects acquire heritage status. Unlike family heritage, collective heritage is not handed down to us from our ascendants; transmission is effected by the recipients of objects rather than their donors. In other words, in the case of cultural heritage, its heirs start from the present and attribute a certain value to specific objects, thereby transforming them into items of heritage. This recognition of value does not merely depend on favourable opinion or a special taste or interest at some given moment. An object must undergo several processes to acquire heritage status: discovery (or rediscovery), knowledge of it, authentication, declaration, presentation to the public and transmission (Davallon 2006). Several of these stages posit the existence of scientific expertise and political recognition, as well as the organisation of exhibitions aimed at sharing this piece of common property.

Though there is a wealth of *chanson* archives in France, there are relatively few exhibitions and museums devoted to it. The political project to establish and highlight any such song heritage is relatively recent and has only been partially realised. Admittedly, there has been an institution in charge of enhancing the status of *chanson* since 1990; it is supported by the Ministry of Culture and Communication and is known as the Hall de la Chanson, but it does not have a real exhibition hall on site, nor is the preservation of the genre its true vocation. As for researchers who venture an analysis of *chanson*, they are still few and far between, and when it has been a subject of study, more often than not, it is only partial or fragmented, so the genre still suffers from a lack of esteem which keeps it firmly outside mainstream research circuits, especially in France.

It would be false, however, to conclude that in the absence of scientific experts and firm political determination, songs are not transmitted by memory. On the contrary, if the research focus can be enlarged to include the broader question of the circulation and consecration of song culture, it will be seen that these points actually depend on a wide range of non-institutional memory structures. The little institutional and scientific attention shown to songs leaves plenty of room for groups of non-academic experts such as fans, collectors, specialised journalists or even simple "amateurs"[2] of *chanson*. The modalities of transmission of this song culture are extremely heterogeneous, and correspond to a wide range of forms, including souvenirs and records passed down from parents to their children, record fairs, TV game shows, reissues and complete works on various formats, biographies and encyclopaedias, TV programmes that include cover versions, films devoted to the stars of song, new versions of old hits by the latest singers, visits to a singer's grave and so on.

Less often, *chanson* finds a place in the *legitimate*[3] structures devoted to transmission—that is, in temporary or permanent exhibitions.

Traditional forms of institutional consecration (i.e., those taken from the world of fine art, such as exhibiting an item in a museum) are not the most widespread, and above all, their existence does not affect the more non-academic forms relying on memory or the expertise of amateurs. The latter are not waiting for cultural institutions to recognize the value of this *tiny cultural object* represented by songs (Cheyronnaud 2002). On the contrary, they invent

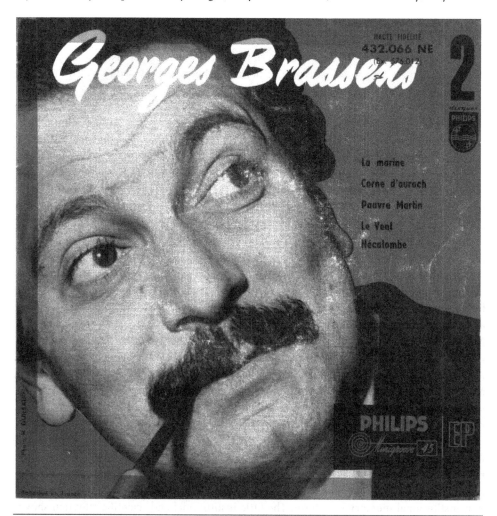

Figure 13.1 Georges Brassens, *La marine*, Philips, 1956, EP front cover.

their own ways of consecration and transmission of the whole song culture, which can either be complementary to or even present a challenge to recognised institutions (Dalbavie 2008).

The city of Sète, birthplace of singer Georges Brassens,[4] gave us the chance to observe *in situ* such links of complementarity and competition that can exist between memory constructs and institutional heritage structures. If we accept the distinction Davallon offers between these two processes, the heritage reconstruction process requires scientific knowledge of the relationship between the object and its original context, starting from our present approach, whereas memory ensures transmission and the continuity of knowledge from its original context through to ourselves (Davallon 2002). However, both these processes stem more often from mythical rather than historical discourse, yet heritage as a construct is relatively stable, whilst the main characteristic of collective memory is its protean nature and its great adaptability to the circumstances in which it is cited (Rautenberg 2003). As a contemporary representation of the past, collective memory "adapts the image of old facts to the spiritual beliefs and needs of the present" (Halbwachs 1971, 7). There is no such thing as universal collective memory, only collective memories insofar as "every collective memory is based on a group defined in time and space" (Halbwachs 1997, 137), which means there are as many memories as there are groups. Yet these memories will die out when their "support groups" vanish, whereas the museum is an institution and, as such, confers a lasting quality on the stabilised version of the past offered by national heritage.

Our study concerned two particular structures: firstly, the Espace Georges Brassens, a museum devoted to the singer's life and work, financed by local authorities, and secondly, the singer's grave just a stone's throw away from the museum. In 1991, on the tenth anniversary of Georges Brassens's death, the municipality of Sète in the south of France, thanks to financial aid from the Hérault General Council and the Languedoc-Roussillon Region, decided to create a museum devoted to the singer right opposite the Cemetery of Le Py, where Brassens is buried. Since then, the Espace Georges Brassens receives some 50,000 visitors every year. Before or after seeing the permanent exhibition, most of them include another short trip to visit the singer's grave on their circuit.

Our ethnographical survey at the museum and near the grave led us to observe the behaviour of Brassens lovers, to describe both these structures and to give an account of the various forms of *attachment* prompted in each of them (Hennion 2004, 11). It also shows how the two places actually form a single unit and a single structure under local authority management, the grave encouraging and completing the national heritage approach. In fact, it is not impossible to put *chanson* on exhibition, as the museum scenographers show by the various strategies employed. However, putting *chanson* on show is never a neutral process: this form of legitimisation is bound to have some effect on the actual nature of this cultural product and the status of the singer who has brought it to life. Indeed, even when *chanson* does manage to become part of national heritage, it does not shed its memorial aspect so easily and song lovers will not necessarily give up their own modes of consecration.

The Consequences on the Status of *Chanson* when Displayed Inside a Museum: From Songs to Poems

The permanent exhibition on show at the Espace Georges Brassens takes the form of a guided tour that follows the chronology of the singer's life, beginning with his birth and childhood years in Sète, and ending with the area devoted to the famous song, "Supplique pour être enterré à la plage de Sète" ("Request to Be Buried on the Beach at Sète"). The story of his life is organised into three parts, of which the first, *The Life of Georges Brassens*, is mainly focussed on biographical data. The second part consists of a video room where several documentaries, including TV programmes, interviews and the singer's live performances, are shown. Then the third and last part offers an approach to Georges Brassens's work through several important themes: Non-conformism, The Artist's Way of Life, Poets, Women and Death. The latter concludes the visit and is treated with ironical humour, such as that which Brassens used in the song "Request to Be Buried on the Beach at Sète." Brassens's death is only evoked by that one song; otherwise, there is no direct reference to it.

The headphones provided on the spot to be used throughout the museum visit enable visitors to listen to excerpts from interviews with the artist and of him singing his own songs so that it is Georges Brassens himself and not an outsider who guides each visitor on his or her tour round the exhibition. What the visitor hears is the edited result of an interview with Brassens conducted by a journalist in 1979.[5]

The exhibition uses two types of written material: the contents of the information panels posted along the itinerary and the texts actually on show (i.e., all the manuscripts and typescripts Brassens produced himself and which are presented as authentic, including rough copies of certain songs, amongst other things). Typed texts of poems chosen by Brassens to be set to music are also exhibited, revealing a surprising reversal on the part of the curators,

Figure 13.2 "L'impasse Florimont," as presented in the Espace Georges Brassens. Photo: J. Dalbavie.

since they take these texts back to their initial form, thus leaving out all the singer's compositional work. But by exhibiting the lyrics of Brassens's songs in the same way as the texts of poems by François Villon, Victor Hugo, Louis Aragon or Paul Fort, this arrangement puts Brassens on the same level as these poets; the scenography deliberately chooses, then, to have Brassens change status from singer to poet. Several documents in the Espace Georges Brassens present the museum explicitly as a place dedicated to the "*poet*" and not to the singer.

It must be emphasised here that exhibiting the songs in their written form implies that the text is more important than the music. By highlighting the lyrics of Brassens's songs, the designers are taking the French contrast between "*chanson à texte*" and "*chanson de variété*"[6] to an extreme; classifying the singer in the first category somehow legitimizes the entry of *chanson* into a museum. This classification not only ratifies this step but also goes further and presents Brassens's songs as poems, a gesture largely justified by some of the events and reviews that already ensured the singer's consecration during his lifetime (e.g., his early career in a cabaret, the volume on the singer published in the Seghers collection "Poètes d'aujourd'hui" ["Poets of Today"] series in 1963, the Grand Prix de Poésie [Grand Prix for Poetry] awarded by the French Academy in 1967, the fact that certain of his lyrics were studied as poetry in the competitive entry examination to the Ecole Normale Supérieure in 1969, etc.).

Of course, the lyrics of a song can be reduced to a set of words and phrases, or rather a set of rhyming lines. But song reduced to its written text in this way loses all its performative dimension, and becomes a simple linguistic statement; for the reader, it narrates and describes. The ephemeral nature of performance gives way to the lasting quality of writing. What we are faced with now is a simple statement in words and no longer the utterance of a song (Kerbrat-Orecchioni 1980, 29).

Brassens's Persona Reinvented: From Singer to Guide

Georges Brassens's voice guiding the visitor and the broadcast of a few excerpts from some of his songs inside the visitors' headphones compensate a little for the loss created by this artificial passage from sound to written mode. The device of headphones and the editing done by the designers has a certain effect on the Brassens persona[7]: the singer is turned into a guide whose voice and songs go with the visitors as they walk round the museum. Brassens talks in the present tense—and apparently the visitors accept this anachronism without a qualm. The specific choice of individual headphones, as a pose to a possible group device, transforms the relationship between Brassens the guide and each visitor into a highly individual experience. The designers put them both inside the same bubble of sound that no one else can enter, and plunge them into a softly lit ambiance where each visitor becomes Brassens's special confidant and the singer plays host, welcoming him or her as he would a friend into his own home, and revealing part of his private life. So, in the museum, Brassens is presented as a much more expansive and generous character than the one usually described by legend. His role is not to display a neutral or self-effacing point of view; on the contrary, he is there to give a subjective one on his own life and songs. In this manner, the guide here is also a character in and a witness to his own life. The tone is one of total commitment and the guide's memories guarantee the authenticity of whatever is narrated. This autobiographical account, brimming with human experience and events, gives spirit and soul to a place that is nothing more than a reconstitution and cannot present all the features of a real place (Gellereau 2005, 130). Brassens is no longer just the singer who has a special way of singing his own songs, but also the man who explains and gives meaning to a place and his own works.

The Resurgence of Cult-Like Attitudes in the Museum

Thus, although *chanson* and its singer can be placed in a museum, there is a clear price to pay for this consecration: the alteration, major in some cases, to the status of both this cultural product and the person who embodies it. Museums are part of the heritage structures that elevate a social memory considered as a reference, but this does not mean exhibition designers can just ignore the individual and collective memory certain visitors carry inside them and which, in the case of *chanson*, can turn out to be persistent. Similarly, they cannot put an end to the forms of consecration invented by song lovers themselves and which very often involve the appropriation of objects of attachment (Esquenazi 2004, 97). The multitude of cult-like attitudes expressed inside the museum shows that giving heritage status to songs does not imply the process has been irretrievably completed, even in Brassens's case (Le Guern 2002, 16). From our very first visit to the museum, we observed that the literary approach to Brassens's songs offered by the museum to its visitors did not in any way stop them from doing things outside usual museum behaviour patterns and rules, such as pilfering. In the belief that certain Brassens manuscripts on show are original documents, some visitors actually try and steal them. By "pinching" these texts (or just certain parts of them), the visitors change these museum objects into cult objects. After repeated attempts at theft of some of the singer's personal items (pen, pipe, pair of glasses, etc.), the designers have been obliged to install a video surveillance system in the exhibition.

Even the visitors' book tells us about these cult-like attitudes. This book, supposedly designed to receive all kinds of criticism, negative and positive, as well as visitors' complaints, is, in this case, transformed into something like a fanzine. Visitors write as though they are talking directly to Brassens; whether they use the familiar "*tu*" or the more formal "*vous*" for "you," they have no compunction about speaking to him in the present tense, even though they are fully aware he will never read their comments. So one comes across such remarks as, "A very fine exhibition, Georges, you'll never die!" "Georges, you will always be here with us. The stupid bastards will just have to get used to it!" "After that, everything that needs to be said has been said. Hats off to the poet and bravo for the expo!" "Thanks, Georges. We don't believe you're dead either." "I hope that up there you've still got that mischievous look on your face when you see some of the things going on down here. Bravo for all you've given me."[8] These personal statements show just what an important part some artists can play in the life of their fans, not only because they go on living in the media, but also because the fans themselves continue to make the artists live on in their memory.

The interesting thing with Georges Brassens is that these cult-like practices occur more spontaneously inside the museum than at the singer's grave. It could even be said that the strategies and devices deliberately incorporated into the museum exhibition encourage and support such attitudes. The commissioners have not merely put Brassens's songs on show; they have turned the artist into a living guide and are very careful not to mention his death inside the museum, as we have noted previously. They also encourage visitors to make the singer live on outside the museum, thanks to the cards available at the end of the exhibition, with the reproduction of a note in Brassens's handwriting that he used to hang on his door when he was composing his songs: "Unless it's a question of life or death, please do not disturb me right now, whilst I'm working. I've locked myself in. Best regards, Brassens." These cards taken home by visitors mean that Brassens is still alive in each of the places where they are posted.

Régine Monpays, the museum director,[9] has a very interesting point of view about these cult-like attitudes. Rather than condemn them out of hand, as many cultural institutions sometimes do,[10] she has understood that she must learn to make the most of them. It is also noteworthy that her role as museum director of the Espace Georges Brassens gives her a status that is not limited to the missions usually allotted to this function. She is regularly consulted as an expert and as such, receives artist's demo tapes with a cover version of a Brassens song; her opinion is sought on the quality of what has been sent in, and she is asked to say whether they haven't "betrayed the master too much," which makes the *Espace Brassens*, in the eyes of many amateurs, a foundation ensuring respect and long life to the singer's values. The fact that his museum is sited in Sète means it has become the *family home*, to quote Régine Monpays, whose role as director is sometimes very close to that of president of a fan club. She keeps up a correspondence with the many visitors who send her a postcard every year. She has managed to create and maintain successful links with many of those close to the singer, and this, too, has enhanced her reputation amongst the amateurs. After the lectures she gives in festivals and secondary schools, members of the public go as far as to ask for her autograph, or even try and have bodily contact by shaking hands with her or touching her shoulder, as if being the director of the Espace Georges Brassens has conferred her with a special status; she is now the living incarnation of the singer's values. It seems as if her own body could make up in some way for the absence of Georges's body. Therefore the museum's success also resides in the singular personality of its female director who has understood the futility, impossibility even, of rejecting these cult-like attitudes and has thus decided to make the most of them.

Conclusion

If Brassens has become "one of the symbols of France, alongside perfumes, *haute couture*, and the great wines of Bordeaux" (Calvet 1993, 8), his case may not be radically different from that of other singers regarding the heritage process. It would be wrong to believe that the heritage process of his repertoire or his persona has been made simpler by the legitimacy he may have acquired over time and his being classified as a *chanteur à texte*. If we try and list the various arrangements that allow us to recapture the memory of Brassens's songs or his persona, we arrive at the same conclusion as we already reached on a larger scale concerning access to song culture: patrimonial arrangements play an anecdotic role compared to memory constructs. Brassens is no exception even though he ranks amongst the rare singers in France to have his own museum.[11] Alongside this heritage structure, there also exists a wealth of non-institutional arrangements dedicated to his name. There are so many of them that establishing a full list is a piece of research in itself. Attempts have been made at this task by clubs of Brassens "admirers" through their websites, including *Le mot de passe* (founded by Jean-Paul Sermonte in 1991) and *Auprès de son arbre* (founded by Pierre Schuller in 1997), to give only two examples. *Le mot de passe*, which publishes a bi-monthly magazine, *Les Amis de Georges*, entirely devoted to the latest news on Brassens and Brassens-related events, lists the following for the period between 2004 and 2008: 47 festivals devoted to the singer (including 5 outside France), 589 shows concerts of new versions of old songs or plays (3 outside France), 32 records (cover versions by current singers, the complete songs and reissues of documentaries on DVD about the singer, etc.) and 24 books (biographies, books detailing the singer's TV appearances, song lyrics, detective novels, etc.). The association also keeps track of articles about the singer, websites, musical comedies, current Brassens singers (41 according to them), a wide variety of tributes (commemorative plaques, pictures inspired by the songs, etc.) and so forth. There are numerous clubs for Brassens lovers in a number of French towns and cities, and even in cities abroad.

Where *chanson de variétés* is concerned, then, the case of Brassens is in no way an exception when we examine the complex relationships linking living memory and the heritage process, or amateurs and cultural institutions. The only difference with other singers is that the legitimacy he acquired during his lifetime has given rise to a wider range of mediations, allowing access to the memory of the singer's persona and his repertoire, and one of them is a heritage structure. In studying this museum, we intended to explore the reasons for its success, which remains exceptional: how and why did Brassens and his repertoire manage to cross over into what belongs to heritage?

Formal analysis of the exhibition clearly shows that entry into a museum is confirmation that his songs had first to be considered as poems. The scenography also establishes a special relationship with the character, even if it means creating new aspects of his personality or attributing new functions to him. Brassens is no longer just a singer, but also the person who explains and gives meaning to a place and his own songs. This structure has one distinctive quality: it encourages a resurgence of cult-like actions and practices inside the museum, or at least it does not condemn them. The force of the Espace Georges Brassens lies precisely in the way it makes the most of the amateurs' memory and their modes of consecration, rather than seeing them as an awkward burden.

The analysis of this permanent exhibition shows there is no simple and definitive answer to the question of the heritage process. This never-ending tension between two apparently contradictory logics—that of the heritage process which aims to institutionalise, designate and legitimise but which rationalises at the same time, and that of the memory process which enables the amateurs not to relinquish the cultural object to which they are so attached—remains at the heart of all heritage arrangements. Integrating songs into the national heritage, even in Brassens's case, is not yet firmly and definitively established, for amateurs can appropriate the designated heritage for themselves in a cult-like way.

Notes

1   French journalists and music critics habitually use two contrasting categories of song when describing *chanson*: *la chanson à texte* and *la chanson de variété(s)*. The first category elevates "good songs"—that is, ones where words and tune have been worked on with care and attention—whereas the second category refers pejoratively to more commercial songs. The expression *chanson de variétés* must not in any way be understood

in this derogatory sense here. The word *variétés* (*varieties*), an Anglicism at first, was used by Joseph Oller (1839–1932), one of the founders of *music-hall* and the man who set up the Olympia and the Bal du Moulin Rouge in Paris, to describe the new form of show comprising several acts of different kinds (songs, sketches, dances, *music-hall* turns), usually unrelated. We found it pertinent to use the expression *chanson de variétés* in spite of its pejorative connotations from the 1940s on, because it can describe a genre starting from the time of the great changes wrought by industrialisation, thus marking a clear distinction between modern songs and songs from the oral tradition. It also reminds us how certain types of establishments such as the music hall (and the *café-concert* before that) prepared listeners for the records to come by offering "a new kind of relationship to the musical show, based on intense but fragmented listening to short pieces, often all with a similar structure, but each with a different content" (Tournès 2002).

2   The notion of *amateur*, as understood by Hennion, Maisonnneuve et Gomart (2000), designates and assembles "all those who actively practise a love of music," whether this be through playing an instrument, following a group, going to concerts, listening to records and so on, and does not just refer to amateur instrumentalists as opposed to professional musicians and the ordinary public. This means that such things as listening are not denigrated, whilst others (e.g., playing an instrument) are not over-estimated either.

3   In the sense that Bourdieu gave this word (Bourdieu 1979).

4   Georges Brassens (1921–1981) is a French singer-songwriter. He set words to music and accompanied himself on the guitar for over a hundred songs. As well as his own lyrics, he also set to music poems by François Villon, Paul Verlaine, Paul Fort and Louis Aragon.

5   *Georges Brassens Talks*, an interview with Philippe Némo, publ. by Editions Le livre qui parle/*Institut national de l'audiovisuel/productions Jacques Canetti, 200924–6*, 1990, two compact discs.

6   It would seem that this contrast in aesthetics, still maintained nowadays by music critics, was originally based on the idea of the different places where *chanson* could be heard. Whereas, historically speaking, the *chanson de variétés* was linked to places like the *café-concert*, then its successor, *music-hall*, the "*chanson à texte*," had its origins, it would seem, in *cabaret*, which was in fashion during the last twenty years of the nineteenth century. This type of establishment arose out of the *café-concert* but became strikingly different. Cabaret was a place where the recognised literature of the time met oral and popular forms, whilst the *café-concert* was first and foremost a visual show with a whole range of different acts in succession, such as pantomimes, *tableaux vivants*, performing dogs, acrobats, songs and so forth. What counts for the audience here is the singer or performer, much more than the words or their author. On the smaller stage of a cabaret, on the other hand, there is no room either for a grand show or a full orchestra (a piano or a single guitar can suffice). More often than not, singers sing their own lyrics; these play a central part in the performance, just as the personality and style of the author does (Pillet 1992).

7   The word *persona* refers here to the public character gradually built up over the course of a career. This *persona* is incarnated in an easily identified look, which in Brassens's case can be resumed by his pipe, moustache and guitar. The *persona* is nourished by public appearances and speeches in the media, as well as biographical tales and values and other fictitious characters constructed in the course of the songs.

8   Noted on 3 February 2006.

9   Note that she does not have the status of curator, as is usually the case in museums.

10   In Delphine Guzowski-Saurier's thesis devoted to Marcel Proust's work achieving heritage status, which she studied by way of La Maison de Tante Léonie and its visitors, she clearly shows how visitor-admirers of the writer are considered either as positive or negative figures, according to who is at the head of this structure, whereas lovers of Proust's work are always seen in a positive light (2003).

11   A museum dedicated to Édith Piaf does exist in Menilmontant, but it is not financed by the state or the local authorities. It is a private museum managed since 1977 by a club of amateurs of the singer, and is situated in one of her earliest apartments. In Narbonne, rather on the model of the Espace Georges Brassens, the municipality has set up a permanent scenography about the life and work of the singer Charles Trenet, in the house where he was born. In both cases, it would be more appropriate to talk about "a singer's house," just as we do in the case of certain writers, rather than a proper museum. The existence of these structures shows how hard it is to dissociate the song and the singer.

Bibliography

Bourdieu, Pierre. 1979. *La distinction: Critique sociale du jugement*. Paris: Ed. de Minuit.

Calvet, Louis-Jean. 1993. *Georges Brassens*. Paris: Payot.

Cheyronnaud, Jacques. 2002. *Musique, politique, religion: De quelques menus objets de culture*. Paris: l'Harmattan.

Dalbavie, Juliette. 2008. "La patrimonialisation de la chanson, entre musée et mémoire collective: L'exemple de Georges Brassens à Sète." PhD diss., University of Avignon.

Davallon, Jean. 2002. "Tradition, mémoire, patrimoine." In *Patrimoines et Identités*, compiled by Bernard Schiele, 42–64. Québec: Musée de la Civilisation, Éd. MultiMondes.

———. 2006. *Le don du patrimoine: Une approche communicationnelle de la patrimonialisation*. Paris: Ed. Hermès Science Publications.

Esquenazi, Jean-Pierre. 2004. "Structure du champ de la réception: publics et non-publics." In *Les non-publics, Volume I*, compiled by Pascale Ancel and Alain Pessin, 83–99. Paris: L'Harmattan.

Gellereau, Michèle. 2005. *Les mises en scène de la visite guidée: Communication et médiation*. Paris: L'Harmattan.

Guzowski-Saurier, Delphine. 2003. "Médiations et co-construction du patrimoine littéraire de Marcel Proust, La Maison de Tante Léonie et ses visiteurs." PhD diss., University of Avignon.

Halbwachs, Maurice. 1971. *La Topographie légendaire des Evangiles en Terre sainte*. Paris: PUF.

———. 1997. *La mémoire collective*. Paris: Albin Michel.

Hennion, Antoine. 2004. "Une sociologie des attachements: D'une sociologie de la culture à une pragmatique de l'amateur." *Sociétés* 85:9–24.

Hennion, Antoine, Sophie Maisonneuve, and Emilie Gomart. 2000. *Figures de l'amateur: Formes, objets, pratiques de L'amour de la musique aujourd'hui*. Paris: Dep, Ministère de la Culture/La Documentation Française.

Kerbrat-Orecchioni, Catherine. 1980. *L'énonciation: De la subjectivité dans le langage*. Paris: Armand Colin.

Le Guern, Philippe, ed. 2002. *Les cultes médiatiques: Culture fan et œuvres cultes*. Rennes: Presses Universitaires de Rennes.

Pillet, Elisabeth. 1992. "Cafés-concerts et cabarets." *Romantisme* 75:43–50.

Rautenberg, Michel. 2003. *La Rupture patrimoniale*. Bernin: À la croisée.

Tournès, Ludovic. 2002. "Reproduire L'œuvre: la nouvelle économie musicale." In *La culture de masse en France de la Belle Epoque à aujourd'hui*, compiled by Jean-Pierre Rioux and Jean-François Sirinelli, 220–258. Paris: Fayard.

14
Tecktonik and *Danses Électro*
Subculture, Media Processes and Web 2.0[1]

Anne Petiau

Introduction

Danses électro took on the character of a movement in France at the beginning of the 2000s. Inspired by other European dance movements, this specific current, danced to electronic music, went on to be influential in its own right across the world. Tecktonik, registered as a trademark in France in 2002, played an important role in the spread of the movement. The Tecktonik trademark branded nights in clubs, compilation albums and various tie-in products (clothes, alcoholic drinks, energy drinks, etc.). The term *danses électro* was upheld by amateurs who made a distinction between the movement and the brand.[2] *Danses électro* were at their height between 2002 and 2009, and the movement has continued to exist since, albeit in a more discreet form. It brought together a large cross section of young people: pre-teenagers, teenagers and young adults, with post-teenagers seeming to have been most instrumental in carrying it forward through participation in national and international championships.

Danses électro formed part of the musical and cultural current of electronic music, at the same time as it contributed certain specificities. These included the place of brands in the development of cultural movements, the involvement of pre-teenagers and new, participatory celebrity creation processes. Popular music thus seems to have been affected by developments affecting the cultural practices of young people more generally, in France and beyond, which have gone hand in hand with the use of information technologies and in particular Web 2.0 applications.

This chapter draws extensively on a survey composed of semi-directive interviews carried out from 2008 to 2009 with twenty of the movement's contributors: fifteen dancers aged 14 to 20 (four girls and eleven boys, reflecting the greater involvement of male dancers) and five industry professionals (managers, artistic directors, event organizers).[3] The study is also based on observations of websites, content-sharing sites, social networks and roughly thirty blogs dedicated to *danses électro*.

Forms of Dances That Emerged From Clubbing and Electronic Music

A Development of Jump Style

Danses électro are part of the cultural continuum of electronic music. Born in the United States, the first manifestations of house came in the mid-1980s and techno around 1988

(Bara 1999; Poschardt 2002). Electronic music hit England in 1987–1988, then arriving in France and other European countries. It spread through networks of clubs, concert venues and festivals, never in fact leaving club floors, house music's original birthplace. In England and France, it also gave rise to the rave and free party movement (Racine 2002; Petiau 2004; Pourtau 2009). Several sub-genres developed out of the two principle genres of house and techno. Two of these fostered the practice of *danses électro*: electro and hardstyle.

Danses électro originate, to a large extent, in clubbing. A useful point of reference in situating their emergence is the first "Tecktonik Killer" events organized in 2002 in the club Metropolis, located in Val-de-Marne on the edge of Paris. Artistic directors Alexandre Barouzdin and Cyril Blanc invited Belgian and Dutch hardstyle DJs to mix at these events (Petiau 2011). Hardstyle is an electronic music sub-genre that appeared in the wake of gabber and of happy hardcore. These styles of music have a distinctively rapid tempo and a "hard"[4] electronic sound, also incorporating vocals and melodies from dance and Eurodance. They took off initially in the Netherlands and spread around Europe, notably in Germany, Belgium and the north of France. Young clubbers in Belgium then developed a specific dance, Jumpstyle,[5] to the sound of hardstyle (Latour 2008). Until then, while dancing to electronic music was certainly distinctive, it hadn't been much codified.

Through the "Tecktonik Killer" events and later the "Black Out" and "Dance Floor" nights, at which dancers faced off against one another in a ring set up in the club, Metropolis popularized hardstyle and therefore played an important role in the emergence and spread of codified electronic dances in France. These dances also spread to other clubs already playing electro, techno and hardstyle, more specifically the Mix Club and the Redlight in Paris. This expansion, initially in Paris and its surroundings, gave rise to two specifically French names for new forms of codified dances: Tecktonik and *danses électro*. On arrival in France, these codified dances took on new forms. While only the feet and legs are used in Jumpstyle, electro was mainly based on arm and upper-body movements.[6] The principle of the competitive confrontation of dancers was maintained in the form of dance *battles*.

The Tecktonik Brand and the Danses Électro *Movement*

In 2002, the Tecktonik night's artistic directors registered the event's name to prevent its use by others[7] (Zawisza 2008). The same year, they set up a company (Tecktonik Event, later to be replaced by Tecktonik) and rolled out the concept with compilations and tie-in products. The music industry rapidly became interested: the first two Tecktonik compilations were produced by independent label 3em, and were distributed by Sony in 2006. The following volumes were released as part of an international production and distribution contract with EMI. The brand also produced DVDs and tie-in products (clothes, bags, phone accessories, etc.) (Kessous 2008; Petiau 2011).[8] From 2007, it was promoted through a dedicated team of dancers, this format being directly inspired by existing "*teams*" created spontaneously by young people through their shared experience of the dance in clubs.

In summer 2007, the print media and television became interested in this youth movement that seemed to be very much on the rise, popularizing the term "tecktonik" (Khelifi 2007; Couvez 2007; Bouchet-Petersen 2007; Mauger 2007; Koly 2007). Young people began posting videos under the name "tecktonik" on YouTube and Dailymotion; the brand name

Figure 14.1 Flyer for an *"electro tecktonik aprem"* in Limoges.

lost its capital letter and became a common term used to refer to the entire movement. The founders of the brand willingly presented themselves as the inventors of the dance and the style (Petiau 2011).[9] As the brand targeted commercial development, the founders clearly had no objection to their trademark being popularized and used to name the entire movement.

Nevertheless, not all amateurs identified with the Tecktonik brand. The name *danses électro* was claimed by some of them who drew a distinction between the movement and the brand. The members of the Dance Generation collective were among those who sought to impose the term "*danse electro*." This small group of young musicians and dancers contributed greatly to the popularization of the dance through the blog Dance Generation, set up in 2006 on the Skyblog[10] platform. The collective included Fozzie Bear, a DJ and composer, Ristourne, a young film director and several dancers. On their blog, they recounted the recent history of the dance, sharing videos of performances and music, posting news items and giving lessons on the movements (Dance Generation 2014). The collective also pioneered "dance afternoons" ("*aprems électro*," Figure 14.1), meetings among dancers in public spaces, which also become opportunities to produce videos to be shared on the Internet. Eponymous collectives appeared at this time in many French cities and abroad. The idea of "dance afternoons" also spread: young people gathered to dance in cities across France (Lyon, Montpellier, Toulouse, etc.) and also on Reunion Island, in Italy, Portugal, Belgium, Switzerland, Morocco, Senegal, Russia and so on. Dance Generation USA remained the most active and continued to post new videos on YouTube (YouTube 2014a).

Thus, the young electro dance amateurs came together in dance teams. They were involved in the spread of these dances through the organization of events and battles and by creating blogs and websites and sharing videos and dance performances on the Internet.

Battles and the Occupation of Public Space

Tecktonik and *danses électro* were also danced in public spaces: in the streets and on public squares. In Paris, for example, Les Halles and the gardens around Châtelet, in the heart of the first arrondissement and La Place du Trocadéro in the sixteenth, in the west of Paris, were popular gathering points. These public spaces were places where both clubbers and a younger generation gathered who would not legally be allowed to go into clubs. In France, those under the age of 16 are not allowed into clubs except on afternoons where alcohol isn't served.[11] In 2007 and 2008, this occupation of public space was very frequent both in Paris and in the other main French cities: Montpellier, Lyon, Marseille, Toulouse, Lille and so on. To the sound of a mobile phone or wearing headphones, young people would practice their skills in small groups. They also challenged one another in battles: two dancers facing off against each other in the centre of a circle of spectators. In *danses électro*, dance takes a central place, like in hip hop. Dance played a highly important role in hip hop's popularization: dancers teamed up, occupied the street and public spaces and competitions were organized (Bazin 1995, 137–142). In electronic music generally, the DJs and composers monopolize the attention. With *danses électro*, they became secondary and the dancers and teams took centre stage. The links between *danses électro* and hip hop (the importance of dance, the occupation of public space, the structuring of dance teams, the challenges between dancers and teams) explain why hip hop practitioners got interested. In 2007, organizers of hip hop events started to include these dances alongside their own activities. Hagson, Youval and Steady took advantage of the opportunity of these new forms of expression and this new audience in order to organize a championship especially for these dances, the Vertifight (Figure 14.2). From October 2007, Vertifight teams organized a monthly event with national reach. From 2010 on, they also organized world championships, involving the participation of more than twenty countries, and set up a system of international licensing.[12] In this way,

Figure 14.2 Team Blackout, France Championship, Vertifight 2010, in Paris. Photo: Anne Petiau

the organizers introduced to *danses électro* the practice of competitions and championships at which dancers and teams faced off against each other in front of a jury.[13]

A Non-Subversive Subculture

Forms of Expression Well Integrated Within the Cultural Industry

Various cultural industries showed great interest in *danses électro*, notably during the period 2006–2008. The French music industry is dominated by four large companies, who control 90% of the market (Benhamou 2003, 77–82; SNEP 2008). Each of these majors marketed formats based around *danses électro*. This process followed a path that had been well trodden in France since disco in the middle of the 1970s, whereby the majors mined the capacity for innovation of independent producers by joining forces with them to release or distribute their productions (Guibert 2006, 141–151). In the case of *danses électro*, this "cooperation" between majors and independents mainly took the form of marketing by majors of compilations mixed by DJs of titles produced by independent labels. Thus, Sony-BMG and EMI marketed Tecktonik compilations and DVDs, and Universal and BMG produced other CD-DVD projects staging electro dancers (e.g., Mondotek 2007; Various 2008; DJ Fozzie Bear and Kevin Tandarsen 2007 and 2008). CDs of electronic music mixed by a DJ came with DVDs featuring either dancers or teams facing off in battles, or tutorials by famous dancers breaking down the steps for young amateurs.

During a time of recession in the market for music recorded in France (Curien and Moreau 2006, 45–46), *danses électro* represented an opportunity for the major labels. Selling CDs and DVDs together, the promotion of famous dancers and dance lessons were new promotional channels and included audio CDs that valued the importance of dancers over musicians.

The cultural industry thus succeeded in keeping up with social changes. Pre-teens were now laying claim to cultural independence. When starting secondary school, they took (relative) distance from their families in order to affirm a sense of belonging to their generation and new cultural tastes and practices specific to their age group (De Singly 2006). Tecktonik and *danses électro* came as an opportunity for the major labels to address a following that was younger than the traditional one for electronic music. This wasn't originally a commercial phenomenon but the majors took advantage of it to respond to changes in age-group lifestyles.[14]

A Subculture Led by Amateur Practice

Danses électro were partially led by the practice of young amateurs. The movement appeared as an "interstitial space" in which young people could engage and participate in cultural creation, through a relationship with themselves and others (Bazin 2002). It is easier to get involved in a cultural trend led by amateurs than in a professional world, in an emerging style rather than a well-established one. There are fewer constraints to development in a social world that is not yet institutionalized (Petiau 2004 and 2012). The occupation of public space, the organization of events like "dance afternoons" and dances that do not require formal

Figure 14.3 Yelle, "À cause des garçons," TEPR remix, Source Etc., 2007, compact disc front cover. The CD includes a video clip of the song, showing Tecktonik dancers.

training have no need to respect particular legal frameworks. More generally, the easiness of engaging in an activity is an important aspect of what attracted young audiences to this or other musical currents. In the case of *danses électro*, engagement could take the form of dance, the creation of a team or a blog or website for the production of videos or the distribution of images and other content.

Teams began to appear in 2005 (Petiau 2011) as part of *clubbing* culture. Their names echoed techno culture: Piratek, Fanatek, Wantek, Hooliteck, Diablotek, Fluotek, Gladiatek, Buffalotek and so forth. Later, they were created in order to participate in Vertifight championships, with names that evoked, rather, electro dance: Rythmik or RK, Electro Street, Electro Famous, Artifice Style and Electro Addicte. As with other popular-music-related groupings, young people came together through friendship and shared passions, developing common activities, giving themselves a common name and creating a logo or brand much like hip hop *crews* (Bazin 1996) or *tribes* and techno *sound systems* (Pourtau 2009). An innovation brought by the teams was their use of the Internet. The teams often created blogs, Facebook profiles, Myspace pages and so on and shared their videos online. Another specificity was their hierarchal structures: teams were led by *leaders* and *co-leaders*, and grew through the active headhunting of talented dancers. They were thus a mixture between common affinities and performance goals.

Danses électro can, then, be seen as a subculture, in that they consisted of a coherent set of values, attitudes, musical styles, clothes and meanings attributed to the world around them (Clarke et al. 2005). They offered a way of being part of a cultural generational ensemble, whilst affirming individual identities. Personal distinction was achieved by the way in which individuals appropriated a look and musical preferences—subtleties that could be invisible to the uninitiated (Muggleton 2008). The subculture developed on the margins of professional music and performance networks and was led by young people engaging in activities in a spontaneous way. This sort of dynamic was first introduced by alternative cultures: first by punk and its DIY philosophy in the 1970s (O'Hara 2003, 179–193), and later in France in the 1980s with alternative rock and its development of an independent production and distribution network (Guibert 2006, 99–325). Even though alternative musicians often did eventually work with the media or music industry, most had a profoundly ambivalent attitude towards the commercial dimension of their practice and fame (Seca 2001). In this sense, electro dance was not an alternative or subversive subculture. The commercial aspect and integration within the cultural industry was not rejected but rather valued and appreciated. Thus, the Dance Generation collective was able to refuse to be amalgamated with Tecktonik, and affirm its own role in the development of the movement whilst at the same time recognising the brand for its marketing qualities and commercial approach. In electro culture, self-promotion came with the territory (e.g., the "Dance Generation et les médias" section on the collective's blog, promoting their presence on television, in the press and on radio [Dance Generation 2014]).

Popularity Mechanisms

Their development in parallel with digital culture is another distinguishing characteristic of *danses électro*. Dancers and teams created blogs, websites and social networking profiles. Young dancers also filmed dance sessions with their mobile phones or camcorders, sharing them on the Internet on sites such as YouTube or Dailymotion. This was the first time in the history of youth culture that such synergy between dance, music, fashion and Internet culture had been seen.

Those who connect most frequently to the Internet and engage most with social networks are in the 18–24 age group (84% of them) (Bigot and Croutte 2012). Blogs are typically set up by a younger age group. By 2009, more than half of 12- to 17-year-olds had already created a blog (Bigot and Croutte 2009).

It is also because *danses électro* was a dance movement that was inseparably linked to the Internet that it became so popular amongst youngsters. Thanks to videos and blogs, under-16s, who had not yet had the chance to go to clubs, could discover electro dance and become part of it. Simply on the basis of observation, we can say that at its strongest, in 2007–2008, *danses électro* touched a wide cross section of young people spanning from pre-teens to young adults. Later, electro dance seems to have remained most popular among teenagers and young adults, notably through the Vertifight championships.

Becoming famous was a common goal in electro dance. Dancers actively sought out popularity. They aspired to stand out and be recognised in clubs, on the street and online. This is why they shared their images and videos online so energetically. Content-sharing sites, blogs and social networking sites offer tracking tools, and in addition to being a space for expression, the youth blogosphere is a network that functions around the search for popularity and fame, measurable in terms of scores and accolades (Orban de Xivry et al. 2007). The Skyrock platform, popular among teens and pre-teens,[15] also used mechanisms for tracking popularity by creating "tops" (top 100, top 7 days and top 24 hours) according to numbers of visits, and promoting "Blog Stars" on the platform home page. Becoming a "Blog Star" was very desirable, a form of recognition, as the thanks given by bloggers and the congratulatory comments left show. Thus, media processes and aspirations—such as audience measurement—penetrated youth culture by means of social networks and "Web 2.0," through the online sharing of images and videos and popularity measurement on platforms.

Peer Networks and Mass Media

On the Internet, horizontal networks created by Internet users coexist with vertically structured transmissions from the cultural industry (Rebillard 2007, 104–105). These are not two separate universes. The phenomenon of *danses électro* is a perfect example of these dynamics, of the meeting of peers with hierarchical mass media. When, in the summer of 2007, the print media, popular television and radio began to take an interest in Tecktonik and *danses électro*, they gave a public stage to dancers who already had a certain popularity online.[16] In return, this sudden visibility on traditional media platforms increased the interest of young audiences in the movement. The combination of the youth-created online networks with the mass media of print, television and radio led to a real media explosion in the summer of 2007.

Web 2.0 platforms developed Internet users' possibilities for expression. Up until its appearance, audiences were merely receptors of media messages. In the areas of news, music, and more generally cultural production and distribution, people could now react to content published on the web and also produce their own. We have witnessed the development of horizontal networks, where users address other users (Castells 2001, 72–73). Blogs and social networks constitute community spaces in the sense that groups can form around common tastes or practices, but they may also form parallel spaces for distribution, promotion and recognition.

That being said, they are not so much in opposition to as in intimate entwinement with traditional media. The traditional media also uses the new means of promotion via the Internet. In the age of Web 2.0, economists talk of the move from scarcity of production to the issue of garnering audiences: the difficulty lies less in access to content production than in how to gain an audience in the midst of a glut of content (Chantepie 2009). From this point of view, the traditional media benefits from a legitimacy that allows it to attract attention more easily than ordinary users. Moreover, these media continue to represent the most significant platform in terms of artistic recognition or success.[17] Although user networks and traditional channels do intertwine and fame can be acquired in online spaces, the mass media of the press and television remain the most important platform for stardom. Becoming a star remained the end goal for electro dancers.

Stars Become Ordinary

The young stars of *danses électro* promoted on social networks very much resembled their admirers in terms of age and style. Thus, among the dancers interviewed who gained a certain level of popularity, Lili Azian from the Fanateck team, Fozzie Bear from the Dance Generation collective and Picolo and Alystar from the Hooliteck team were all between 16 and 18 years old. Celebrity appeared as a status to which everyone could aspire: no training or qualification was required, and you no longer had to wait for recognition by traditional media for popularity to begin to build, as it could be achieved through networks, blogs and content-sharing sites.

The "secularization" of stars was diagnosed as far back as the 1970s: at the same time as being idealized and worshipped, stars got closer to reality and the ordinary human condition (Morin 1972, 26). This process was further accentuated in the 1990s, as stars became increasingly ordinary: on one hand, celebrity became a widely shared aspiration and, on the other, celebrity figures could now be ordinary people. This process was revealed in the 1990s through the new reality TV heroes who were elevated from being ordinary young people by the media and could return to being so just as quickly (Tisseron 2001, 101–127, Jost 2007).

Stars are media figures: identification figures, symbols of a condition or the means of experiencing a magical existence by procuration (Morin 1972, 17–35). The creation of stars also creates focal points around which communities can take shape, through the collective emotions that they evoke in the group (Maffesoli 1988). In *danses électro* and no doubt in a more general sense, we can speak of a diffraction of celebrity, functioning through this particular aspect: every individual can imagine one day becoming a celebrity inspiring enthusiasm, an identification figure around which the group takes shape. Thus, the youngest dancers interviewed, between the ages of 14 and 16, were able to identify with dancers who were only slightly older, whose popularity was built using the Internet.

Conclusion

Neither a fashion exactly, nor a cultural movement *per se*, *danses électro* can be identified as a trend in electronic music generally. Inspired by Belgian Jumpstyle, this codified dance was born in France in clubs and on the blogosphere. The Tecktonik brand played an important role in its spread across France, before ceasing its activities in 2011. *Danses électro* was then carried forward on social networks (particularly Facebook) and through amateur practice, more specifically around the Vertifight championship. Today, nearly thirty countries organise local championships and participate in the world championships in Paris (Vertifight 2014). Dance Generation collectives have also been founded in other countries following the

French example. Some of these are still active (notably Dance Generation USA). This spreading of the trend is very much "long tail" (Anderson 2006): the circulation of these dances on the Internet, notably using horizontal networks created by young people themselves, has allowed the propagation of the dances in various places around the world, while remaining under the radar nevertheless.

Several points stand out in the development of this movement. Firstly, the lowering of the age of those participating in youth culture. Media attention and the spread of the dances online were factors in attracting a very young following. This is an example of how pre-teens are now gaining their own cultural autonomy, following in the footsteps of teenagers. Secondly, this age group's strong online presence in the form of content, pages and blogs shows how new communication technologies now shape young people's everyday social interactions. Finally, the third point to be mentioned is the movement towards diffraction of celebrity, and the way in which young people are creating their own spaces for the creation of stars. The increasingly commonplace nature of stars has gone hand in hand with the development of social networks and the participative application of Web 2.0. We can thus observe a reconfiguration of spaces for the creation of stars, spaces in which social networks of peers intertwine with the hierarchical logic of mass media.

Mass media popularity mechanisms can today be seen at work within youth culture itself. Since the arrival of rock 'n' roll, young people have always been actors in the cultural movements in which they engage, giving them life through amateur practice, shaping them and embodying them in their lifestyles and daily social interaction. With Internet networks, young people are now participating in the construction of popularity and the creation of stars of musical and cultural trends in a new way.

Notes

1 I would like to thank Victoria Davis for her thorough re-reading of this chapter.
2 Amateurs distinguished other sub-genres within electro dance: electro-popping, house, milky-way, vertigo, Jumpstyle, shuffle and so on. Here we use the term "electro dance" as a generic category that encompasses all these sub-genres.
3 Including Cyril Blanc (cofounder of Tecktonik with Alexandre Barouzdin), Mathieu Solard (head of marketing at Tecktonik), Youval and Steady (creators of the Vertifight championship). In the following text, I refer to my book (Petiau 2011) for the data derived from interviews.
4 On "hardness" (static, stridency, grinding sounds, extreme high frequencies, white noise, filtered sounds, etc.) in electronic music, see Grynszpan (1999, 40–62).
5 In Belgium and France, there were websites dedicated to Jumpstyle (Belgian Jumpstyle 2010; France Jumpstyle 2014).
6 These movements were called "phases."
7 Registered with the official French body for trademarks (Institut National de la Propriété Industrielle, or INPI).
8 Interview with Mathieu Solard.
9 Interviews with Cyril Blanc and Mathieu Solard.
10 The platform has since been renamed Skyrock.
11 At the height of the movement, certain clubs, like Le Gibus in Paris, organised "electro afternoons" for pre-teens.
12 Almost thirty countries organised their own local Vertifight championships (interviews with Steady and Youval, the originators of Vertifight; Vertifight 2014).
13 Interviews with Youval and Steady.
14 Indeed, we can extend De Singly (2006, 22), for whom "fashion knows how to use this demand [for independence from children], it does not create it," to the various other cultural industry offerings. Our translation of *"la mode sait utiliser à son profit cette demande [d'autonomie des enfants], elle ne la crée pas."*

15   Ninety-seven percent of users are between the ages of 12 and 19 (Delaunay-Téterel 2008).
16   Such as Jey Jey dancing in his garage, a video posted in 2006 that became famous and that has been viewed more than 15 million times to date (JeyJey91 2006).
17   Analogue processes have been studied in the music industry. In spite of the rise of social networks and crowd-funding sites, record industry majors remain the path to national and international careers, with social networks being above all a tool for local promotion (Beuscart 2007 and 2008).

Bibliography

Books and Journals

Allard, Laurence. 2007. "Emergence des cultures expressives d'Internet au mobile." *Mediamorphose* 21.
Anderson, Chris. 2006. *The Long Tail: Why the Future of Business Is Selling More of Less*. New York: Hyperion.
Bara, Guillaume. 1999. *La techno*. Paris: EJL.
Bazin, Hugues. 1995. *La culture Hip Hop*. Paris: Desclée de Brouwer.
———. 2002. "Jeunesses messianiques et espaces populaires de création culturelle." *Agora Débats/Jeunesses* 29:22–26.
Benhamou, Françoise. 2003. *L'économie de la culture*. Paris: La Découverte.
Beuscart, Jean-Samuel. 2007. "Les transformations de l'intermédiation musicale." *Réseaux* 142:143–174.
———. 2008. "Les usages de Myspace par les musiciens autoproduits." *Réseaux* 26:139–168.
Bigot, Régis, and Patricia Croutte. 2009. *La diffusion des technologies de L'information et de la communication dans la société française*. Paris: CREDOC Editions. www.arcep.fr/uploads/tx_gspublication/etude-credoc-2009-111209.pdf.
———. 2012. *La diffusion des technologies de l'information et de la communication dans la société française*. Paris: CREDOC Editions. www.credoc.fr/pdf/Sou/Credoc_DiffusiondesTIC_2012.pdf.
Castells, Manuel. 2001. *La galaxie Internet*. Paris: Fayard.
Chantepie, Philippe. 2009. "Web 2.0: les économies de L'attention et L'insaisissable internaute-hypertexte." *Esprit* 353:107–127.
Clarke, John, Stuart Hall, Tony Jefferson, and Brian Roberts. 2005. "Subcultures, Cultures and Class: A Theoretical Overview." In *Resistance Through Rituals: Youth Subcultures in Post-War Britain*, edited by Stuart Hall and Tony Jefferson, 9–74. Oxon and New York: Routledge.
Curien, Nicolas, and François Moreau. 2006. *L'industrie du disque*. Paris: La Découverte.
Delaunay-Téterel, Hélène. 2008. "La communication juvénile à travers les blogs de lycéens." *Agora Débats/Jeunesses* 46:44–56.
De Singly, François. 2006. *Les adonaissants*. Paris: Hachette.
Grynszpan, Emmanuel. 1999. *Bruyante techno: Réflexion sur le son de la free party*. Nantes: Mélanie Seteun.
Guibert, Gérôme. 2006. *La production de la culture: Le cas des musiques amplifiées en France*. Paris and St Amant Tallende: Irma/editions Seteun.
Hebdige, Dick. 1979. *Subculture*. London and New York: Methuen.
Jost, François. 2007. *Le culte du banal*. Paris: CNRS Editions.
Latour, Alexandre. 2008. *Electro dance*. Paris: Hors Collection.
Maffesoli, Michel. 1988. *Le temps des tribus*. Paris: Le Livre de Poche.
Morin, Edgar. 1972. *Les stars*. Paris: Seuil.
Muggleton, David. 2008. "Individualité distinctive et affiliation subculturelle." In *Cultural studies: Anthologie*, edited by Hervé Glévarec, Eric Macé and Eric Maigret, 232–250. Paris: Armand Colin.
O'Hara, Craig. 2003. *La philosophie du punk*. St Mury-Monteymond: Rytrut.
Orban de Xivry, Anne-Claire, Sarah Gallez, and Julie Matagne. 2007. "Vous tous chez moi." In *Objectif blogs!*, edited by Annabelle Klein, 163–183. Paris: L'Harmattan.
Petiau Anne. 2004. "L'expérience techno, des raves aux free-parties." In *La fête techno*, edited by Béatrice Mabilon-Bonfils, 28–43. Paris: Autrement.
———. 2006. "Marginalité et musiques électroniques." *Agora Débats/Jeunesses* 42(1):128–139.
———. 2011. *Technomedia: Jeunes, musique et blogosphère*. Bordeaux: Editions Mélanie Seteun.
———. 2012. "Free parties et tecknivals: Dans les marges du marché et de L'Etat, système de don et participation." In *Festivals, raves parties, free parties*, edited by Nicolas Bénard, 587–610. Paris: Camion Blanc.
Poschardt, Ulf. 2002. *DJ culture*. Paris: Kargo.
Pourtau, Lionel. 2009. *Techno: Voyage au cœur des nouvelles communautés festives*. Paris: CNRS Editions.
Racine, Etienne. 2002. *Le phénomène techno*. Paris: Imago.
Rebillard, Franck. 2007. *Le web 2.0 en perspective*. Paris: L'Harmattan.
Seca, Jean-Marie. 2001. *Les musiciens underground*. Paris: Presses Universitaires de France.
SNEP. 2008. *L'économie de la production musicale 2008*. Paris: Editions du SNEP. http://proxy.siteo.com.s3.amazonaws.com/www.snepmusique.com/file/guidesnep2008.pdf.
Tisseron, Serge. 2001. *L'intimité surexposée*. Paris: Hachette.

Websites

Belgian Jumpstyle. 2010. "Historique." Accessed August 2. www.belgian-jumpstyle.com/.

Dance Generation. 2014. Accessed March 15. http://dancegeneration.skyrock.com/.

Dance Generation Portland OR and TekNahLow-G. 2008. *Dancegenerationusa*. Accessed March 15, 2014. www.youtube.com/user/dancegenerationusa.

France Jumpstyle. 2014. "Historique." Accessed January 29. www.france-jumpstyle.com/.

JeyJey91. 2006. "Jey jey Wantek Danse électro!!!". Accessed January 29, 2014. www.youtube.com/watch?v=ZkGum 1YYkGk.

Vertifight. 2014. Accessed March 15. www.vertifight.com/.

Articles in Newspapers

Bouchet-Petersen, Jonathan. 2007. "La tecktonik fait vibrer les ados." *Le journal du dimanche*, August 16.

Couvez, Cédric. 2007. "Jumpstyle vs. Tecktonik." *20 minutes*, July 11.

Kessous, Mustapha. 2008. "Tecktonik (la danse): TCK (la marque)." *Le Monde*, January 17:3.

Khelifi, Raja. 2007. "Tecktonik, la nouvelle vague." *Libération.fr*, June 14.

Koly, Saran. 2007. "La tecktonik dépote." *Libération*, August 31.

Mauger, Léna. 2007. "La tecktonik, danse sismique." *Le nouvel observateur* 2233, August 23.

Zawisza, Marie. 2008. "Les agités de la Tecktonik." *Le Monde*, January 9.

Musical Recordings

DJ Fozzie Bear and Kevin Tandarsen, *Electro Dance Generation Vol. 1 and 2*, Warner, 2007, 2008, compact disc and digital video disc.

Electro Mix Vol. 1/Vertifight: le battle électro de référence, Warner Music France, 2008, compact disc and digital video disc.

Mondotek. *Alive*. Mercury/Universal, 2007, compact disc and digital video disc.

Various. *Tecktonik*. Sony Music, 2006, compact disc.

Various. *Tecktonik Vol. 6*. EMI Music France, 2008, compact disc.

15

My Dealer Is a Rock Star

Digital Piracy and Social Networks in the Context of the French Three-Strikes Law and HADOPI

Sylvain Dejean and Raphaël Suire

Since the end of the last decade, the French government has been attempting to prevent Internet users from illegally downloading digitized cultural content. Precisely, a law, known as "Creation and Internet," was voted in 2013 by the parliament in order to set out a public agency in charge of technically monitoring and punishing illegal online behaviour: HADOPI.[1] When a user illegally downloads or uploads a digital file using a BitTorrent protocol, he uses a peer-to-peer (P2P) platform. In this case, and only in this case, HADOPI can, upon request by rights holders, detect the computer's Internet protocol (IP) address and contact the Internet service provider (ISP) to identify the owner of the Internet subscription. If some files violate copyright laws, the user can be punished, depending on the quantity downloaded and recidivism. Its legal motivation is based on the "idea" that what is stolen is not purchased. By 2013,[2] only one user has been punished following the gradual three-strikes procedure. Yet, HADOPI defended this result as proof of success, signalling that illegal behaviour had been dissuaded or stopped.

The theoretical relationship between the illegal and legal consumption of cultural goods is well founded. With a focus on the case of the music industry, Peitz and Waelbroeck (2006) analysed the impact of the "sampling effect" on sales when piracy exists. The main result of their research was that some illegal activities enable commercial players to gain higher profits thanks to this effect. In a nutshell, cultural goods are regarded as experience goods where ex ante uncertainty about features is strong. Sampling through piracy helps to reduce uncertainty about some, if not all, features.

Empirical evidence is more ambivalent. Some highlight a complementarity effect between offline and online behaviour (Bounie et al. 2006; Smith and Telang 2010). As predicted, illegal downloading favours the sampling effect and helps consumers discover characteristics of cultural and experience goods. Others point out a substitution of illegal for legal consumption (Liebowitz 2008; Zentner 2006). Under budget constraints, what is "stolen" online is not purchased online or offline. Whereas a recent report published by the European Commission (Aguiar and Martens 2013) and based on the online habits of 16,000 Europeans claims that music web piracy does not harm legitimate sales, the International Federation of the Phonographic Industry (IFPI) keeps arguing that this kind of research is "flawed and misleading."[3]

En France, **450 000 films** piratés chaque jour.

Plus d'un milliard de fichiers pirates sont échangés chaque année.

1 nouveau talent sur 5 ne peut être produit...

PIRATER TUE LES ARTISTES
ET TOUS LES MÉTIERS DU CINÉMA DE LA MUSIQUE ET DU JEU VIDÉO

Je ne pirate pas !

J'♥LESARTISTES.FR

www.jaimelesartistes.fr

SITE MOMENTANÉMENT INDISPONIBLE

Figure 15.1 "J'aime les artistes" government website opening page (2009).

Academic evaluations of HADOPI are still very rare. As far as we know, Danaher et al.'s study (2014) is the most recent empirical work on this issue. Basing their study on Apple's iTunes Store, the authors show that since the implementation of HADOPI, legal sales in France have been a bit higher than in other European countries. From a certain point of view, they do not reject the preventive aspect of HADOPI nor a substitution effect of legal for illegal downloading. Another work (Dejean, Pénard and Suire 2010) highlights different issues. Indeed, based on a representative French sample, its pioneering results show that a majority of downloaders and pirates no longer use P2P technology. They prefer consuming digital contents such as MP3s or videos via streaming, cyberlockers or newsgroups. In a word, they seem to have anticipated the legal threats and thus changed their behaviour. This conclusion suggests a limited impact of HADOPI in an environment where alternative ways to illegally access copyrighted contents exist.

Based on an original 2012 survey of a representative sample of French users, we show that the illegal consumption of digital music files now occurs largely offline, thanks to exchanges via USB keys, hard drives or mobile devices. This makes the cost of monitoring illegal behaviour higher than ever, if not infinite. Secondly, using an econometric analysis, we show that the exchange of music files relies on a social network where some users are "wholesalers," risk lovers who still illegally download online, whereas others are more risk adverse and simple users who consume via offline swapping.[4] Our results show that the HADOPI threat can account for part of the offline swapping network.

This chapter is organized as follows. The following section presents HADOPI and the legislative context. The second section presents the joint dynamics that link piracy behaviours and social networks. The third section proposes econometric results based on an original French database and the last section concludes.

HADOPI: Some Insights

HADOPI is the name of the former administrative agency[5] created to monitor P2P networks and manages the "three-strikes" sanction addressed at pirates. This ad hoc authority is part of a law named "Creation and Internet" which aims at promoting and protecting creative works on the Internet. The procedure supposed to deter digital pirates is a three-step process. The first time an individual is caught downloading or sharing copyrighted content on the Internet, a warning email is sent to his or her mailbox asking him or her to stop illegal downloading. The second time the presence of the pirate is detected on a P2P network, a certified letter is sent, and upon the third infringement, the ISP is supposed to suspend the pirate's Internet connexion. This first version of the three-strikes law was submitted to many criticisms. The two major ones made were, first, that the IP address (which is supposed to identify the pirate) is only related to the computer. As a result, those who suffer from the disconnection of Internet access are not necessarily those who trespass the law. This is especially true in the case of children or teenagers using their parents' computers. Furthermore, IP addresses can easily be hacked, and thus, identifying the real pirate may be impossible in many cases.

The second major criticism concerns the ability of the three-strike process to disconnect Internet users. This sanction is in contradiction with the "telecom package" reform submitted to the European Parliament. This text was supposed to unify EU telecom rules, and one of its amendments (voted in May 2009) says that "no restriction may be imposed on the fundamental rights and freedoms of end users, without a prior ruling by the judicial authorities." For the same reason, the Constitutional Council of France decided in June 2009 that an administrative authority was not empowered to take the decision of disconnecting Internet users and thus rejected the first version of HADOPI. The law has since been changed and has been voted in its new version in September 2009 by the French National Assembly. In the so-called HADOPI 2, the decision to disconnect Internet users is made by judicial intervention. The second major evolution is that users won't be prosecuted for copyright infringement but rather for neglecting to protect their computer from potential hackers. However, the general purpose was still the same: to deter pirates from using P2P networks, and P2P networks only.

After four years of existence, the assessment of HADOPI is balanced. On the one hand, almost 2 million first warnings and 186,000 second warnings have been sent to Internet users, while 51 files are waiting for a judge's decision, suggesting that HADOPI is the illegal file-sharing watchdog. On the other hand, there is little evidence that Internet users massively stopped downloading and sharing illegal content, as a lot of alternatives exist: streaming, cyberlockers, offline swapping and so on (Arnold et al. 2014). As a result, many people claimed that the cost/benefit ratio was too high and that the measures wasted public money, and accused their designers of failing to understand that only the development of an attractive legal offer could deter resorting to illegal platforms.

Digital Pirates and Social Networks

Basically, one assumes that illegal behaviours are rational (Becker 1968). This means that each user will balance piracy's costs and benefits before taking a decision. The cost of piracy is obviously sensitive to the three-strikes law and proportional to the number of digital cultural files downloaded through P2P protocols. But this threat is considered more or less credible because some users may perfectly know how this monitoring works and how to circumvent it. The individual level of knowledge on HADOPI can help decrease this cost to zero when some of the pirates use virtual private networks (VPNs),[6] for instance. This cost can be significantly reduced if pirates know what types of files are monitored.[7] Put differently, the threat is not perceived homogeneously, and some pirates can doubt its credibility. In the HADOPI context, we should observe these differences, meaning that the position in the social network of illegal exchange is a function of the perceived threat. We can consider two opposite types of HADOPI violators. First, those who consider it a credible threat, as they are risk adverse, have thus stopped using P2P networks. We shall name them "simple consumers," which doesn't mean that they have abandoned all forms of illegal behaviours. "Simple consumers" can still watch movies, series and listen to music on streaming platforms or, as we mentioned earlier, duplicate files from a friend or a relative's hard drive.

Second, those who perfectly know how to circumvent the threat and consider HADOPI non-credible are "the wholesalers." They have no fear of HADOPI and keep on downloading illegal content before sharing it with friends on the offline swapping network. This leads to the first research hypothesis which we are going to test in the following section.

> Hypothesis 1: The position in the social network of illegal exchange is a function of the perceived threat.

Benefits of illegality are often less clear. We know that digital piracy is dominated by symbolic rewards and impure altruism (Rehn 2004). Pirates are passionate and like to receive attention from peers for what they do. Direct benefits are proportional to the quantity of digital files consumed. One can reasonably expect that individual preferences can explain the amount of cultural goods that people consume. A strong taste for culture can lead to a more intense and frequent consumption of cultural goods (Peterson 1992). In the context of digital piracy, this means that a positive correlation exists between the declared taste for digital cultural goods and the intensity of consumption. P2P protocols are a way of accessing various and unlimited content sources. These can be new, niche or back catalogues that perfectly match preferences and cultural tastes. P2P users can keep this stock for themselves and share it with relatives through offline swapping. We therefore expect a positive correlation between a higher position in the value chain of offline swapping networks and P2P usage. This leads to the second research hypothesis.

Hypothesis 2: Wholesalers keep using P2P platforms and monitor digital channels, whereas simple consumers don't.

Indirect benefits are trickier to take hold of. Indeed, this means that asymmetrical exchanges between protagonists of the black market are motivated by symbolic rewards, the quest for legitimacy or the demonstration of skills to relatives and peers. Therefore, some users can give larger quantities than they actually receive because they have access to huge stocks of digital files or because they are able to find very highly desirable content for others.

Data and Empirical Strategy

We used a representative survey carried out among 2,000 French Internet users in May 2012. Quotas were determined based on age, socioprofessional category, gender and size of the urban area. Among these Internet users, 1,015 are engaged in offline swapping, and constitute the basis of our empirical analysis. Internet users were questioned about their online consumption of cultural goods (music, movies, series) and the illegal channels that they use (streaming, P2P, etc.), as well as their feelings about the HADOPI law.

The Offline Swapping Network

Piracy is often a synonym for P2P, streaming, cyberlockers or even newsgroups, but a large part (if not the majority) of the sharing of illegal content now takes place offline. Of our respondents, 51% declared that they traded illegal files on a person-to-person basis using USB keys, hard drives or mobile devices. At the same time, only 15% used P2P platforms, 18% cyberlockers, 29% streaming websites and 16% alternative platforms (probably VPNs and newsgroups). By far, in the HADOPI era, offline swapping is the most popular way to obtain illegal files. The Recording Industry Association of America (RIAA) made a similar discovery in their 2011 annual music survey (cf. Table 15.1).

In offline swapping activity, people differ depending on what they give and what they receive. We asked our informants if they received more than they gave, if they shared less

Table 15.1 Statistics on the rise of offline swapping activities

	Our survey, May 2012[8]	NPD 2011 annual music study, mentioned by the RIAA
Offline swapping	51%	65%
P2P	15%	15%
Cyberlockers	18%	4%
Streaming	29%	–
Others	16%	16%

Note: The large difference in downloading from cyberlockers is probably due to the fact that our study took into consideration not only music but also movies, which are largely downloaded from such platforms.

than they gave or if the quantities were approximately the same. Based on their answers, the following figure (Figure 15.2) shows the organization of the offline swapping network and the number of respondents that belong to each category of "sharers." "Wholesalers," who give more than they receive, represent 10% of the sample, while "simple consumers," who exclusively receive without giving anything, are 27% of people involved in offline swapping. Finally, we defined an intermediary position for the respondents who declared that they give but not more than they receive; these "middlemen" represent the largest share of the sample (63%).

Econometric Modelling

To measure how the HADOPI law impacts user behaviours, we determined the threat perceived by each individual. This feeling was collected by asking, "On a scale of 1 to 5, to what extent do you feel threatened by the HADOPI law with 1 being no threat at all and 5 a high threat?" Among the 1,015 individuals engaged in offline swapping, 60% responded that the

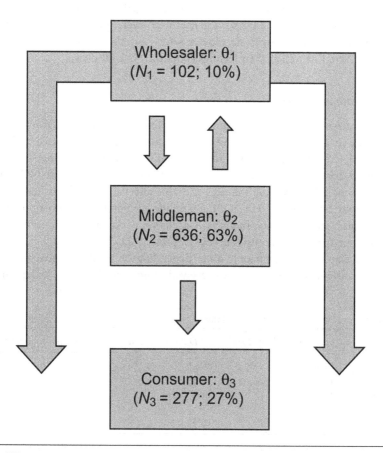

Figure 15.2 Offline swapping network.

law does not represent a threat. Only 4% of our sample responded more than 4 on the threat perception scale, which prompted us to build a dichotomous variable named THREAT which had the value of 1 if the user responded that HADOPI represented a threat (at least 2 on the scale of the threat perception), and 0 otherwise.

As hypothesized previously, we expected that people who feel threatened by HADOPI are less liable to be at the top of the offline swapping network and conversely are less willing to take the risk of offering content to others (Hypothesis 1).

To test this assumption, we also built an ordered variable reflecting the position in the offline swapping network. Following the organization described in Figure 15.2, the variable named OFF_SWAP spans from 1 to 3, with 1 representing a consumer at the bottom of the offline swapping network, 2 representing the middleman and 3 the wholesaler at the top. Another way to understand the ordered nature of this variable is to consider that the higher the users' positions in the network, the more they circulate content.

Dealing With the Issue of Endogeneity

Estimating HADOPI's impact on users' position in the offline swapping network can lead to different biases, and we used the method of instrumental variables to assess potential endogeneity.

In the survey, Internet users were asked to evaluate the probability for someone who illegally downloads on the Internet of being caught by HADOPI. We think that this variable, named PROB_DETECTION, satisfies both the inclusion and exclusion restrictions. The former one implies that people who think that HADOPI effectively controls the network feel more threatened than those who think that the probability of being detected by it is low. The exclusion restriction is satisfied if there is no direct correlation between the position in the offline swapping network and the perceived efficiency of HADOPI. Put differently, PROB_DETECTION should have an impact on OFF_SWAPPING only through THREAT. This means that a change in the position in the offline swapping network is caused by a change in the feeling of threat, and this change is (only) the consequence of a variation in HADOPI's estimated efficiency. The key point of this reasoning is that HADOPI's estimated efficiency only impacts choices at the top or the bottom of the sharing network because users feel threatened (or not) by HADOPI. We consider this assumption as reasonable.

The Model

The final model estimated is as follows:

$$OFFSWAP = X\beta_1 + THREAT + \varepsilon_2, \quad OFFSWAP = \begin{cases} 1 \; if \, 0 < OFFSWAP^* < \mu 1 \; (a\,wholesaler) \\ 2 \; if \, \mu 1 < OFFSWAP^* < \mu 2 \; (a\,middleman) \\ 3 \; if \, \mu 2 < OFFSWAP^* < \infty \; (a\,consumer) \end{cases} \quad (1)$$

$$THREAT = X\beta_2 + PROB\_DETECT \, \beta_3 + \varepsilon_2 \quad THREAT = 1 \; if \; THREAT^* > 0, 0 \; otherwise \quad (2)$$

OFF_SWAP* and THREAT* are the latent variables of the model. ε_1 and ε_2 are the error terms of the two equations, while X is the vector of control variables. This vector is composed of controls for sociodemographic attributes such as age, education, gender and income. The P2P variable has the value of 1 if the respondent has downloaded a cultural file (music, movies or series) at least once per month on a P2P network. We expected this behaviour to be found among those at the top of the offline swapping network. We also controlled for taste, as music or cinema lovers are more liable to feel threatened by HADOPI or even more engaged in offline swapping activities, as they probably have more content to share. The variable FRAUD is a proxy for individual acceptance of illegal behaviours based on a question originally implemented in the word value survey which asked whether respondents "find that tax cheating is justifiable" on a ten-point scale spanning from 1 (tax fraud is immoral) to 10 (tax fraud is acceptable). We suspected that being comfortable with illegal behaviour can favour the position of the "wholesaler." Finally, we asked people if many of their friends or relatives downloaded and shared illegal content, as we know that peer effect and social contagion are important determinants of illegal online and offline sharing networks. Table 15.2 recapitulates these different variables.

The first stage estimates the reduced form of the model (equation 2) and the second stage estimates the parameters of the structural model (equation 1). The structural model is our main model, which describes the position of Internet users in the offline swapping network, and the reduced form is the estimation of the perceived threat regressed on the instrument, as well as on the other control variables.

Table 15.2 Variable descriptions

Variables	Details of coding
OFFSWAP	1 for "consumers" (receiving but never sharing), 2 for middlemen (sharing and receiving) and 3 for wholesalers (sharing more than receiving).
P2P	1 if the informant has downloaded digital content on a P2P network at least once a month, 0 otherwise.
THREAT	1 if the informant responds that HADOPI represents a threat (at least 2 in a 1–5 scale), 0 otherwise.
PROB_DETECT	1 for someone for whom the estimated probability of being notified by HADOPI for illegally downloading is less than or equal to 30%, 0 otherwise.
MALE	1 if the respondent is male, 0 otherwise.
AGE24	1 for ages 15–24, 0 otherwise.
AGE39	1 for ages 25–34, 0 otherwise.
AGE59	1 for ages 35–50, 0 otherwise.
AGE+	1 for ages above 50, 0 otherwise.
EDUCATION1	1 for primary or secondary education.
EDUCATION2	1 for first level of tertiary education.
EDUCATION3	1 for second level of tertiary education.
INCOME1	1 for low incomes, 0 otherwise.
INCOME2	1 for acceptable incomes, 0 otherwise.
INCOME3	1 for comfortable incomes, 0 otherwise.
TASTE1	1 for strong taste in music or videos, 0 otherwise.
TASTE2	1 for important taste in music or videos, 0 otherwise.
TASTE3	1 for moderate taste in music or videos, 0 otherwise.
TASTE4	1 for no or limited taste in music or videos, 0 otherwise.
FRAUD	1 for informants who consider tax cheating acceptable.
PEERPIRACY	1 for informants who have a pirate in their close social network.

Table 15.3 Ordered probit with and without endogenous variable

Variables	Ordered probit	Ordered probit with endogenous variable	
	(1)	(2)	(3)
	OFFSWAP	OFFSWAP	THREAT
THREAT	0.270***	−1.186***	
	(0.0809)	(0.293)	
PROB_DETECT			−0.231**
			(0.0922)
P2P	0.311***	0.473***	0.483***
	(0.0840)	(0.0787)	(0.0883)
MALE	0.125	0.0919	−0.0138
	(0.0776)	(0.0746)	(0.0910)
AGE24	0.278**	0.456***	0.434***
	(0.129)	(0.122)	(0.143)
AGE39	0.331**	0.402***	0.285*
	(0.137)	(0.128)	(0.151)
AGE59	0.104	0.123	0.0596
	(0.125)	(0.118)	(0.142)
AGE+	Ref	Ref	Ref
INCOME1	0.119	0.161	0.0803
	(0.108)	(0.101)	(0.118)
INCOME2	0.0301	0.0990	0.139
	(0.0971)	(0.0918)	(0.105)
INCOME3	Ref	Ref	Ref
EDUCATION1	−0.210*	−0.178	−0.0796
	(0.121)	(0.115)	(0.137)
EDUCATION2	−0.0765	0.0352	0.169*
	(0.0853)	(0.0847)	(0.0922)
EDUCATION3	Ref	Ref	Ref
TASTE1	0.565***	0.530***	0.224
	(0.140)	(0.138)	(0.156)
TASTE2	0.424***	0.415***	0.192
	(0.129)	(0.124)	(0.146)
TASTE3	0.202	0.227*	0.137
	(0.131)	(0.123)	(0.147)
TASTE4	Ref	Ref	Ref
FRAUD	0.0196	0.0400**	0.0508**
	(0.0182)	(0.0173)	(0.0197)
PEERPIRACY	0.428***	0.477***	0.336***
	(0.0861)	(0.0828)	(0.0940)
Constant			−1.198***
			(0.207)
LogLikelihood	−807	−1424	
AthRho (1_2)		1.267**	
X^2 for LR test			
Observations	1,015	1,015	

Standard errors in parentheses. Ref stands for "reference variable." In the case of AGE, the variable AGE+ (older than 50 years old) is fixed, and the interpretation of the causality is based on this fixed variable. So, the youngest users (ages 24–39) are positively and significantly correlated compared to the variable AGE+.

*** $p < 0.01$, ** $p < 0.05$, * $p < 0.1$

Results and Comments

The main results are given in Table 15.3. Column 1 is the ordered probit regression without taking into account the potential endogeneity of the perceived threat of HADOPI. Column 2 and 3 show the estimates of the model that consider THREAT an endogenous variable—in this specification, the estimated probability of HADOPI catching an illegal downloader is the instrument.

The first interesting result is the difference between both regressions: the coefficient associated with the variable THREAT is positive and significant when we don't take into account the endogeneity, but becomes negative and still significant when we control for potential endogeneity bias. As expected, the instrument is significant and negatively correlated with the endogenous variable, meaning that people who think that an illegal downloader has a low probability of being detected by the HADOPI are less liable to feel threatened by HADOPI.[9]

Our two main hypotheses cannot be disproven by the results of Table 15.3 (column 2): Internet users who do not feel threatened by HADOPI share more content on offline swapping networks while still sourcing from P2P networks. As expected, being young, as well as having a strong taste for audio and video contents, also favours top positions in the swapping network. Young generations are more comfortable with digital devices that lower the cost of sharing; they also have a dense social life which promotes opportunities to share digital files through social contagion. This last assertion can be legitimated by the positive effect of having pirates among their friends and relatives. The positive and significant sign of the variable FRAUD shows that sharing behaviours can be associated with a certain tolerance towards illegal behaviours. To some extent, here we suspect a stabilized deviant norm (Becker 1997) among younger generations.

We also derived interesting insights from the reduced form equation (column 3 in Table 15.3), as some variables which have a direct and positive effect on sharing behaviours also have an indirect negative one on the same variable because they increase the perceived threat generated by HADOPI. For instance, downloading on P2P networks, having pirates within one's social network or being young increases the probability of feeling threatened by HADOPI and thus indirectly lowers the position within the swapping network.

Discussion and Conclusion

In this chapter, we have proposed a simple empirical test to evaluate how HADOPI reinforces a parallel and unmonitored offline swapping network where cultural and music goods are exchanged. Basically, illegal behaviours are strongly socially embedded. There are three types of downloaders: simple consumers, middlemen and wholesalers. Each is typified by an online behaviour and an attitude towards the threat represented by HADOPI.

Limitations to these findings are obvious. For sure, this social network existed prior to HADOPI but cross-sectional data does not allow us to say anything about its structuring. Indeed, we know not only that consumption of cultural goods is often socially embedded (Bourdieu 1979) but also that many cultural goods, such as books, move from hand to hand (Dalli and Corciolani 2008).

Previous results on HADOPI evaluation have shown that many users rationally antici-pate monitoring and therefore modify their illegal cultural and digital practices. P2P is now largely overrun by streaming, which in turn is also often overrun by offline swapping.

Notes

1 HADOPI stands for Haute Autorité pour la Diffusion des Oeuvres et la Protection des droits sur Internet (High Authority for the Distribution and Protection of Creativity on the Internet).
2 For readers comfortable with French, an annual report of HADOPI's 2013 activity can be downloaded here: www.HADOPI.fr/sites/default/files/page/pdf/HADOPI_RapportAnnuel_2013.pdf.
3 Music Week, "IFPI slams EU piracy study as 'flawed and misleading,'" March 20, 2013.
4 In 1980, the major label CBS had claimed that the illegal exchange of audio cassette tapes was killing the music industry's profits. With the help of the RIAA, a large "Home Taping Is Killing Music" campaign was launched in order to implement a tax on blank media. A Copyright Royalty Tribunal study published the same year showed that audio cassette tape users were also the biggest buyers of vinyl records. Later, it appeared that the decreasing of sales was largely due to the appearance of a new format, the compact disc, and evolving usages (Coleman 2004). With HADOPI, in a digital era, history repeats itself.
5 In September 2013, the French government announced the abolition of HADOPI per se. But all of its missions and in particular the three-strikes law have been transferred to a state agency: the Superior Audio-visual Council (CSA) in charge of media and content regulation.
6 A VPN allows a user to hide his personal IP address by giving him a random one. It is, then, impossible for any technical monitor to locate the user and his or her illegal behaviour.
7 In fact, rights holders pay a fee for each file that HADOPI has to monitor. Thus, they tend to prefer popular contents like blockbusters because many pirates share them. From a pirate's perspective, downloading long-tail and niche contents is less risky than very recent movies or just-released music albums.
8 The sum is above 100% as respondents can declare multiple usages.
9 Following Wooldridge's recommendation (2009), we used a simple probit to confirm that the inclusion condi-tion is satisfied.

Bibliography

Aguiar, Luis, and Bertin Martens. 2013. "Digital Music Consumption on the Internet: Evidence From Clickstream Data." Working paper European Commission, Institute for prospective technological studies.
Arnold, Michael A., Eric Darmon, Sylvain Dejean, and Thierry Pénard. 2014. "Graduated Response Policy and the Behavior of Digital Pirates: Evidence From the French Three-Strike (hadopi) Law." SSRN, https://papers.ssrn.com/sol3/papers.cfm?abstract_id=2380522.
Becker, Gary S. 1968. "Crime and Punishment: An Economic Approach." Journal of Political Economy 76(2):169–217.
Becker, Gary S., Kevin M. Murphy, and Michael Grossman. 2006. "The Markets for Illegal Goods: The Case of Drugs." Journal of Political Economy 114:38–60.
Becker, Howard S. 1997. Outsiders: Studies in the Sociology of Deviance. New York and London: Free Press.
Bhattacharjee, Sudip, Ram D. Gopal, Kaveepan Lertwachara, and James R. Marsden. 2006. "Impact of Legal Threats on Online Music Sharing Activity: An Analysis of Music Industry Legal Actions." Journal of Law and Eco-nomics 49(1):91–114.
Bounie, David, Marc Bourreau, and Patrick Waelbroeck. 2006. "Piracy and the Demand for Film: Analysis of Piracy Behavior in French Universities." Review of Economic Research on Copyright Issues 3:15–27.
Bourdieu, Pierre. 1979. "Les trois états du capital culturel." Acte de la Recherche en Sciences Sociales 30:3–6.
Coleman, Mark. 2004. Playback: From the Victrola to Mp3, 100 Years of Music, Machines, and Money. Cambridge: Da Capo Press.
Dalli, Daniele, and Matteo Corciolani. 2008. "Releasing Books Into the Wild: Communal Gift Giving at bookcross-ing.com." SSRN, http://ssrn.com/abstract=1292852.
Danaher, Brett, Michael D. Smith, Rahul Telang, and Siwen Chen. 2014. "The Effect of Graduated Response Anti-Piracy Laws on Music Sales: Evidence from an Event Study in France." Journal of Industrial Economics 62(3):541–553.
Dejean, Sylvain, Thierry Pénard, and Raphaël Suire. 2010. "Une première évaluation des effets de la loi HADOPI sur les pratiques des Internautes francais." Working paper MARSOUIN—University of Rennes 1.
Goldfarb, Avi, and Jeff Prince. 2008. "Internet Adoption and Usage Patterns Are Different: Implications for the Digital Divide." Information, Economics and Policy 20:2–15.

Granovetter, Mark. 1985. "Economic Action and Social Structure: The Problem of Embeddedness." *American Journal of Sociology* 3:481–510.

Kardefelt-Winther, Daniel. 2014. "A Conceptual and Methodological Critique of Internet Addiction Research: Towards a Model of Compensatory Internet Use." *Computers in Human Behaviour* 31:351–354.

Larsson, Stefan, Måns Svensson, and Marcin de Kaminski. 2013. "Online Piracy, Anonymity and Social Change: Innovation Through Deviance." *Convergence* 19:95–114.

Liebowitz, Stan J. 2008. "Testing File-Sharing's Impact on Music Album Sales in Cities." *Management Science* 53:852–859.

Peitz, Martin, and Patrick Waelbroeck. 2006. "Why the Music Industry May Gain From Free Downloading: The Role of Sampling." *International Journal of Industrial Organization* 24:907–913.

Peterson Richard. A. 1992. "Understanding Audience Segmentation: From Elite and Mass to Omnivore and Univore." *Poetics* 21:243–258.

Rehn, Alf. 2004. "The Politics of Contraband: The Honor Economics of the Warez Scene." *Journal of Socio-Economics* 33:359–374.

Smith, Michael D., and Rahul Telang. 2010. "Piracy or Promotion? The Impact of Broadband Internet Penetration on DVD Sales." *Information Economics and Policy* 21:289–298.

Thornton, Mark. 1991. *The Economics of Prohibition.* Salt Lake City: University of Utah Press.

Zentner, Alejandro. 2006. "Measuring the Effect of File Sharing on Music Purchases." *Journal of Law and Economics* 49(1):63–90.

16

At the Intersections of Popular Music
From Background Music to Localized Alternative Musical Experiences

Vincent Rouzé

> When I was a housewife, I just had Muzak on
> —background music—'cause it relaxes you.
>> (Interview with John Lennon, *Playboy*, 1980)

Introduction

"At the intersections of popular music" is a phrase that is both voluntarily referential and ambiguous. To speak of popular music in France means inviting a discussion, thanks to the very ambivalence of the term.[1] Far from the institutional expression "current popular music" marked by styles, singers, and singer-songwriters known nationally and internationally, from "*chanteurs à texte*" like Édith Piaf to the DJ David Guetta, or groups like Phoenix or Daft Punk, we will propose in this chapter not a status report on styles or musical genres— over time and in the geographical area of France—but instead a consideration of popular music in the light of its daily and professional uses: background music. While this expression has negative connotations in France and recalls saccharine instrumental productions from the American firm Muzak, it has multiple meanings and covers different realities between specific styles and particular situations of music being played and listened to.

A study of popular music in light of its quality as background sound can be justified in at least two ways. The first is tied to the dearth of existing studies and interest from the French academic world. The second is the fact that this music participates in historic, economic, political, and social mediation (Hennion 1993) at the core of popular music. Whether they are integrated in 360-degree-style economic strategies or they generate value from back catalogs, the creation of original territorial sound identities, or by the imposition of silence, they include other types of popular music that are not often analyzed in France, such as mood music, easy listening, or relaxation music.

In this chapter, we will show that the current status of this background music in France can be found at the intersection of the evolution of French radio broadcasting, the history of past forms of background music, of Muzak, and the logics of globalization and homogenization, as well as an ecological and artistic value enhancement of geographic territories.

Light Music as a Starting Point

If it is accepted that music has a functional character (Supicic 1988), it's only with the development of modern techniques of reproduction and distribution that it acquired its ubiquitous nature, as properly noted by poet Paul Valéry as of 1928. In fact, music is no longer dependent on musicians to exist in space and time. Thus, the concept of "background music" is first and foremost found in "light music" in the context of radio broadcasts.

"Light music" as opposed to "serious music" began in France in 1921 with the creation of Radio Tour Eiffel, and was of two types. Some music came from recordings. Other music was produced by radio orchestras, both at and outside the station. This practice offered national broadcasts, for example, of the Orchestre national de la Radiodiffusion française, as well as local broadcasts in major cities, for example, of the orchestra of Radio Strasbourg. In each case the radio programming varied and included serious music, contemporary music, and light music (Méadel 1994; Cheval 1998).

Between 1931 and 1934, the programming of provincial station Radio Strasbourg, for example, devoted 4,912 hours to light music, 1,560 hours to serious music, and 2,096 hours to the broadcast of various concerts (Bennet 2010, 18). The fruit of the criticism of the philosopher Theodor Adorno (1994 [1968]), "light music" developed at the crossroads of classical orchestration and the repetitive patterns of "industrialized" popular music. It participated in the creation of everyday sound atmospheres heard primarily in a private setting, becoming an accompaniment to daily activities for a broad and diverse audience, an audience that would later become fragmented and plural as radio stations multiplied and specialized.

After the Second World War, these forms of light music declined with the development of albums, the so-called peripheral radio stations (stations ostensibly broadcasting from outside of France to the French market, in competition with the French national stations), private radio stations (Europe n° 1 would broadcast *yéyé* hits in the program *Salut les Copains*), and, beginning in the 1970s, pirate radio stations. With the recognition of "free radios" in 1981 and the control of the FM frequencies by national authorities (today the Conseil Supérieur de l'Audiovisuel, or CSA, the French broadcasting authority), light orchestral music disappeared in favor of thematic or generalist musical programming inherent to the identity of the particular FM radio station.

The expression "light music" and the compositions it refers to have given way to rationales of commercial interest and brand identity. It seems thus that today background music is less tied to effects of orchestral compositions than to variable forms of listening (attentive or not), reinforced by effects of rotations and repetitions of play of various works, and of a sound compression that marks the audio identity of the radio station.

Easy Listening, Relaxation or the Clichés of Background Music

Background music would thus be found in the continuity of "easy listening" music, based on two conceptions of musical creation: to be heard rather than listened to, and to accompany activities rather than to exist for its own sake. It therefor encounters the conception of "furniture music" proposed in 1920 by iconoclastic composer Erik Satie. The French musician saw himself as part of the tradition of music composed as forms of accompaniment, such as Telemann's Tafelmusik, and defined this utilitarian music as "[c]rystallized around pivot notes, it is a repetition of sequences, it creates vibration, it has no other goal; it fills the same role as light, heat, and comfort in all its forms" (cited by Rey 1974, 170, our translation). This is what led Marc Bredel to say that "furniture music is characterized by the obsessive repetition of a given theme. No event in these works, but a single cell that seems recorded on an endless loop" (our translation). This allusion to the loop recalls the practices of sampling and looping that are found in today's electro music, as well as in many pop music works. Thus, we can say that Erik Satie announces as of the 1920s what will become today's popular music: something industrial, repetitive, and commercial. This continuity can also be seen in the influence it holds over many contemporary or pop musicians, whether French or foreign. Thus, it is cited or taken up by composers such as the American John Cage, producer-performers such as the Briton Brian Eno, or current French singer-songwriters like Arthur H, the son of singer Jacques Higelin, or Yann Tiersen, who composed the music for the film *Amélie Poulain*.

A recognizable musical style, an "*exhaustive* compilation of the cliches of *post-Renaissance* music," cleverly complemented by sweet formulas, on which rests background music, as defined by Glenn Gould (1983 [1966]), these instrumental compositions known as "easy listening" make a further shift. They began in the 1950s in the United States and a few years later came to Europe. Immortalized by American composers Burt Bacharach or Henry Mancini, they gave rise to collections such as *Music for Gracious Living* from Columbia or *Background Music* from Capitol Records.[2] In France, this musical style was primarily used to accompany films by creating atmospheres like those produced by pianists who accompanied silent movies. Sometimes known as "*musique au mètre*" ("music by the yard," given its pricing and the lack of royalties), it would find a second life in the 1980s in corporate films and advertising.

At the same time, this easy listening music was being revisited in France as of the end of the 1970s in the form of low-cost compilation records sold at large retailers, most often in the form of instrumental arrangements of pop and classical works. These recordings were the subject of stinging criticism in France, where they were seen as the continuation of the compositions of performers like Richard Clayderman or André Rieu, who had also popularized classical music by arranging works in the style of pop hits and who sold millions of records in France and abroad. Often decried and criticized because they were derived from a more complex esthetic composition, these "easy" works would see new interest in the 1990s, with the support of the music press (e.g., the cultural magazine *Les Inrockuptibles*), and by being programmed by Paris radio station Nova, aimed at a well-informed and trendy audience. In a program like *Cocktail Time*, hosts Ariel Wizman and Jean Croc would offer original programming and remixes that modernized the concept of easy listening. This musical style thus became "trendy" and "alternative," as illustrated by the label Tricatel, founded by musician and producer Bertrand Burgalat, who did the music for the album *Présence humaine* from writer Michel Houellebecq.

Another intersection is found when the "ambient" style, born of the musical experimentation of Brian Eno as of 1978 (Eno 1996), is included in original creative logics. Starting as an experimental and little-known form, it would develop and become more legitimate by being programmed by club DJs to offer moments of rest for dancers, in particular in the hip clubs of Paris. During the 1990s, this style reached a broader audience with the recording of DJ compositions. The "ambient" and "lounge" styles used the format of easy listening music, remixing them as did Gilles Pompougnac for the Hôtel Costes or the compilations of the Buddha Bar published under the label George V Record. In a callback to furniture music, Satie's *Gnossienne* would be remixed in a compilation from the Buddha Bar.

While this music offers yet more variants on the concept of mood music, here in the form of "chic" and "trendy," it also shows the fluidity of the boundaries between alternative music and economic logic. These labels work for brands so as to personalize and adapt music to their brand image, and aim to be part of "a genuine trend, integrated in a total marketing concept" (our translation).[3] This mixture of aims calls for a local and territorial compositional originality tied to the place where the music is heard, and its identity (bars, hotels, specialized retailers), while being part of worldwide marketing strategies for its diffusion.

Crossing boundaries and genres is illustrated by another type of mood music found in relaxation music. Relaxation music is at the intersection of easy listening and world music and arrangements of classical works. Being one of the most important New Age music composers, the American Steven Halpern, who holds a PhD in psychology, has theorized the main compositional traits of that music.[4] By studying and then calling on the benefits of the "healing powers" of music, he became a leading proponent of therapeutic music. In this continuity, many French artists and records have taken on this aspect of music. In France, composers such as Zoralkia, Michel Logos, Thierry Morati, Jean-Marc Staehle, and Michel Pépé propose relaxing music made mainly by using synthesizers or classical instruments, to which are added natural sounds from a variety of samplings (waves, bird songs, traditional singing such as that of Native Americans). These musical productions generated a myriad of labels of various sizes, beginning with defunct label DIEM, and included labels with evocative names such as Biosphere, Ellébore, Oréade Music, and Narada, which were more often than not distributed by specialized firms such as DG Productions, focused on the "well-being" market. This musical response to the stress and demands of urban life became a fixture of certain types of public spaces like macrobiotic restaurants or esoteric bookshops in Paris and the provinces.[5] In France, it became widespread in the 1990s via the national chain of retailers Natures et Découvertes, which not only sold the recordings, but played them in their stores.

Mood Music in Public Spaces: Marketing and Revenue-Generation Strategies

Unlike styles arising from light music and individual listening formats, the concept of "mood music" also developed in France by its daily presence in public or semipublic spaces. In the line of rearrangements of existing pieces, from the patented method of "stimulus progression"[6] and its worldwide expansion (Lanza 1994; Rouzé 2004), the French firm Mood Music was founded in 1960. It played music in luxury hotels in Paris's Eighth Arrondissement, and it soon expanded its strategy to supermarkets to create an audio presence in these "nonplaces" built on the edges of cities, as well as to increase consumption, if possible. To do so, many works of popular music were rearranged, renewing the easy-listening mood music already mentioned. Due to increased demands from supermarkets and to respond to the technical difficulties tied to vinyl records, Mood Music bought the firm DIMA, which allowed the use of magnetic tape. Specialized in "Tapes Top," with reliable and long-playing tapes, it offered compilations of original light "orchestral" music, differentiating itself from its American competitor Muzak that was trying to gain a foothold in France. This primacy of atmosphere over "business music" led the American firm, after a brief collaboration with Mood Music, to leave the French market.[7]

The firm changed its name to Mood Media in the 1990s to highlight the diversification of its activities, its investment in visual and audio marketing, and its international focus, with the firm being bought in 2003 by the Canadian-based international group Fluid Media Canada and taking the name Mood Media Corporation. The story returned to its beginnings with the acquisition by this group of Muzak in 2011.

Today, present in most public places, mood music (defined institutionally in France by the rights organization for music authors and composers as "background-sound music") has now become thematic presentations mixing French- and English-language works, pop and classical music, with specific themes, played from digital recordings that avoid the repetition inherent to former media (vinyl records, tapes, CDs) and that reject musical styles considered intrusive. Because background music needs to be consensual in terms of melody and tempo, this leads to the exclusion of certain musical styles that are aimed at specific audiences (metal, contemporary, etc.). Some venues that host a diverse public choose, often at the initiative of the manager, a national radio broadcast focused on golden oldies, or else a broadcast aimed at an audience aged 30 to 50 (Chérie FM, Nostalgie, RFM), recalling in a new fashion the concept of light music already discussed. Others prefer customized or thematic musical programming produced by firms such as Mood Media. Such is the case, for example, of supermarket chain Monoprix, which has developed its own "Radio Monop" (Mood Media), made up of fashionable hit songs, or of Vinci ("a global player in concessions and construction, employing close to 191,000 people in some 100 countries"),[8] which has created multiple radio stations adapted to the places the music is played (toll roads, parking structures). In the case of parking structures, the programming is a succession of pieces designated as "classical," such as Dvořák, so as to create an aural presence that is reassuring and unobtrusive.

As did Muzak for decades, Mood Media Corporation today is participating in the globalization of diffusion, with a catalog of 5 million songs, free from digital rights management restrictions, coming primarily from its subsidiary Somerset Entertainment, which itself comprises labels such as Solitudes, Avalon, and Fisher Price. But unlike Muzak, which offered new arrangements of existing pieces, Mood Media has built strong relations with the major record companies, which see background music as a way to generate revenue from their catalogs and their artists. As part of overall rationales of worldwide total value generation, these musical atmospheres offer a soundtrack to daily urban life, and form part of the economics of the French and international music industries. The annual reports of the Société des Auteurs, Compositeurs et Éditeurs de Musique (SACEM), which collects royalties via SPRE,[9] shows constant growth of the use of music in public places, with a total revenue of €57.5 million in 2012 as compared to €13.9 million in 2000. According to SPRE, the constant growth[10] of this sector allows "60,000 performers and 2,000 producers to exercise their profession."[11] The issue is thus one of creating a general or specific sound identity, but also of making the most of music catalogs.

Les Halles de Paris or the Paradox of the Globalized Local

Under the cover of background music and music played in public places, there is also the intent to create sound identities, transforming music into a marketing and communications tool. To illustrate this point, we'll speak now of the ethnographic study we carried out at the Forum des Halles from 2004 to 2006 (Rouzé 2006). Today, the Forum des Halles is undergoing a major renovation. This shopping center is the heir to a long tradition of commercial activity, with the central markets located here until the 1970s, right in the heart of the capital of France. After the market was transferred to Rungis in the southern suburbs of Paris, the site was modernized to become a station of the RER suburban express rail network and a three-level shopping center.

Thus, the place has different kinds of sound systems. The Forum shopping center plays music in the corridors, while each store has its own musical selection for its own premises. In each case, the music played through the loudspeakers is different, depending on the location and size of the store. While national and international chains (H&M, Gap, etc.) have a rhythmic selection played at high volume aiming to produce a localized international identity, smaller stores offer a more heterogeneous choice of music. Paradoxically, the music serves as a masking sound to cover the other sounds of the venue or even completely eradicate them. This music can thus be perceived as a sort of pollution. Even though the music can be found in various formats, it transforms identity-based ambiances into homogenizing and consensual atmospheres.[12] Thus each location contributes to the creation of a multiple-sound space that is difficult to understand: first, because their repetition is perceived only by those who work there and not by those passing through, and second, because the sound goes beyond the space intended, mixing with other sounds and interfering with the ability to listen to any one sound. In this setting, background music mixes with ambient noises to become a patchwork of sound. This is what Murray Schafer (1979) calls hi-fi "schizophonia"—that is to say, the blurring of the cognition and meaning of music, lost in the flow of sound, as sounds are superimposed on each other, become clear then not, and mix with each other. As tools, this music becomes circular and repetitive, drowning in this "ocean of sound" described by David Toop (2000), or becomes just noise that aims to stultify and silence walkers and consumers (Attali 1977).

Background Music as a Revenue Generator in the Era of the Web

This problem of background music in public spaces has been exacerbated by the arrival of digital music and the Internet. We can see this in the development of Sound Deezer, a service that provides music for retail outlets, created by the French streaming music service Deezer. Thanks to its agreements with major record companies, it is able to provide sound service to the 700 McDonald's restaurants in France and offer background music for the photos on the website of Getty Images.[13] There's a similar logic for the alternative website Jamendo,[14] created in 2005 by French entrepreneurs and based in Luxembourg. The launch of this site offered "amateur music," aiming to break the vertical integration of the music industry by highlighting amateur productions promoted on the platform. Royalty free so as to strengthen its criticism of the SACEM, this site, bought in 2010 by Belgian firm MusicMatic, developed a catalog for public places and "is listened to in 1500 shops in the world with more than 20,000 hours of music broadcast everyday [*sic*]."[15] The catalog of this collaborative platform includes 2,355 performers and 56,948 titles. They are included in musical programs formatted like those of companies offering background music for public places: eleven radio "stations" are available, updated daily, and classified by genre (lounge, jazz, pop, electro, instrumental, classical, ambient pop) or by atmosphere (relaxation, down tempo, up tempo, mid-tempo).

For its classical offerings, Jamendo has joined forces with the net label OnClassical, which offers royalty-free classical works (Bach, Verdi, Chopin) and soundtrack music. But this has raised objections within the community of amateurs who supported the project at its start. This path toward seeking economic value has generated discontent among those who saw the platform as an alternative to traditional rationales of mediatization. The risk is to transform these productions into a simple flow of background music to the places that play them and also to eliminate the initial philosophy of the project based on exchanges, selection, and recognition by web users. And as is often the case for use in advertising, artists singing in languages other than English are often excluded from this system.

Musical Walks to Crossroads

Even if these musical atmospheres participate in the homogenization of the musical space and transform music into a tool, they can also be claimed as an "artistic" and ecological alternative focused within a particular territory. To consider this possibility, we look at two particular cases emblematic of this trend in France.

The first is found in musical walks. Unlike the many music festivals that have developed throughout France (Eurockéennes in Belfort, Vieilles Charrues, etc.), which show a territorial attachment for music, these "walks" aim to be alternative forms of creation and distribution, outside the mainstream and globalized logics already discussed. They are exemplified in the label BS, Balades Sonores. Born from a collective known as Boutiques Sonores, this label calls for the "liberation of music, seeking out and offering alternative solutions to independent labels, self-produced artists, and the general public."[16] Groups such as Syd Matters organized their "BaladeS SonoreS" tour not in concert venues, but in chapels, theaters, farms, and local festivals.

The second is based on the creation of music inherent to the territory where it is heard, and integrates its sounds, its history, and its architecture. Begun in the 1990s by artists such as Pierre Marietan[17] or Nicholas Frize, these "sound paths" now offer multiple horizons and are at the crossroads between analysis and listening for existing aural identities, musical composition, and enhancement of local heritage. Thus, we find hybrid forms mixing text, walks, music, sound, and voice. We find ourselves at the crossroads of academic, popular, and plastic esthetics, while reinserting music in the heart of daily environments in imagined scenarios. The "sound walks" of the collective MU, for example, mix sounds collected on site with personal compositions. With "Front Pop (Flavitron remix)," by WPMG/Jopo Stereo, in 2006 MU took over the André Citroen Park in Paris. With the project "Cité d'Or" by OttoannA (Sweet Sixteen/Super 16, Paris Quartier d'Été, summer 2007), they took on the densely populated neighborhoods of the Goutte d'Or in Paris's Eighteenth Arrondissement.

This local interest can also be found in a rural setting. The "sound walks" created by musician-artists Pierre Redon and Edmond Carrère in the Limousin region aim to be "hybrid projects, between visual, sound, and documentary creation, revealing a territory through its inhabitants, the sound in the landscape, and human ecology."[18] Blending traditional regional music, natural sounds recorded on the walk, and pop and synthetic sounds, these productions participate in the creation of original sound environments that allow participants to rediscover the existing architectural and visual environment in a new way. Its forms of composition, financially supported by local, regional, and national institutions, are connected to the precepts of sound ecology developed by Canadian musician Murray Schafer (1979). These rely on a sound classification and on daily reflexive listening, which gave rise to research on surroundings carried out by certain French science laboratories such as the Cresson lab in Grenoble beginning in the late 1990s. But by following the line of so-called natural recordings, these walks raise certain issues. While they aim at enhancing local heritage, these projects in sound ecology raise the question of the need to add music to an existing soundscape, transforming the initial sound identity of the places. This process is not so dissimilar to the problems of sound pollution described previously in public places.

In conclusion, this short overview of the various forms taken by so-called background music raises the question of the role of music in our modern communication-based societies. At the intersection of the styles used, they are nourished by logics of sound used in everyday public places reinvented today by personalized musicalization that becomes possible with the use of new digital terminals such as MP3 players and mobile phones.

Notes

1   While there have been a variety of definitions offered in the English-language literature, its existence in France is the topic of some discussion. See, for example, Looseley (2006, 199–204). See also Rouzé (2007), who considers it a paradigm, or Le Guern (2007), who criticizes the use of the term in the context of new technologies because it refers to audiences that can be differentiated in space and time.
2   *L'Express*, "La vogue de l'easy-listening," 2001, accessed July 21, 2017, www.lexpress.fr/informations/la-vogue-de-l-easylistening_642255.html#3D3Ghz3AqWyvdIO6.99.
3   Buddah Bar, "Musique," 2016, accessed December 18, 2013, www.buddhabar.com/fr/music-buddha-bar-musique-album-buddha-bar#.
4   According to him, the following must be sought:

> Harmony and consonance rather than dissonance. Unpredictable melodic lines; i.e., avoidance of progressions that fulfill cultural expectations. Lack of traditional pulsing rhythm. Avoidance of instruments with harsh or shrill sounds. Open texture, creating a feeling of "space" in the listener.
> (Quoted by Blum 1996, 122)

5   France is made up of twenty-two regional authorities and ninety-six *départements*.
6   This method aims to increase production by playing a series of pieces on an ascending rhythmic curve, with a climax, followed by a descending curve, then a period of silence, which is repeated over and over.
7   "L'image du produit" (translated by Michel Chion) in "Le pouvoir des sons," *Cahiers de la Recherche sur la musique* 6:239, 1978.
8   As Vinci defines itself on its corporate website.
9   Société pour la Perception de la Rémunération Equitable (company for the collection of equitable remuneration).
10   But it must be noted that this increase is also due to increased fees and by stricter enforcement of royalties.
11   Document presenting the fees according to the location of use; see SPRE, "Tarifs. Lieux sonorisés," 2011, accessed November 9, 2013, www.spre.fr/document/tarif_lieux_sonorises.pdf.
12   This observation corresponds to those of scholars such as Ola Stockfelt (1998) in Sweden, Jonhathan Sterne (1997) in Canada, or Tia DeNora (2000) in the United Kingdom.

13 Getty Images, "Collection musicale. Musique d'ambiance. Musique d'attente," 2013, accessed December 2, 2013, www.gettyimages.fr/music/collection/background-music-on-hold.
14 Jamendo Music, "Streaming gratuit. Téléchargement gratuit," 2013, accessed December 2, 2013, www.jamendo.com/fr.
15 Jamendo Licensing, "Musique d'ambiance libre de droits," 2013, accessed December 2, 2013, http://pro.jamendo.com/musique-ambiance.
16 Balades Sonores, "Qui sommes-nous?" 2013, accessed December 18, 2013, www.baladessonores.com/infos.
17 We'll refer here to his work that summarizes the problems discussed and makes clear the implementation of this "music of place." Pierre Marietan, "La Musique du Lieu. Musique, Architecture, Paysage, Environnement," Swiss National Commission for UNESCO, Bern, 1997.
18 Pierre Redon, "Marches sonores," 2013, accessed May 18, 2013, www.pierreredon.com/marches_sonores.html.

Bibliography

Adorno, Theodor W. 1994 [1968]. *Introduction à la sociologie de la musique*. Genève: Ed. Contrechamps.
Anderson, Tim J. 2006. *Making Easy Listening: Material Culture and Postwar American Recording: Commerce and Mass Culture Series*. Minneapolis and London: University of Minnesota Press.
Attali, Jacques. 1977. *Bruit*. Paris: PUF.
Bennet, Christophe. 2010. *La musique à la radio dans les années 30: La création d'un genre particulier*. Paris: L'Harmattan.
Blum, Peter C. 1996. "Typification, Transcendence and Critique: On the Social Construction of New Age Music." In *All Music: Essays on the Hermeneutics of Music*, edited by Fabio B. Dasilva and David L. Brunsma, 117–132. Aldershot: Avebury Press.
Bredel, Marc. 1982. *Erik Satie*. Paris: Éditions Mazarine.
Cheval, Jean-Jacques. 1998. "Les radios en France, histoire, état et enjeux." *Communication et langages* 115(1):123.
Delalande, François. 2001. *Le son des musiques: Entre technologie et esthétique*. Paris: INA-Buchet/Chastel.
DeNora, Tia. 2000. *Music in Everyday Life*. Cambridge: Cambridge University Press.
Gauthier, Laure, and Mélanie Traversier, eds. 2008. *Mélodies urbaines: La musique dans les villes d'Europe (XVIᵉ–XIXᵉ siècles)*. Paris: Presses Universitaires de la Sorbonne.
Gould, Glenn. 1983 [1966]. "L'enregistrement et ses perspectives." In *Le Dernier puritain: écrits I*, edited by Bruno Monsaingeon, Paris: Fayard.
Hennion Antoine. 1993. *La Passion musicale*. Paris: Metailié.
Lanza, Joseph. 1994. *Elevator Music, a Surreal History of Muzak, Easy-Listening and Other Moodsong*. New York: St Martin's Press.
Le Guern, Philippe. 2007. "En arrière la musique! Sociologies des musiques populaires en France." *Réseaux* 2(141–142):15–45.
Looseley, David. 2006. "Musiques populaires: une exception francophone?" *Volume! La revue des musiques populaires* 5(2):199–204.
Maisonneuve, Sophie. 2009. *L'invention du disque, 1877–1949: Genèse de L'usage des médias musicaux contemporains*. Paris: Éditions des archives contemporaines.
Méadel, Cécile. 1994. *Histoire de la radio des années 30*. Paris: Anthropos-economica.
Rey, Anne. 1974. *Satie* Paris: Seuil, Coll. "Solfège."
Rouzé, Vincent. 2004. "Les musiques diffusées dans les lieux publics: analyse et enjeux de pratiques communicationnelles quotidiennes." PhD diss., Université Paris 8.
———. 2007. *Populaire, vous avez dit musique populaire*. Louvain la Neuve: IASPM BFE. Online: http://iaspmfrancophone.online.fr/colloque2007/Rouze_2007.pdf.
Schafer, R. Murray. 1979. *Le paysage sonore*. Paris: J.C. Lattès.
Supicic, Ivo. 1988. "Les fonctions sociales de la musique." In *Musique et société, hommages à R. Wangermée*, 173–182. Brussels: Editions Université de Bruxelles.
Toop, David. 2000. *Ocean of Sound, Ambient Music, mondes imaginaires et voix de l'éther*. Paris: Kargo editions.
Valery, Paul. 1928. "La conquête de l'ubiquité." Online: http://classiques.uqac.ca/classiques/Valery_paul/conquete_ubiguite/valery_conquete_ubiquite.pdf/.

Coda
Rethinking the Popular?
Some Reflections on Popular Music
in France and Britain

David Looseley

In March 2014, shortly before municipal elections, France's "socialist" president Francois Hollande appointed a new speech-writer, Pierre-Yves Bocquet. There would be nothing remarkable in this were it not for the fact that Bocquet, a senior civil servant in his day job, moonlights as the seriously cool "Pierre Evil," a critic specialising in US gangsta rap. Amusing or trivial, this snippet does tell us something about the public status of popular music in contemporary France. The stylistic differences between French and British popular musics have long been obvious. But the appointment of Bocquet points out the different ways the music is actually thought about in the two countries. The present volume does much the same. Decades after the rise of popular music studies in the Anglophone world, the sociologists, musicologists and historians who feature in *Made in France* are still pioneers in French academia, although change is coming fast now. They represent a new generation of French scholars who admirably challenge established orthodoxies about French music and have clearly engaged with cultural studies in ways that previous generations from more traditionally minded disciplines did not. Yet there is still to some extent a kind of "French cultural exception" about the kinds of questions they pose, as distinctive in some ways as the music itself.[1]

My intention, however, is not to analyse either that musical or that academic distinctiveness. The "coda" format calls instead for a consideration of how a local popular music is perceived and evaluated "elsewhere." That "elsewhere" implies, first, an ethnographic distance: an outside gaze which defamiliarises local perceptions. It may also entail a linguistic, transcultural distance, as in my own case. A French-speaking British scholar in the field of French cultural studies, I inevitably bring to that field my own form of cultural difference. This is partly a difference of academic training and viewpoint; but it is also born of my being a participant observer of the Anglophone popular music and culture I grew up with in the 1960s. My approach therefore will be broadly comparative in the hope of drawing out at least some of what makes French attitudes to popular music distinctive and different from British ones.

Semantics and Discourse

Any Anglophone observer confronts the semantic problems caused by long-standing French appropriations of Anglo-American musical taxonomies: *le music-hall, le jazz, le rock, la pop, le hard, la techno, les boys' [sic] bands* and so on. As that genitive apostrophe conscientiously but incorrectly inserted into "boy bands" hints (see Looseley 2013a, 4), terminological borrowing in France is rarely direct or transparent. We cannot assume that such loan words connote or even denote in the same way. *Le rock* is a case in point, since it has (at least) two related but distinct meanings. As in English, it can designate a harder-edged, louder, more personally expressive sub-genre within pop music, from which UK and US rock began to distance itself in the late 1960s. Secondly, *le rock* can be a very broad generic category, "a portmanteau concept" and "the originator of a prolific and undifferentiated family of descendants" (Hein 2011, 156). This would seem close to the similarly elastic English classification "pop and rock," sloppily employed to distinguish American-influenced, usually electrified styles of popular music since the mid-1950s from equally unsatisfactory bundles such as classical, jazz, big band, or easy listening. I shall use it in this second sense.

These questions of transcultural naming, which I will return to, suggest that "popular music" is a dynamic rhetorical artefact more than a stable aesthetic category. Its "nature" changes with use, reconstructed over time by public discourse—"public" here covering not the individual music user but institutionalised discourses: critics, presenters, educationists and the cultural and political establishments as a whole. In France, I would argue, the cultural and political establishments are especially influential, because the social construction of popular music is in part a national-cultural one. And in this respect, comparison with the United Kingdom can be illuminating.

A Middlebrow Culture?

It is often said that the old hierarchy of "high" and "low" cultural practices, legitimate and illegitimate, is outdated. The argument is that social, economic and technological change has radically transformed those practices in a post-Bourdieu, neo-liberal age, turning them into readily available commodities whose social value lies, much more than in the past, in their economic usefulness rather than in the cultural capital associated with them. To this can be added the common perception that today's cultural consumers are omnivores, as much at ease with Bach or Bartok as with Bieber or Beyoncé. This is all true, of course. But in France, it seems to me, there is still a residual, subterranean tendency to deplore the erosion of aesthetic and national boundaries brought about by democratisation, globalisation, migration and the digital revolution. The judgmental terminology of "high" culture (*la haute culture, la culture cultivée*) and "mass" culture (*la culture de masse*) remains in relatively common use, suggesting that a binary vision of cultural value survives, albeit discreetly.

We should not overstate this case. Cultural levelling is as much a fact of life in France as in most advanced Western societies and there are no doubt many French fans of popular culture who wouldn't even recognise my description of a persistent binarism. But there is a difference between grass-roots cultural practices and institutionalised discourse. For centuries, the perceived value of classical French culture has been part of a resilient national sense of self, an awareness of sharing a material and written cultural heritage of global importance and a history of avant-garde or intellectual revolt involving the constant search for new creative forms and languages. And this collective sense refuses to give up the ghost entirely, resolutely shapeshifting and adapting to contemporary circumstance. The diligent ethnographer may still catch a glimpse of its comings and goings, sometimes in unexpected locations. The uproar caused by Nicolas Sarkozy's disdain for France's great classical novel *La Princesse de Clèves* (Looseley 2013b, 198) offered one such opportunity.

As candidate, then president, Sarkozy projected himself as a no-nonsense representative of the unassuming French citizen, whose down-to-earth tastes he purported to share. He affably admitted to liking the reality singing show *Star Academy* and he listed amongst his favourite singers middle-of-the-road stars like Mireille Mathieu and Johnny Hallyday. He enjoyed action films like *Saving Private Ryan* and anything featuring Sylvester Stallone. Unusually for a French president, of whom eloquence is expected, his spoken register was similarly populist. This confected self—along with some controversial policies of course— elicited remarkable hostility. For many, he became the political agent of an undesirable ingress of the lowbrow at the heart of national culture. The historian Antoine de Baecque (2008) contended that, whereas in the past French cultural crises had always been resolved by a reassertion of culture's importance, the crisis caused by Sarkozy "is about imposing a quite different 'culture,' the culture of results, at the very heart of public policy." Sarkozy, he went on, has lost sight of the fundamental belief system underpinning the national culture, namely that:

> to be French is to share the conviction that culture makes us better people. [. . .] The sovereign in France, whether he reigns over a monarchy, leads an empire or presides over a republic, has always been the protector of the arts and the propagator of the national culture. [. . .] With Nicolas Sarkozy, we are entering a new era.

Journalist and cultural policy specialist Jean-Michel Djian (2010) took much the same apocalyptic view of the Sarkozian "cultural revolution": "It's all over: the utopia of sharing, the humanist dream and critical thinking. It's time for technocultural realism, for converting 'high minds' ['*belles âmes*'] to the virtuous paradigm of sound and image."

Djian touches here on the ultimate meaning that Sarkozy assumed for many: his shamelessly declared tastes drilled into a seam of anxiety about the shift from a culture of the word to one of sound, vision and virtuality. And sociologist and blogger Frédéric Martel (2012, 222) gives a name to those tastes: "*la culture 'middlebrow'*" (Martel 2012, 222).

For Martel, "middlebrow" is pejorative, designating a culture neither crassly populist nor particularly demanding, just reassuringly moderate. As we will see, this reading of the middlebrow is incomplete in the French context (Holmes and Looseley 2013). But we need first to understand its relevance for the rise of rock and pop in France and Britain.

Histories

Until the 1980s, French intellectual attitudes to home-grown rock and pop were largely dismissive. This was due in part to a dominant Adornian pessimism about mass culture generally, combined with anti-Americanism. But even among those who welcomed rock and pop as a new source of popular creativity, the more discriminating commentators and fans were often embarrassed by the derivative nature of French rock 'n' roll and *yéyé* (lightweight pop)—both epitomised in Johnny Hallyday's chameleon-like subservience to Anglo-American fashions.

Instead, they favoured the American or British originals, supposedly more authentic. With hindsight, this blanket disapproval was shortsighted, since some *yéyé* adaptations of those originals were skilfully executed and became meaningful for French adolescents (see Saladin, Chapter 1 in this book). But a third factor comes into play here. The rejection of Americanised culture and the concern with authenticity come together in the perception of *la chanson française*[2] as a criterion of evaluation.

La chanson française is a slippery term, for, as Catherine Rudent rightly maintains (Rudent, Chapter 9 in this book), it has no single, over-arching definition. Certainly, it is too diverse and dynamic to be a genre. And I have argued elsewhere (Looseley 2003, 63–86) that it only becomes fully itself, self-aware, in opposition to Anglo-American popular musics. *Chanson française* discourse hinges on the assumption that *le rock* signifies rhythm, dance, sexuality, the body as agent; and that pop lyrics—"text" is the term revealingly used in French—are largely incomprehensible because they are in English or the accompaniment makes them inaudible. Accordingly, it assumes that French *chanson* involves the foregrounding of lyrics in French and clearly articulated, emotion tempered by intellect and the primacy of the head and heart over the body. *Le rock*, then, is not *chanson française*, and, in the early days at least, inauthentic and un-French. A simple version of this binary mode is voiced by the lyricist Pierre Delanoë (1993, 109–110), who adapted a good deal of Anglo-American pop into French but evidently drew the line at *yéyé*, which he sees as "a retreat from the text [. . .] *chanson* today has degenerated into sound, rhythm, dance music."

Early French attitudes to pop and rock are further illuminated by music journalist Patrice Bollon (1987 [1981]) reviewing the first twenty years of *le rock* in France:

> French rock is a colonised rock, which has no roots other than imported and (or) strictly mythical ones. A "country-bumpkin" rock whose capital is a fantastical "New York" or an imagined "London" and which retains of its models only a "form" completely devoid of real "meaning."

With any former imperial power, a colonial metaphor takes on particular resonance. Here, it is especially revealing of the cultural-historical trope I am examining. Around 1960, France was losing the 130-year-old imperial identity which, as postcolonial studies emphasises, had been so closely imbricated with its national sense of self. Anglo-American rock 'n' roll was therefore experienced by some as a second humiliation: the coloniser colonised. French culture, once admired throughout the world, was now dancing grotesquely to its master's voice, that of a foreign civilisation economically and culturally more powerful. But Bollon's position is more sophisticated than this. He doesn't take *chanson française* as a positive point of reference and he doesn't see Anglo-American pop as an invader. Rather, the rhetoric of colonisation is used as a metaphor for a self-inflicted abdication of creative input, the colonised culture's compliance with domination and fear of moving from imitation to a creative appropriation that would reinvest the dominant form "with a meaning which was not there before in the original." Through the colonial metaphor, then, popular-musical authenticity becomes a national, ideological matter.

Now, whatever assessment we might make of such reactions, one aspect of Bollon's subtle argument can easily pass unnoticed: the automatic association of the United States and the United Kingdom. As the familiar French epithet *anglo-saxon* reveals, these two Anglo-phone countries are assumed to be brothers-in-arms in a concerted colonial enterprise. And yet, rock 'n' roll was partially experienced as a colonisation in the United Kingdom too, still struggling with economic crisis after the abrupt ending of American wartime aid ("Lend-Lease") in 1945 and imperial crisis after Suez in 1956. And, as in France, there was conservative resistance to Americanisation by rock 'n' roll.

Once again, we have to distinguish between grass-roots practices and public discourse. British audiences had enjoyed American songs and dances since Victorian times but particularly since the Second World War, with big band music, jitterbugging and jiving. But cultural guardians like the BBC and vested interests in the UK entertainment business were less accommodating. The Musicians' Union, for example, was hostile to touring American dance bands from the 1930s. Government protectionism meant it was nigh impossible to buy an American electric guitar in 1950s Britain. And as early as 1949, the BBC, in its internal guidelines known as the "Green Book" (BBC 1949), loftily stated,

> American idiom and slang frequently find their way quite inappropriately into scripts, and dance band singers for the most part elect to adopt pseudo American accents. The BBC believes that this spurious Americanisation of programmes—whether in the writing or the interpretation—is unwelcome to the great majority of listeners.

Although governments and organisations like the BBC were effectively telling the public what it should and shouldn't like, it is also important to realise that the real America was not particularly well known in Britain in the 1950s, where overseas holidays were rare and Hollywood, Tin Pan Alley and the GIs stationed there during the war provided the major images of the United States. So, in Britain as in France, when American artists started singing about teenagers owning cars and going to drive-in movies to smooch in the back seat, these were exciting but alien references. Similarly, the racial implications of that marriage of Black and White cultures which had so controversially produced rock 'n' roll in the rural southern states of America meant little to the White working class from the London or Paris suburbs. Hence the sense that Tommy Steele, Cliff Richard, Johnny Hallyday and Eddy Mitchell were, as Bollon recognises, impersonating an imperfectly understood American cultural reality. Nevertheless, the backlash that the music encountered in Britain was to a degree religious, nationalist and ultimately racist. Dominic Sandbrook (2005, 461) quotes a 1956 piece on the subject in the *Daily Mail*—still today a major tabloid influence on Britain culture: "[Rock 'n' roll] is deplorable. It is tribal. And it is from America. It follows ragtime, blues, dixie, jazz, hot cha-cha and the boogie-woogie, which surely originated in the jungle. We sometimes wonder whether this is the Negro's revenge."

So, Americanisation through pop did not come about more smoothly in Britain because of some mythical linguistic and cultural family likeness. Even so, what does strike me as different in the two countries is the *intensity* of the French response. Americanised mass music was constructed as the very antithesis of French republican humanism, as the sociologist Edgar Morin (1963) recognised when reflecting on the sociocultural meanings of a live music festival held at the Place de la Nation in Paris in 1963, which had attracted heated disapproval in the adult press. For the fascinated Morin, the pop and rock on display there represented what cultural studies would later call a subculture, whose styles and tastes expressed values that interrogated the dominant culture—though for him it was the expression of values specific not to a dominated working-class fraction but to an entire "age class." The music and dance styles particular to this subculture were, he argued, homologous with French baby boomers' happy immersion of the rational self in an irresponsible, bodily present:

> What frightens [the adult world] is the exaltation without content. For there is indeed a gratuitous frenzy triggered by the rhythmic singing, the "yeah yeahs" of the twist. [. . .] In the rhythm—this chanted, syncopated music, these cries of yeah yeah—there is a form of participation in something elemental, biological.
>
> (Morin 1963)

All this, as he puts it, has reached France via the infusion of "uprooted negritude" into American culture.

Of course, in France as in the United Kingdom, the initial reaction of stunned negativity that Morin described would quickly evolve. For the last fifty years in fact, the history of French pop and rock has been of its naturalisation, appropriation and segmentation into an ever more complex mosaic of genres, sub-genres, cross-fertilisations and tastes. All the same, I have a hunch that it is still possible to detect a form of binary thinking on the subject, barely visible below the surface of otherwise unexceptional attitudes and judgments. The discourse of *la chanson française* is still at work, reshaping itself constantly in response to myriad new styles and genres emerging or re-emerging from 1950s rock 'n' roll and 1960s pop. French *chanson* has long defined itself against the commercial music known as *variétés*. It similarly knows itself to be different from *le rock* though it has absorbed influences from it. It has successfully negotiated hip hop and stood out against electronic dance music. But today, I suggest, what makes *la chanson française* most sure of itself, stiffening its sinews and summoning the blood, is the reality singing show.

What condemned *Star Academy* when it first launched in 2001 on the TF1 TV channel[3] was that the long-established codes of *la chanson française* were not respected. Contestants do not have to write their material in the way that the deities of *chanson française*—Jacques Brel, Georges Brassens, Léo Ferré, Barbara—once did, or have songs written for their stage persona like Édith Piaf or the later Hallyday. On the contrary, students at the "Academy" are required to sing indiscriminately, in English or French and in a range of styles. What's more, by the very nature of the show, they have not followed the established path of apprenticeship, the long, hard struggle to the top. During the controversy caused by the first two series (2001 and 2002), Juliette Gréco (2002, 4), *chanson française* star par excellence, exclaimed, "You don't become a singer in three months. Barbara, Brel, Ferré or Brassens spent years becoming what they have become." The young hopefuls on *Star Academy*, then, have no credentials; their musical identity is visibly concocted. This is no doubt why the few who have subsequently achieved success tend to play down their debt to the show, hoping to slip unnoticed through the back gate of *chanson* paradise. And it is here that we come back to the notion of middlebrow.

A New Middlebrow?

Distinguished since the early twentieth century from songs and singers deemed inferior (Looseley 2013a, 47–84), *la chanson française* has acquired a special legitimacy. Its perceived merit is its aspiration to what we might call the high popular, to being both artistically and democratically demanding. Thus elevated, it has become a gold standard against which other musics in France are judged and obliged to position themselves. This is how an impenitent rocker like Hallyday ends up being labelled *chanson*, with all the national monumentality this grants him.

So what about Britain? Of course, the same drive to upward mobility exists to a degree. Simon Warner (2011) shows how the "pop group" of the first half of the 1960s evolved into the "rock band" of the second, with different connotations. "Pop," he argues, connoted superficiality, simplicity, fabrication; "rock" signified a creative seriousness and an auteurist conception of the singer. To this I would add that, around the time of the Beatles' rise to fame, "group" connoted a loose affiliation of self-taught lads, often school friends, who had started out as amateurs playing low dives and dances and who retained an edge of amiable amateurism, whereas "band," adopted for later, more adventurous ensembles like Cream or Traffic, meant professional, even artistic seriousness. The Beatles illustrate this evolution. They set out as a boyish "group" whose sound was still rough round the edges and whose backwards-looking eclectic repertoire of covers consisted of US rock 'n' roll mixed with newer R&B material, rejecting the slick variety-tinged pop (Tommy Steele, Cliff Richard, Adam Faith) that rock 'n' roll had been turned into by music publishers, producers and impresarios (Gillett 1996, 256–257 and 262–263). They ended as a mature "band," whose three songwriters had become experimental creatives, keen to pursue their individual auteurist aspirations.

Even so, I would suggest that in the United Kingdom, broadly speaking, these processes of distinction and legitimation are less important, less intellectually charged, than in France. France simply cares more about them. In a chapter examining British pop and rock historiography, Simon Frith (2011) concludes that the dominant historical narrative in pop histories is not progress but nostalgia, regret of time passing. One hypothesis—deriving for the moment from no more than my ethnographic distance—is that in France the opposite might apply: a persistent linear aspiration upwards, towards progress, improvement, growth: in short, towards a middlebrow. If this hypothesis could be verified, what might explain this divergence between the two countries? One key factor might be that the British, like the Americans, simply do not have a gold standard like *la chanson française*. And I think this in turn might have to do with the respective national meanings of popular music.

Martin Cloonan (2007) maintains that the first cultural-policy initiatives for pop and rock in Britain, introduced by New Labour under Tony Blair, failed to conceptualise what was British about British popular music. The primary concern of policy makers were the economic benefits of "British" music whatever it might be. No doubt the same can be said of France to a point. But French governments since 1981 have arguably adopted a more comprehensive understanding of the worth of popular music, drawing on two values that look beyond markets. One is the centuries-old identification, evoked earlier, of culture with nation, even today when the newer notions of cultural diversity and intercultural dialogue have (at least theoretically) been worked in. The other is the republican aspiration to democratisation—democracy being assumed to be built into the very notion of "popular" music.

These two values inform the development since the 1980s of an evaluative system for French popular music, essential to which is the existence of a Ministry of Culture. Comparatively powerful, albeit less so than thirty years ago, this institution established in 1959 has, alongside the more obviously powerful Ministry of National Education, served as an institutional point of reference for discriminating between good and bad art. And since 1981 the ministry has taken various steps to formulate a more positive take on French pop and rock music in its multiple forms, which the ministry has grouped together and tried unsuccessfully to find a universally agreed name for: "today's musics," "present-day musics," "amplified musics."

But naming pop and rock has always been a complex issue for French institutions. This might very well be because of its original foreignness, that fundamental alterity which Morin pointed out and which appeared to challenge the deeply rooted cultural values of the republic: reason, intelligence, moderation, the word. Hence, perhaps, the tendency to fall back on the reassuring familiarity and literariness of *la chanson française*, which sounds less ambiguous (though quite wrongly). Still, the persistence of the discursive category *chanson française* suggests a desire to mark out a homelier space within the global music scene and to invest that space with a superior, middlebrow value. Some of the cooler commentators make fun of this desire, interpreted as parochialism. Benoit Sabatier (2003) detects it particularly in the aspirational print media, summarising the binary model with forensic irony:

> France is split in two. You have to choose which side you're on: quality (Vincent Delerm, Carla Bruni, Benjamin Biolay, Keren Ann, Émilie Simon, Coralie Clément . . .) or crap (Star Academy). It's highbrow France versus lowbrow culture.

But in so doing, of course, they confirm that it lives on.

Conclusions

Ultimately, it would seem, *la chanson française*, middlebrow par excellence, is less an objectively verifiable aesthetic category than an ideological narrative. Beyond this, we probably can't draw firmer conclusions about so dynamic a phenomenon as French popular music. But I think that the discursive history of that music and comparison with the United Kingdom can at least point out some important shifts in the classic French binary between highbrow and lowbrow. First, this binary has worked its way into popular music itself, with *la chanson française* separated from the rest as a desirable (rather than pejoratively construed) middlebrow, like jazz. Second, the opening up of this middlebrow space represents a concern with French specificity, national authenticity, in a global music environment. This concern can be seen at work in the hostility of musicians, critics and other institutional standpoints to the lowbrow *Star Academy*, though the popularity of the talent-show format with the TF1 public continues with *The Voice: la plus belle voix* (2012–).

But what of pop and rock specifically? I would suggest that binary thinking is gradually asserting itself here too, as their more explicitly inventive forms reach the threshold of middlebrow legitimation: "alternative rock,"[4] hip hop, world music. Might this even come to apply to electronic synthpop and disco, bearing in mind the current standing of Daft Punk after the huge international success of their album *Random Access Memories* (2013)? Perhaps, but the band's global reach nonetheless creates a curious anomaly, as yet unresolved. Daft Punk are the most enduring exponents of what became known in the 1990s as "French Touch." Yet ironically, they have been assiduous in avoiding any associations with Frenchness by using English for their lyrics, band name and track titles. As Philippe Poirrier (2015) notes, their success in fact stems from their having "liberated" themselves from both the "linguistic constraint that French represents" and the commercial constraint of national markets by astute use of the web. Much the same could be said of the rock band Phoenix, who have also achieved international fame by singing in English. All of which suggests that in the early twenty-first century a question that has been present, implicitly or explicitly, since the early twentieth has become much more acute: what exactly is meant by "French" popular music?

Notes

1 The distinctiveness of French academic approaches to popular music studies is especially evident in Dauncey and Le Guern (2011), which pairs French and British scholars discussing specific themes.
2 Literally "French song." But I shall retain the French expression (or the variant "French *chanson*") to indicate that it carries special meanings; see the following paragraphs.
3 The series now airs on NRJ12.
4 For the French connotations of *le rock alternatif*, see Lebrun (2009, 15–16).

Bibliography

Baecque, Antoine de. 2008. "Sarkozy nous conduit à la 'catastrophe culturelle.'" *Prise de Baecque* February 6. Accessed April 16, 2014. http://blogs.rue89.com/prise-de-baecque/sarkozy-nous-conduit-a-la-catastrophe-culturelle.
BBC. 1949. "Variety Programmes Policy Guide for Writers and Producers." Accessed April 15, 2014. www.g4dmp.co.uk/bbc-guide.pdf.
Bollon, Patrice. 1987 [1981]. "Le Grand Sommeil du rock français." In *1968–1988: Histoire de chansons: de Maxime Leforestier à Étienne Daho*, edited by Sylvie Coulomb and Didier Varrod, 239–245. Paris: Balland.
Cloonan, Martin. 2007. *Popular Music and the State*. Aldershot: Arena.
Dauncey, Hugh, and Philippe Le Guern, eds. 2011. *Stereo: Comparative Perspectives on the Sociological Study of Popular Music in France and Britain*. Farnham: Ashgate.
Delanoë, Pierre. 1993. *La Chanson en colère: entretiens avec Alain-Gilles Minella*. Paris: Mame.
Djian, Jean-Michel. 2010. "La Politique culturelle en toutes lettres." *Le Monde diplomatique*, July 29. Accessed April 15, 2014. www.monde-diplomatique.fr/carnet/2010-07-20-Politique-culturelle.
Frith, Simon. 2011. "Writing the History of Popular Music." In *Stereo: Comparative Perspectives on the Sociological Study of Popular Music in France and Britain*, edited by Hugh Dauncey and Philippe Le Guern, 11–21. Farnham: Ashgate.
Gillett, Charlie. 1996. *The Sound of the City: The Rise of Rock&Roll*. 3rd edition revised and enlarged. London: Souvenir Press.
Gréco, Juliette. 2002. Quoted in *Le Monde. Télévision* supplement, December 14.
Hein, Fabien. 2011. "The Issue of Musical Genres in France." In *Stereo: Comparative Perspectives on the Sociological Study of Popular Music in France and Britain*, edited by Hugh Dauncey and Philippe Le Guern, 153–171. Farnham: Ashgate.
Holmes, Diana, and David Looseley, eds. 2013. *Imagining the Popular in Contemporary French Culture*. Manchester: Manchester University Press.
Lebrun, Barbara. 2009. *Protest Music in France: Production, Identity and Audiences*. Farnham: Ashgate.
Looseley, David. 2003. *Popular Music in Contemporary France*. New York and Oxford: Berg.
———. 2013a. "Authenticity and Appropriation: A Discursive History of French Popular Music." In *Imagining the Popular in Contemporary French Culture*, edited by Diana Holmes and David Looseley, 47–84. Manchester: Manchester University Press.

———. 2013b. "Culture and the State Under Sarkozy." In *The Sarkozy Presidency: Breaking the Mould?* edited by Gino Raymond, 183–207. Houndsmill: Palgrave Macmillan.

Martel, Frédéric. 2012. *J'aime pas le sarkozysme culturel*. Paris: Flammarion.

Morin, Edgar. 1963. "Salut les copains." *Le Monde*, July 6 and 7–8.

Poirrier, Philippe. 2015. "Daft Punk, la Toile et le disco: revival culturel à L'heure du numérique." *Contemporary French Civilization* 26(3):368–381.

Sabatier, Benoît. 2003. "Le Charme discret de la chansonnerie." *Technikart*, April 1.

Sandbrook, Dominic. 2005. *Never Had It So Good: A History of Britain From Suez to the Beatles*. London: Abacus.

Warner, Simon. 2011. "Genres and the Aesthetics of Popular Music in the UK." In *Stereo: Comparative Perspectives on the Sociological Study of Popular Music in France and Britain*, edited by Hugh Dauncey and Philippe Le Guern, 137–151. Farnham: Ashgate.

Afterword
"We Freed Ourselves From the Band Format": A Conversation With Nicolas Godin (Founding Member of the Duo Air)

Gérôme Guibert

Air is a band formed in Paris in the mid-1990s by Nicolas Godin and Jean-Benoît Dunckel. Both from Versailles, by the end of the 1990s, they were seen as being among the most important representatives of French Touch, gaining international recognition. In comparison with other French Touch artists, their music was more atmospheric and less specifically for dance. From the start, they referenced a forgotten section of French musicians such as Jean-Jacques Perrey. Their debut album, Moon Safari *(1998, Figure A.1), the cover of which was designed by American graphic designer and film director Mike Mills, was a hit in Britain, and the duo toured extensively after its release, taking in a major US tour. They were then contacted by Sofia Coppola and wrote the soundtrack for the film* The Virgin Suicides *(2000), which they brought out on the label they'd just set up with Marc Teissier du Cros, a friend from Versailles who had previously signed them to Source/Virgin. They would also contribute to the music of the films* Lost in Translation *(2003) and* Marie Antoinette *(2006), also by Coppola (the latter feature being shot at the Château de Versailles). In all, Air have recorded seven albums and numerous singles, along with several collaborations with other musicians, dancers and visual artists. They wrote and played the music on Charlotte Gainsboug's album* 5:55 *(Because Music, 2006).*

In September 2015, Nicolas Godin released his first solo album Contrepoint *(Because Music). He was enthusiastic about doing an interview for* Made in France, *the idea being that during the conversation, we would address his own positioning as an artist and his views on French popular music.*

If we were to ask you what stands out as particularly French in French music, especially popular music, what would you say?

French music was amazing before rock music came along. For me, rock music is something typically English speaking—and I say that as a fan of rock. I have no issue with rock, I love rock! But for me, from a creative point of view, rock music is an English, American and Black American phenomenon . . . and what I see at the same time is that, historically, there are some great French records from artists like Ferré, Brassens and Brel, albums that have a wonderful

Figure A.1   Air, *Moon Safari*, Virgin, 1998 (deluxe re-release from 2008). Album cover designed by Mike Mills.

sound. And I think many foreigners who don't like French rock worship French *chanson*: Édith Piaf, Jacques Brel, people like that.

So, you would say that it's *chanson* rather than any other form that is truly French?

Not only *chanson*! Classical music too, especially from the last century, when the music had real personality. France provided a real counterpoint to German classical music, as well as to British. I'm primarily talking about the Ravel and Debussy period at the turn of the twentieth century, but musicians such as Messiaen a little later and even Schaeffer also contributed. The French were able to come up with something quite avant-garde, quite romantic, beautiful and spacey and this was a real specificity. I, who am such a fan of Bach, who am particularly sensitive to the construction of artistic worlds, really think that these composers took music somewhere else, into other universes—even I would say a kind of "outer space."

Yet musicologically or even historically or in terms of shared spaces or networks of people who knew each other, there doesn't seem to have been a real connection between the people you mention: Ravel, Debussy, Messiaen, Schaeffer?

Yes, but it's a kind of lineage, with a heavenly element, that was destroyed by pop music. I mean that from the time the record business embraced rock/pop celebrity culture, French music became outdated. The popularity of records from the 1950s on changed everything. Before that, every generation still brought a development, in artistic terms, in the concept of music itself. Afterwards, when vinyl appeared and started to generate millions and millions of dollars of revenue, music became a consumer product. And I don't think the French were as good when music became a consumer product. The English earned this new medium its stripes. The albums by The Beatles, for example, are classics. With records establishing themselves as a widespread medium, the product went beyond song and music. The challenge now involved image, objects and so on.

Is sound, texture and timbre something you excel at?

Now timbre and sound are different things. And, yes, I have expressed myself through records, but at the same time retaining a specificity in my musical approach. I was very limited musically. I wouldn't have been able to make music just with a pen and paper. I needed recordings. This type of technique has, in fact, been a renaissance in music, because some kind of shamanic something takes place during recording that you have to catch in the moment. And when you manage to do that, people get to experience that moment again when they listen at home after buying the record.

It's as if you think a bit like Gainsbourg. The greats came before me, "I do low art" [*art mineur*].

No doubt it's a bit conservative to talk about the greats . . . but I do think it was harder to make music with a pen and paper than in the studio, yes. Studio music seems easier. Even if we're talking apples and oranges. As far as I'm concerned, I know my level. I knew I could never be primarily a music composer, but nor did I want rock star status. I didn't start a rock band to be famous. So many of us in France were bent on doing that and it dated us . . . right from the start of the process.

So how did Air manage to do something we consider to be quintessentially French using the medium of recorded music?

As a matter of fact, historically, something was happening in music at the time. I would date it to the early 1990s, from the first album by Massive Attack.[1] For a little over a decade, we went from being singer-songwriters or performers to producers. The spotlight was put on producers. What I mean is record companies started selling producers as artists. Massive Attack, Portishead, The Chemical Brothers, Daft Punk, us . . . and all the way to The Strokes if you want, there were ten years of "producer-composers." I mean people like me, who came up with their records in their heads: if I needed a singer, I got a singer; if I needed a drummer, I got a drummer. We mixed records together and came up with something new. We freed ourselves from the band format with drummer, guitarist, singer and keyboard player. This gave total artistic freedom, which was solely oriented towards making a great song, a great record. And I came onto the scene at that time. Getting rid of the band format opened up new possibilities.

But you mention artists from quite diverse backgrounds, and it's often said of your music that it has a specifically French thing about it.

This moment in the history of music, when records made by producers were sold as products composed by artists, is what allowed me to find my own way in to coming up with specifically French records. If I had had to form a rock band to get known, things would never have worked out for me. But here, suddenly, record companies gave us the means to promote our music. And suddenly we thought, well, let's go! You simply made a record with what you knew. And we managed to make a pretty good career out of it.

Is it through the impact of your music abroad (and more immediately through touring overseas, particularly in the United States) that you realised that your music was seen as French? Did that lead you to question yourselves about the French aspect of your music?

I think so, yes. Except that I love film music and I think that what feeds you as an artist is your childhood. And I was pretty surprised that I was one of the first people who had the idea of making records inspired by film music. Many people could have done it before us! I mean, both you and I, when we were little, watched TV before buying records and listening to them. The Barbapapas and Starsky and Hutch as well as Michel Legrand, Ennio Morricone and westerns, et cetera. A lot of the references that were cited to describe Air's music were indeed these sorts of influences! From age 2 or 3, when I started to watch TV, these were the programs I watched. And later, when I was a teenager, I started buying records, but that was ten years later. Ten years of pop culture came out at me through a CRT [cathode ray tube].

Musical instruments like the Rhodes keyboard, the Fender Rhodes, were used on all the soundtracks of the TV series! If you listen to David Bowie or Iggy Pop, there's no Rhodes . . . you do find it in soul music of course, but you didn't hear it in rock music. But it was in all the soap operas. I'm thinking about French series like *Pause-Café* in which Véronique Jannot played the social worker Joëlle Mazart, or the *Papa Poule* series. There were Fender Rhodes everywhere. So when I first played this instrument, I saw my whole childhood pass in front of my eyes and I incorporated the instrument in my recordings. I must have started with it in 1990 or 1991.

And more specifically, the day I put an electric bass and a Rhodes keyboard together I saw something come together in front of me. A bit like the genie from Aladdin's lamp! At first it was just a bass octave played in parallel to the keyboard. The sound from Gainsbourg's *Melody Nelson* album [1971] combined with layers of Air bass came a few years later. I can date it from when Nicolas Dufournet, former the bassist from Oui-Oui [a band he was in in Versailles in the 1980s with the future director Michel Gondry], lent me his electric bass. It had flatwound strings and the muffled sound that was reminiscent of the *Melody Nelson* album. And it was then, in 1996, that I did the bass parts for the Air tracks "J'ai Dormi sous l'Eau," "Talisman" and "La Femme d'Argent."

What is a historical fact is that *Melody Nelson*, although it was recorded by English musicians (at least in part), really had an impact on French pop as a whole. I don't know why, but that bass sound accompanied by arpeggios [used by Gainsbourg in the first half of 1970s] is now seen as a specifically French way of playing. I'm thinking for example about the guitar arpeggios on "Je suis venu te dire que je m'en vais" [1973]. It may be a session-musician thing, I don't know. And the recordings were played on by English or American session musicians, but as it was Gainsbourg who made hits with that sound, I think Americans in particular associate it with France.

Some years before French Touch, the English media had associated "alternative rock" bands like Les Negresses Vertes and Mano Negra with French culture (there was even a David Byrne Luaka Bop world music collection compilation of French alternative rock).[2] Their music was very different from yours, however, as are the attributes you associate with "French culture."

What's so great with Les Negresses Vertes is the "gypsy clan" thing, which is also part of French culture! The Gipsy Kings also had great international success in the late '80s. People have a somewhat folkloric vision of France, and Jean-Benoît and I were just one of its incarnations. I have a sort of bourgeois physique, the sort of face that easily fits in with the image of 1960s French New Wave cinema. And Jean-Benoît also has a bit of a Gavroche look with his cap and all that! So between us, we had something of the Gavroche, the little Montmartre *poulbot* street kid . . . and something of the New Wave bourgeois. The English saw this . . . and it corresponded to their idea of France, if you see what I mean! And also we came from Versailles! This means that the English thought we lived with carriages and servants everywhere, that sort of thing. In reality, Versailles is a bit of a sad garrison town . . . It's a non-town. All it has is the chateau, the rest of Versailles is . . . We absolutely did not experience it as somewhere glamorous when we were young. Except now, in recent years, with Sofia Coppola's film

[*Marie Antoinette*, 2006] in particular, it has become glamorous again. I think we gave some-thing contemporary to Versailles, and then Sofia made her film about Marie Antoinette, and now Americans *really* think that Versailles is a kind of magical French place. They don't see the sad side at all. Tourists imagine opulence when they think of Versailles. They see festivals, colour, Molière. For a Californian, Versailles is a hyper-glam thing! When we say we're from Versailles, they imagine . . . they see the Three Musketeers. I don't know how to put it exactly but when we started touring, we really felt that gap. While we grew up in a rather rainy, cold Parisian suburb, the Americans and Japanese imagined we lived on the Cote d'Azur. They thought we drove around in sports cars and drank champagne cocktails every night. Talking with them, I tell you, they really thought France was like that. In any case that was the image that we conveyed, the stereotypes that we triggered.

Obviously, Les Negresses Vertes have another image. But foreigners can see both sides. The English and Americans love Godard and Truffaut's New Wave films, even *Un homme et une femme*, but on the other hand, you also have *Les Misérables*. Two completely coherent images. Les Negresses Vertes also managed to leave rock behind to make something that was inspired by, let's say, continental culture. That's how I experienced it from the inside.

What does French Touch represent for you? And Versailles?

It's our generation. It started with Daft Punk, who pioneered things in the mid '90s. Then we got in on the act and Phoenix came after us. At the same time we set up our label, Record Makers, in 2000 to release the soundtrack for the movie *Virgin Suicides* (Figure A2).

Among others we signed Sébastien Tellier. He made "La Ritournelle" [2005], which was played all around the world and the *Sexuality* album in 2008, produced by Guy-Manuel de Homem-Christo, one half of Daft Punk . . .

Then with Justice, the new French Touch generation appeared. And now there's yet another generation, a third, but we were the pioneers. We played in the US, did gigs there . . . But we went to the same middle school [Collège Pierre et Marie Curie] as the members of Phoenix in the '80s. They were a little younger than us. When we were in the last year of middle school they were just starting. And they then went to Lycée Hoche, while we went to the other Versailles high school, Jules Ferry. Jean-Benoît Dunckel and others, such as Alexis Latrobe—the future Alex Gopher, Etienne De Crécy and Arnaud Rebotini went to these two schools around the same time. They were our comrades-in-arms. We left to conquer the world.

At the end of your first album tour, you made the much-talked-about *Eating, Sleeping, Waiting and Playing* film, produced by Mike Mills, that shows both your environment [Versailles, the Rough Trade record shop in the Bastille district in Paris, your studio, etc.] and follows you on tour. I remember seeing you on the *Moon Safari* [1998] tour in Nantes at L'Olympic.[3]

It's funny because I remember that concert very well. It was part of the *Les Inrockuptibles* festival, and there weren't many people there. I felt a real disconnect between my musician's fantasy and the audience expectations. I think there was a big misunderstanding between us and the audience at the Inrocks Festival concert that year. There weren't many people there,

Figure A.2 Air, *The Virgin Suicides*, Record Makers/Virgin, 2000, compact disc front cover.

about 200. We were dressed all in white . . . and when the concert ended I went backstage, got dressed and went out into the lobby at L'Olympic to hang out and talk. This guy came up to me and said, "Who do you think you are?" It felt pretty violent . . . What he said really hit me.

I have a theory. People had been waiting for thirty years for a French group to make it big abroad. And a lot of them said, "How did these two guys from Versailles do it? We've been waiting for thirty years, for fuck's sake!" And I think people, especially a whole section from the milieu of French music, would have liked to see some rockers make the breakthrough . . . but I agree with John Lennon who said, "French rock is like English wine." I don't see the point of doing a bad imitation. Anyway, that's just my taste, and frankly my taste is no better than anyone else's. There's music for all tastes. There are people who are bored by Air. But anyway, our debuts in France were hard. Playing to 200 people wasn't easy when, at the same time, in New York or Los Angeles, you're playing in front of thousands of people.

At first we were quite naïve; we just made music with our hearts. Lots of people think that we're trendy hipster Parisian *bobo*[4] snobs, but in fact not at all. I think our success was built on a form of artistic innocence. That may be why it worked in fact! We made music without thinking about the fact that it might get on the radio. We really did what we wanted to. But all the film and TV music of my childhood and time spent in the park of Versailles meant I had a really psychedelic vision of music, inspired by unreal locations. The castle grounds and gardens really are a wonder, crazy! And this was not conducive to having a hold on real life . . . and if people have an issue with Air, it's this "music that's not connected with reality" thing. We're more on the side of the dreamers.

But above and beyond what inspired the music, in terms of the French Touch movement that exploded in the second half of the 1990s, what you talk about as being the common ground between the different artists, in addition to the fact that they knew each other [remixing each other, Phoenix musicians who played as the backing band for Air, the Phoenix guitarist who started by playing with Daft Punk, etc.], there was the technical aspect, production, as you argued earlier in the interview.

Yes, but there was also a "making the most of what we've got" thing. I'm not a singer; I don't have a Mick Jagger side. So what was left? I loved music and I came up with some totally phantasmagorical stuff. My belief is that when you record something that you really feel, later, even in other contexts, people can feel the intensity when they listen to the music. For example, when I recorded "Ce matin là" [1998] in my little room in Montmartre with an old tuba that I'd found in a flea market . . . well, when we were recording it, when I was playing, I imagined we were in Hollywood being produced by Burt Bacharach at Capitol with all the best equipment, the best compressors, et cetera. And when I was playing, I played in that spirit. I had a real mental strength at the time that allowed me to move forward. I did not see Paris around me; I was in my fantasy world, my song, and I think when people listen to it, the feeling I had comes through. That's alchemy. I don't know how to explain it. I think the world you're in when you create something comes through if you're really inhabited by it the day you do it.

And French as a language?

No, I love literature, but I have no talent for writing. The song titles, you mean? I'm not sure why some of the tracks have French titles. "Le soleil est près de moi" was a phrase that sounded good in the vocoder. First you go "na na na," and then the words come, phonemes, and then it sounds good. That was just a mic test. We just used to sing along with nonsense words and then they'd sometimes develop in French and sometimes in English.

Maybe foreigners like the titles to be in French?

Yes, but, you know, for them, even when we're singing in English, it sounds French! It's like a German who speaks French: it'll always sound German for us, it will remind us of their country, their culture. Having a French accent is awesome though . . . It stimulates people's imagination.

You say you've even got typically French body postures?

We, the French, make an effort in terms of clothes; we wear smart shoes and shirts. In the United States, they put on the first T-shirt that comes to hand. There's not much refinement. Often they seem to have mutated. Their feet are so big they have to wear sneakers, you know what I mean? From the perspective of food, the portions they serve up are so big you get enough for several days. That's why they've invented doggie bags, so they can take the leftovers home with them.

Do you talk about these experiences abroad with other artists, or more generally other French people who have also experienced them?

We'd meet expatriates at times, but for us, it wasn't like Patrick Bruel playing at the Royal Albert Hall in London! I don't know if there were many English people there for his concert. When we play the US, our crowd is American. We're not Johnny [Hallyday], we can't hire a charter to fly French fans over to see us in Las Vegas, when we give a concert. And I'm not saying that to speak ill of Johnny! Phoenix are the people you should talk to because they did a Johnny cover at the Hollywood Bowl.[5]

What about being decorated by the Ministry of Culture?[6]

The Americans love all that stuff. But they don't understand how you can be "knighted" in that way in a republic. So I explain by saying that we're like the Jedi. In any case, for them, we deserve it because they know us and before Air and Daft Punk, the French were, for them, a disgrace musically speaking. We accepted the award because it's part of French folklore but they, the Americans and the English, they take it very seriously. The English tell us, you really deserve it, you rendered a service to French music. Before you, French music was a joke.

The first piece you wrote alone, for Air, was "Modulor" in 1995, which got international attention when it was included on the English instrumental compilation *Headz 2*, which came out on Mo'Wax in 1996 [alongside artists like Massive Attack, The Beastie Boys, DJ Krush, U.N.K.L.E. and Tortoise].

Yes, Mo'Wax had the idea of selling funky instrumental trip hop albums in the early '90s and "Modulor" was a good piece of sound design. I used a sampler at the time that only had a few seconds of memory. So I played two chords I'd sampled and then I did a bass line. After that I just introduced some cuts with echo, stuff like that, because I didn't have enough memory to record other bits of music! The song title is a reference to the work of architect Le Corbusier, who is not French by birth but was naturalised, much like Godard. But that wasn't really thought through. I'd studied architecture . . . and I was looking for ideas.

Actually, this first Air track to come out had originally appeared on the first volume of a series of three Source Lab compilations, which came out on Virgin [recently acquired at the time by the major EMI]. Combining experimental hip hop, drum 'n' bass, down tempo experiments and electronics, these compilations were to feature most of the first

wave French Touch musicians [including Daft Punk, Etienne de Crécy, Bob Sinclar, Gilb'r, Arnaud Rebotini, Alex Gopher, La Funk Mob and Motorbass] and launch the movement.

We were lucky in that at that time, record labels were able to sell adventurous records . . . with promotion, work and the support of the specialised music press. At that time, even for little, three-minute instrumental pieces, they could put the sort of money on the line that they would if they were promoting Johnny. That's what was great. At Virgin, we were treated as "normal" artists, though, as you know, the Source Lab compilations were pretty obscure!

At that time I had given up music but Marc Teissier Du Cros, who had just been hired by Source, asked me to write a track. He headed up the Source Lab compilations project and was a friend from Versailles.

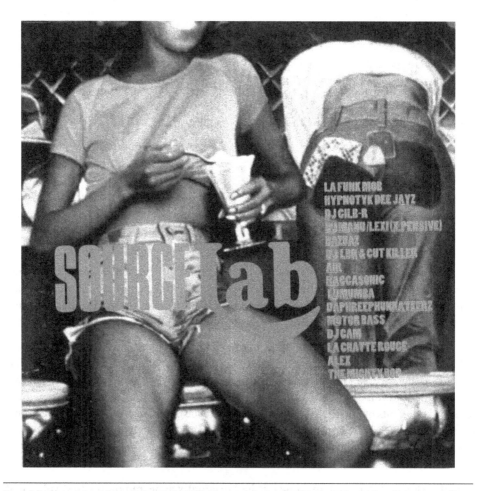

Figure A.3 *Source Lab*, vol. 1 compilation, Virgin, 1995. Album cover by Jean Baptiste Goude. Excerpt from the back cover: "An authentic compilation with carte blanche given to young, French sound innovators, well-known or otherwise [. . .]. When you put it all together, French hip hop, techno, funk and ragga/jungle all seems to be moving in the same musical direction." Compact disc cover by Jean Baptiste Goude.

I think that even more importantly than the Source compilations, French Touch was born with the Channel Tunnel [opened in 1994]. All of a sudden English journalists, who'd had enough of what was going on in the UK came to see what was going on in Paris. And they came to the Respect nights at Queen and all that. And they decided that Paris had more going for it at that time than London. In fact, French Touch existed already, through the engineers at Airbus and all that. This Channel Tunnel engineering project meant that the TGV [high-speed train] brought a continuous stream of journalists over. There really were a lot of them. They really enjoyed themselves for two or three years. They invented any excuse to come to Paris. It was a kind of French *Movida*, and Paris was exotic for them. Three hours by train, and bam! We used to see them all in Montmartre. I don't think that French Touch would have come about without the Eurostar.

When I was on tour and when I said I was French, people would often talk about Montand's "À bicyclette," as well as newer titles like "Quelqu'un de bien," which was written by Kent and sung by Enzo Enzo, with jazz musicians. Many people I've met around the world, particularly in Australia, have talked about this song. They must have heard it on compilations. This is the somewhat musette side we mentioned in connection with the Les Négresses Vertes; accordion, dogs and *guinguette* [cabaret].[7]

Notes

1   Massive Attack, *Blue Lines*, 1991, Virgin.
2   Luaka-bop, "Cuisine non-stop: Introduction to the French nouvelle generation," 2002, accessed 23 July 2017, http://luakabop.com/catalog/cuisine-non-stop-introduction-to-the-french-nouvelle-generation.
3   8 November 1998, the *Les Inrockuptibles* festival: Air, Lo-Fidelity All Stars, Sean Lennon, Mellow, in Nantes, L'Olympic.
4   A term that results from the contraction of the expression "*bourgeois bohème*" (or bourgeois bohemian), meaning, often pejoratively, a person who is financially well-off but holds left-wing views. We refer you to David Brooks, *Bobos in Paradise: The New Upper Class and How They Got There*, Simon and Schuster, 2001.
5   Phoenix covered "La fille aux cheveux clairs" by Johnny Hallyday on 18 September 2010 at the Hollywood Bowl and other dates on the Wolfgang Amadeus Phoenix tour.
6   On 17 February 2005, Renaud Donnedieu de Vabres, the French minister of culture, gave the Chevalier des Arts et des Lettres award to Nicolas Godin and Jean-Benoît Dunckel. In doing so he recognised Air's contribution to French music and, at least indirectly, the French Touch movement. Philippe Zdar (from La Funk Mob, Motorbass and Cassius) and Dimitri from Paris were also decorated at the same ceremony.
7   Interview (by Gérôme Guibert), Thursday, 10 March 2016 at the Le Walt hotel bar, 37 avenue de La Motte-Picquet, Paris.

A Selected Bibliography on French Popular Music

General Books

History and Cultural Practices

Baudrillard, Jean. 1970. *La société de consommation*. Paris: Denoël.
Berstein, Serge, and Pierre Milza. 1996. *Histoire du XXe siècle, tome 2, Le monde entre guerre et paix. 1945–1973*. Paris: Hatier.
———. 2010. *Histoire du XXe siècle, tome 3, La fin du monde bipolaire: 1973 aux années 1990*. Paris: Hatier.
Bourdieu, Pierre. 1979. *La distinction: Critique sociale du jugement*. Paris: Les Editions de Minuit.
Braudel, Fernand. 1986. *L'identité de la France. 1: Espace et histoire*. Paris: France Loisirs.
———. 1987. *L'identité de la France. 2: Les hommes et les choses*. Paris: France Loisirs.
Cheyronnaud, Jacques. 2002. *Musique, politique, religion: De quelques menus objets de culture*. Paris: L'Harmattan.
De Certeau, Michel. 1974. *La culture au pluriel*. Paris: UGE.
———. 1990 [1980]. *L'invention du quotidien: Essai sur les nouvelles classes moyennes. I: Arts de faire*. Paris: Gallimard.
———. 1990 [1980]. *L'invention du quotidien: Essai sur les nouvelles classes moyennes. II: Habiter, cuisiner*. Paris: Gallimard.
Donnat, Olivier. 1997. *Les pratiques culturelles des Français: Enquête 1997*. Paris: La Documentation Française.
———. 2008. *Les pratiques culturelles des Français à l'ère numérique: Enquête 2008*. Paris: La Documentation Française.
Dubet, François. 1987. *La galère: jeunes en survie*. Paris: Fayard.
Dubois, Vincent. 1999. *La politique culturelle: Genèse d'une catégorie d'intervention publique*. Paris: Belin.
Fabiani, Jean-Louis. 2015. *La sociologie comme elle s'écrit: De Bourdieu à Latour*. Paris: Éditions de L'EHESS.
Flichy, Patrice. 1991. *Une histoire de la communication moderne: Espace public et vie privée*. Paris: La Découverte.
Galland, Olivier. 1985. *Les jeunes*. Paris: La Découverte.
Guibert, Gérôme, and Nelly Quemener. 2015. "Cultural studies et économie politique de la communication: Quel rapport au marxisme?" *Réseaux* 192:87–114.
Halbwachs, Maurice. 1997 [1950]. *La mémoire collective*. Paris: Albin Michel.
Heinich, Nathalie. 1996. *Être artiste*. Paris: Klincksiek.
Kalifa, Dominique. 2001. *La culture de masse en France. 1: 1860–1930*. Paris: La Découverte.
Latour, Bruno. 1991. *Nous n'avons jamais été modernes: Essai d'anthropologie symétrique*. Paris: La Découverte.
Macé, Eric. 2006. "Actualité de *L'esprit du temps*." In Preamble to the new edition of *L'esprit du temps*, edited by Edgar Morin, 1–7. Paris: Armand Colin.
Maigret, Eric. 2003. *Sociologie de la communication et des médias*. Paris: Armand Colin.
Mendras, Henri. 1994 [1988]. *La seconde révolution française, 1965–1984*. Paris: Gallimard.
Morin, Edgar. 1962. *L'esprit du temps*. Paris: Grasset.
Ozouf, Jacques, and Mona Ozouf. 1989. *La république des instituteurs*. Paris: Gallimard.
Prévost-Thomas, Cécile. 2010. "Les nouvelles perspectives en sociologie de la musique." *L'Année sociologique* 60(2):403–417.
Rioux, Jean-Pierre, and Jean-François Sirinelli. 2002. *La culture de masse en France: De la Belle Epoque à nos jours*. Paris: Fayard.
Shusterman, Richard. 1993. "Légitimer la légitimation de l'art populaire." *Politix* 24:153–167.
Souriaux, Etienne, ed. 1999. *Vocabulaire d'esthétique*. Paris: Presses Universitaires de France.

Music

Barthes, Roland. 1972. "Le grain de la voix." *Musique en jeu* 9:57–63.
Brunschwig, Chantal, Louis-Jean Calvet, and Jean-Claude Klein. 1972. *100 ans de chanson française*. Paris: Éditions du Seuil.
Cecchetto, Céline, ed. 2011. *Chanson et intertextualité*. Pessac: Presses Universitaires de Bordeaux.
Guiu, Claire, ed. 2006. "Géographies et musiques: quelles perspectives?" *Géographie et cultures* 59.
Guibert, Gérôme. 2006. *La production de la culture: Le cas des musiques amplifiées en France*. Paris and St Amant Tallende: Irma/editions Seteun.
Hennion, Antoine, Émilie Gomart, and Sophie Maisonneuve. 2000. *Figures de l'amateur: Formes, objets et pratiques de l'amour de la musique aujourd'hui*. Paris: La Documentation Française.
Hirschi, Stéphane. 2008. *Chanson: L'art de fixer l'air du temps. De Béranger à Mano Solo*. Paris and Valenciennes: Société d'édition Les Belles Lettres/Presses universitaires de Valenciennes.
Lesueur, Daniel. 1999. *Hit parades: 1950–1998*. Paris: Alternatives et Parallèles.
Looseley, David. 2003. *Popular Music in Contemporary France: Authenticity, Politics, Debate*. London: Berg.
Martin, Denis-Constant. 2006. "Le myosotis, et puis la rose . . . Pour une sociologie des 'musiques de masse.'" *L'Homme* 177–178(1):131–154.
Mignon, Patrick, and Antoine Hennion, eds. 1991. *Rock, de l'histoire au mythe*. Paris: Anthropos.
Morin, Edgar. 1965. "On ne connaît pas la chanson." *Communications* 6:1–9.
Roland-Manuel. 1963. *Histoire de la musique, tome 2, du XVIIIᵉ siècle à nos jours*. Paris: Gallimard, La Pléiade.
Spyropoulou-Leclanche, Maria. 1998. *Le refrain dans la chanson française: De Bruant à Renaud*. Limoges: Presses Universitaires de Limoges.
Szendy, Peter. 2001. *Écoute: Une histoire de nos oreilles*. Paris: Minuit.
Vian, Boris. 1997 [1958]. *En avant la zizique . . . et par ici les gros sous*. Paris: Pauvert.

Popular Music in France Before the 1950s

Chanson

Amaouche-Antoine, Marie-Dominique. 1984. "Espéraza 1870–1940: Une ville ouvrière qui chante." *Ethnologie Française* 14(3):237–250.
Basile, Giusy, and Chantal Gavouyère. 1996. *La chanson française dans le cinéma des années 30*. Paris: Bibliothèque Nationale de France.
———. 1999. "La chanson et la musique des rues à travers la production phonographique et cinématographique." *Ethnologie Française* 29(1):11–21.
Condemi, Concetta. 1992. *Les Cafés-concerts: Histoire d'un divertissement*. Paris: Quai Voltaire.
Deniot, Joëlle, and Catherine Dutheil, eds. 1997. "La voix et son document." *Sociologie de L'Art* 10:53–69.
Duneton, Claude. 1998. *Histoire de la chanson française, 1780–1860, tome 2*. Paris: Éditions du Seuil.
Dutheil-Pessin, Catherine. 2004. *La chanson réaliste: Sociologie d'un genre: le visage et la voix*. Paris: L'Harmattan.
Hélian, Jacques. 1984. *Les grands orchestres de music-hall en France: Souvenirs et témoignages*. Paris: Filipacchi.
Klein, Jean-Claude. 1985. "Emprunt, syncrétisme, métissage: la revue à grand spectacle des années folles." *Vibrations* 1:39–53.
———. 1988. "Chanson et music-hall des années 20." In *La chanson française et son histoire*, edited by Rieger Dietmar, 299–305. Tübingen: Gunter Narr Verlag.
Naudin, Marie. 1968. *Évolution parallèle de la poésie et de la musique en France: Rôle unificateur de la chanson*. Paris: Nizet.
Rypko Schub, Louise. 1976. "La chanson naturaliste: Aristide Bruant, ou le revers de la Belle Époque." *Cahiers de l'Association internationale des études françaises* 28:195–212.

Jazz

Cugny, Laurent. 2014. *Une histoire du jazz en France, tome 1, Du milieu du XIXᵉ siècle à 1929*. Paris: Outre Mesure.
Guerpin, Martin. 2013. "Bricktop's: un centre névralgique du jazz parisien." In *La catastrophe apprivoisée: Regards sur le jazz en France*, edited by Vincent Cotro, Laurent Cugny and Philippe Gumplowicz, 33–56. Paris: Outre Mesure.
Martin, Denis-Constant, and Olivier Roueff. 2002. *La France du jazz: Musique, modernité et identité dans la première moitié du XXᵉ siècle*. Marseille: Parenthèses.
Ory, Pascal. 1985. "Notes sur l'acclimatation du jazz en France." *Vibrations* 1:93–102.
Schaeffner, André. 1997 [1926]. *Le jazz*. Paris: Jean Michel Place.

Popular Music, Folk Music and Society

Cheyronnaud, Jacques. 1984. "Musiques et institutions au 'village.'" *Ethnologie Française* 14(3):265–280.

Cordonnier, Pierrick. 1994. "Harmonies, fanfares et danses populaires." *Marsyas* 29:7–9.

Defrance, Yves. 1984. "Traditions populaires et industrialisation: Le cas de l'accordéon." *Ethnologie Française* 14(3):223–236.

De Langle, Henry-Melchior. 1990. *Le petit monde des cafés et débits parisiens au xixᵉ siècle*. Paris: PUF.

Gasnault, François. 1986. *Guinguettes et lorettes: Bals publics et danse sociale à Paris entre 1830 et 1870*. Paris: Aubier.

Gétreau, Florence, ed. 1997. *Musiciens des rues de Paris*. Paris: RMN.

Goffre, Annie. 1984. "Exploitation raisonnée de la musique folklorique en France et ses artisans depuis la fin du xixᵉ siècle." *Ethnologie Française* 14(3):295–318.

Gumplowicz, Philippe. 2001 [1989]. *Les travaux d'Orphée: Deux siècles de pratique musicale amateur en France (1820–2000). Harmonies, chorales, fanfares*. Paris: Aubier.

Maisonneuve, Sophie. 2006. "De la machine parlante au disque: une innovation technique, commerciale et culturelle." *XXᵉ siècle* 92:17–32.

Mussat, Marie-Claire. 1992. *La belle époque des kiosques à musique*. Paris: Éditions du May.

Tournès, Ludovic. 2002. "Jalons pour une histoire internationale de l'industrie du disque; expansion, déclin et absorption de la branche phonographique de Pathé (1894–1936)." In *Histoire des industries culturelles en France, XIXᵉ–XXᵉ siècles*, edited by Jacques Marseille and Patrick Eveno, 465–477. Paris: ADHE.

Zalko, Nardo. 1998. *Un siècle de tango: Paris-Buenos Aires*. Paris: Éditions du Félin.

Popular Music in France Since the 1950s

Chanson

Borowice, Yves. 2007. "La chanson française: un art de métèques?" *Amnis* 7. http://amnis.revues.org/804. doi: 10.4000/amnis.804.

Calvet, Louis-Jean. 1981. *Chanson et société*. Paris: Payot.

Frith, Simon. 1989. "Why Do Songs Have Words?" *Contemporary Music Review* 5(1):77–96.

Gainsbourg, Serge. 1963. "Serge Gainsbourg . . . et la nouvelle vague" (interview by Denise Glaser). *Discorama* (3DVD): INA, 2008.

Gastaut, Yvan, Naima Yahi et Michael Spanu, eds. 2015. "Avec ma gueule de métèque: Chanson et immigration dans la France de la seconde moitié du XXᵉ siècle." *Volume! la revue des musiques populaires* 12(1).

Guibert, Gérôme. 2005. "Is the French Word 'chanson' Equivalent to the English Term 'popular music'?" In *Making Music, Making Meaning, IASPM International Conference Proceedings*, edited by Geoff Stahl, 275–282. Rome: IASPM. www.iaspm.net/archive/IASPM05LIGHT.pdf.

Morin, Edgar. 1963. "Salut les copains I. Une nouvelle classe d'âge." *Le Monde* 6 juillet:1.

———. 1994 [1984]. "Salut les copains." In *Sociologie*, 399–407. Paris: Éditions du Seuil.

Penet, Martin. 1999. "L'âge d'or de la chanson littéraire." *Revue de la Bibliothèque Nationale de France* 3:61–67.

Rudent, Catherine. 2000. "L'analyse du cliché dans les chansons à succès." In *Musique et sociologie: Enjeux méthodologiques et approches empiriques*, edited by Anne-Marie Green, 95–121. Paris: L'Harmattan.

———. 2008. "Le premier album de mademoiselle K: Entre création individuelle et coopérations négociées." *Ethnologie Française* 38(1):69–78.

———. 2011a. *L'album de chansons entre processus social et œuvre musicale: Juliette Gréco, Bruno Joubrel, Mademoiselle K*. Paris: Honoré Champion.

———. 2011b. "Une intimité très médiatisée: les paradoxes de 'J'ai dix ans' (Souchon—Voulzy)." *Contemporary French Civilization* 36(1–2):81–96.

Schlesser, Gilles. 2006. *Le Cabaret "rive gauche": De la Rose rouge au Bateau ivre (1946–1974)*. Paris: L'Archipel.

Jazz

Béthune, Christian. 2008. *Le Jazz et l'Occident*. Paris: Klincksieck.

Coulangeon, Philippe. 1999. "Les musiciens de jazz: les chemins de la professionnalisation." *Genèses* 36:54–68.

Fabiani, Jean-Louis. 1985. "Carrières improvisées: théorie et pratique de la musique de jazz en France." In *Sociologie de l'art*, edited by Raymonde Moulin, 231–246. Paris: La Documentation Française.

Roueff, Olivier. 2013. *Jazz, les échelles du plaisir*. Paris, La Dispute.

Sklower Jedediah. 2006. *Free jazz, la catastrophe féconde*. Paris: L'Harmattan.

Tournès, Ludovic. 1999. *New Orleans sur Seine, Histoire du jazz en France*. Paris: Fayard.

Rock, Pop, Punk and Metal

Baubérot, Arnaud, and Florence Tamagne. 2016. *This Is a Modern World: Histoire sociale du rock*. Lille: Presses du Septentrion.
Escoubet, Stéphane. 2013. "French Pop Bands of the 2000s Singing in English." Paper presented at the 17th IASPM biennial conference, Gijon (Spain).
Guibert, Gérôme. 2004. "Chantez-vous en français ou en anglais? Le choix de la langue dans le rock en France." *Volume!* 2(2):83–98.
Guibert, Gérôme, and Fabien Hein, eds. 2006. "Les scènes metal: Sciences sociales et pratiques culturelles radicales." *Volume!* 5(2).
Guibert, Gérôme, and Jedediah Sklower. 2012. "Hellfest: The Thing That Should Not Be? Local Perceptions and Catholic Discourses on Metal Culture in France." *Popular Music History* 6(2): 100–115.
Hein, Fabien. 2003. *Hard rock, heavy metal, metal: Histoire, culture et pratiquants*. Nantes and Paris: Mélanie Seteun/IRMA.
———. 2006. *Le monde du rock: Ethnographie du réel*. Clermont-Ferrand and Paris: Mélanie Seteun/IRMA.
———. 2012. *Do It Yourself! Autodétermination et culture punk*. Paris: Le Passager clandestin.
Mastor, Wanda, Jean-Pierre Marguénaud, and Fabien Marchadier, eds. 2010. *Droit et rock*. Paris: Dalloz.
Rudent, Catherine. 2013. "Anglo-American Mermaids: The Troubled 'anglo-saxon' Fantasy in French Pop Song." Paper presented at the 17th IASPM biennial conference, Gijon (Spain).
Seca, Jean-Marie. 1988. *Vocations Rock*. Paris: Klincksieck.

Rap and Hip Hop

Béthune, Christian. 1999. *Le rap: une esthétique hors la loi*. Paris: Autrement.
———. 2004. *Pour une esthétique du rap*. Paris: Klincksieck.
Boucher, Manuel. 1999. *Rap, expression des lascars: significations et enjeux du rap dans la société française*. Paris: L'Harmattan.
Hammou, Karim. 2012. *Une histoire du rap en France*. Paris: La Découverte.
Lapassade, Georges, and Philippe Rousselot. 1990. *Le rap ou la fureur de dire*. Paris: Loris Talmont.
Marc-Martinez, Isabelle. 2008. *Le rap français, esthétique et poétique des textes (1990–1995)*. Bern: Peter Lang.
Martin, Denis-Constant, ed. 2010. *Quand le rap sort de sa bulle: Sociologie politique d'un succès populaire*. Bordeaux and Paris: Mélanie Seteun/Irma.
Molinero, Stéphanie. 2009. *Les publics du rap: Enquête sociologique*. Paris: L'Harmattan.
Pecqueux, Anthony. 2005. "Le rap français comme pratique chansonnière: Réponse à Christophe Rubin." *Volume! La revue des musiques populaires* 4(1):151–154.
———. 2007. *Voix du rap: Essai de sociologie de L'action musicale*. Paris. L'Harmattan.
Rubin, Christophe. 2004. "Le rap est-il soluble dans la chanson française?" *Volume! La revue des musiques populaires* 3(2):29–42.

Techno and Electronic Music

Gastaut, Amélie, ed. 2012. *French touch: Graphisme, vidéo, électro*. Paris: Les Arts Décoratifs.
Guibert, Gérôme. 2009. "Versailles and the French Touch: When a Virtual Local Scene Becomes Real." Paper presented at the 15th IASPM biennial conference, Liverpool (United Kingdom).
———. 2012. "'La classe rémoise': À propos du traitement médiatique des musiques populaires émergentes en France." *Contemporary French Civilization* 36(1–2):97–112.
Jouannais, Jean-Yves, and Christophe Kihm, eds. 1998. "Techno: Anatomie des cultures électroniques." *Art Press hors-série*. Paris: Art Press.
Julien, Olivier. 2002. "La technologie de la French touch: Les Paul ou Pierre Schaeffer?" *Musurgia* 9(2):71–84.
Petiau, Anne. 2006. "Marginalité et musiques électronique." *Agora débats-Jeunesse* 42(1):128–139.
Sevin, Jean-Christophe. 2004. "L'épreuve du dance floor. Une approche des free parties." *Sociétés* 85(3):47–71.

Other Genres

Constant, Denis. 1982. *Aux sources du reggae: Musique, société et politique en Jamaïque*. Roquevaire: Parenthèses.
Gayou, Evelyne. 2007. *GRM: Groupe de recherches musicales: Cinquante ans d'histoire*. Paris: Fayard.
Laborde, Denis, ed. 1996. *Tout un monde de musiques: Repérer, enquêter, analyser, conserver . . .* Paris: L'Harmattan.

Olivier, Emmanuelle, ed. 2012. *Musiques au monde: La tradition au prisme de la création*. Sampzac: Éditions Delatour.
———. 2013. "Composer avec le monde." *Volume! La revue des musiques populaires* 10(2).

Popular Music and Society

Belleville, Pierre. 1985. "Demain l'éducation populaire." In *Guide de L'éducation populaire*, edited by Benigno Caseres, 220–225. Paris: La Découverte.
Dorin, Stéphane, and Gérôme Guibert. 2008. "Le secteur des musiques actuelles: Les paradoxes de la professionnalisation." In *Les arts moyens aujourd'hui*, edited by Florent Gaudez, 67–78. Paris: L'Harmattan.
Farchy, Joëlle, and Fabrice Rochelandet. 2002. "Le droit d'auteur dans les industries du disque et du cinéma en France." In *Histoire des industries culturelles en France, XIXᵉ–XXᵉ siècles*, edited by Jacques Marseille and Patrick Eveno, 157–182. Paris: ADHE.
Farchy, Joëlle, and Dominique Sagot-Duvauroux. 1994. *Economie des politiques culturelles*. Paris: Presses Universitaires de France.
Ferment, Fabrice, and le SNEP. 2001. *40 ans de tubes: Les meilleures ventes de 45 tours et CD singles*. Clichy: Éditions Larivière.
Girard, Augustin. 1978. "Industries culturelles." *Futuribles: Analyse—prévision—prospectives* 17:597–605.
Glevarec, Hervé, and Michel Pinet. 2009. *La radio et ses publics: Sociologie d'une fragmentation*. Paris: Seteun/Irma.
Grenier, Line. 1991. "*Vibrations: musiques, médias, sociétés*. Nos. 1–6. Paris: Privat, 1985–1988." *Popular Music* 10(1):93–97.
Guibert, Gérôme. 2006. *La production de la culture: Le cas des musiques amplifiées en France. Genèse, structuration, industries, alternatives*. Paris and St Amant Tallende: Irma/editions Seteun.
Guibert, Gérôme, and Philippe Le Guern. 2007. "Faire l'histoire des musiques amplifiées en France." In *Stereo: Sociologie comparée des musiques populaires France/G.B.*, edited by Hugh Dauncey and Philippe Le Guern, 27–44. Paris: Seteun/Irma.
———. 2010. "Charting the History of Amplified Musics in France." In *Stereo: Comparative Perspectives on the Sociological Study of Popular Music in France and Britain*, edited by Hugh Dauncey and Philippe Le Guern, 23–42. London: Asghate.
Hennion, Antoine. 1981. *Les professionnels du disque: Une sociologie des variétés*. Paris: Métailié.
Heurtebize, Frédéric. 2010. "Washington face à l'Union de la gauche en France, 1971–1981." *Revue française d'études américaines* 124:82–102.
Huet, Armel, Jacques Ion, Alain Lefebvre, Bernard Miège, and René Peron. 1978. *Capitalisme et industries culturelles*. Grenoble: Presses Universitaires de Grenoble.
Lebrun, Barbara, ed. 2012. *Chanson et performance: Mise en scène du corps dans la chanson française et francophone*. Paris: L'Harmattan.
Menger, Pierre Michel. 2005. *Profession artiste: Extension du domaine de la création*. Paris: Textuel.
Neyrand, Gérard, and Caroline Guillot. 1983. *Entre clips et looks: Les pratiques de consommation des adolescents*. Paris: L'Harmattan.
Penasse, Jean-Philippe. 2008. "Mick Jagger et les camarades." *Rue Descartes* 60:94–105.
———. 2011. "Le parti communiste et la pop." Interview by Guillaume Heuguet and Etienne Menu. *Vox Pop* 20: 20–21.
Perrenoud, Marc. 2007. *Les musicos: Enquête sur des musiciens ordinaires*. Paris: La Découverte.
Poirrier, Philippe. 2000. *L'État et la culture en France au XXᵉ siècle*. Paris: Le Livre de Poche.
Prévost-Thomas. 2006. "Dialectiques et fonctions symboliques de la chanson francophone contemporaine." PhD diss., Paris X-Nanterre University.
Rouzé, Vincent. 2005. "Musicaliser le quotidien: analyse et enjeux de mises en scène particulières." *Volume! La revue des musiques populaires* 4(2):41–50.
Rudent, Catherine. 2000. "Le discours sur la musique dans la presse française: l'exemple des périodiques spécialisés en 1993." PhD diss., Paris-Sorbonne University. www.theses.paris-sorbonne.fr/these-%20Rudent.pdf.
———. 2006. "La télévision française et les 'voix québécoises' populaires: le trompe-l'œil d'un étiquetage médiatique." *Intersections: Canadian Journal of Music/Revue canadienne de musique* 27(1):75–99.
Sohier, Alice. 2010. "Le rôle de l'expérience vécue et de ses antécédents sur la satisfaction envers un spectacle vivant. Le cas des festivals de rock." PhD diss., Caen University.
Sohn, Anne-Marie. 2001. *Âge tendre et tête de bois: Histoire des jeunes des années 60*. Paris: Hachette.
Teillet, Philippe. 2002. "Éléments pour une histoire des politiques publiques en faveur des 'musiques amplifiées.'" In *Les collectivités locales et la culture: Les formes de l'institutionnalisation, xixᵉ–xxᵉ siècles*, edited by Philippe Poirrier, 361–393. Paris: La Documentation Française/Comité d'Histoire du Ministère de la Culture—Fondation Maison des Sciences de l'Homme.
———. 2003. "Publics et politiques des musiques actuelles." In *Le(s) public(s) de la culture*, edited by Olivier Donnat and Paul Tolila, 155–180. Paris: Presses de Sciences Po.

Touché, Marc. 1994. *Connaissance de l'environnement sonore urbain: L'exemple des lieux de répétitions.* Vaucresson: Research survey CRIV-CNRS.

Contemporary Topics

Public Policy and Management

Guibert, Gérôme. 2011. "Détourner le contrôle: Le cas de la fédération des lieux de musiques actuelles." *Sociologies Pratiques* 22(1):79–92.
Lallement, Michel. 2015. *L'âge du faire: Hacking, travail, anarchie.* Paris: Le Seuil.
Le Rendu-Lizée, Carole. 2014. "Enjeux et conditions de la mise en oeuvre d'un groupement d'employeurs dans le secteur culturel: une application aux musiques actuelles." PhD diss., Angers University.
Lizé, Wenceslas, Delphine Naudier, and Olivier Roueff, eds. 2011. *Intermédiaires du travail artistique: A la frontière de l'art et du commerce.* Paris: La Documentation Française.
Menger, Pierre-Michel. 2003. *Portrait de L'artiste en travailleur: Métamorphoses du capitalisme.* Paris: Éditions du Seuil.
Poirrier, Philippe. 2006. *L'État et la culture en France au xxᵉ siècle.* Paris: Le Livre de Poche.
Saez, Guy. 2014. "La métropolisation de la culture." *Cahier Français* 382:10–15.

Technology and Digital

Auray, Nicolas. 2011. "La consommation en régime d'abondance: La confrontation aux offres culturelles dites illimitées." *Revue Française de Socio-Économie* 8(2):85–102.
Bacache-Beauvallet, Maya, Marc Bourreau, and François Moreau. 2011. *Portrait des musiciens à l'heure du numérique.* Paris: Rue d'Ulm.
Beuscart, Jean-Samuel. 2007. "Les transformations de L'intermédiation musicale: La construction de l'offre commerciale de musique en ligne en France." *Réseaux* 25(141–142):143–176.
———. 2008. "Sociabilité en ligne, notoriété virtuelle et carrière artistique: Les usages de MySpace par les musiciens autoproduits." *Réseaux* 152:139–168.
Beuscart, Jean-Samuel, and Thomas Couronné. 2009. "La distribution de la notoriété en ligne: Une analyse quantitative de MySpace." *Terrains & Travaux* 15:147–170.
Bouquillion, Philippe. 2012. "Mutation des industries musicales et actualité des industries culturelles." In *Sound Factory: Musique et logiques de l'industrialisation*, edited by Stéphane Dorin, 125–140. Saffré: Mélanie Seteun.
Bouquillion, Philippe, and Jacob T. Matthews. 2010. *Le Web collaboratif: Mutations des industries de la culture et de la communication.* Grenoble: Presses Universitaires de Grenoble.
Constantini, Stéphane. 2015. "De la scène musicale aux réseaux musicalisés: Les inscriptions territoriales et socio-économiques de l'activité artistique." *Réseaux* 192(6):143–168.
Dejean, Sylvain, Thierry Pénard, and Raphaël Suire. 2010. "La gratuité est-elle une fatalité sur les marchés numériques? Une étude sur le consentement à payer pour des offres de contenus audiovisuels sur internet." *Économie et Prévision* 194(3):15–32.
Flichy, Patrice. 2009. "Comment Internet est devenu un marché." In *Traité de sociologie économique*, edited by Philippe Steiner and François Vatin, 451–492. Paris: Presses Universitaires de France.
Hesmondhalgh, David. 2008. "La musique et le numérique: au-delà du battage." In *Sound Factory: Musique et logiques de l'industrialisation*, edited by Stéphane Dorin, 141–151. Saffré: Mélanie Seteun.
Jouvenet, Morgan. 2006. *Rap, techno, électro . . . Le musicien entre travail artistique et critique sociale.* Charenton-le-Pont: Éditions de la Maison des Sciences de l'Homme.
Lizé, Wenceslas, Delphine Naudier, and Séverine Sofio, eds. 2014. *Les stratèges de la notoriété: Intermédiaires et consécration dans les univers artistiques.* Paris: Éditions des Archives Contemporaines.
Matthews, Jacob, and Lucien Perticoz, eds. 2013. *l'industrie musicale à L'aube du xxiᵉ siècle.* Paris: L'Harmattan.
Moreau, François. 2014. "L'industrie de la musique aujourd'hui." *Cahiers Français* 382:39–45.
Moulier-Boutang, Yann. 2007. *Le capitalisme cognitif: La nouvelle grande transformation.* Paris: Éditions Amsterdam.
Nowak, Raphaël. 2013. "Consommer la musique à l'ère du numérique: Vers une analyse des environnements sonores." *Volume! La revue des musiques populaires* 10(1):227–228.
Pecqueux, Anthony, and Olivier Roueff, eds. 2009. *Écologie sociale de L'oreille: Enquêtes sur l'expérience musicale.* Paris: Éditions de l'EHESS.
Petiau, Anne. 2006. "Marginalité et musiques électroniques." *Agora: Débats, Jeunesse* 42(1):128–137.
———. 2011. *Technomedia.* Saffré: Mélanie Seteun.
Rouzé, Vincent. 2010. *Mythologie de l'ipod.* Paris: Le Cavalier Bleu.

Culture and Society (Race, Class, Genre)

Amselle, Jean-Loup. 2001. *Vers un multiculturalisme français*. Paris: Flammarion.
———. 2011. *L'ethnicisation de la France*. Paris: Lignes.
Ervine, Jonathan. 2011. "Kamini's Rural Rap: A Study of Minority Identities, New Media, and Music." *Contemporary French Civilization* 36(1–2):127–140.
Gaulier, Armelle. 2014. "Zebda, Tactikolectif, Origines Contrôlées: la musique au service de l'action sociale et politique à Toulouse." PhD diss., Bordeaux University.
Laplantine, François, and Alexis Nouss. 2014 [1977]. *Le métissage*. Paris: Téraèdre.
Lebrun, Barbara. 2002. "A Case Study of Zebda: Republicanism, Métissage and Authenticity in Contemporary France." *Volume! La revue des musiques populaires* 1(2):59–69.
———. 2009. *Protest Music in France: Production, Identity and Audiences*. Farnham: Ashgate.
———. 2012a. "Carte de Séjour: Re-visiting 'Arabness' and anti-racism in 1980s France." *Popular Music* 31(3):331–346.
———. 2012b. "Hybridity, Arabness and Cultural Legitimacy in Rock Métis." In *Music and Protest*, edited by Ian Peddie, 473–499. Farnham: Ashgate.
Mathis-Moser, Ursula. 2003. "L'image de 'l'Arabe' dans la chanson française contemporaine." *Volume! La revue des musiques populaires* 2(2):129–144.
Raibaud, Yves. 2011. "Armstrong, je ne suis pas noir . . ." *Volume! La revue des musiques populaires* 8(1):223–232.
Ramdani, Karima. 2011. "Bitch et Beurette, quand féminité rime avec liberté. Représentation du corps féminin noir et maghrébin dans la musique rap et le R'n'B." *Volume! La revue des musiques populaires* 8(2):13–39.
Sutcliffe, Ellie. 2011. "Managing the Media, the Music and 'métissage': Compromise in the Music of Faudel and Magyd Cherfi." *Contemporary French Civilization* 36(1–2):97–112.
Tinker, Chris. 2015. "Genre, Gender and the Republic: Televising the Annual Charity Concert Les Enfoirés." *French Cultural Studies* 26(3):343–353.

Cultural Heritage, Archives, Memorabilia and Nostalgia

Dalbavie, Juliette. 2003. "Exposer des objets sonores: le cas des chansons de Brassens." *Volume! La revue des musiques populaires* 2(2):145–161.
Guibert, Gérôme. 2013. "The Sound of the City: À propos du colloque 'Pop Music, Pop Musée. Un nouveau défi patrimonial.'" *Musée et Collections Publiques de France* 268:28–33.
Guibert, Gérôme, and Emmanuel Parent. 2015. "When Folk Meets Pop: DIY Archives in the Making of a Punk Rock DIY Community in Western France." In *Preserving Popular Music Heritage: Do-It-Yourself, Do-It-Together*, edited by Sarah Baker, 104–113. New York: Routledge.
Le Guern, Philippe. 2012. "Un spectre hante le rock: L'obsession patrimoniale, les musiques populaires et actuelles et les enjeux de la 'muséomomification.'" *Questions de Communication* 22:7–44.
Tinker, Chris, and Hugh Dauncey, eds. 2014. "Souvenirs, souvenirs. La nostalgie dans les musiques populaires." *Volume! La revue des musiques populaires* 11(1):7–17.
Touché, Marc. 2007. "Muséographier les musiques amplifiées: Pour une socio-histoire du sonore." *Réseaux* 25(141–142):297–325.
———. 2012. "Les musiques amplifiées s'exposent . . . et s'invitent dans les musées." *Questions de Communication* 22:57–86.
Warnier, Jean-Pierre, ed. 1994. *Le paradoxe de la marchandise authentique*. Paris: L'Harmattan.
———. 1999. *La mondialisation de la culture*. Paris: La Découverte.

Live Music

Guibert, Gérôme, and Dominique Sagot-Duvauroux. 2013. *Musiques actuelles, ça part en live: Analyse économique d'une filière culture*. Paris: Irma/DEPS.
Heuguet, Guillaume. 2014. "Le smartphone et le concert." *Esprit* 409(11):125–127.

Index

Note: Page numbers in *italic* indicate a figure on the corresponding page.